# *ADVANCED* UNDERWATER PHOTOGRAPHY

## TECHNIQUES FOR DIGITAL PHOTOGRAPHERS

LARRY GATES

Amherst Media, Inc. ■ Buffalo, NY

## DEDICATION

This book is dedicated to Lucy
and in memory of Hans DeJager, June 9, 1949–June 22, 2010.



Published by:
Amherst Media, Inc.
P.O. Box 586
Buffalo, N.Y. 14226
Fax: 716-874-4508
www.AmherstMedia.com

Publisher: Craig Alesse
Senior Editor/Production Manager: Michelle Perkins
Assistant Editor: Barbara A. Lynch-Johnt
Editorial assistance provided by Sally Jarzab, John S. Loder, and Carey A. Miller.
Business Manager: Adam Richards
Marketing, Sales, and Promotions Manager: Kate Neaverth
Warehouse and Fulfillment Manager: Roger Singo

ISBN-13: 978-1-60895-253-3
Library of Congress Control Number: 2011924263
Printed in Korea.
10 9 8 7 6 5 4 3 2 1

# CONTENTS



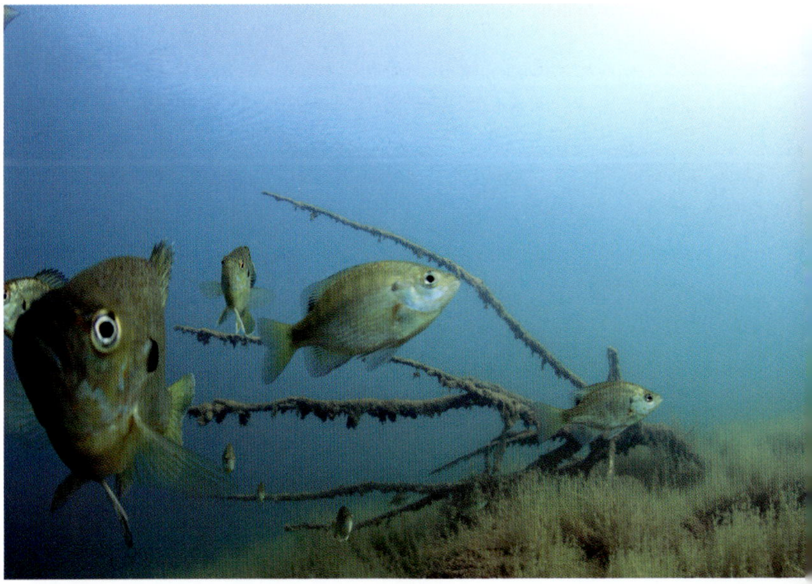

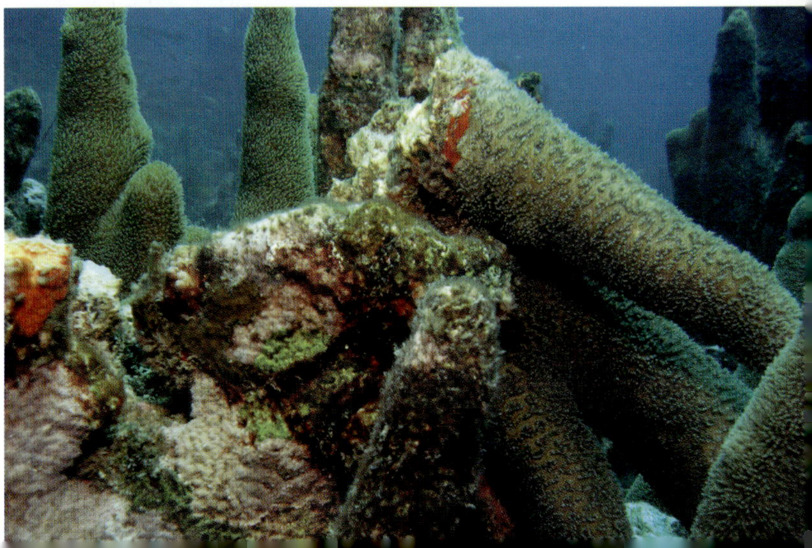

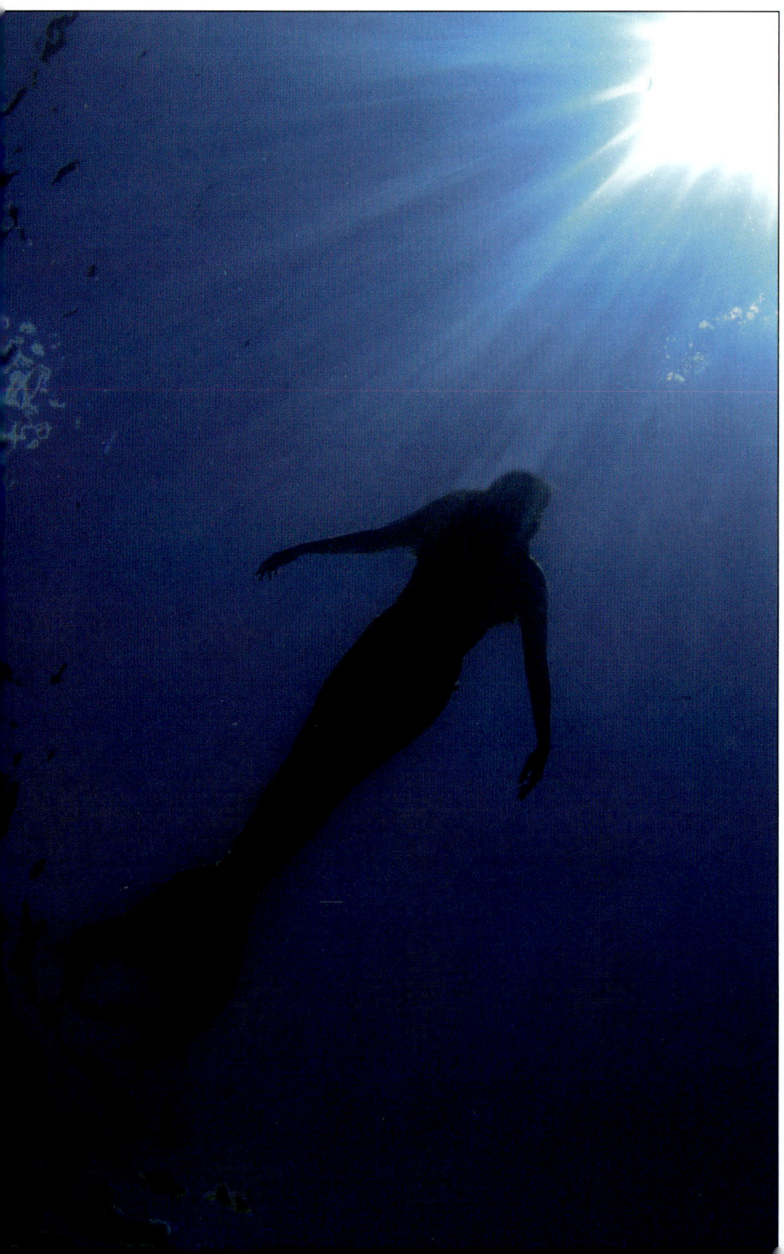

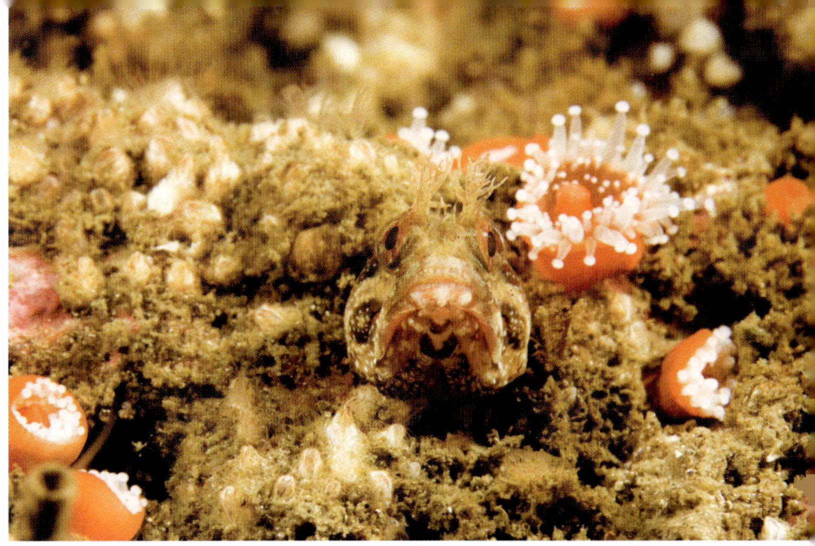

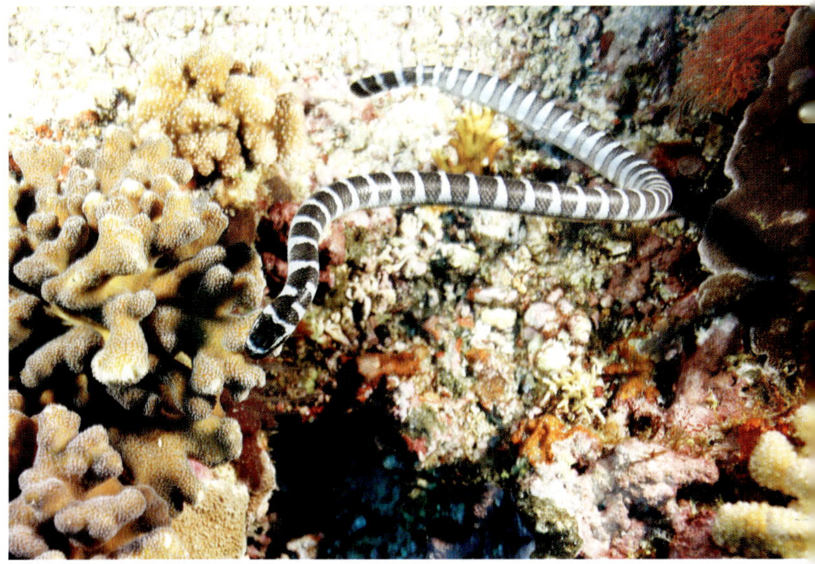

# ABOUT THE AUTHOR

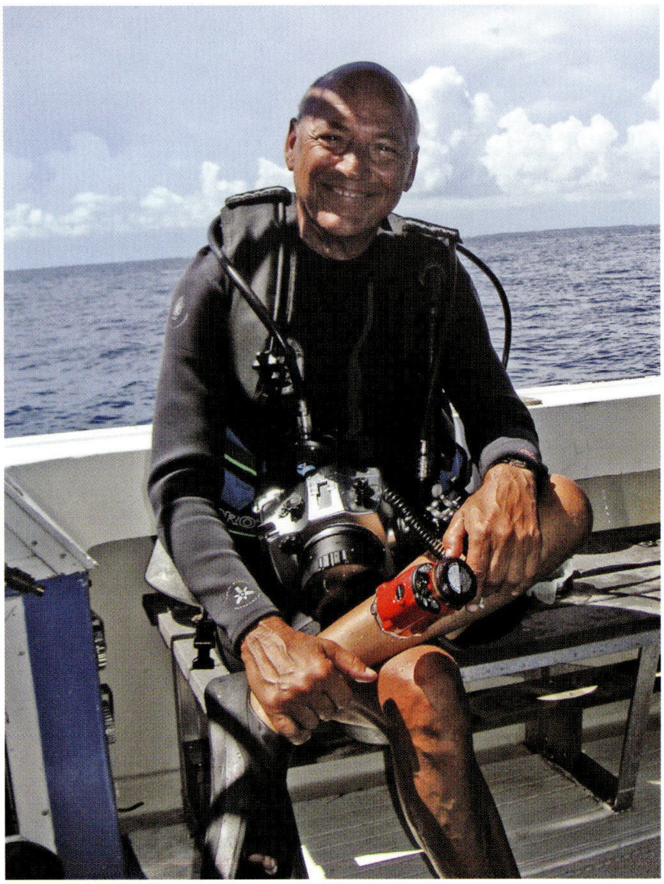

Author Larry Gates. Photo courtesy of Gene Condon.

Larry Gates began shooting underwater photography in 1992, when he took his first photograph while scuba diving in Lake Oahe near Pierre, South Dakota. Within a couple of years, he became a scuba instructor in Maui in the Hawaiian Islands. In 1994, Larry moved from Maui to Key Largo, Florida, where he teaches underwater photography. He is a PADI Master Instructor with credentials in teaching underwater photography, and he has done over 5000 dives and taught underwater photography to hundreds of individuals. He has photographed subjects in the Bahamas, the Turks and Caicos Islands, the Cayman Islands, Cozumel, Bonaire, and Belize, and he shares his experiences shooting in those locations with his readers and students.


### THANKS

I'd like to acknowledge several people who helped make this book possible.

I thank my publisher, Craig Alesse, for his faith and confidence in me. Thank you, Barbara A. Lynch-Johnt, my editor, for your tireless effort in assembling my manuscript into a readable book.

I thank Jennifer Maksymiak, Chris Edson, and Battle Vaughn for their reviews, critiques, ideas, and suggestions during my writing of this book.

I thank Mary Moyer, Connie Z, Ali Gracey, Jan McGarva, Rob Stein, Steve Minor, Brian Bolton, and John Yasaki, all of whom generously contributed their images and technical and artistic insights for use in this book. I also thank Steve Philbrook, Ryan Marchese, Jeff Baerlocher, and Hans DeJager for contributing photographs used here.

My thanks also go out to the following dive charter operators and their staff for their support: Ocean Divers, Scuba-Do, and Pleasure Diver (all of Key Largo).

A big thank you also goes out to all of my students of underwater photography, who have over the many years, perhaps paradoxically, taught me something. Most of what we discovered together is found in this book and its older sister, *The Beginner's Guide to Underwater Digital Photography,* also from Amherst Media.

# INTRODUCTION

This book was written for underwater photographers who have learned the basics of digital underwater photography. While this book's title includes the word "advanced," it is not all-encompassing. Covering every possible facet of underwater photography would require numerous volumes written by several authors. Additionally, such a book would be outdated upon its publication, given the rapid changes in the technology and equipment we dive with and use in making digital images in the underwater environment.

This book will define what advanced underwater photography is and what makes a photographer an advanced underwater photographer. I will outline the equipment used in advanced underwater photography and will present strategies for using that equipment, plus solid technique, to create advanced underwater photographs. This book also provides various techniques used by other advanced underwater photographers. All in all, the book is a little more in-depth than its sister, *A Beginner's Guide to Digital Underwater Photography.* Think of it as your next fin-kick forward into the fun and challenge of underwater photography!

As beginning underwater photographers, we learned about focus, exposure, and composition. With time and experience, we made improved captures. This book will expand on these key topics to help you take a mission-orientated approach to your underwater photography.

When one enters the advanced arena of underwater photography, the good ole point & shoot cameras are left at the gate. We use a full-featured digital camera (one that offers full manual exposure control), and more likely the housed digital Single Lens Reflex (dSLR) cameras are employed. This book provides information about the myriad equipment choices and the

**Left**—Sometimes it's possible to use fish behavior to your advantage when photographing. In this case, the fish's curiosity allowed for a great photo opportunity. Exposure: f/8, $^{1}/_{125}$, and 200 ISO. **Right**—Large coral heads like this Brain Coral offer the opportunity to create wonderful compositional studies. Shoot these from many angles and vantage points to ensure the best-possible composition. Exposure: f/8 $^{1}/_{100}$, and 100 ISO.

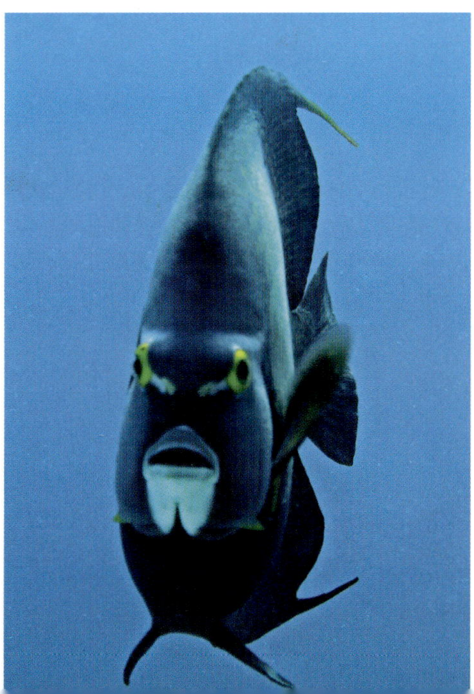

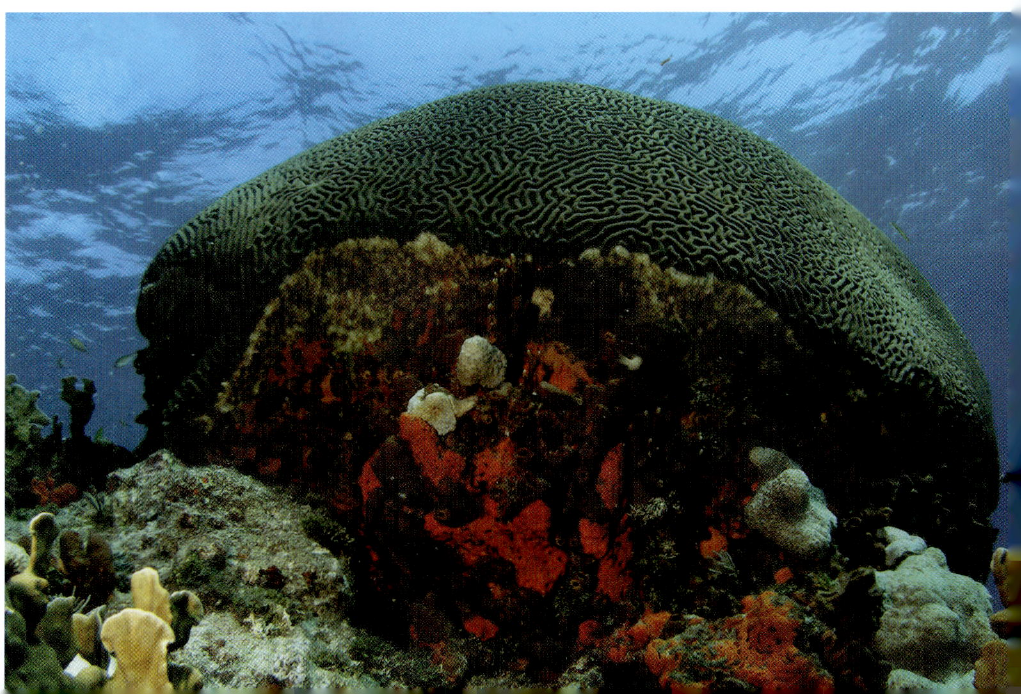

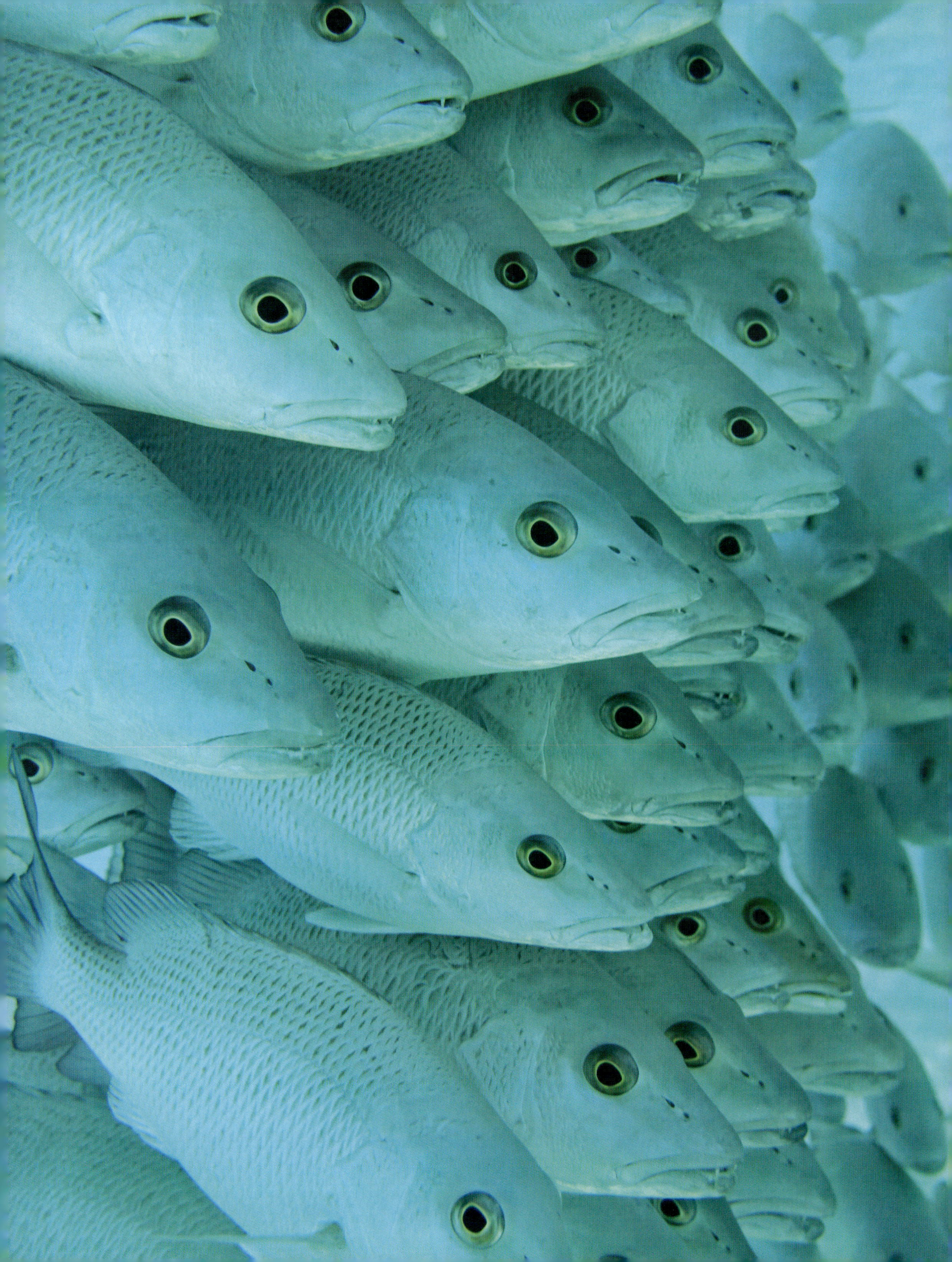

advantages the gear offers underwater photographers. While more elaborate, robust, and typically higher-cost equipment is used, this equipment, in and of itself, will not make you a more advanced shooter. It may make you more capable, but a capable photographer can take an advanced underwater photograph with virtually any type of camera. Good technique is critical.

Because even advanced underwater photographers have equipment-related issues from time to time, this book also offers a troubleshooting section.

Underwater photography is enjoyable and fun to engage in, and it becomes even more rewarding as we advance our knowledge and skills. I've made a conscious decision to make this book enjoyable to read; it is not void of humor, but it does lack charts, graphs, equations, and diagrams, which can be difficult to grasp. When technicalities are discussed, they are presented in layman's terms.

A goal of this book is to teach what is necessary, in terms of equipment and technique, to get a particular capture. This book will detail some of the problems encountered in making a given capture and how those problems were addressed. In short, it will try to answer the question: "How can I take such a photograph?"

In these pages, you will find numerous photographs taken by myself and other photographers, mostly my students of underwater photography. In some cases, they have provided a description of how a given capture was made.

**Facing page**—Schoolmasters are schooling fish. They apparently find safety in numbers, which allows for a close approach. Exposure: f/5.6, 1/125, and 200 ISO. **Left**—Seafans over the ridge. Exposure: f/5.6, 1/80, and 100 ISO. **Right**—Deep water reef scenic, shot with a wide angle lens. Exposure: f/5.6, 1/125, and 100 ISO. Photo courtesy of Mary Moyer.

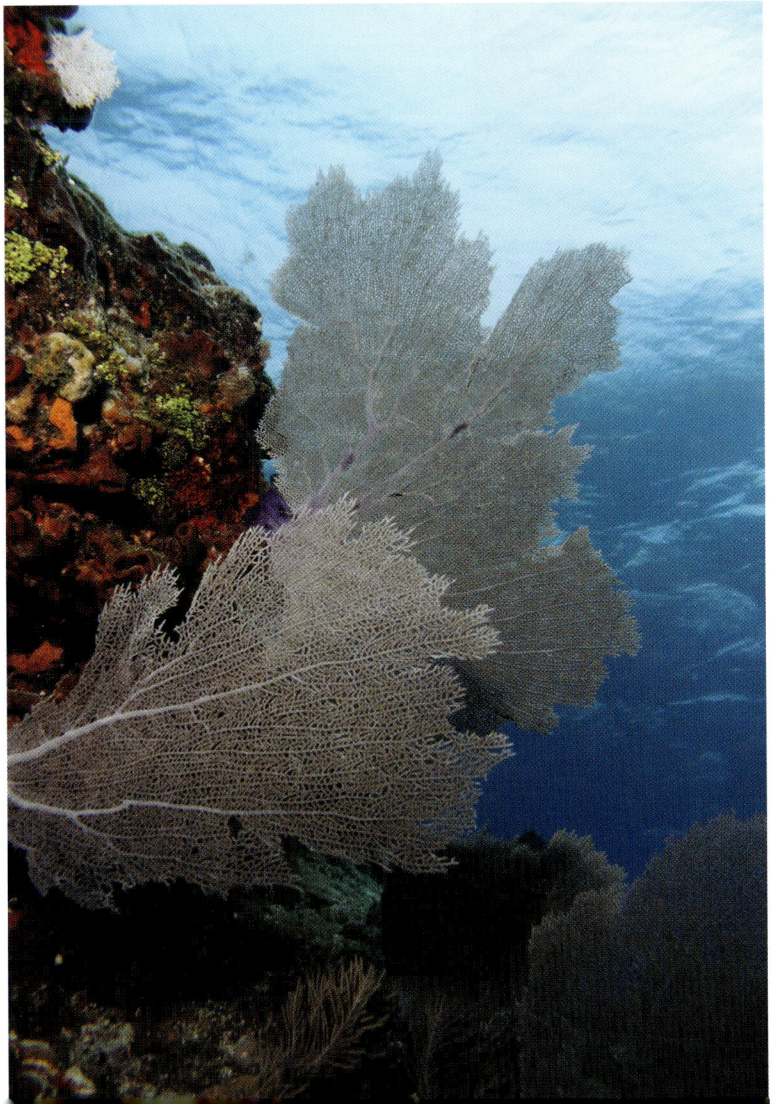

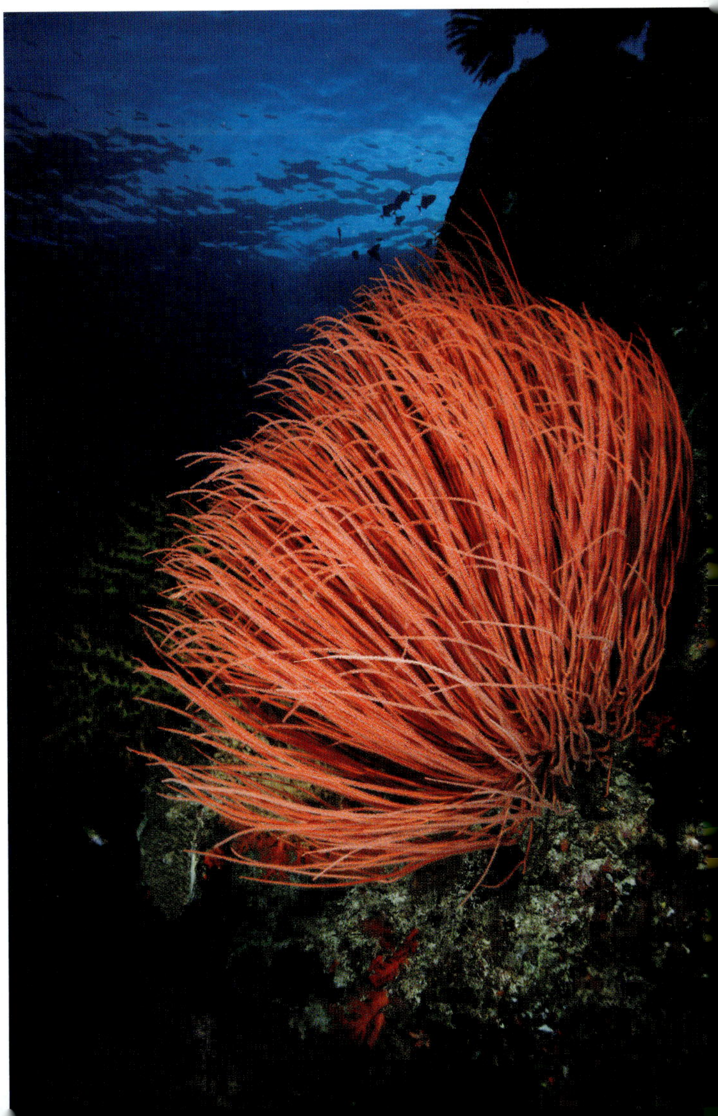

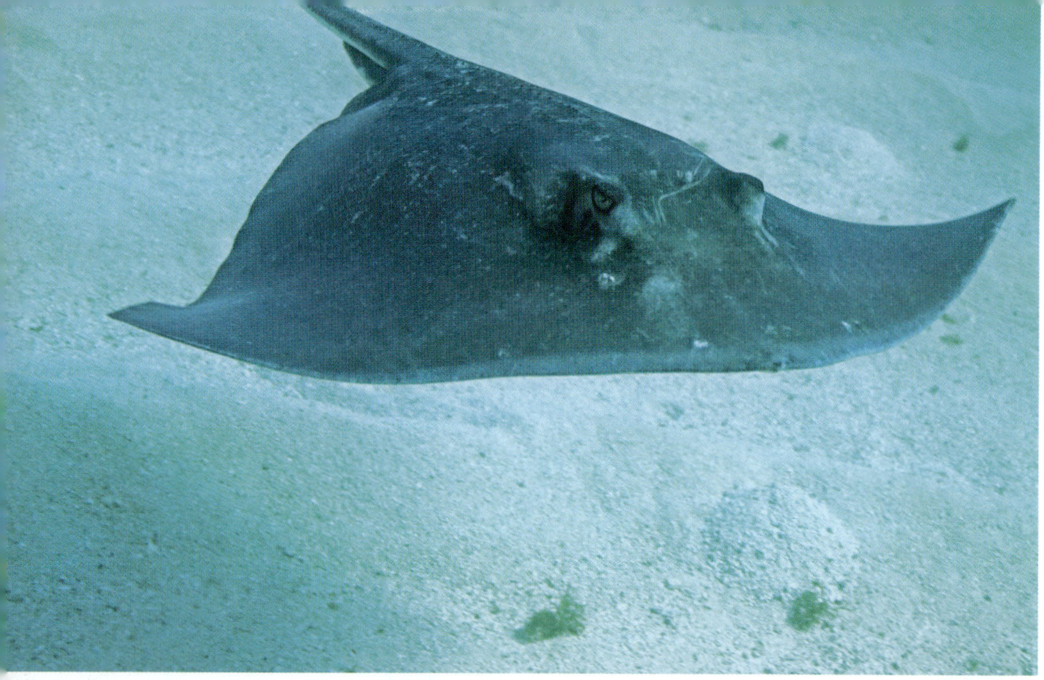

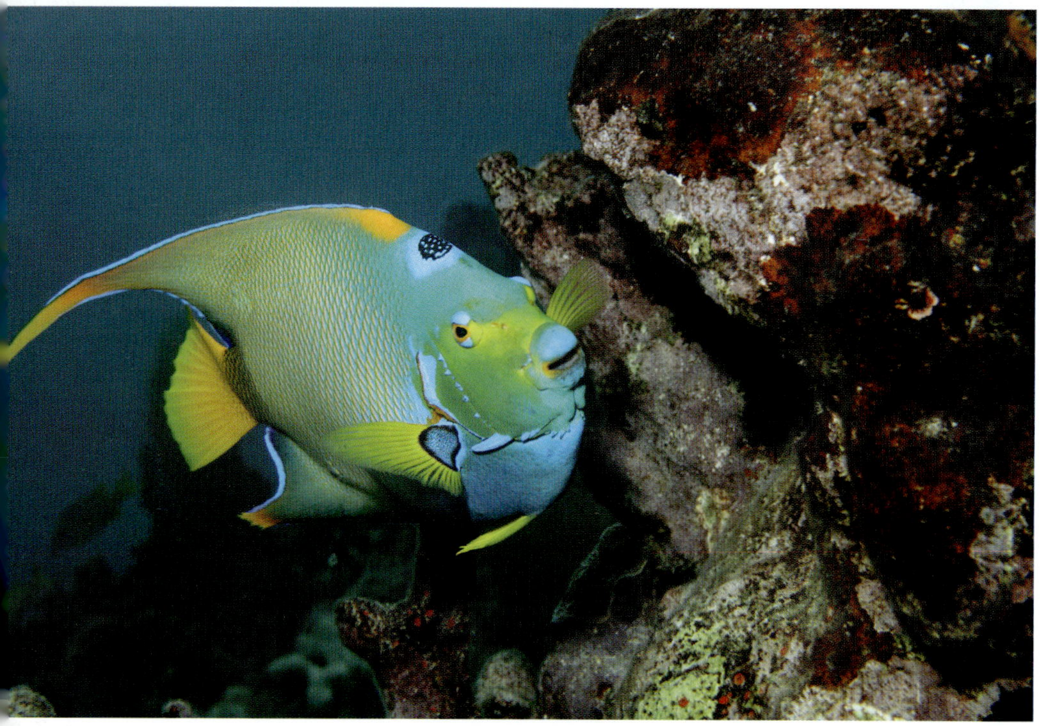

**Top**—Being ready to take a photograph enabled me to get this quick grab shot of a Southern Stingray. Exposure: f/5.6, $^{1}/_{125}$, and 100 ISO. Focal length 55mm. **Bottom**—Queen Angelfish are the most ornate of the Angelfish. They are also the most "diver skittish," so luck plays a role when it comes to capturing one. Exposure: f/6.3, $^{1}/_{125}$, and 100 ISO. **Facing page**—This image was composed to include a secondary subject. The colors and variety of corals is the primary subject, and the dive boat and its ladders is the secondary subject. Exposure: f/5.6, $^{1}/_{125}$, and 100 ISO.

This book assumes the reader is very comfortable with their scuba diving and has experience, skills, or training well beyond the limits of the open-water diver. Successful underwater photography depends more on one's scuba diving skills than the underwater photographic equipment used.

Always remember that as an underwater photographer, beginner or advanced, you are first and foremost a scuba diver. Always adhere to the fundamentals, tenets, and teachings of your certifying agency. Dive within your limits and from the standpoint of your experience, mental comfort level, physical capabilities, air consumption, navigational skills, and your training in the different underwater environments we dive in. You are also a dive buddy to your dive partner. As a scuba diver, you are responsible for your own safety

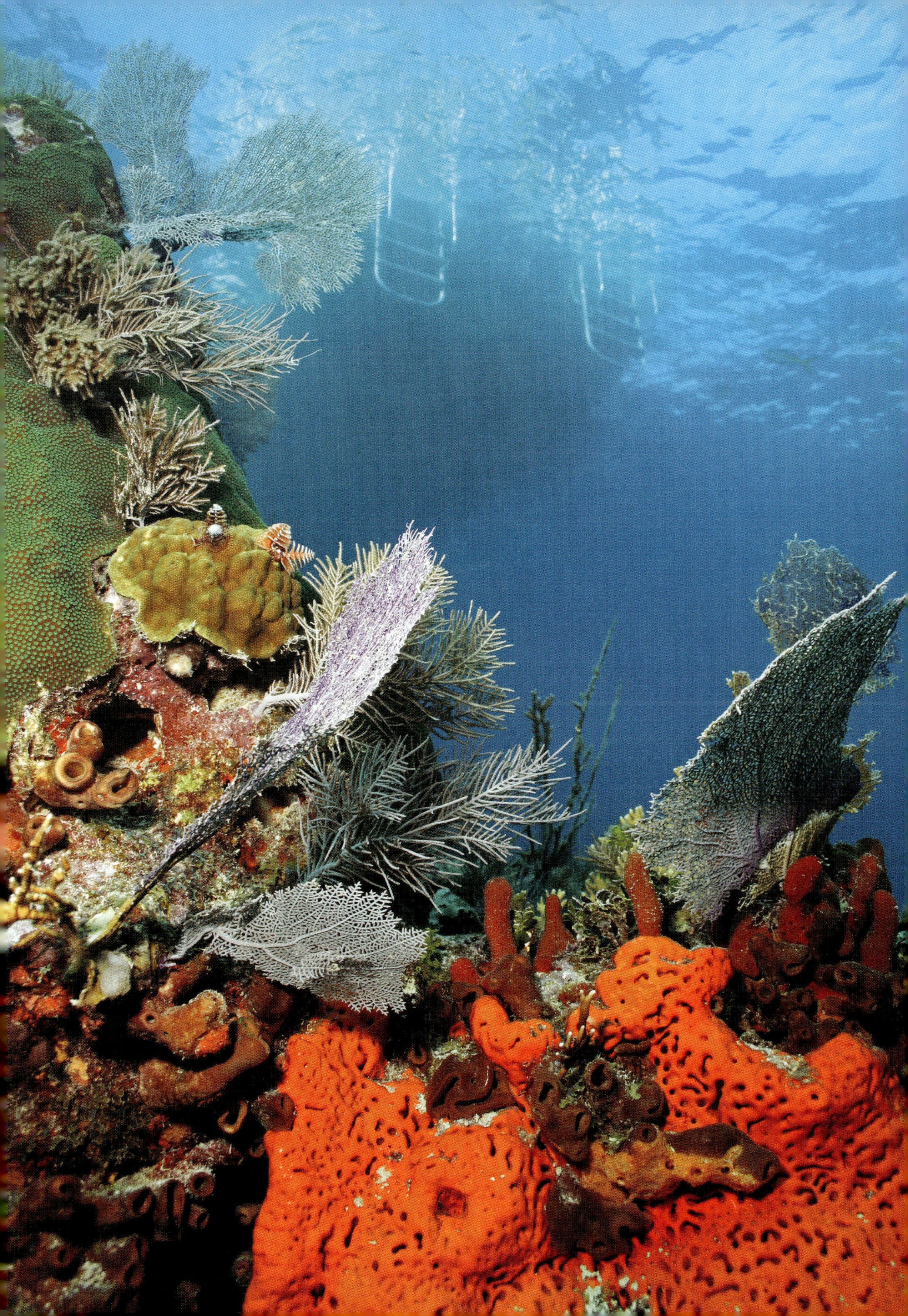

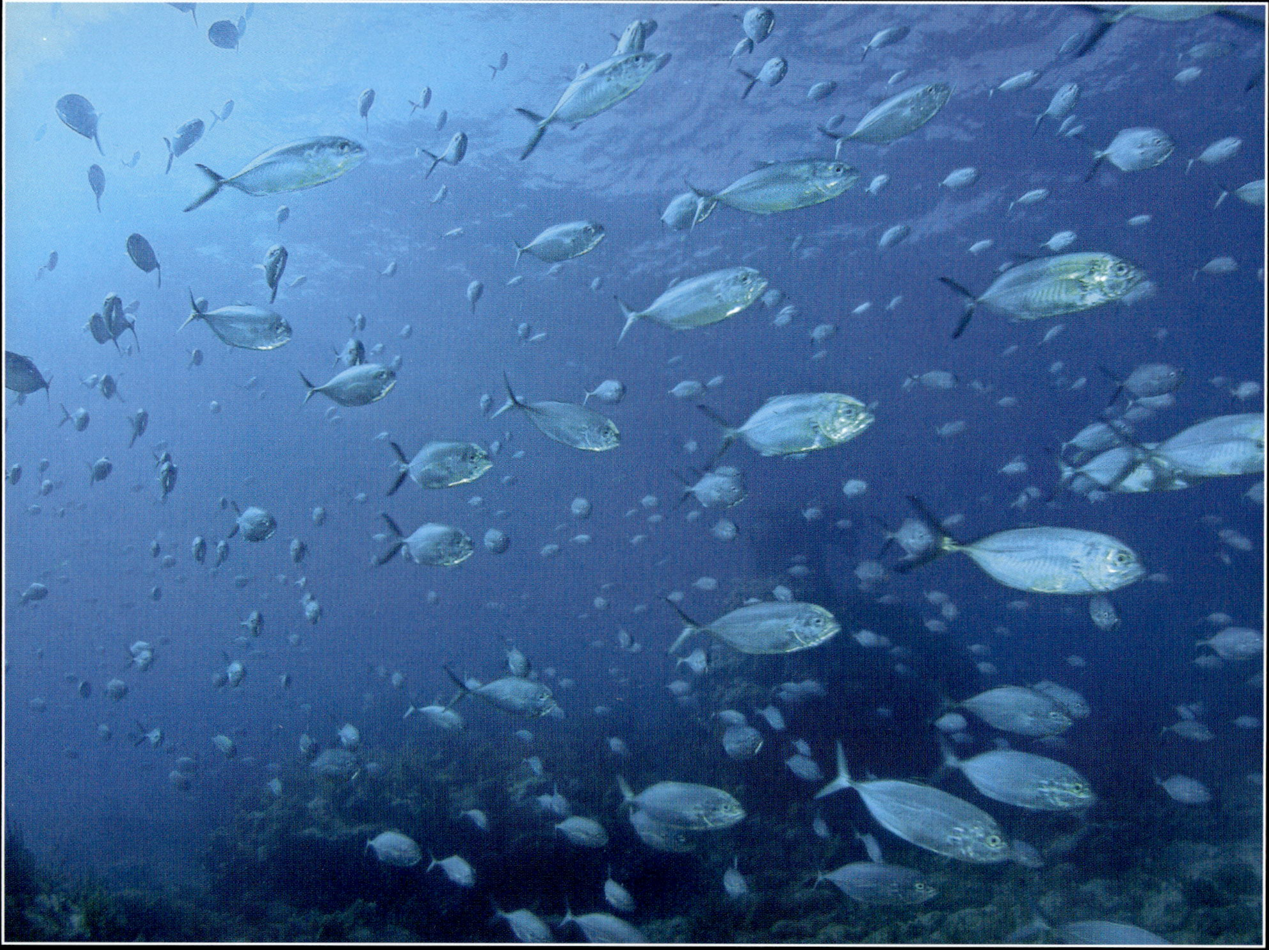

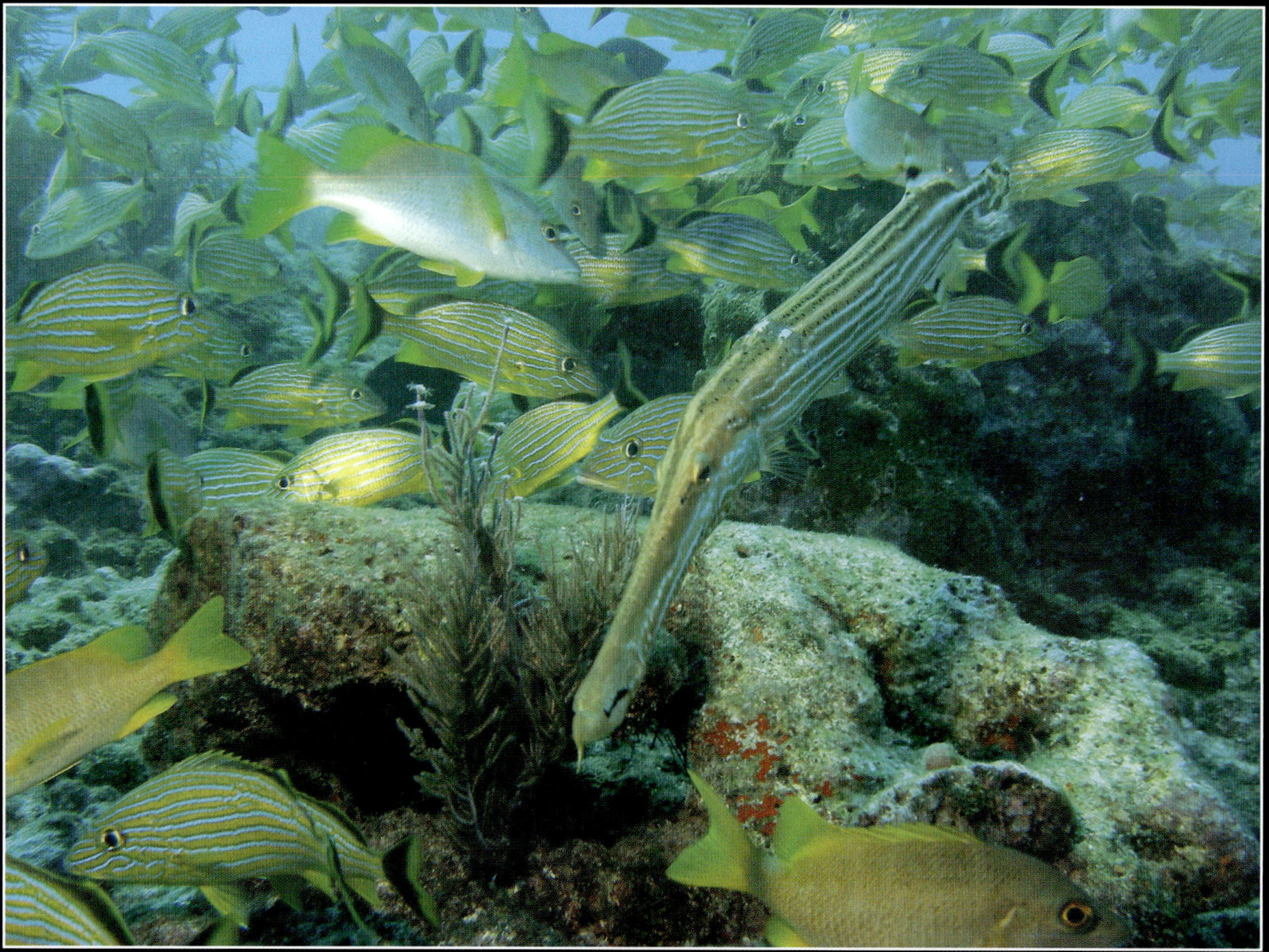

**Facing page**—(Top) The reflectivity of the fish and scene being backlit in this fish attack made lighting tricky. The solution was to use the edge of the cone of light of a diffused, TTL flash. Exposure: f/5.6, 1/125, and 100 ISO. Focal length 20mm. (Bottom) Trumpetfish seem to think they are invisible. This makes them easy to approach and get close to. Just pretend you're not interested and approach them slowly. Exposure: f/5.6, 1/100, and 200 ISO.

and welfare, as well as the safety and welfare of your dive partner. We can all take a photograph underwater; the trick is to bring it topside. Never attempt to take a photograph in a situation that is not suited to your experience and/or dive training. The more challenging situations and circumstances discussed in this book are directed only at readers who have the proficiency to handle such experiences with ease.

Among our goals as underwater photographers is to visit various underwater environments, experience the wonderful sights, and create the best-possible photograph of these sights—in a safe way that does no harm to the aquatic life we visit. We are guests on the reef, and we are its caretakers.

This book's approach to underwater photography is somewhat mission-oriented, but the mission will be a fun one. The overall goal of this book is to help you move from creating an ordinary photograph to capturing an extraordinary image of that subject, and be able to repeat the performance.

### DEFENDING THE TITLE

This book is about advanced underwater photography and is geared toward advanced underwater photographers. What does this mean?

An advanced underwater photograph is easily defined: it is technically perfect. In other words, the critical, in-focus area of the image is tack-sharp; the photograph is correctly exposed and thoughtfully composed; and the subject is rare or otherwise compelling.

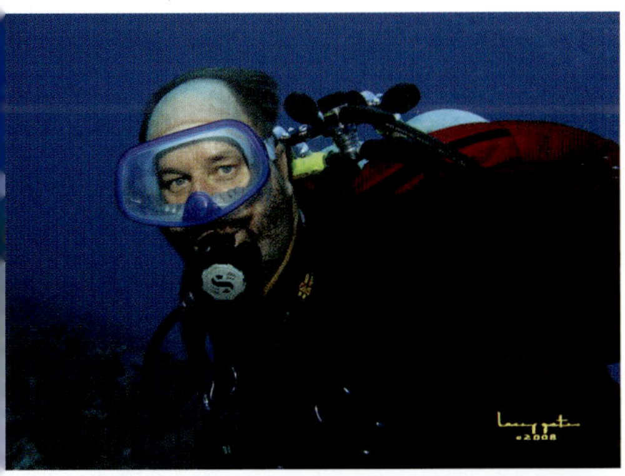

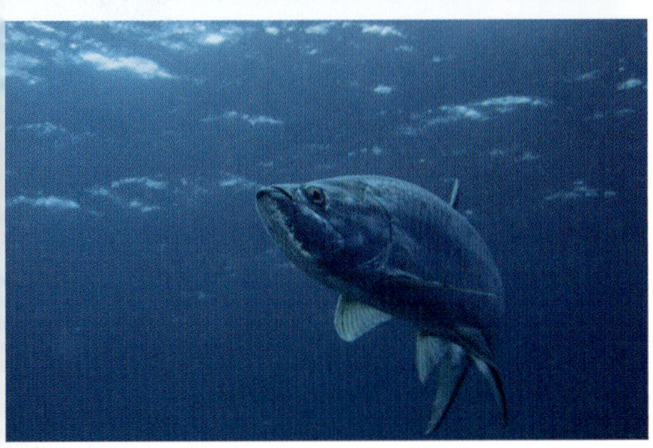

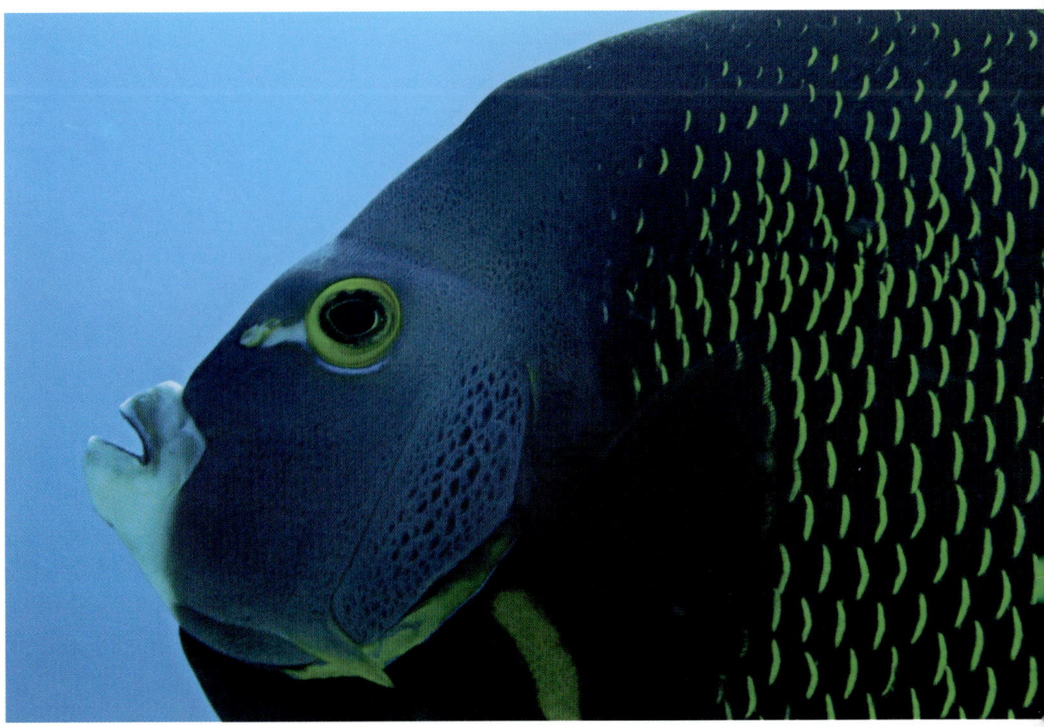

**Top left**—Diver portrait. Exposure: f/5.6, 1/125, and ISO 100. Flash fill. **Bottom left**—Photographing this Tarpon from below empowered the subject and added drama to the scene. Exposure: f/8, 1/125, and 100 ISO. **Right**—This French Angelfish offered a portrait opportunity. Exposure: f/8, 1/125, and 200 ISO.

The term "advanced underwater photographer" is harder to define. A beginner can take a photograph. An advanced photographer can consistently capture a more pleasing photograph of the same subject. A highly advanced photographer can consistently and creatively capture a pleasing image. An advanced underwater photographer should know ahead of time what photograph(s) he wants to make and what equipment he needs to get the job done. He shoots with a goal in mind: to do more than simply get an image, to take the best picture he can.

### EQUIPMENT NOTE

In writing this book, I have made some equipment references to Canon products. I am not implying that Canon is better; it's just that I am most familiar with their products. Keep in mind that Nikon, Olympus, and other major manufacturers offer similar products.

Each manufacturer offers a range of models, from point & shoots to professional-level gear with all of the bells and whistles. Generally speaking, the better the tools you have, the easier it is to do the job or do it more efficiently or effectively. However, not all professional photographers use professional-level cameras. There are picture takers and picture makers, and the camera is just a tool. When you see an intriguing photograph, it is more important to ask how that photograph was made than to determine what kind of camera the photographer used. When you reach that point, you will have truly begun your journey into advanced underwater photography.

The portrait I shot of my friend, yacht boat captain Fred Hammond (page 13), is an example. I could have used any of many underwater cameras, from an entry-level model to one with all the bells and whistles. I simply used the one I had at hand.

**Below**—Feeding time is a great opportunity to photograph sharks. However, the sharks are very busy and move quickly, presenting an element of difficulty in getting the shot. Exposure: f/5.6, 1/125, and 200 ISO. Focal length 20mm. Photo courtesy of Ali Gracey. **Facing page**—(Top left) A single, simple subject can make for an elegant image. Exposure: f/8, 1/125, and ISO 100. (Top right) The purple color of the Stovepipe Sponge is complemented by the blue water background. Exposure: f/6.7, 1/125, and 100 ISO. (Bottom) Conflict can present an interesting photographic opportunity. This image from Connie Z Photography, LLC, shows a turf battle between two Spotted Eels. The one on the left owns the home, but the one on the right wants to take it over. Exposure: f/5.6, 1/125, and 100 ISO. Focal length 55mm.

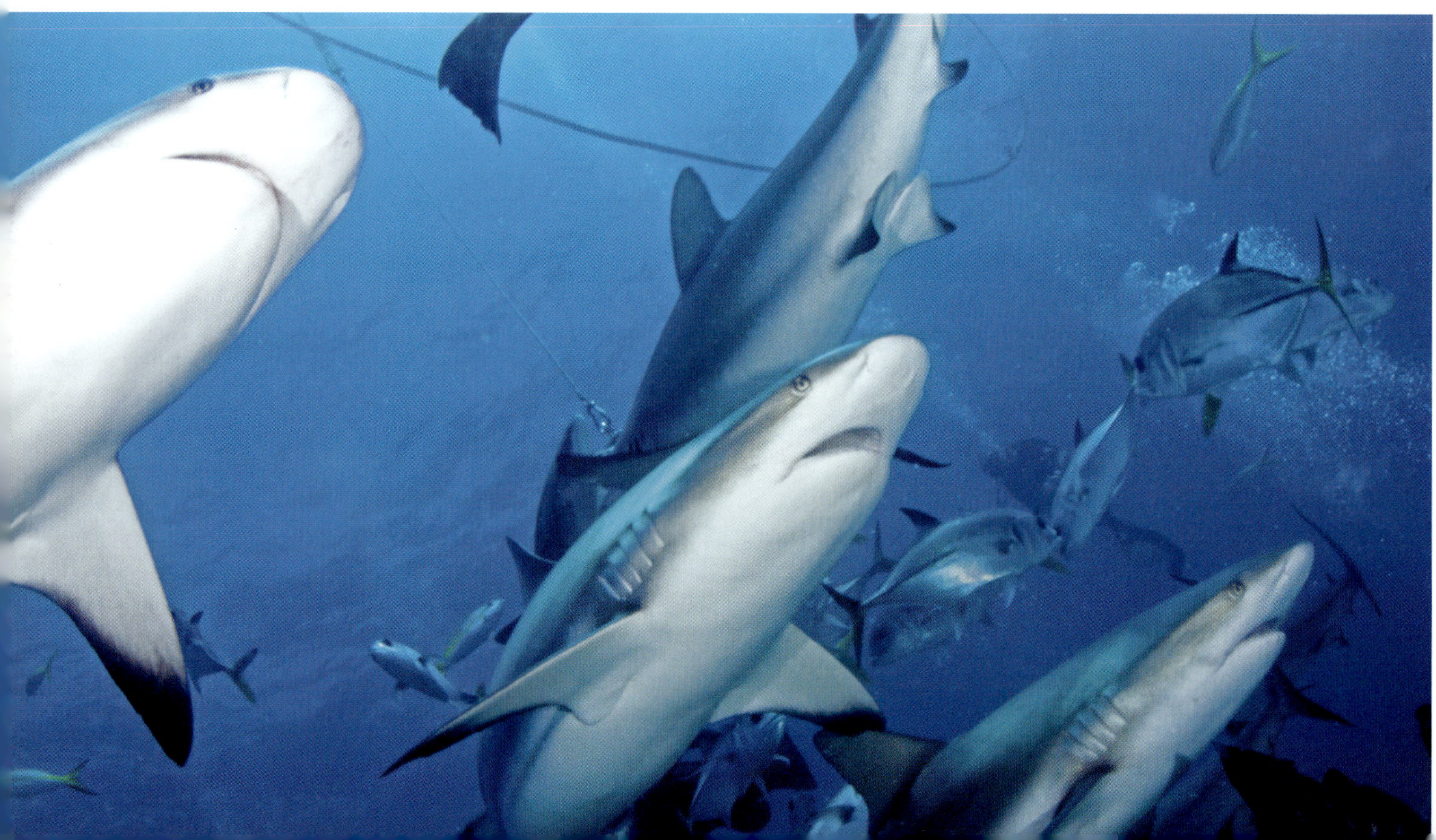

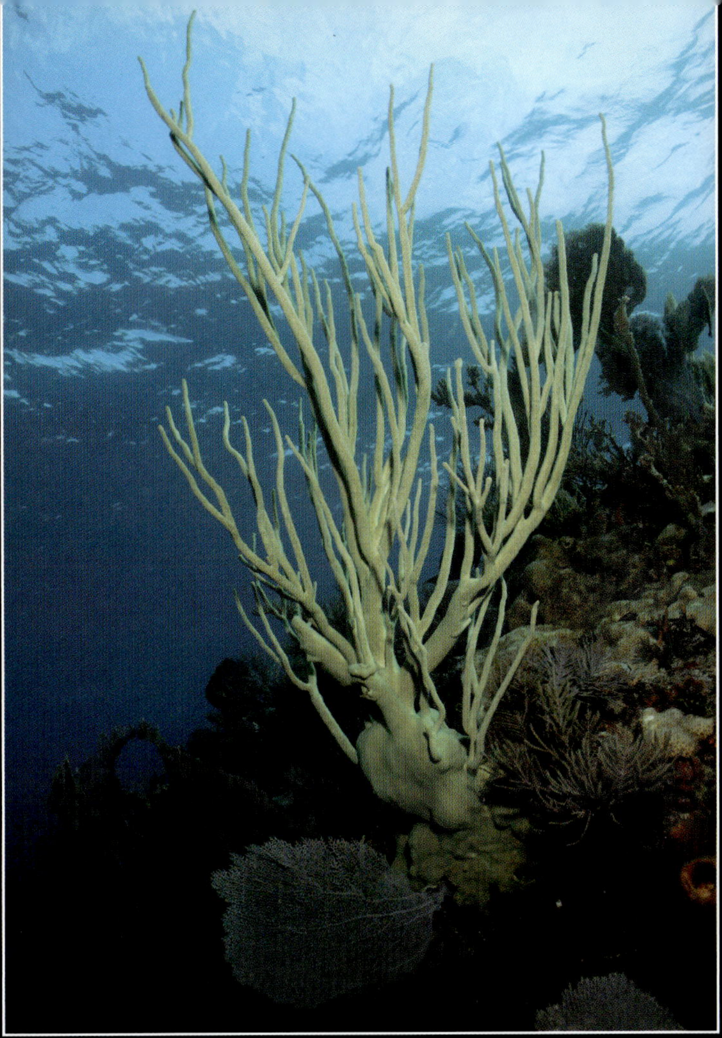

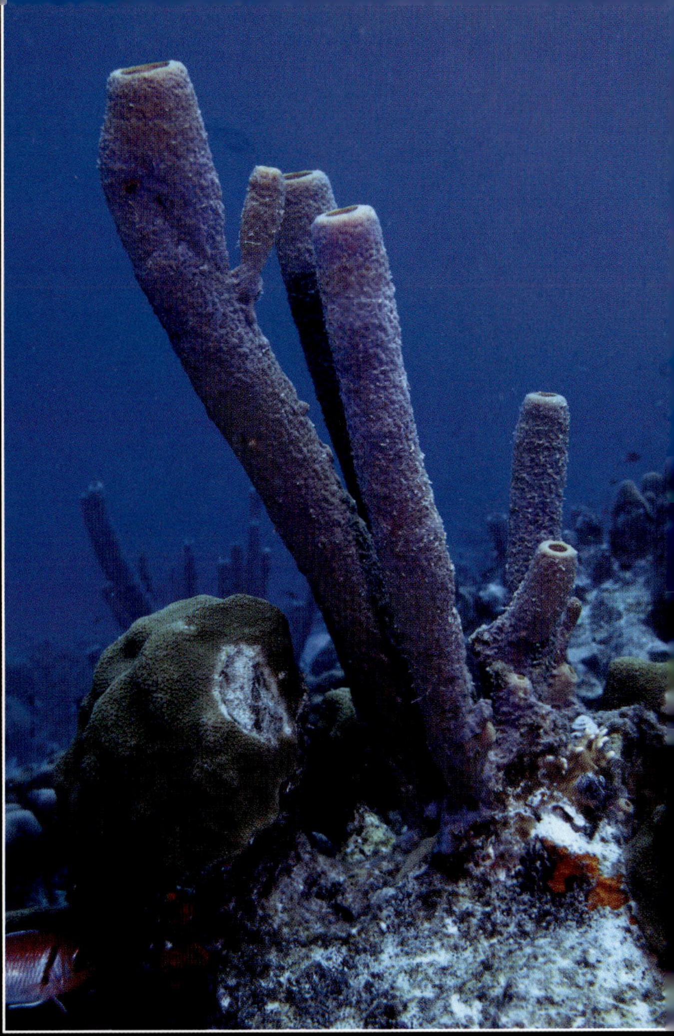

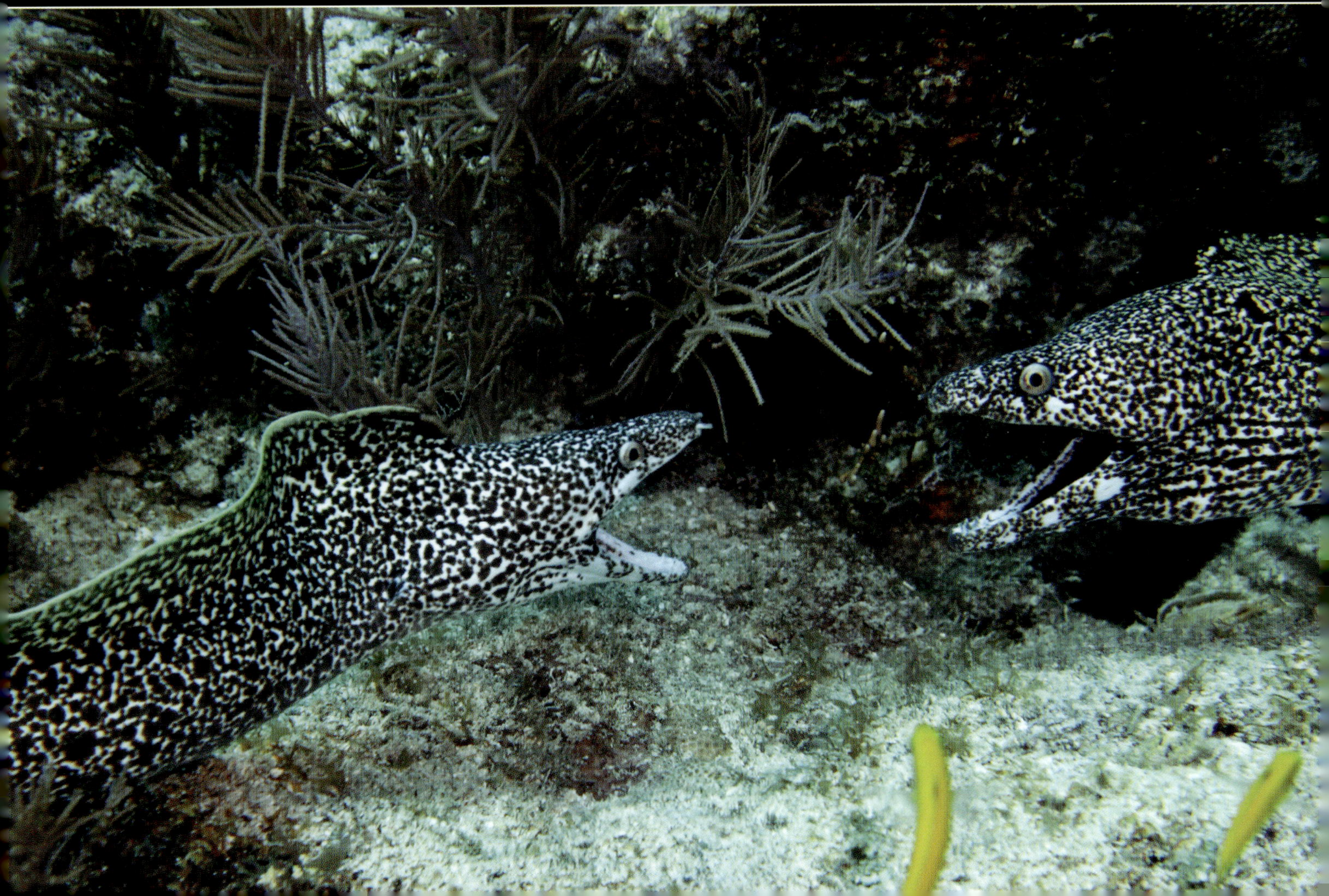

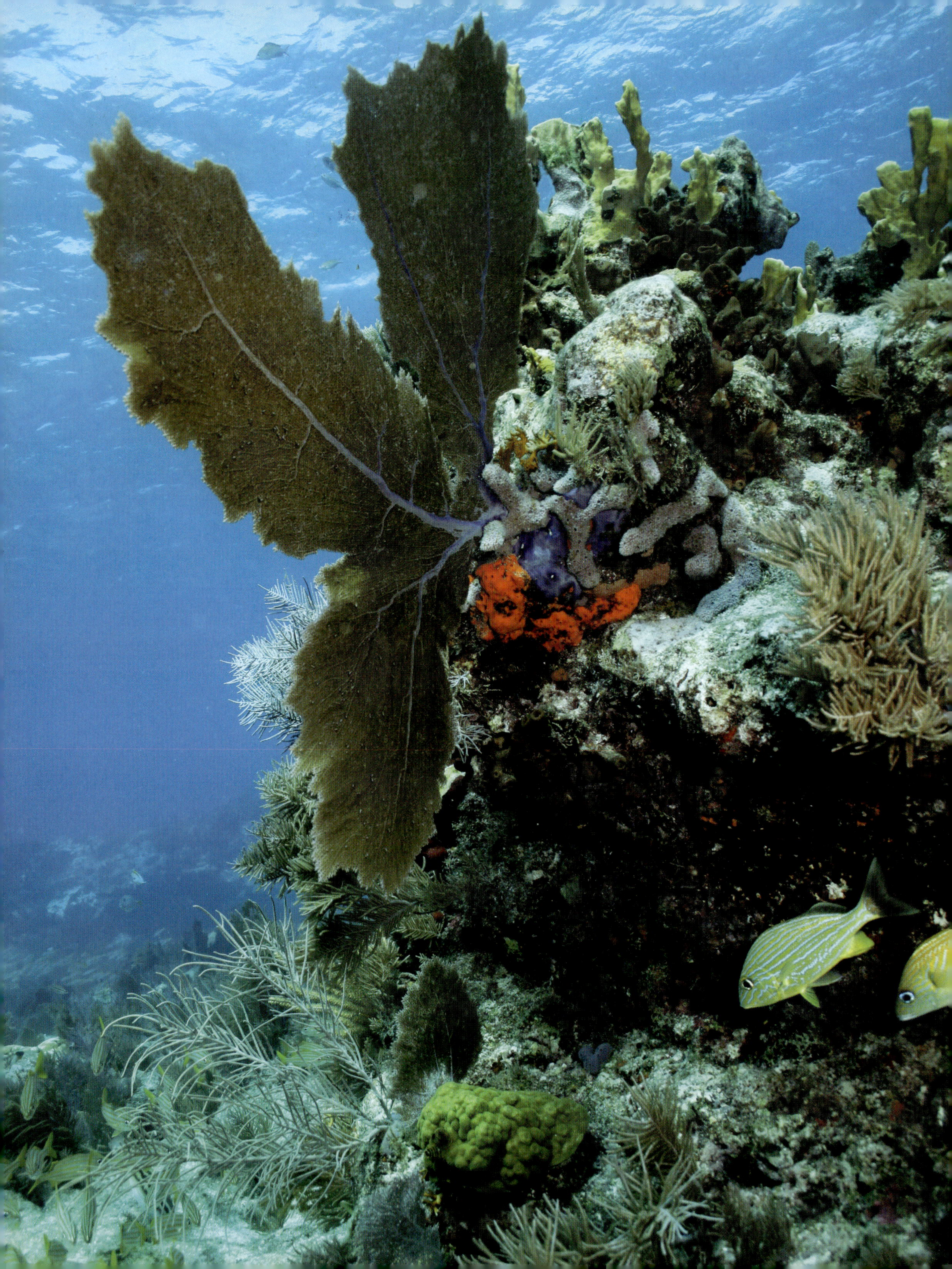

# 1. A TECHNICALLY PERFECT IMAGE

There are four elements that comprise a technically perfect or advanced underwater photograph: focus, exposure, composition, and subject. This chapter provides a quick review of those topics, plus some additional insights.

These four elements, while desirable in image making, should not be considered in a vacuum when determining how acceptable an image is. A photo that does not meet these criteria may still be a keeper. It may document a sentimental experience, or it may be your only capture of a subject. Sometimes the subject can be so compelling or rare, or the difficulty of capture so great, that it does not matter that it was not the nicest composition or perfectly exposed. If you like the image, keep it!

That said, the advanced photographer's goal is to create a technically perfect image, so let's review the four critical elements that comprise such a shot.

**Facing page**—Complementary and contrasting shapes, colors, and textures of multiple corals make for a splendid photo of the coral reef environment. Exposure: f/5.6, 1/125, and 100 ISO. **Below**—Another subject photographed from below. Note how this perspective seems to empower the subject and add a sense of drama to the image. Exposure: f/5.6, 1/125, and 100 ISO.

## FOCUS

I begin with focus because, of the four criteria, it is probably the most important. A lack of focus has been the ruin of many otherwise great photographs. It rivals backscatter as a reason why many photographs end up in the trash.

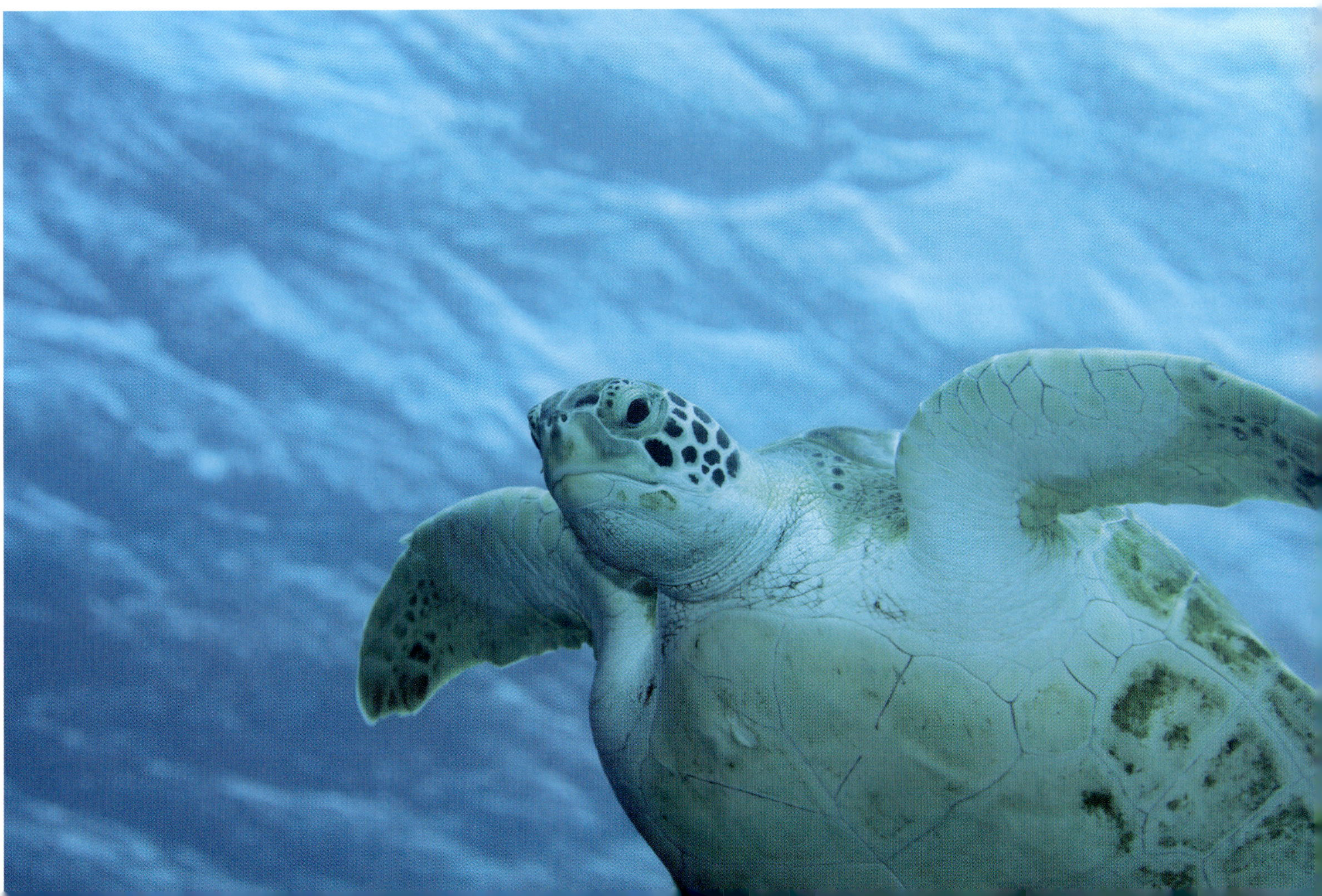

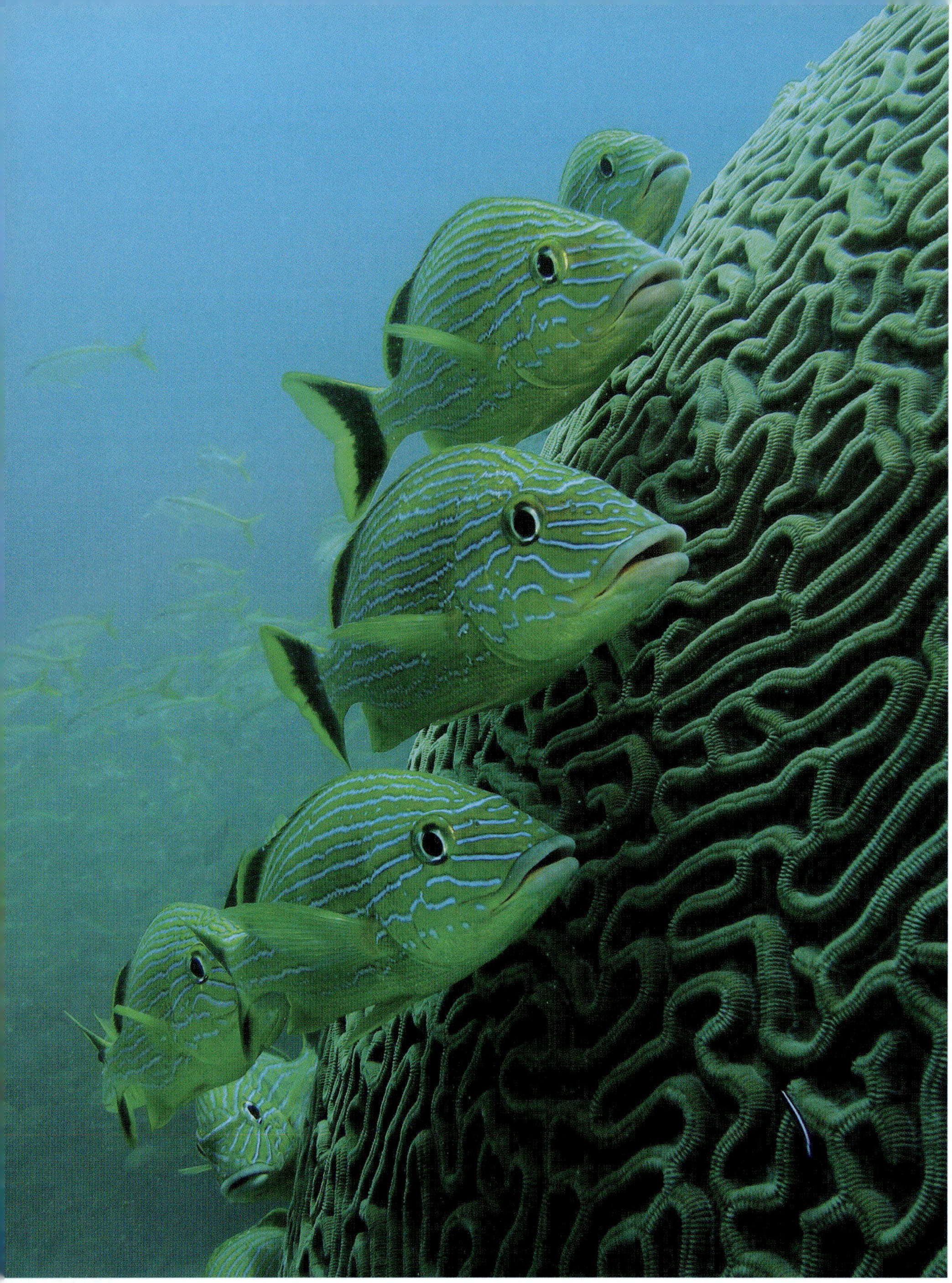

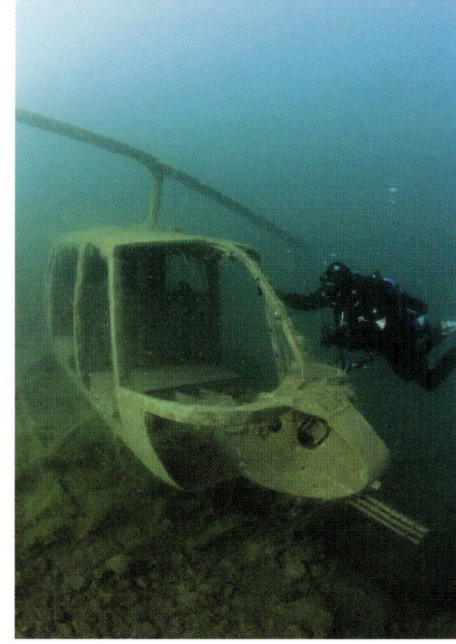

**Left**—Congregated fish will stay where they want to be if you approach slowly and patiently. You'll have better luck if you approach them from the front than if you sneak up on them from behind. Exposure: f/5.6, 1/125, and 100 ISO. **Above**—Fresh-water image. Exposure: f/8, 1/100, 400 ISO. No strobe. Photo courtesy of Steve Philbrook.

When a photograph is in focus, the subject can be viewed clearly and detail can be easily seen. When an image lacks focus, it can be frustrating to view—and frustration is not a feeling we want to elicit in our images.

We can achieve focus by using the camera's auto focus feature or manually focusing the lens. When shooting underwater, we primarily use auto focus. We rely on manual focus when using auto focus is not an option.

While we certainly know how to engage our camera's auto focus system, what we may not know is how it works and when we should employ the different auto-focus options our cameras offer. With a better understanding of the mechanics, we can better predict when auto focus will do the job and when we're better off using manual focus.

**The Focus Point.** A camera has one or more focus sensors (a light-sensitive strip). Cameras either employ a vertical line sensor, which collects data from one dimension, or a cross-type sensor, which is made of two sensors working in tandem to collect data from two dimensions.

In a camera with a single sensor, the focus point is the center of the viewfinder or image frame. When focus is acquired, a confirmation light typically shows in the viewfinder, indicating the area where focus was achieved. Many cameras will emit a tone indicating the lens is in focus.

High-end dSLRs utilize multiple sensors. Some high-quality auto-focus systems use the better-quality cross sensors, which allow for quicker focusing, in all sensor areas of the frame. More often, however, a cross sensor is used in the center of the frame and vertical sensors are used in other areas of the frame. When using a camera with multiple focusing sensors (some models offer up to forty-five as of this writing), the photographer has choices. In the underwater environment, most photographers, myself included, opt to use the center-of-frame sensor—typically the cross sensor.

*Locking the Focus Point.* To achieve focus, you can simply depress the shutter button halfway. Once focus is achieved, fully depressing the shutter button will capture the image. Alternatively, focusing can be assigned to another camera control, such as the "*" button on Canon cameras. Focus is then achieved by depressing that button. Once focus is achieved or "locked," the photographer can press the camera's shutter button, without the prerequisite half-press.

**Passive versus Active Auto Focus.** Today's cameras rely on one of two types of auto-focus capabilities: passive or active. Most modern cameras use

**Below**—This is an example of a technique called "macro wide angle." It's similar to a close focus/wide angle shot but in this approach, the foreground subject is smaller. Thanks to Steve Philbrook and Aquaventure Dive and Photo Center of Minneapolis, MN.

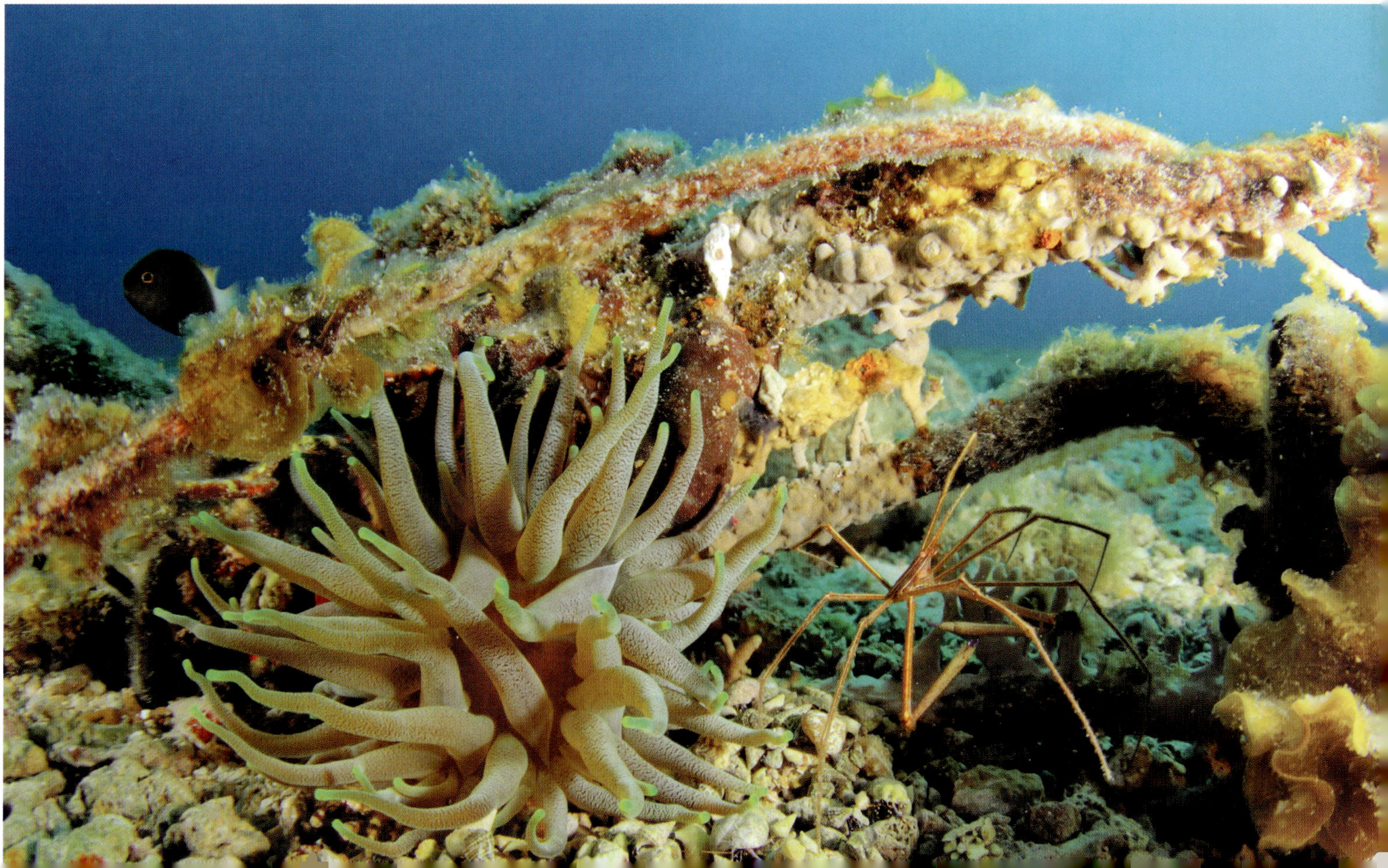

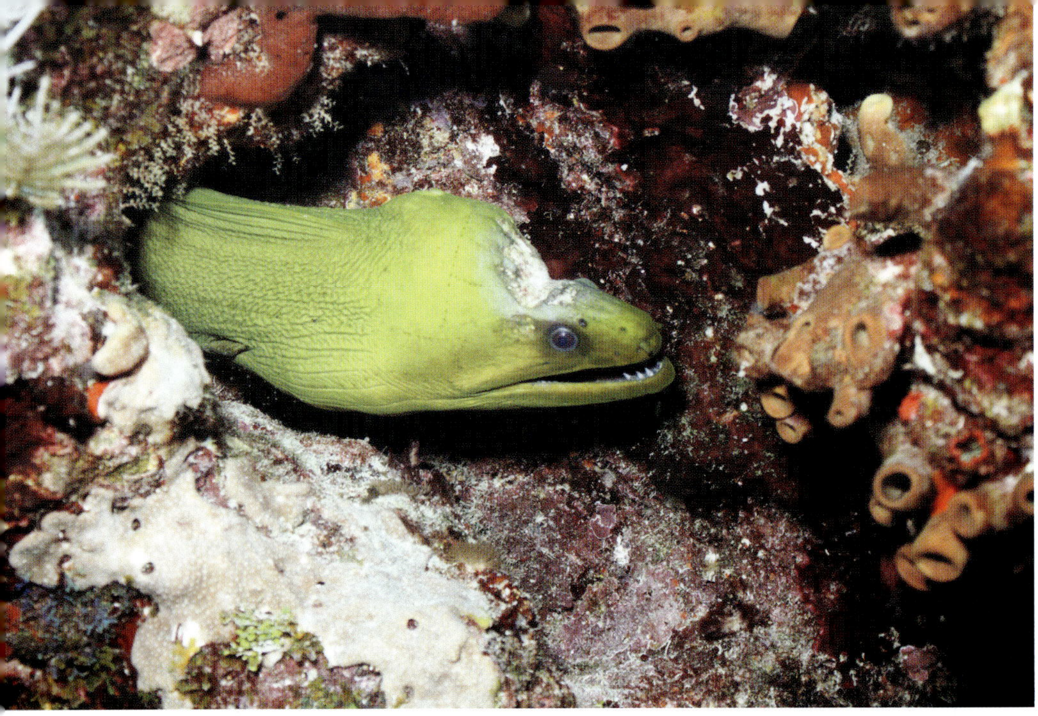

**Left**—Photographing diseased or sick corals or any aquatic life is an underwater photography niche that aids in marine study and conservation awareness. Exposure: f/5.6, $^1/_{125}$, and 100 ISO. Focal length 45mm.

passive focus. In this approach, the camera analyzes the scene and achieves focus via a contrast-detection method. In scenes with insufficient contrast, passive-focus cameras may not be able to produce the amount of sharpness we desire. To improve the odds of success, you can look for an object that has contrast and appears to be the same distance away as is your subject. Then, lock focus on that and return to your subject.

In active focus systems, a beam of light (often infrared) emitted from the camera determines the distance from the camera to the subject. This focus method requires multiple sensors. The upside is that, since it is not an optically based system, the camera can obtain focus in low-contrast situations.

*Overcoming Focusing Problems.* So, we have a dSLR with auto focus, and we know how to use the auto-focus controls. We know about passive and active auto focus, and know that our camera uses a sensor or multiple sensors to achieve focus. We know that in cameras with multiple sensors, we can select the focus area and that most of us will choose the center of the frame or viewfinder.

So, what can go wrong? Well, plenty.

When using auto focus, our success in focusing depends on: (1) the amount of ambient light; (2) the amount of contrast our subject has; and (3) subject and/or camera movement.

As mentioned earlier, auto-focus systems read the contrast in a scene in order to focus the lens. Often, there is little contrast when shooting in low-light situations or dimly lit areas such as caverns, crevices, and recesses in coral reefs. Similarly, there may be little contrast when photographing fish colored to blend in with the water column and located in the water column, or near-translucent subjects, such as Jellyfish.

There are a few work-arounds that can help when shooting scenes with low con or insufficient ambient light. One is to use a focus light (see page

53). Aiming that at your subject can often provide the contrast and light necessary to acquire focus. The second, as mentioned earlier, is to locate something that has contrast and is at the same distance as your subject, focus on it, lock the focus, compose the shot, and take the picture. I've also had some success in switching from my center auto-focus sensor to engaging all of the auto-focus sensors. The camera can then focus on something that one of its sensors picks up on, enabling me to take the photograph. This works great when that "something" the camera focuses on is at the same distance as the subject. When this is not the case, you'll end up with an out-of-focus subject.

If you find yourself photographing very close to your subject and unable to acquire focus, your subject may be too close to the lens. A remedy to this situation is simply to back away from your subject so that your working distance will be equal to, or greater than, the minimum focus distance.

If you find yourself photographing very close to your subject and unable to acquire focus, your subject may be too close to the lens.

Difficulty achieving focus may also be due to the aperture and focal length used. A relatively long focal length, coupled with a relatively large aperture, produces a relatively shallow depth of field. In such cases, any camera movement can make focusing slower, more difficult, or impossible. In these instances, the camera/lens auto-focus system hunts for focus, racking back and forth through the focus range of the system, and may never find it. The solution is to steady the camera, "set" yourself, and/or use a smaller aperture.

Camera movement, also called camera shake, results in an unfocused image, regardless of the type of camera or lens being used. To help alleviate this problem, select a shutter speed that is equal to or greater than the focal length of the lens being used. Another means of reducing or eliminating camera shake is to "set" yourself as solidly as you can.

In some cases, focus is impossible due to the mismatch between the lens and lens port. Most port manufacturers have lens and port charts that list the correct port for the lens being used (provided the port maker supports that lens). Of course, the problem can be avoided if you ensure that the lens and port are compatible at the time of purchase. This issue is discussed in more detail in chapter 2.

**Right**—Our underwater photographer is "set."

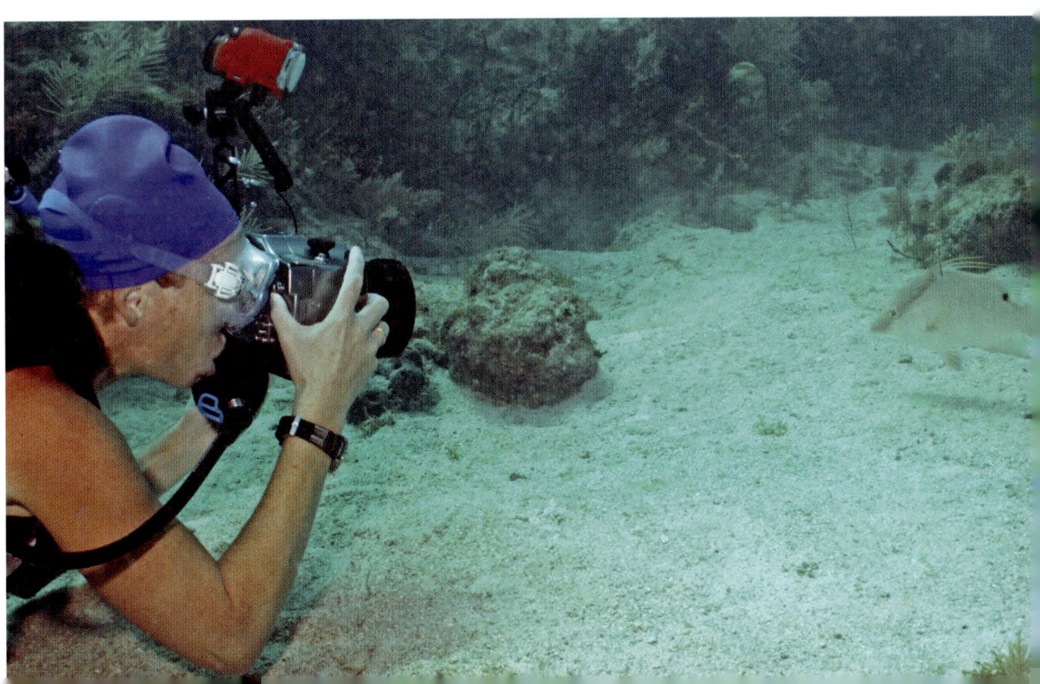

*Focusing on Moving Subjects.* So far I've limited the discussion of auto focus to the plain Jane version. Many modern dSLRs offer a feature that helps photographers capture in-focus images of moving subjects (Nikon calls it continuous focus, while Canon calls it AI focus). Once the photographer locks the focus on the subject, the camera's focusing system will sense the direction and speed in which the subject is moving and will continue to keep the subject in focus.

Another means to creating an in-focus image of a moving subject is to compose the image and track the subject with your camera, keeping it in the desired area of the frame. This is called panning. When the subject reaches the desired distance, shift your aim (if necessary), lock focus on the subject, quickly recompose, and take your photograph. Panning works when the subject is moving left to right or right to left in front of you. It does not work when the subject is moving toward or away from you.

One means to creating an in-focus image of a moving subject is to compose the image and track the subject with your camera, keeping it in the desired area of the frame. This is called panning.

Taking in-focus images of moving subjects requires practice. You can do this above water. Go outside and photograph the cars driving up and down your street. Hold your camera down and in front of you, then look for your subject. Once you see a car, try photographing it. With practice, you will learn how to quickly compose your shot. It's kind of fun, but your neighbors may think you've finally gone off the deep end.

**Manual Focus.** When the auto-focus system isn't doing its job or you don't want to allow for the time it takes for the camera to achieve focus, manual focus is the solution. Manual focus is only possible when the housing or port has a control system that enables you to manipulate the lens's focus ring.

If the lens's focusing ring is inaccessible, you can focus on an above-water subject that is roughly the same distance from your camera as your underwater subject will be, then install the camera/lens into the housing. Using a smaller aperture and a lens with a shorter focal length will allow for a wide depth of field that can help you photograph a fast and furious subject. The downside to this approach is you're committed to photographing subjects that are at that distance and within that depth of field throughout the duration of your dive.

Another strategy is to focus at the lens's hyperfocal point—the point nearest to the camera at which everything is considered acceptably sharp. When the lens is focused at this point, anything from that point to infinity will be in focus. Anything located within the hyperfocal distance (the distance between the camera and the hyperfocal point, which is dependent on the size of the image sensor, focal length of the lens, and the selected aperture) will be rendered acceptably sharp too. This sounds like a panacea, but the approach is not foolproof. The hyperfocal distance changes when the aperture is changed, and the aperture you need to capture the image may result in an unacceptable hyperfocal distance given the distance of your subject.

## EXPOSURE

When light strikes the digital camera's image sensor (a light-sensitive medium), an image is produced or, in other words, an "exposure" is made. Not all exposures are created equal. The amount of light that strikes the sensor can result in a too-dark (underexposed) or too-light (overexposed) image. Ideally, we want an image with a full range of tones and detail in the highlight and shadow areas.

Five influences govern the quality of the exposures we make. We can take full control over four of these, and we can manage the fifth one.

**ISO Rating.** We can control the sensor's responsiveness to light by dialing in a higher or lower ISO setting.

**Aperture.** Choosing a small aperture (high f-number, e.g., f/32) cuts the amount of light that strikes the image sensor. Using a large aperture (low f-number, e.g., f/3.5) will allow more light to strike the image sensor.

**Shutter Speed.** The shutter speed selected—the length of time that light is allowed to strike the sensor—also influences the exposure. A longer shutter speed (e.g., a few minutes) allows much more time for the light to affect the exposure than a shorter shutter speed (e.g., 1/500 second).

**Artificial Light.** Another way that we can control the amount of light used to create an exposure is by adding illumination, typically via a strobe light. (Measurements like guide numbers, watt-seconds, and Kelvin units allow us to gauge the output of the light.) Modern strobes offer settings that allow you to alter the output. The intensity of the light can also be controlled by increasing or decreasing the strobe-to-subject distance. Moving the strobe one foot closer or farther results in a ±1-stop change in exposure value.

**Ambient Light.** Ambient light is not something we can control, although it is measurable, in a sense, by metering it. Metering the ambient light will tell us whether our current camera settings will result in a correct exposure, over-, or underexposure. We can begin to manage ambient light by learning to be sensitive to how much or how little we have to work with and how much of it is used in making the exposure. We manage the impact of ambient light on our exposure by adjusting one of the other four exposure controls.

### DYNAMIC RANGE AND EXPOSURE

The term "dynamic range" refers to the maximum range of tones, from darkest shadow to brightest highlight, that can be captured by a device or perceived in an image.

The human eye has a pretty wide dynamic range—we can distinguish between brightly lit areas and areas of dark shadow quite well. Our camera sensors have a narrower dynamic range. In scenes with a very high contrast range, the camera's sensor will not be able to record faithfully all areas. Photographic paper has an even more narrow dynamic range.

In topside photography, photographers often put a graduated neutral-density filter over the lens to cut the light entering the lens in certain areas, thereby lowering overall contrast. However, such filters aren't very useful for dealing with bright patches and dark patches on an image. One way to cope is to shoot two or more photographs of the scene (exposing for highlight, exposing for shadow, etc.), then combine them digitally. Yet another way is to use a high-end digital camera, which has a higher-quality sensor with a wider dynamic range.

I tend to try to exclude areas of great brightness (e.g., sandy bottoms in shallow water on a sunny day) from my compositions. When this isn't possible, editing the highlights in postproduction may help.

### THE CASE FOR MANUAL EXPOSURE

An exposure can be made manually or automatically. If you're reading this book, don't count on using the automatic exposure setting. It may work great in some situations, but it won't for us since the light we use to make our exposures reflects from objects (like our subject) or is absorbed (by the water column) and finally passes through the lens to strike the image sensor. Automatic exposure will also fail us when objects in the frame reflect light very differently from one another (e.g., a bright silvery, light-reflecting fish photographed against a light-absorbing background like shaded coral).

Using manual exposure will allow you to dial in the appropriate ISO setting, aperture, and shutter speed for your subject and scene and achieve a correct exposure. You can also introduce a strobe if desired for an added level of control over the exposure.

There are three points of departure for achieving an accurate manual exposure:

**The Sunny 16 Rule.** This rule states that on a bright, sunny day you can set your aperture to f/16 and set your shutter speed to (inversely) match the ISO (i.e., your exposure might be f/16 at ISO 100 and 1/100 second) to achieve a correctly exposed image.

The rule serves as a starting point for making the exposure. Underwater, an equivalent of 1 stop of ambient light is lost for every 33 feet of depth. Therefore, if I was using an exposure of f/16, 100 ISO, and 1/100 second and dove to a depth of 33 feet, I would have to open up my aperture 1 stop to compensate for the lost light. I would take a photograph and check the LCD display. If the exposure looked good, I would be all set. If not, I could simply make an adjustment.

**Built-In or Handheld Meter?** Metering can also help you achieve an accurate underwater exposure. When I descend to my diving depth, I usually meter the water column or whatever area will be my background. I adjust my exposure settings until I zero out the meter reading, take a picture, review it on my LCD, and decide whether I need to make any adjustments.

A quick word on metering: most cameras offer multiple metering modes, including spot, center-weighted, and matrix metering. In the spot metering mode, the camera evaluates a very small area of the scene. When set to the center-weighted average metering option, the camera evaluates a larger area around the center of the frame. In the matrix metering mode, the camera analyzes even more of the scene. My personal preference is center-weighted average metering.

**Just Go for It.** Establish a starting exposure. I photograph my buddy to get a starting exposure for the dive, then review the histogram on my LCD screen. When I see data running off either end of the histogram's scale, I know I have underexposed or overexposed. In that case, I adjust my exposure settings and take another photograph.

### EXPOSURE CHALLENGES

When we are challenged to light a scene containing reflective and non-reflective objects, we have to decide which objects will be correctly exposed. The choice is obvious: expose for your main subject.

One of the toughest exposure challenges, in my opinion, is when the subject is highly reflective, or worse, when part of the subject is highly reflective. There are times when we simply will not be able to get a correct exposure. We can blame this on the limits of our digital photographic technology, but the truth is, sometimes the light just isn't right. When this is the case, do not take the shot. Just enjoy the scenery!

Once you get the correct exposure, you can stick with those settings until something noticeable changes. If the ambient light gets brighter or dimmer or if the background changes from something that was absorbing light to a light-reflecting one, you will need to make some adjustments.

### ADDING STROBE LIGHTING

As we advance in our underwater photography, we add an external strobe to the mix. Using an external strobe offers some advantages over on-board camera flash: it is more powerful and its output can often be adjusted, the photographer can change the strobe-to-subject distance, and mounting the light off the lens axis can prevent or reduce image-degrading backscatter. *(Note:* Backscatter results when flash-illumined particulate matter in the water column between the lens and subject reflects light into the lens.)

Unless we are shooting in an environment that lacks ambient light (e.g., at night, inside of a cave, deep inside of a cavern, or inside of a shipwreck), the strobe should serve as a secondary light source.

When photographing deep in the water column, there is a loss of ambient light, and some of the color bands of our subject matter are absorbed. Using a strobe helps to compensate for the lost light and restores the subject's color.

Obviously, adding or subtracting strobe lighting will impact the exposure. When a strobe is used but not needed, the image will be overexposed. If additional light is needed but not added, an underexposed image will result. When used appropriately, the strobe will add the light necessary to allow for a correct exposure. The image will appear natural-looking, and viewers may not even realize a strobe was used.

**Top**—A fully assembled dSLR camera system with strobe and polycarbonate housing. **Bottom**—Here, the photographer takes the time to study the scene before taking the photograph. Exposure: f/6.7, $^{1}/_{125}$, and 100 ISO. Focal length 18mm.

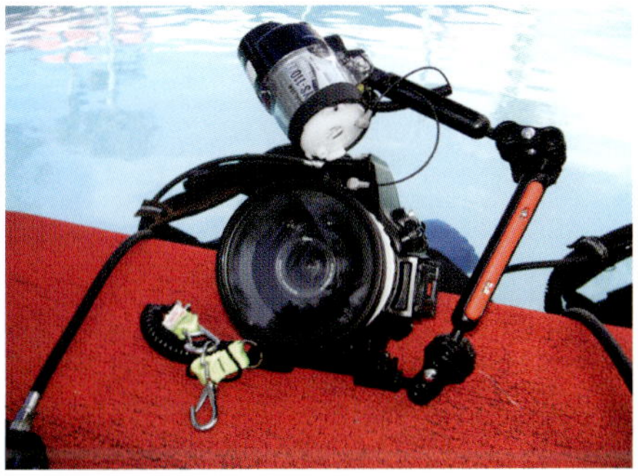

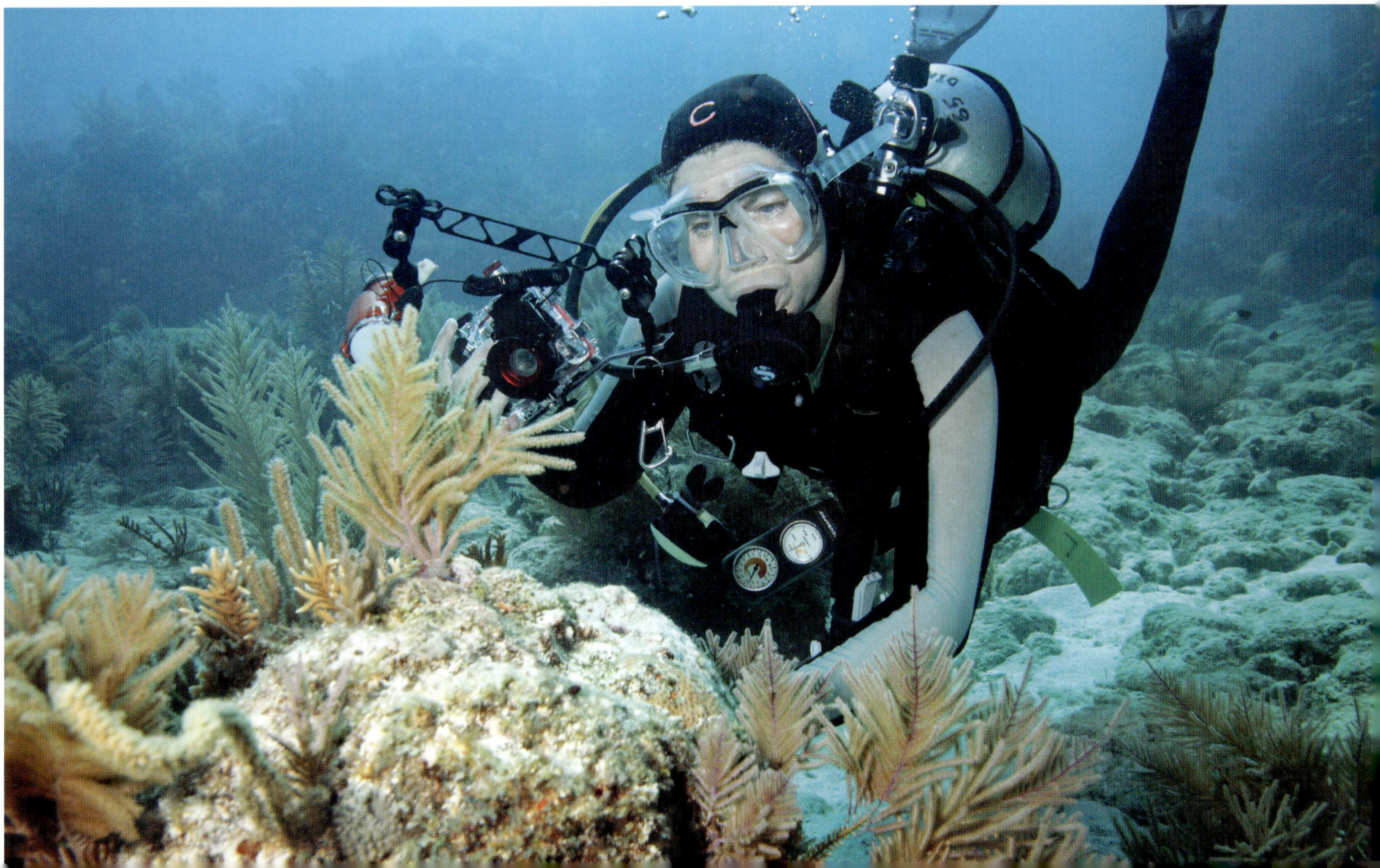

To easily determine how much or how little strobe output is required, check the LCD and the thumbnail and histogram after taking a photograph. If there is too much light in a particular image area, aim the strobe a bit differently, alter the strobe-to-subject distance, shift your position relative to the subject, change the composition or, if your strobe allows, reduce the output.

## COMPOSITION

Effective composition is another element of an advanced underwater photograph. We must decide what elements of the scene we will include or exclude in the frame and how they can best be arranged to engage the viewer. Using the Rule of Thirds, leading lines, extreme blur (bokeh), silhouettes, and close-focus/wide angle approaches are some of the choices we can consider when creating a composition.

### ID SHOTS

Most new photographers take what are referred to as fish ID shots—usually a photo of the whole fish and its broadside. Images like these are used in fish identification books (hence the lingo). They are not creative, per se.

**Top left**—The specimen shot, also known as an ID shot. Nice, but not interesting. **Top right**—Here, the image was composed to make a more interesting photograph of the same subject. **Bottom left**—An example of bokeh. Bokeh is a nice touch in fish or critter portraiture when you don't want other areas of the image to distract from your subject. The design of the aperture and number of blades it uses seem to have an influence over the quality of bokeh. A pleasing bokeh is a very subjective thing. **Bottom right**—Here is an example of a close-focus/wide angle shot. There are two subjects—one is close and in focus and the other is farther away and in the background.

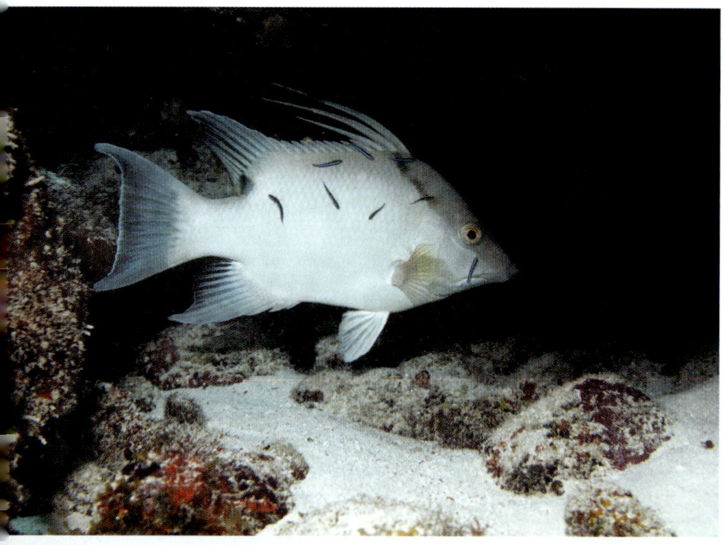

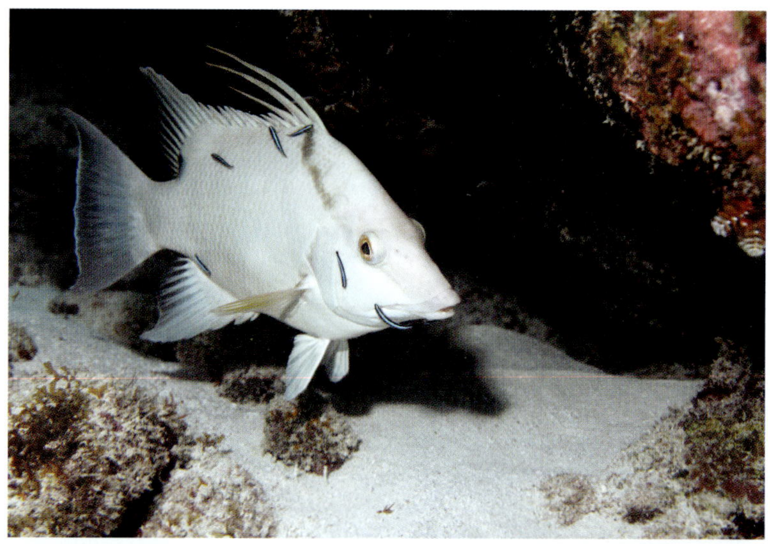

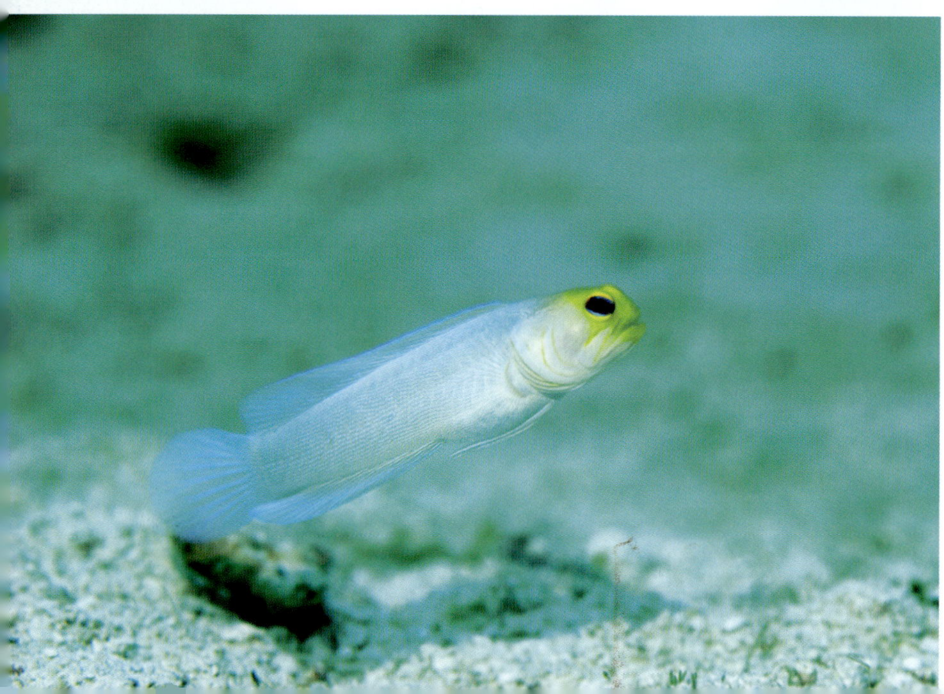

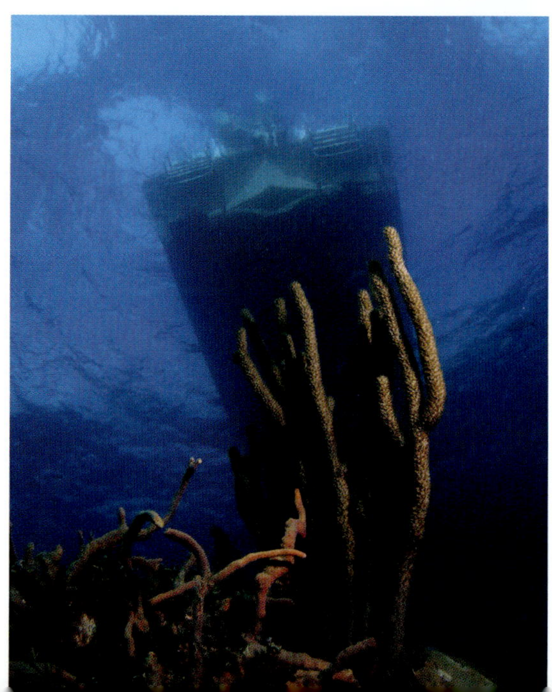

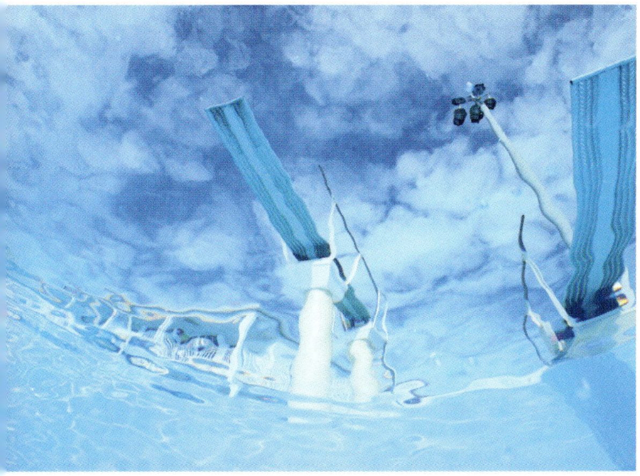

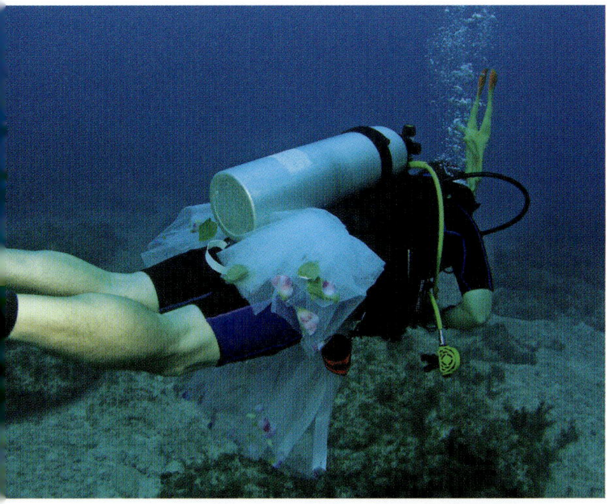

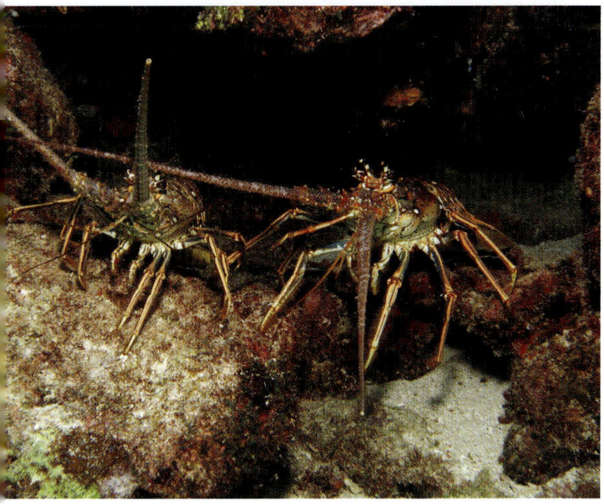

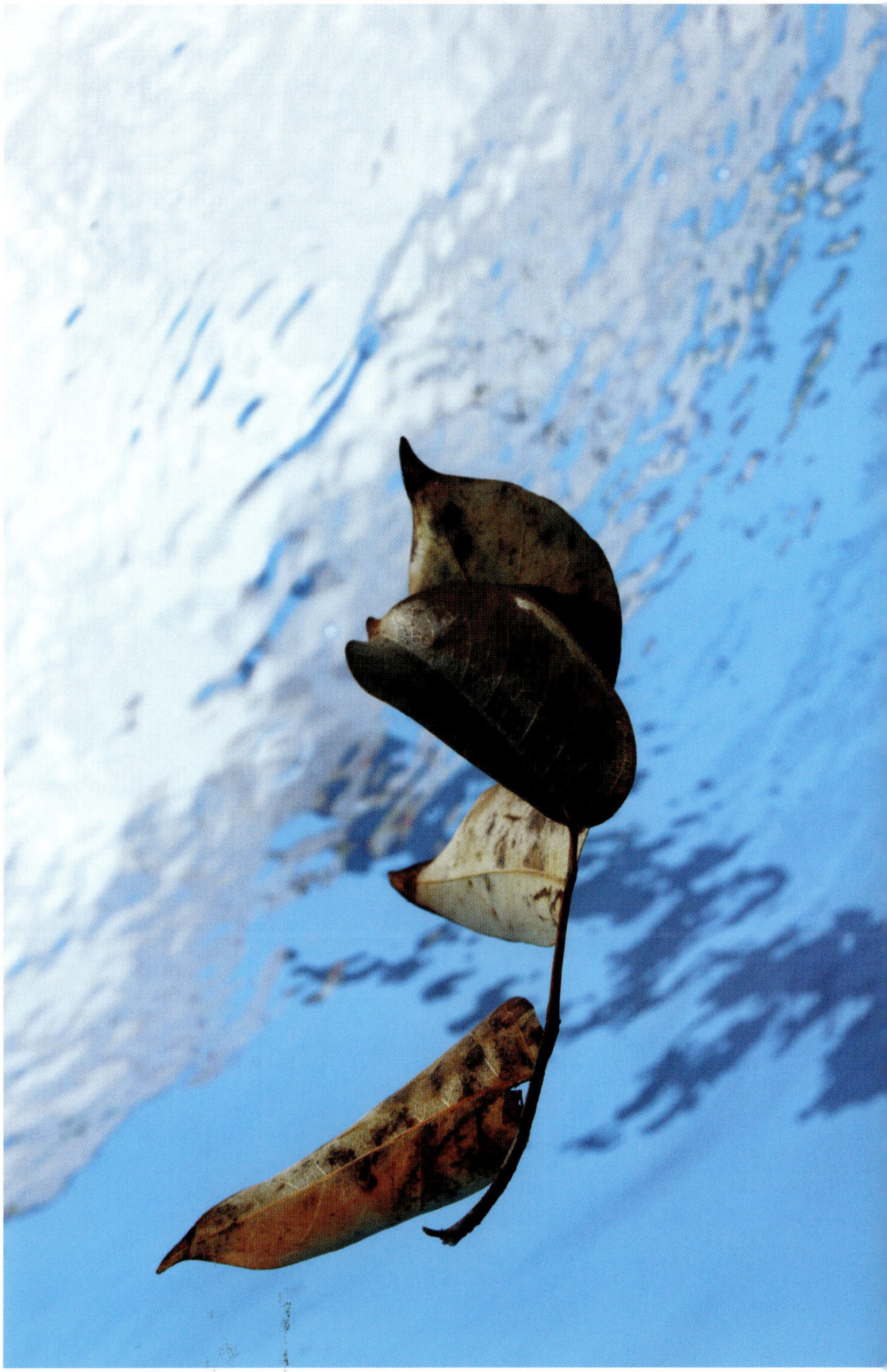

**Left**—(Top) When shooting in shallow water, the photographer sometimes captures some of the surface of the water in the image. The visible surface area is called Snell's window. Here, it is included in the composition. In fact, it is the composition. (Center) The leading lines of my jocular friend Frank's legs lead to the tutu he is wearing. From there, the line of his scuba tank leads the eye to his dive buddy, a rubber chicken! (Bottom) In this image, the Rule of Thirds was used to arrange the composition. The subject's eyes were aligned not with an intersection point, but rather the upper horizontal line of the rule. **Right**—This photo of a leaf was taken in a pool on a cold winter day in Key Largo. The photographer created a great composition in less than optimal conditions. Sometimes we can use our creativity to create a great image. Photograph courtesy of Connie Z Photography, LLC.

### SUBJECT

Underwater photography subjects come in all shapes and sizes. Sometimes they exist in a backyard swimming pool, and other times they are found in distant seas.

Underwater photographers tend to specialize in a certain subject or image style. Keeping our eyes open for new opportunities will allow us to advance our skills and keep our passion alive. As the subject matter in front of your lens changes and your shooting conditions change, you'll need to adapt your technique to create the most effective photographs. We'll take a closer look at some of the strategies we can use to create advanced images later in the book. For now, let's take a look at the equipment used by advanced underwater photographers.

**Facing page**—(Top) Fish are the favored subject for most underwater photographers. (Bottom left) Macro subjects, like Christmastree Worms, make the list of great prospective subjects. (Bottom right) A reef scene is the underwater version of a landscape photograph.

**Left**—Divers make great subjects. **Top right**—Man-made objects, such as wrecks or, as shown here, an undersea habitat, are also popular subjects. **Bottom right**—A photograph of an unusual subject, such as a ray, will usually capture a viewer's interest.

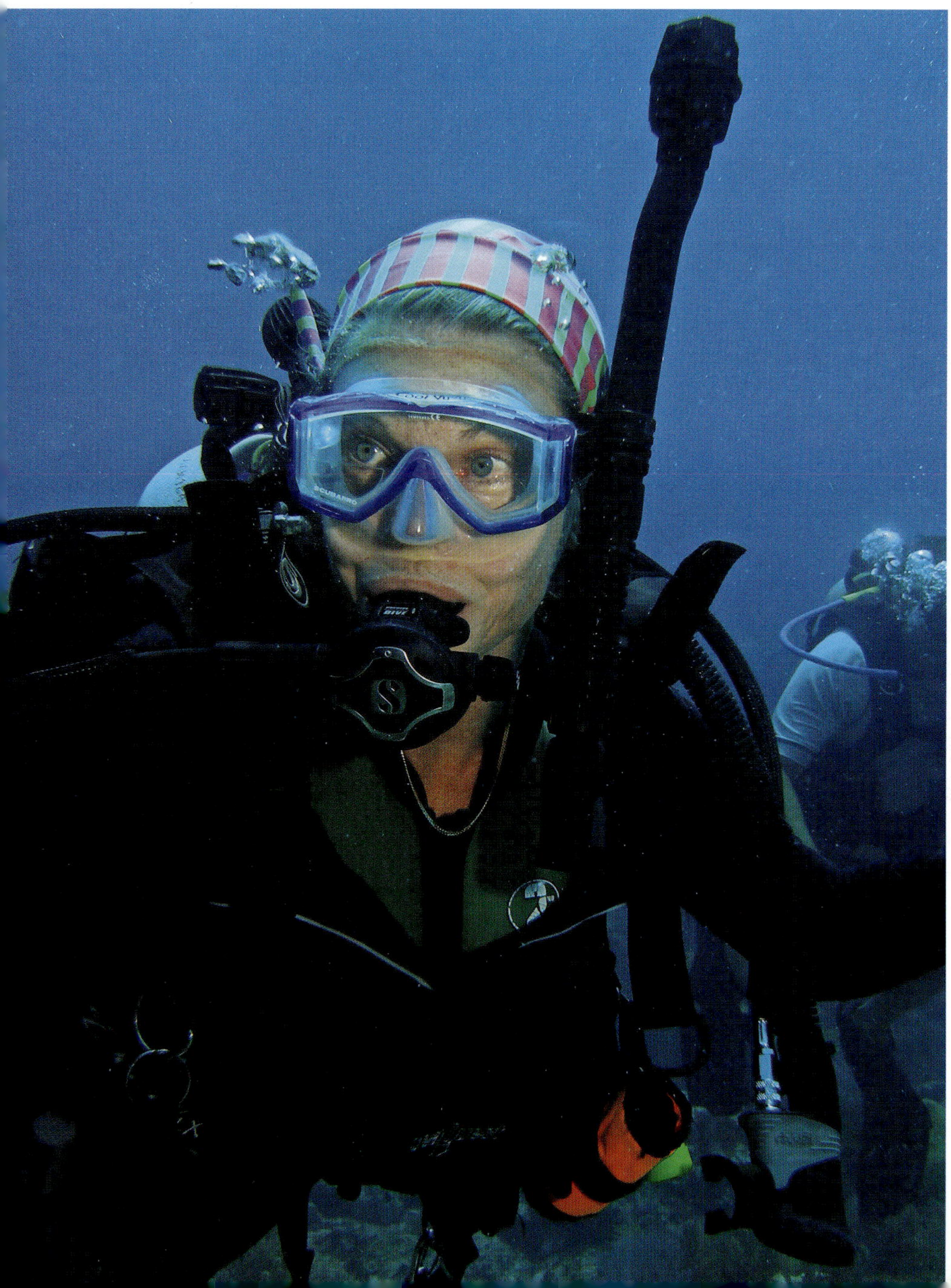

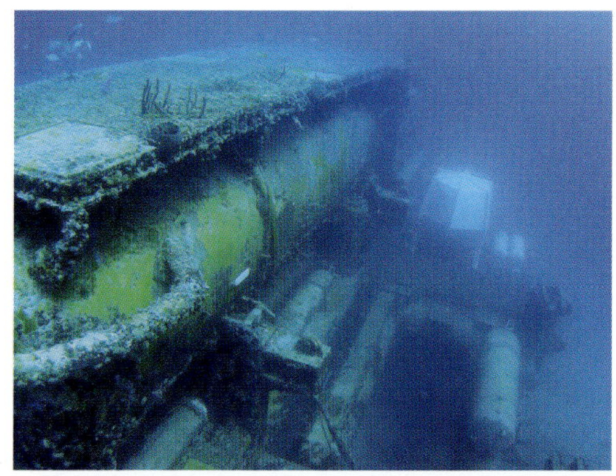

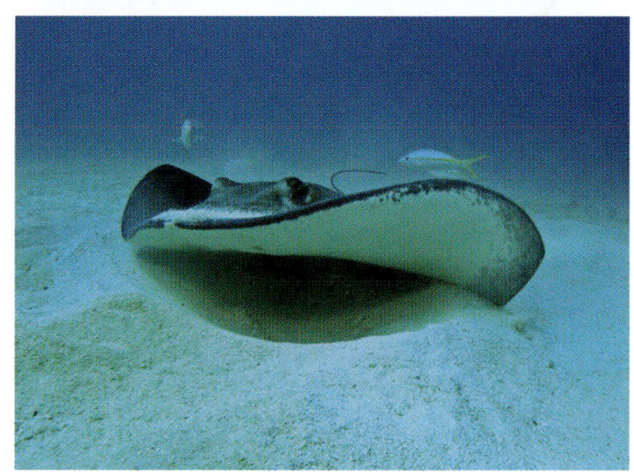

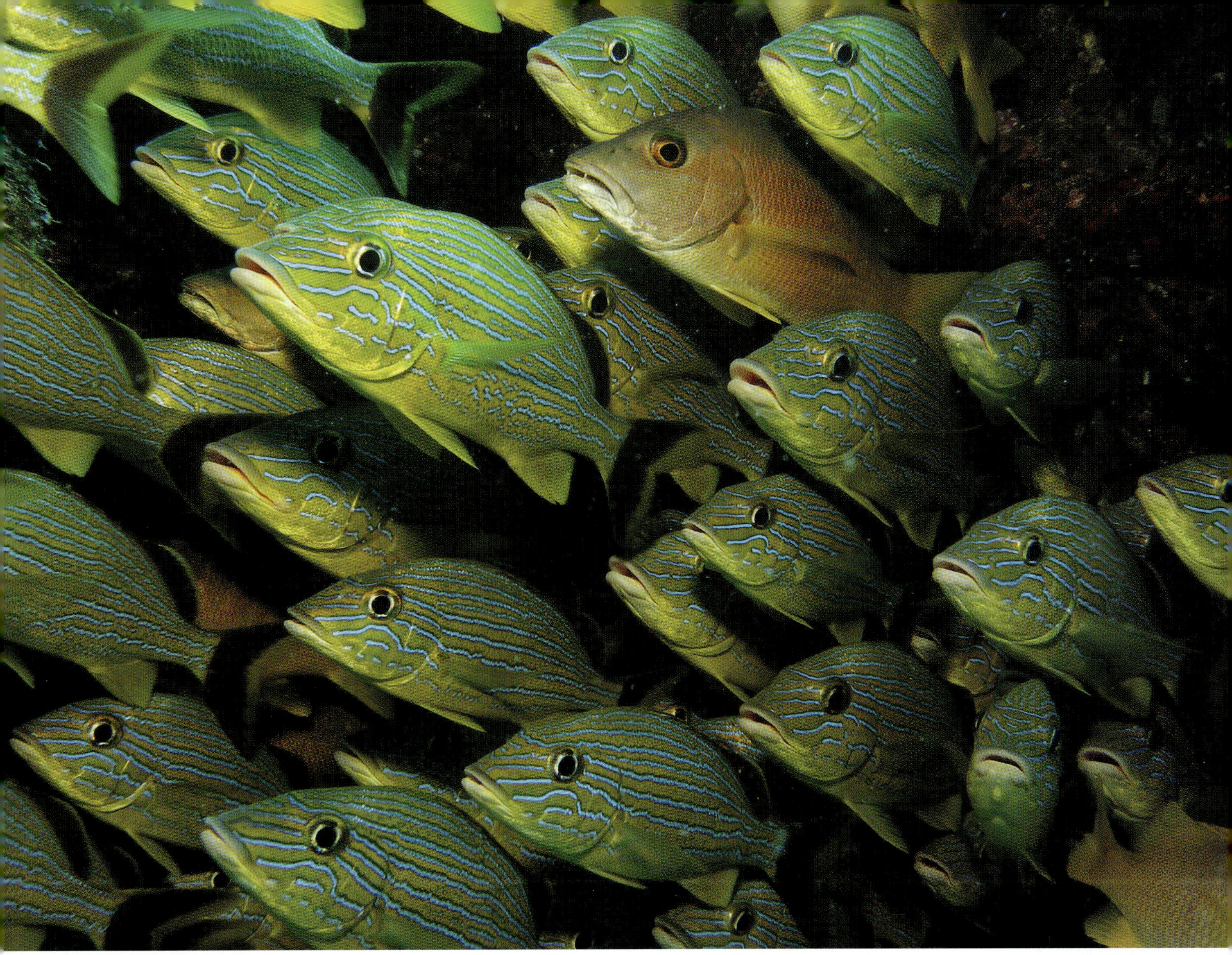
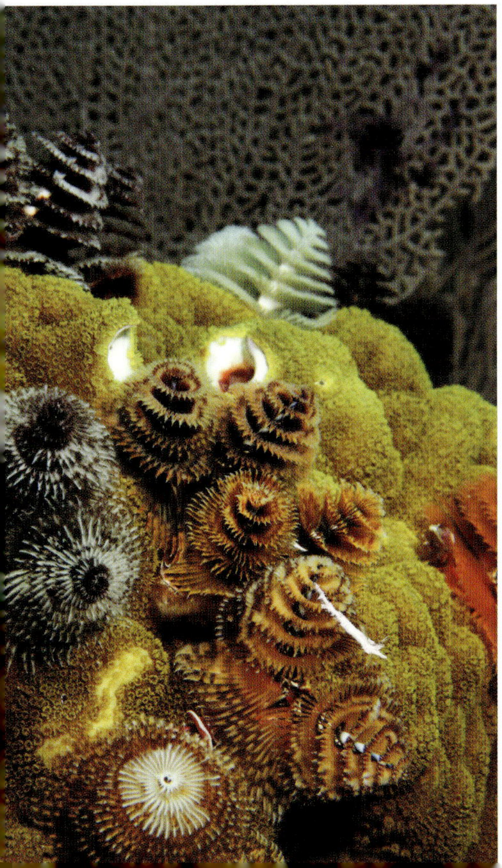
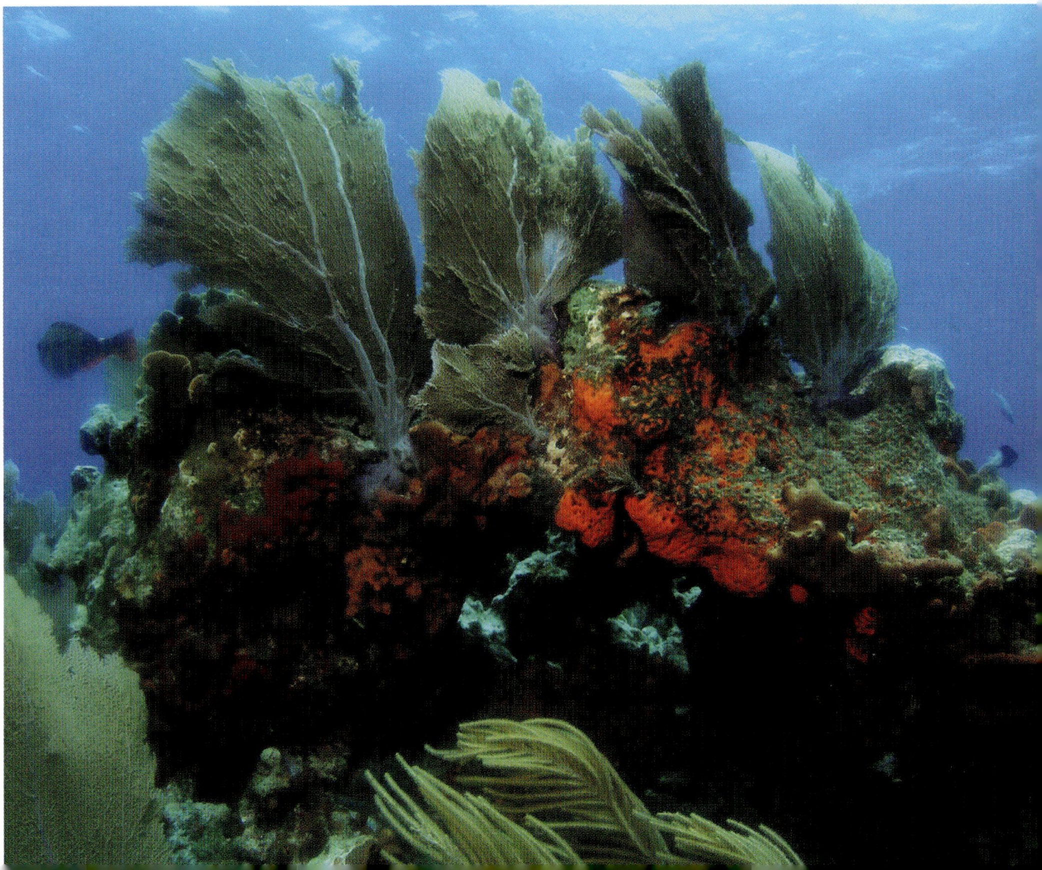

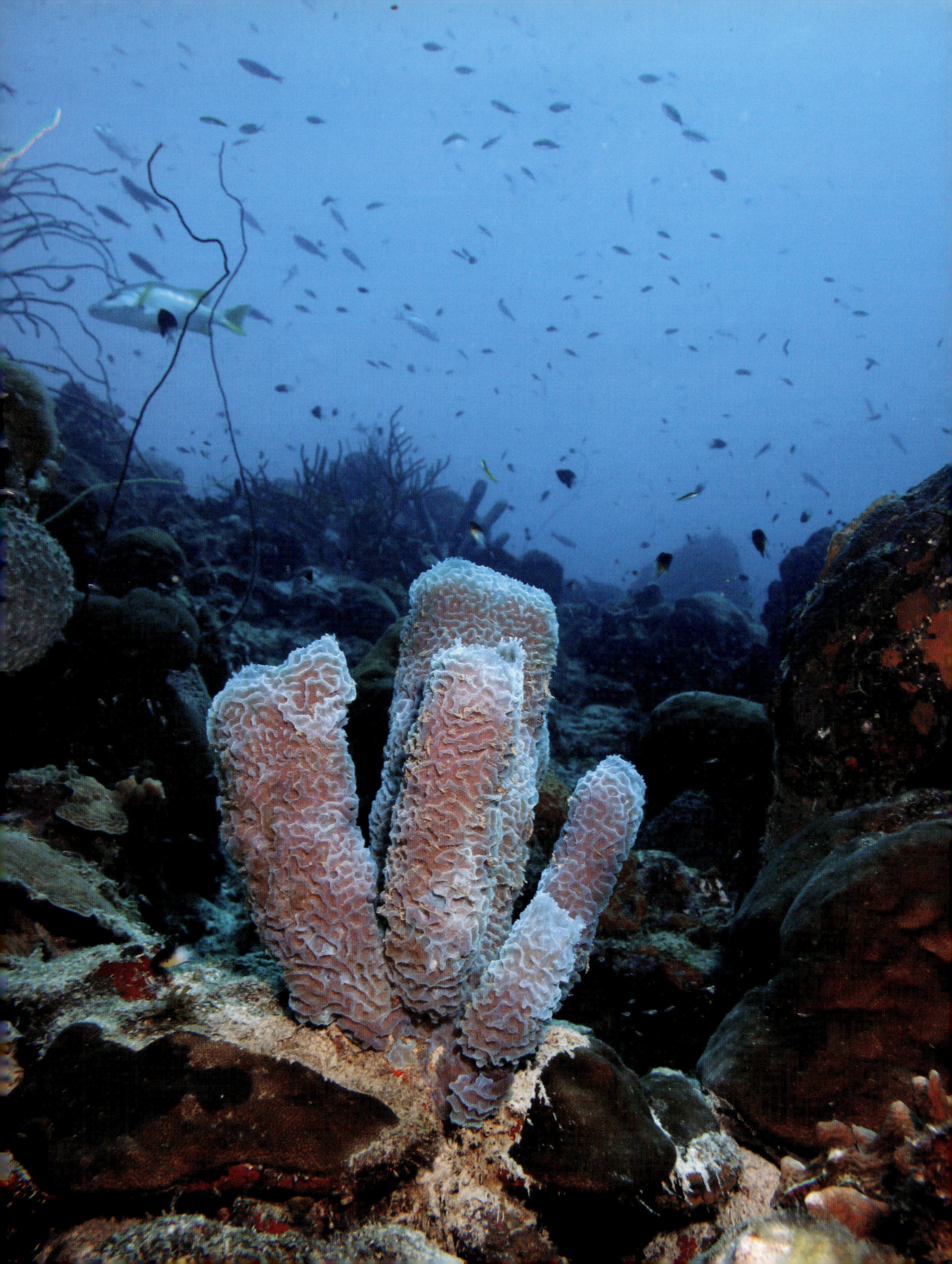

# 2. EQUIPMENT AND TECHNOLOGY

I took up underwater photography so I could share what I saw with friends who did not dive. Taking the pictures was a lot of fun, and I captured many great memories. I never really thought about whether my pictures were any good in the photographic sense. I felt successful if I managed to document the subject in front of my lens.

As time went on, I began to expect more from my images. I began to invest in gear that helped me in my quest for creating more advanced images.

Underwater photography can be a big investment, but it doesn't have to be. Consider your audience and your commitment level before you make purchases. Remember why you are shooting and make purchasing decisions with your goals in mind.

**Facing page**—When shooting during wall dives, it is most effective to photograph from below or alongside your subject. Either vantage point allows you to create subject separation and present negative space. Exposure: f/6.7, 1/125, and 100 ISO.

## THE CAMERA SYSTEM

Underwater photographers have numerous tools at their disposal: cameras, lenses and accessories, housings, lens ports, lens port extenders, ring gears, strobes and their communication links, and the components needed to join

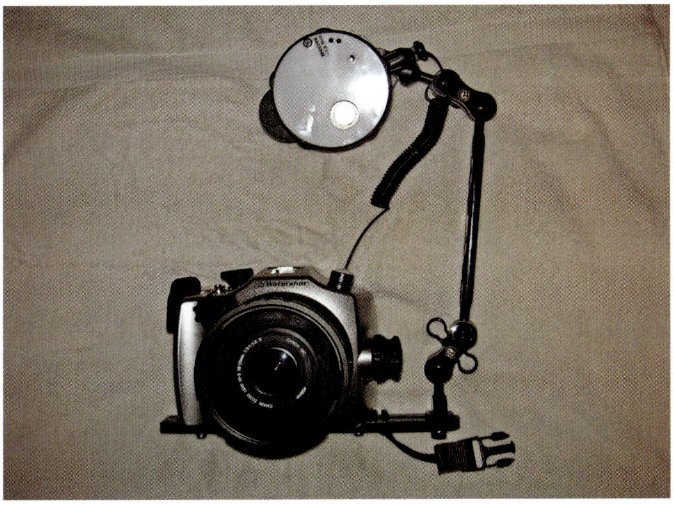

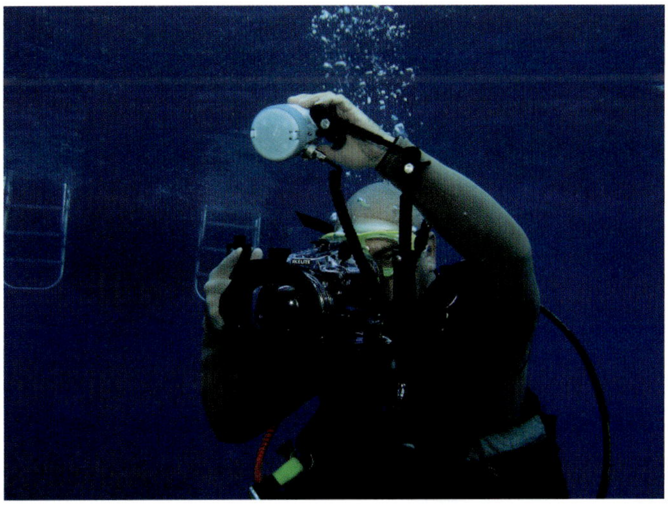

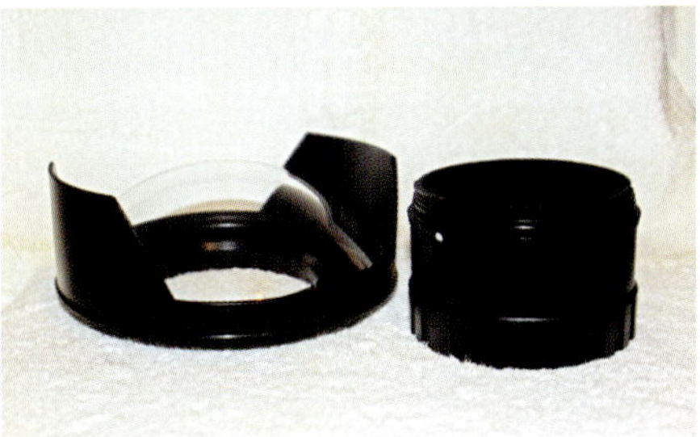

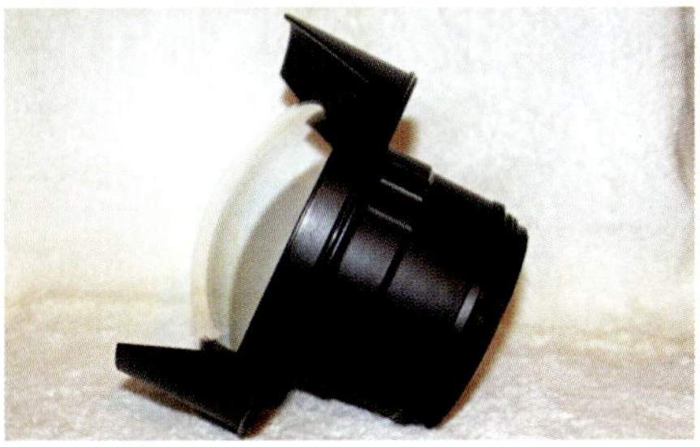

**Top left**—An assembled housed dSLR system with aluminum housing, flat port, tray, adaptors, arm, clamps and strobe with fiber-optic sync cable. **Top right**—An underwater photographer gets ready to function-check his housed dSLR system, comprised of a polycarbonate housing, dome port, tray, handle, clamps, strobe arm, strobe and using an electrical sync cord. **Bottom left**—This image features a dome port with a port extender. **Bottom right**—Here the dome port and extender are assembled.

them. This collection of tools is technically a camera system, but we refer to the system as an underwater camera.

Most beginners start out with a point & shoot camera and housing. As they advance, they add a strobe and the necessary components.

An advanced photographer will typically opt for a more advanced camera—a full-featured digital camera (one that allows for full manual exposure control) or digital single-lens-reflex camera (dSLR). The dSLR is the standard for advanced underwater photographers. Therefore, our discussions will center on dSLR systems.

**The dSLR.** Using a dSLR offers clear advantages for advanced underwater photographers:

- There is no shutter lag. When you push the shutter button, the camera acquires focus and captures what you saw at that very moment in time.
- Using a dSLR allows you to capture two or more images without digital lag in most cases. (There are two instances when it is still a problem: When the buffer fills, there may be a brief lag until the buffer clears and another photograph can be taken. Also, when an on-board flash is needed, time is required for its capacitor to recycle. To address these issues, buy the fastest memory card available and turn down the output of the flash on the camera to cut the recycle time needed.)
- Photographers shooting with dSLRs have a wide selection of high-quality lenses at their disposal.
- DSLRs have a higher-quality auto-focus systems that enable quicker focusing in lower-light, lower-contast scenes.
- Viewfinding. When using a dSLR, the photographer viewfinds through the lens. This allows for a better, clearer view of everything in the scene than does relying on the LCD.
- Power management is less of an issue, as dSLR batteries afford more shots between charges and they are less prone to heat buildup, which can cause condensation inside the housing.

*What to Buy?* There are many dSLRs on the market. Before making a purchase, do some research. Find out whether there are underwater housings made for the camera (this important topic is detailed in the next section). What lenses are compatible with the system? How much support (lens ring gears, port extensions/extenders) is available? Are ports available? You'll want to ensure the camera's ergonomics suit you and that you can easily assemble and disassemble the system components. You will also need to determine whether parts and service will be available should the need arise.

Make sure that there is a selection of strobes that work with the system. If you already own a strobe, ensure it can be used with your new camera and housing.

### FRIENDLY ADVICE

When working underwater, less is often more. If you go overboard, you risk becoming so focused on all of the arms, lights, and clamps that you miss the "Kodak moment." It can be difficult to dive with a lot of equipment. Also, some underwater environmental conditions can make using some of your gear impossible. Start small and build your system as you go.

*Tip:* When you're considering buying new equipment, check out www.dpreview.com. The site features a camera database that you can use to learn about the features various models offer, and you can compare models too.

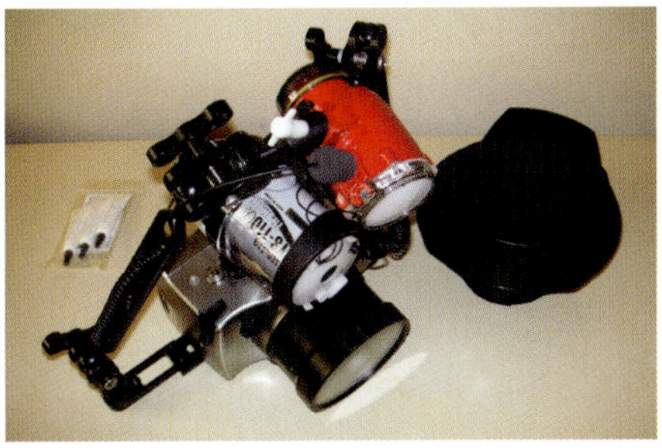

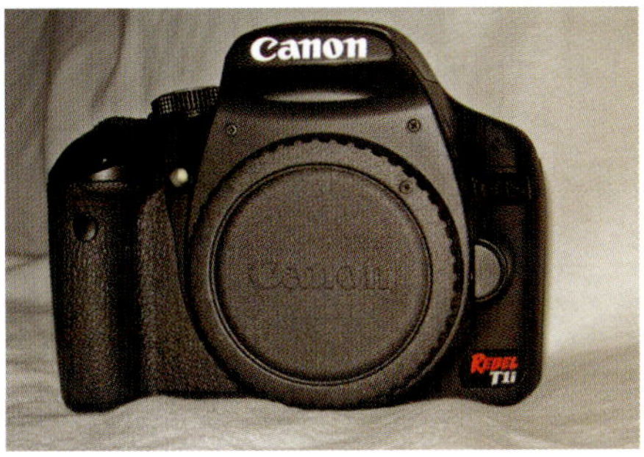


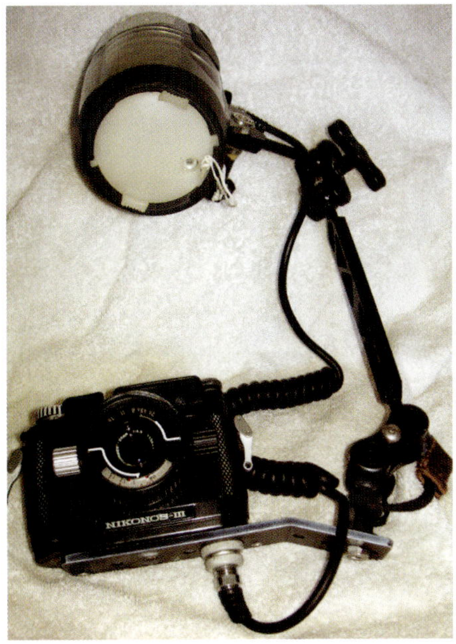


**Top left**—A housed dSLR with two strobes. **Bottom left**—A dSLR camera body. **Right**—An assembled Nikonos III amphibious camera system with tray, strobe arm, clamps, and strobe connected by using an electrical sync cord from the good ole days.

## DEPTH RATINGS

The specifications for every available housing include a depth rating, so take your dive habits into consideration as you shop for a housing.

*Cropped versus Full-Frame Sensors.* A dSLR can be manufactured with a cropped or a full-frame sensor. Cameras with cropped sensors (smaller than the dimension of a 35mm film frame) are less expensive to manufacture than full-frame sensor cameras but may be less durable. These cameras/sensors are often denoted with the letters DX.

Most pros rely on dSLRs with full-frame (36x24mm) sensor. This type of dSLR/sensor is denoted by the letters FX. As larger sensors are more costly to manufacture than smaller ones, these cameras are pricier than the DX models. However, they are built to withstand the day in, day out demands professional photographers place on them. The internal components tend to be of a higher quality. Most of these cameras are built with shutters that will stand the test of time. Unfortunately, FX cameras tend to have a higher price and tend to be weightier than DX models.

No option is inherently better than another. Base your decision on the features you want and the budget you've set for the purchase. Personally, I prefer the DX. They are smaller, lighter weight, and less costly.

**Housings.** To use a dSLR underwater, you'll need to enclose it in a special watertight housing. As of this writing, Olympus, Nikon, and Canon offer the widest selection of underwater housings for their cameras. There are third-party manufacturers that offer housings, but they are not available for every brand or every camera model manufactured.

To choose the best housing for your camera, consider the following:

- Housings are made from metals or plastics. The plastic or polycarbonate housings are lighter in weight. This can be an advantage in both diving and in traveling with your system. They are usually more affordable.
- You will also want to know what the individual components of the housing are made of and how the unit was designed. Take care to choose a housing that is corrosion-resistant and durable.
- Ease of assembly is another factor to consider when shopping for a housing. Are tools required?
- How much trouble is it to maintain the system?
- Is service available? If so, how much does it cost? How quickly can the housing be serviced?
- How easy is it to work the camera's controls through the housing?

- Is the system easy to handle underwater? In some cases, photographers with smaller hands may find it more difficult to reach the controls when larger cameras are housed.
- What strobes can be used with the housed camera? In what manner does the strobe communicate with the camera? Is it via a fiber optic cable or electronic sync cord?
- A housing for your camera may cost more than the camera itself. Can you can afford the camera and housing you are considering? Building a housed dSLR camera system can cost from $3000 to over $20,000.
- What lenses does the housing support? Will your lens(es) fit into the housing's port orifice? Will the port or combination of port and port extension accommodate the lens? If you plan to use a lens with a zoom feature or plan to focus manually, you'll need to make sure there is a zoom ring gear or focus ring available for your lens.

Once you've built your housed dSLR system, resist the urge to "upgrade" it when manufacturers come out with a new model. Upgrade your system when it no longer does the job you want it to do. Most of us get to engage in underwater photography somewhat infrequently, so it will take a long time to outgrow a housed dSLR system.

**Lenses.** Beginning underwater photographers tend to favor photographing a certain subject or creating a certain type of image. They often select a lens with an angle of view that suits that use and stick with it. The more we dive and photograph, the wider our horizons become. We begin to appreciate all of the things we witness underwater, and we want to photograph them.

A photographer can capture an underwater image with any lens, but all lenses are not created equal. Let's look into some of the characteristics of lenses.

Lenses are inscribed with their focal length and maximum aperture. If we look at the specifications, we can learn more about the lens, including

## RAW VERSUS JPEG

The "RAW or JPEG?" debate is ongoing. Some photographers feel that capturing JPEG files is sufficient. They argue that photographers should strive to get the image captured optimally in-camera, so there should be no need to access and correct the data that RAW files give us access to. I agree with that, but what if one wants to bring out the best in a photograph and wants or needs to do some editing?

In these instances, shooting in RAW is a big advantage. This format allows us to access the unprocessed data, giving us more latitude and flexibility to make finer enhancements with our editing tools.

RAW files are many times larger than JPEG files. They take longer to write to memory in-camera. They consume a tremendous amount of disk space and, because of their size, require the computer to have more horsepower to work with.

Fortunately, technology is evolving to handle these large files. Computers are equipped with considerable amounts of memory and faster central processing units these days. One-terabyte hard drives are readily available and affordable. Memory cards have a higher storage capacity, and write times are faster than ever.

Many cameras allow you to shoot RAW + JPEG in-camera. I like this solution. In instances when I get the image right in-camera, I do not have to do any editing because I already have my JPEG for output. In other instances, I have the wonderful extra latitude offered by the RAW file and those adjustment tools.

If your camera does not allow you to shoot both file types simultaneously, I recommend shooting in RAW.

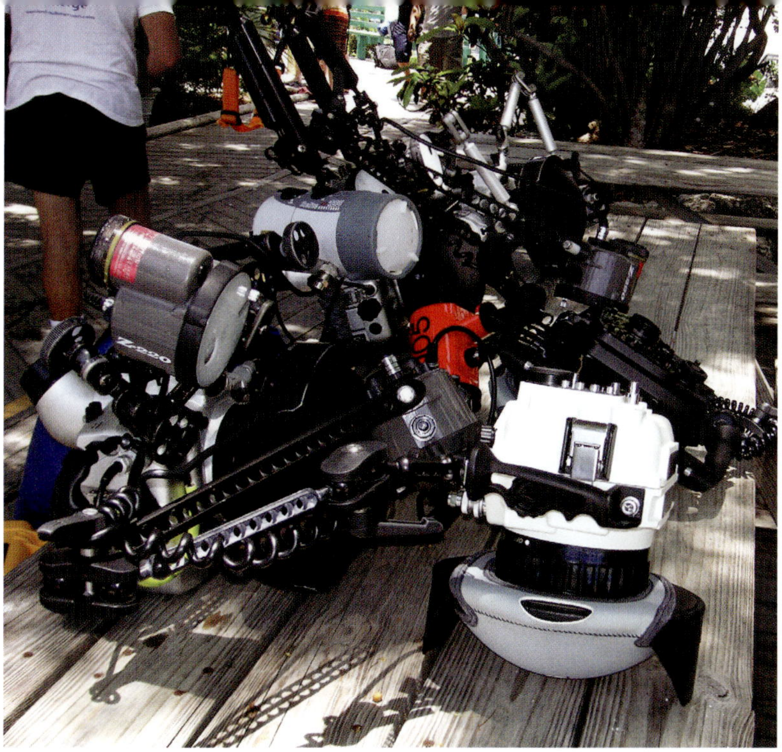

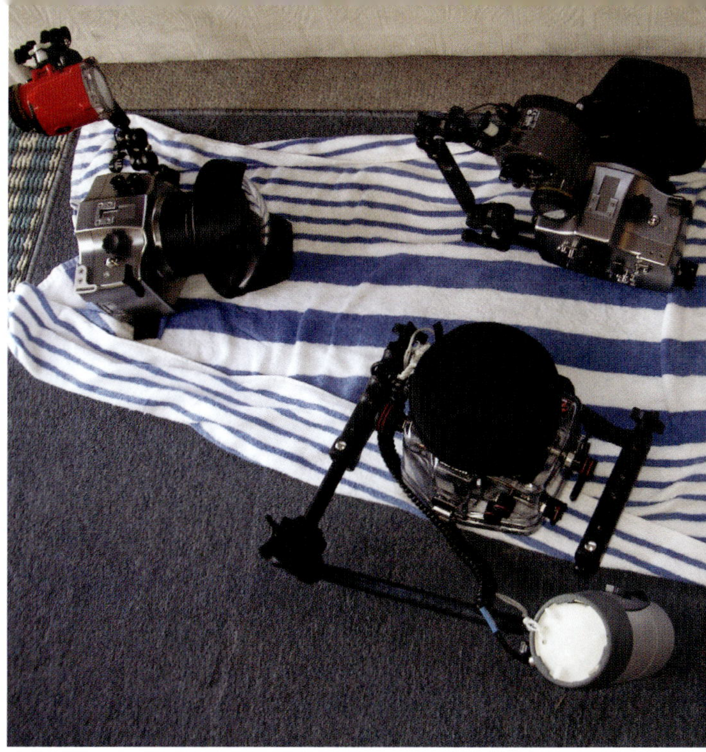

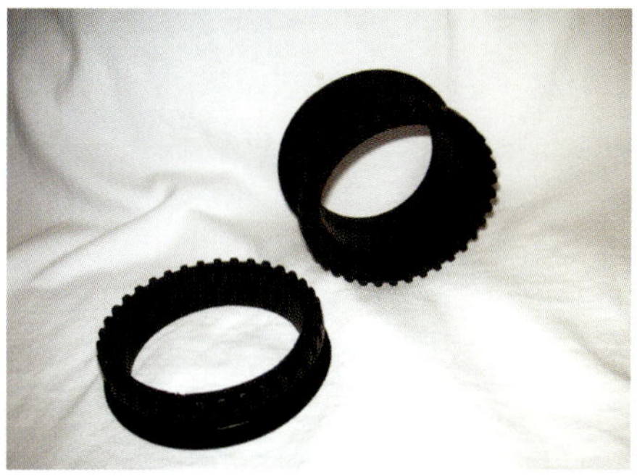

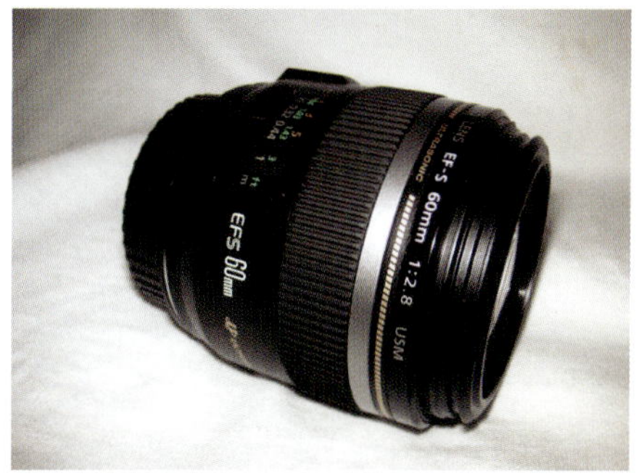

**Top left**—There are a wide variety of housed dSLR camera systems available. **Top right**—Pictured are three dSLR systems. Two housings are made of aluminum, and the third is a polycarbonate housing. **Bottom left**—Zoom ring gears are made for a specific lens. **Bottom right**—The lens component of a housed dSLR camera system.

### BE CHOOSY

If you do not have the perfect lens for the subject you want to photograph, shoot a subject that is well-suited for the lens you have. You can take a picture of anything with any lens—it's just that the angle of view of another lens might be more suitable for the size of the subject.

its angle of view and close-focusing distance. All of these factors affect the way we can capture and render our subjects.

*Focal Length and Angle of View: An Experiment.* The focal length of a lens is the distance, in millimeters, from the rear nodal point to the focal plane (image sensor). The focal length of the lens governs its angle of view.

To understand how focal length governs angle of view, make the scuba diver's okay sign. Now hold your hand half an arm's length from your eye and peer through the okay sign. In your other hand, hold this book at arm's length. The first arm's length represents the focal length. The circular opening made by your thumb and index finger represents your rear nodal point. Your eye is the focal plane. Notice how little of the book you can see when peering through your okay sign. That view is analogous with an angle of view of a lens with a long focal length. How much of the book can you see? Not very much, right? A lens with a long focal length provides a narrow angle of view.

Now move your okay sign closer so that it is just inches away from your eye. You are now effectively using a shorter focal length. Peer through the okay sign and note how much more of the book you can see. You have a

## LENS-RELATED TERMS

**Aberration**—An optical defect in a lens that results in a photograph that is unsharp or otherwise distorted. One example is chromatic aberration, a lens defect that causes various wavelengths of light to be differently focused across the image area.

**Barrel distortion**—A lens aberration that causes straight lines at the edge of the frame to bow toward the center of the image, producing a barrel shape. Fisheye lenses exhibit lots of barrel distortion; the aberration is less of an issue with a rectilinear lens.

**Diffraction**—Light changes direction (i.e., is diffracted) when it passes through a small aperture. (To visualize the effect, imagine pinching the end of a garden hose while water is flowing through it.) We often want to use a small aperture to get a good depth of field, but we must be aware that diffraction can occur and noise can result, affecting the image quality.

**Lens flare**—Lens flare is caused when light enters the lens, gets confused, and bounces (reflects) to and from the internal lens elements. Photographing subjects that are back-lit or shooting into the sun risks lens flare occurring. In these instances, we are introducing two light sources, the light just mentioned and the light of our strobe reflecting from the subject.

**L glass**—Canon's highest-quality lens. "L" does not appear to stand for anything, but I've heard photographers joke that it stands for "luxury." I am confident "L" does not stand for "Larry."

**Depth of field preview**—A camera function that briefly stops down the lens to the selected aperture setting to allow the photographer to gauge the depth of field that will be produced.

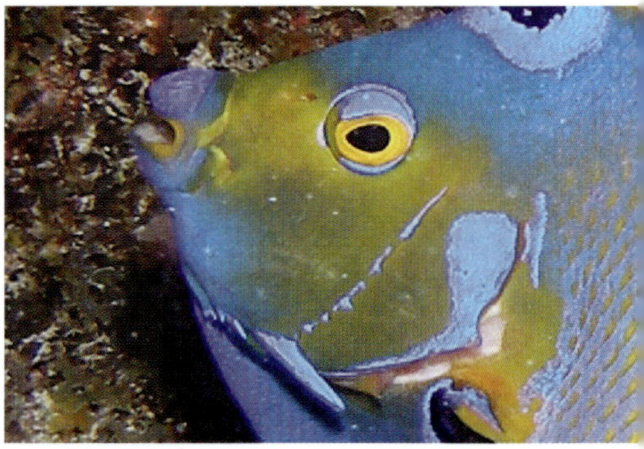

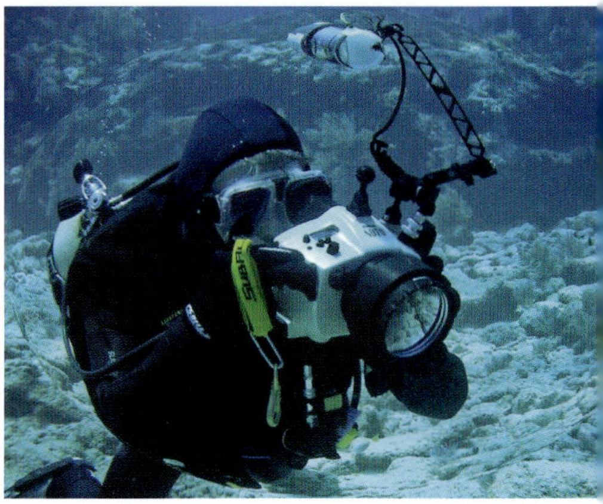

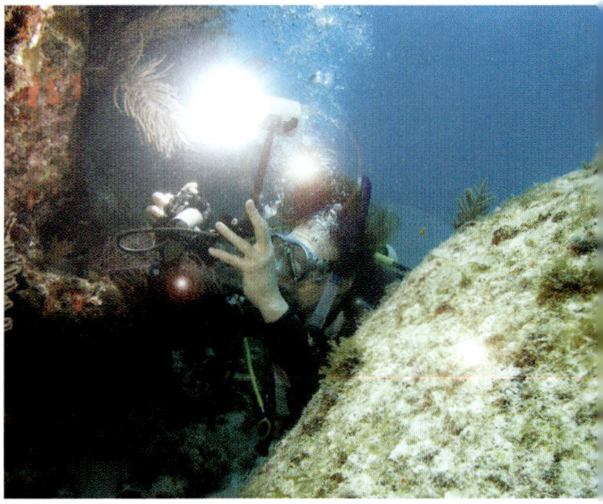

**Top**—Chromatic aberration can be seen along the edges of this photograph. **Center**—An example of barrel distortion. Note the apparent curve of strobe arm. **Bottom**—Lens flare.

much wider view. A lens with a short focal length provides a wide angle of view.

In topside photography, we can easily move closer to or farther from our subject to get the desired angle of view. We might move farther from our friend to create a full-length portrait or closer to create a head shot. Changing our working distance is often quicker and easier than changing the lens to get the desired angle of view.

Underwater photographers are not so lucky. When working from a distance of more than 5 feet, the subject or scene's colors are absorbed by the water column. We must work between our minimum focus point and 5 feet, and we can't do a lens change underwater. Selecting the right lens for the size of the subject, then, is critical to create the best-possible composition.

*Focal Length Factors.* So, now we have a grip on the relationship between focal length and angle of view. Simple, right? Well, there is a complicating factor.

As mentioned earlier, dSLRs are made with cropped or full-frame sensor sizes. Well, when a lens made for a full-frame camera is used on a camera with a cropped sensor, the focal length and angle of view are not what you would expect. Fortunately, manufacturers provide "multipliers" that will allow you to determine an equivalent focal length.

Let's look at an example. The multiplier for a Canon DX dSLR is 1.6. So, if we have a 100mm lens for the camera, we multiply the focal length by the multiplier and determine that the 100mm lens will perform like a 160mm lens would on a full-frame camera (100mm x 1.6 = 160mm). A 100mm lens on a cropped-sensor camera will have an angle of view of a 160mm lens used on a full-frame camera.

Manufacturers now produce lenses specifically for DX cameras. The body of the lenses are marked with the lens's focal length and the specified angle of view, which is accurate for the camera and its sensor size.

Along with this comes the equivalent coverage or angle of view of the lens. A 100mm lens used on the DX sensor camera will provide a smaller angle of view than that achieved when the same lens is used on a camera with an FX sensor.

To figure out what the angle of view of a particular lens will be when used on a cropped-sensor dSLR, you first multiply the focal length by the multiplier. This will result in an equivalent focal length. That equivalent focal length's coverage or angle of view will be the lens's angle of view on the cropped-sensor dSLR.

The coverage angle of a 100mm lens is 24 degrees. The coverage angle of a 160mm lens (if one is made) is around 15 degrees. So when I mount the 100mm lens, which was made to be used with a camera with a full-frame sensor, onto my cropped-sensor dSLR, I am using a lens with an equivalent focal length of 160mm, and it has a 15 degree angle of view.

Now, suppose I have a cropped-sensor dSLR and want to determine what focal length lens I need to use to obtain a 24 degree angle of view. I know that a 100mm lens provides a 24 degree angle of view on a full-frame sensor dSLR. I would divide the focal length by the multiplier (e.g., 100/1.6=62.5) to determine that, to get a 24 degree angle of view, I would need to mount a lens with a focal length of 62.5mm on my cropped-sensor camera.

Manufacturers now produce lenses specifically for DX cameras. The body of the lenses are marked with the lens's focal length and specified angle of view—which is *accurate* for the camera and its sensor size. However, this point is lost on some photographers, who attempt to do the math required to (unnecessarily) determine an equivalent focal length.

So, how does the photographer know when a specific lens was made for use with a camera with a cropped sensor? Manufacturers incorporate a "designator" in the name of the lens. Nikon lenses made for these camera are named with the letters DX (e.g., AF DX fisheye); Canon's lenses are named with the letter S (e.g., Canon's EF-S).

**Lens Selection.** The following lenses are commonly used by topside photographers:

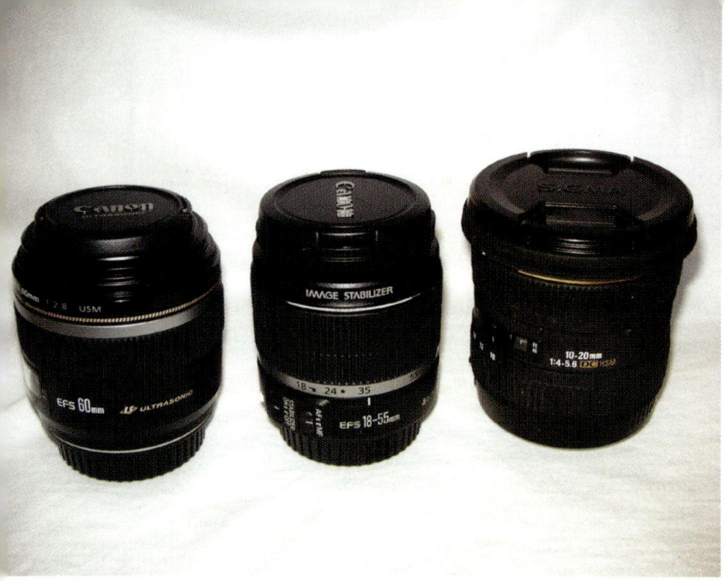

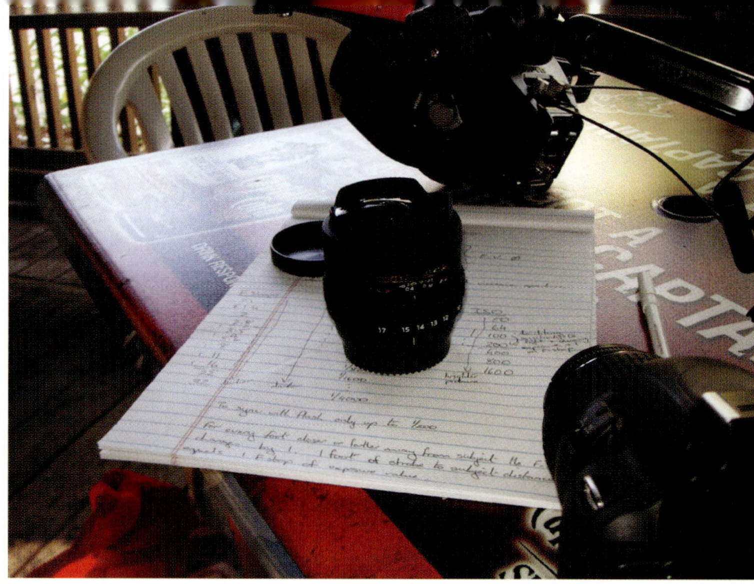

**Left**—A repertoire of lenses, including a wide/ultrawide 10–20mm lens, an 18–55mm midrange zoom lens, and a 60mm macro lens. **Right**—The Tokina 10–17mm fisheye lens for DX cameras.

- **Normal (standard) lens**—A lens with a 50mm focal length (give or take around 10 degrees) and an angle of view of roughly 40 degrees.
- **Telephoto lens**—A lens with a 100mm or longer focal length and an angle of view of roughly 24 degrees (or less when the focal length is longer).
- **Macro lens**—Specialized lenses with focal lengths of 50mm or longer and correspondingly smaller angles of view. A macro lens is made to photograph small subjects from close working distances, so the minimum focusing distance for such lenses is much closer than it is on a normal lens.
- **Wide angle lens**—A lens with a 35mm focal length and an angle of view of around 55 degrees.
- **Super wide angle lens**—A lens with a focal length of around 28mm with an angle of view of approximately 65 degrees.
- **Ultrawide angle lens**—A lens with a focal length around 20mm and an angle of view around 75 degrees.
- **Extreme wide angle lens**—A lens with a focal length of roughly 15 or 16mm or less with an angle of view of about 90 degrees or more.

The lenses described above are all prime lenses (i.e., they have one focal length). Topside photographers also use zoom lenses—a single lens that can be used at a range of focal lengths. For example, Nikon makes a 12–24mm zoom lens.

The following lenses are often used in underwater photography:

- **Wide angle prime lens**—A lens with an angle of view of 70 degrees or more.
- **Macro lens**—Again, a lens with a comparatively long focal length and a narrow angle of view. This type of lens allows for close focusing. Four examples of macro lens focal lengths are 50mm, 60mm, 100mm, and 105mm. A true macro lens can render a subject at 1:1 (lifesize) magni-

fication or greater. *(Note:* Some manufacturers use the term to describe lenses that cannot achieve this level of magnification, so check the specifications to determine whether or not the lens you are considering is truly a macro lens.)

- **Fisheye lens**—A specialized lens with a focal length of around 10mm that produces an angle of view in the neighborhood of 180 degrees. Fisheye lenses have shorter (closer) minimum focusing distances, which enable the photographer to get closer to the subject yet still get the whole subject framed and focused. This minimum focus distance also allows photographers to work closer to smaller subjects, which means that the subject will fill more of the image frame. Fisheye lenses can be prime or zoom.
- **Zoom lenses**—Underwater photographers primarily use two types of zoom lenses: midrange wide angle zooms (e.g., 15–85mm) and ultrawide angle zooms (e.g., 10–20mm).

A collection of three lenses—a macro lens, a midrange zoom lens, and a wide/ultrawide angle prime lens or wide/ultrawide angle zoom lens—will serve most of your needs. Consider picking up a fisheye lens or extreme macro setup to handle any scenarios not served by those three lens types.

When I am not on a mission to photograph a specific subject, I mount my midrange zoom lens. This gives me a reasonable range of focal lengths and angles of view that I can use to photograph subjects of various sizes.

I recommend that you work with a single lens when you are starting out and continue to use it exclusively until you have a good understanding of the subject matter it is best suited for. Learn one lens at a time.

Buy the best lens you can afford so that you can avoid the optical shortcomings of lower-quality lenses. For more information on lenses, go to www.photozone.de. The site contains comprehensive reviews on most lenses used in underwater photography.

*Diopters, Extension Tubes, and Teleconverters.* When photographing macro subjects, some underwater photographers use diopters (also called close-up lenses) to decrease the minimum focus distance of a lens and magnify the view. They are available in different strengths (+1 to +4) and attach to the lens like filters do. Other photographers add an extension tube to their lens to increase its focal length when shooting macro.

Teleconverters are sometimes used in macro photography. These optical devices are mounted between the camera body and lens. They come in two strengths: 1.4x and 2x. A 1.4x teleconverter will increase the focal length of a 100mm lens to 140mm. A 2x teleconverter will double the lens's focal length.

Using a teleconverter narrows the lens's angle of view. They also reduce the lens's widest aperture. A 1.4x teleconverter will cost us one f-stop and a 2x teleconverter will cost us two f-stops.

### PRIME VERSUS ZOOM

Sure, zoom lenses are convenient. However, not everyone is sold on using them. Some photographers believe that the image quality is better with prime lenses, and they enjoy never having to play with various focal lengths. Other photographers enjoy the ability to zoom in or out. When I am using a zoom lens, I have the lens set at its widest angle as a starting point and go longer if need be.

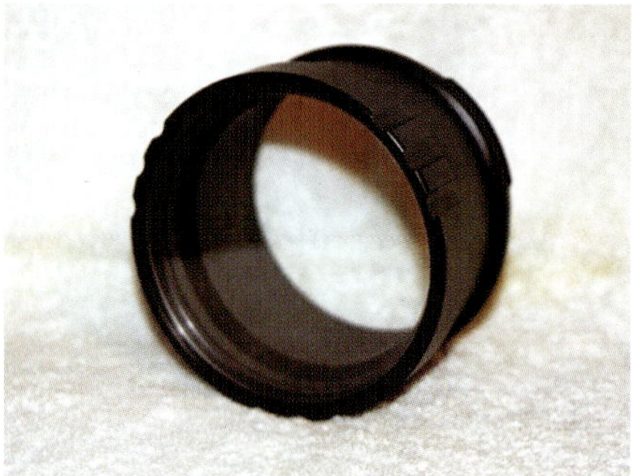

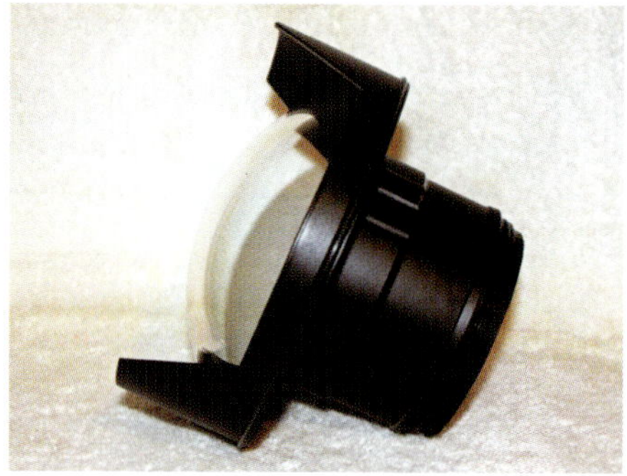

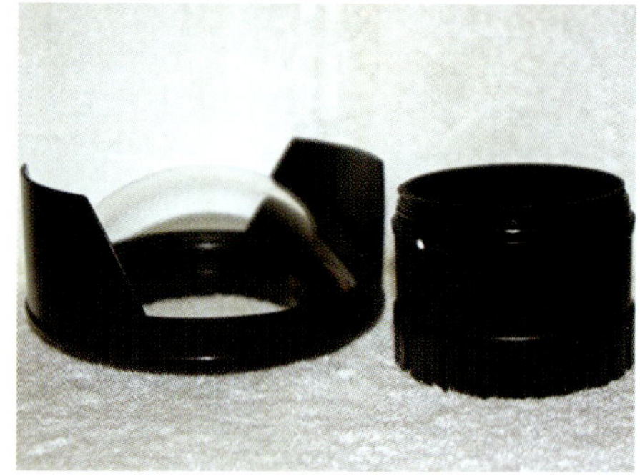

**Left**—A flat port. **Center**—A dome port. **Right**—A dome port with a lens port extender.

**Lens Ports.** Lens ports encase the lens and attach to the camera's housing. There are two types of lens ports—flat and dome. Flat ports are used with lenses with narrow angles of view. They are considerably less expensive than dome ports. Dome ports are used with lenses with wide angles of view. They are concentric, meaning their inner surface is parallel to their outer surface and its thickness remains the same throughout its shape. Dome ports can cost as much as or more than some camera bodies.

Neither type of port is intrinsically better than the other. Rather, the correct choice depends upon which lens is used.

Most lens ports are made by housing manufacturers and only fit that company's housings. This is partially because various manufacturers use different-sized openings (orifices) in their housings to accommodate lenses and associated apparatus, such as ring gears and crown gears. Also, the various manufacturers use different means of mounting the lens ports to the housings. Aftermarket ports are available to fit the housings as well. They often need to be used with a lens port-to-housing adaptor.

Like housings, ports themselves (not necessarily their bodies, mounts, and shades) are made of optical glass or acrylic (or acrylic-like materials). Port bodies, their mounts, and shades are made of various materials, from metals to plastics. While there are advantages and disadvantages to metal and plastic ports, it is difficult if not impossible for an untrained eye to discern any difference in image quality. Because manufacturers make both housings and ports, they tend to make metal-bodied ports for metal housings and plastic-bodied ports for plastic housings. Therefore, we underwater photographers may be locked into which material our port is made from.

Some underwater photographers have a preference for either one of these materials. This is because of their measured judgment of advantages or disadvantages, perceived or real, between these materials.

Acrylic ports are usually more affordable than those made with optical glass. Acrylic ports are more easily scratched, but when that happens, they can be more easily and affordably repaired. Some shooters prefer glass ports and consider them to be "better" from an image quality point of view. I think it's debatable. This is because we're not shooting through pure, clean air—we're shooting through water. The better quality that glass affords is erased by the medium we are shooting in. Proponents of using only optical quality glass ports agree but suggest that glass helps overcome the degradation in image quality that occurs underwater.

Lenses differ in diameter and length. Ports are made to accommodate a specific lens or lens length. If the port does not accommodate the lens length, port extenders can be added between the lens port and housing. Lens ports and extenders also have to accommodate the lens's diameter. Some lenses are so wide that they will not fit inside the lens port or the housing's port orifice. Before buying a lens, ensure your port and housing can accommodate it.

It is easier to accommodate a lens that can be used behind a flat port than one that needs to be used behind a dome port. This is because the chief consideration is only whether the port (with or without an extender) will be long enough and wide enough in diameter to fit the lens being used.

It is also easier to port a prime lens than a zoom lens. This is because a prime lens's length does not change (although some will, but only slightly when focusing). The length of zoom lenses can increase in inches when changing the focal length throughout the zoom range.

*Flat Ports.* Flat ports are generally used in front of lenses with longer focal lengths (and narrower angles of view). Lenses with wider angles of view can vignette when used behind flat ports because their angles of view can be greater than what the face of the port will allow the lens to "see."

Most underwater photographers will start out with a flat port, as they are less expensive than dome ports. Also, flat ports will work with a macro lens and some midrange zoom lenses. The flat port will also accommodate some standard prime lenses, other than wide angle.

Dome ports are larger in diameter than flat ports and are considerably more expensive. They will accommodate midrange zooms, normal lenses, and wider angle lenses.

Flat ports, whether made of optical-quality glass or acrylic, are not optics per-se. They behave much as our masks do with respect to refraction. Objects will appear 1.33 times closer and larger. This can be advantageous when shooting macro, as using a macro lens behind a flat port further reduces the lens's angle of view, while concurrently magnifying the subject's size. On the other hand, using a prime lens or midrange zoom lens with a flat port will result in a 25 percent reduction in the lens's angle of view.

*Dome Ports.* Dome ports are not subject to refraction. They do not produce a magnifying effect; rather, the dome acts as sort of a de-magnifier. The lens's native angle of view is unchanged when used behind a dome.

Dome ports were developed to prevent the vignetting that occurs when using wide angle lenses behind flat ports. They are larger in diameter than flat ports and are considerably more expensive. They will accommodate midrange zooms, normal lenses, and wider angle lenses. While a dome can be used in front of a macro lens, there are two reasons why this is discouraged: First, a dome does not offer the advantage of refraction that a flat port allows when shooting macro. Second, the dome's larger diameter makes it difficult to get close to macro subjects, which are often surrounded by delicate coral.

Domes are described and measured in terms of the diameter of the dome's sphere. Some manufacturers provide this measurement in inches, while others describe the size in millimeters.

It is harder to port a lens that requires a dome port, as the lens has to fit inside the dome port, and, when necessary, also within an extender.

An improperly configured dome port will prohibit optimal or optical performance of the lens used behind it. The lens's entrance pupil should be aligned and located at the center of the sphere from which the dome was created. This distance is achieved by using either the proper dome and/or a port extender of the correct length. If this distance cannot be achieved, the lens will not perform properly behind the dome port.

When an object is at infinity, a virtual image of that object will be created by the dome and located, not at infinity, but, closer than infinity. The rule of thumb is that it will be located three times the distance of the sphere's radius in front of the outside of the dome when an object is focused at infinity. For example, if we were focusing our object at infinity and using a 6-inch (diameter) dome port, the virtual image would appear at 9 inches in front of the dome. (A 6-inch diameter dome has a 3-inch radius. 3x3=9.) When the object is not focused at infinity (in underwater photography, when is it?), the virtual image will be closer to the dome.

The distance at which the mysterious virtual image can appear can pose a challenge when selecting a dome port, extenders, and for that matter, the lens. The lens has to be able to focus on the virtual image, so it must have a relatively short minimum focus distance. The minimum focus distance of most lenses used behind a dome port is sufficient to focus on a virtual image created when the object is focused at infinity. If the object focused on is closer than infinity, however, the virtual image could be located just outside of the front of the dome. This means that if I am using a dome port, I need a lens with a minimum focus distance equal to or less than the distance from my camera's focal plane (sensor) to the outside of my dome port, to be able to focus. This is a problem because not all lenses used with dome ports have the needed minimum focus distance.

Another issue we face is that while our subject (whether photographed at infinity or closer) may be flat, the dome will render the virtual image in a spherical shape or form. The object's outer edges will appear closer than the object's center. This means that while we are focusing on the center of our object, its outer edges may be out of focus, and the edges or corners of our images may appear soft. Fortunately, to resolve this issue, we can use smaller apertures to allow for greater depth of field, and/or use diopters to give the lens closer focusing ability.

Another means to overcome a lens's ability to focus is to use a larger dome. Because focus distance is related to the dome's size, sometimes getting a larger dome will remedy the focus issue. Some lenses simply perform better

## ABOUT DIOPTERS

Diopters come in various strengths. What strength to use is oftentimes cited by the makers of housings and ports, and depends upon the specific lens and dome size. When this information is not available, experimentation is needed. Diopters can be stacked (threaded into each other), so, if a diopter with a power of +1 is not enough, one can add a +1 diopter to obtain a +2 diopter, and so on. There is a more scientific approach to determining the ideal diopter strength as well. To determine the strength, simply take the number 1000 and divide it by the dome's radius in millimeters times four. For example, a dome port with a 170mm diameter has a radius of 85mm. So, our formula would be 1000/(4x85) or 1000/340, which equals 2.94. Therefore, we would select a +3 diopter strength.

Right—A .8x pick-up viewfinder.

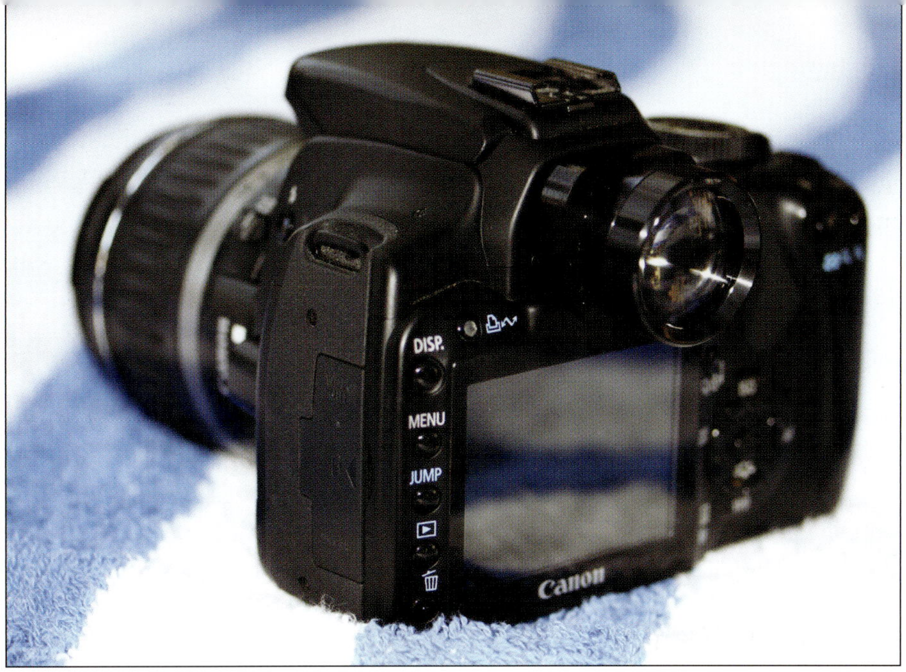


behind a dome port of a specific size. Of course, larger domes are heavier, have different handling characteristics with respect to buoyancy, are not easily used in tighter spaces, and are more expensive than smaller domes.

*Ring Gears.* Once we have a port, we may need to add a zoom ring gear and/or focus ring gear to our shopping list.

Zoom ring gears are made to fit specific lenses. They fit around the zoom ring on the lens. If we want to manually focus our lens, we would need to buy a focus ring gear. Focus ring gears are also made to fit specific lenses. They fit around the focus ring of the lens and are driven by a crown gear, which is built into either the housing or port. Fixed to the crown gear is a shaft which runs through either the housing or port. A control is fixed to the other end of this shaft. The zoom or focus can be manipulated by working the control.

### BUYER BEWARE

Housings, ports, extenders, and ring gears are not available for every lens on the market. Before you buy a lens, be sure that it can be correctly ported.

**View Ports.** A view port is located on the back of the camera and covers the viewfinder. Every camera is designed so that, when the eye rests against the viewfinder, the photographer can see, corner to corner, everything that appears within the viewfinder's frame. In some cases, when the camera is housed, this view is compromised. To compensate for the issue, housing manufacturers build a magnifier into their view ports or offer a "pick-up" viewfinder that enables the photographer to again view all four corners of the camera's viewfinder.

Some housing manufacturers and third-party vendors offer accessory viewfinders. These come in two types: straight and 45 degree. A straight viewfinder allows the photographer to look right through the viewfinder. A 45-degree viewfinder is a device that attaches to the camera at a 45 degree angle to the lens. It allows the photographer to look through the camera's viewfinder via a window located above the camera. This viewfinder rotates 90 degrees so it can be used when shooting in the portrait mode. It also allows you to shoot very near or on the ocean floor without harming the coral.

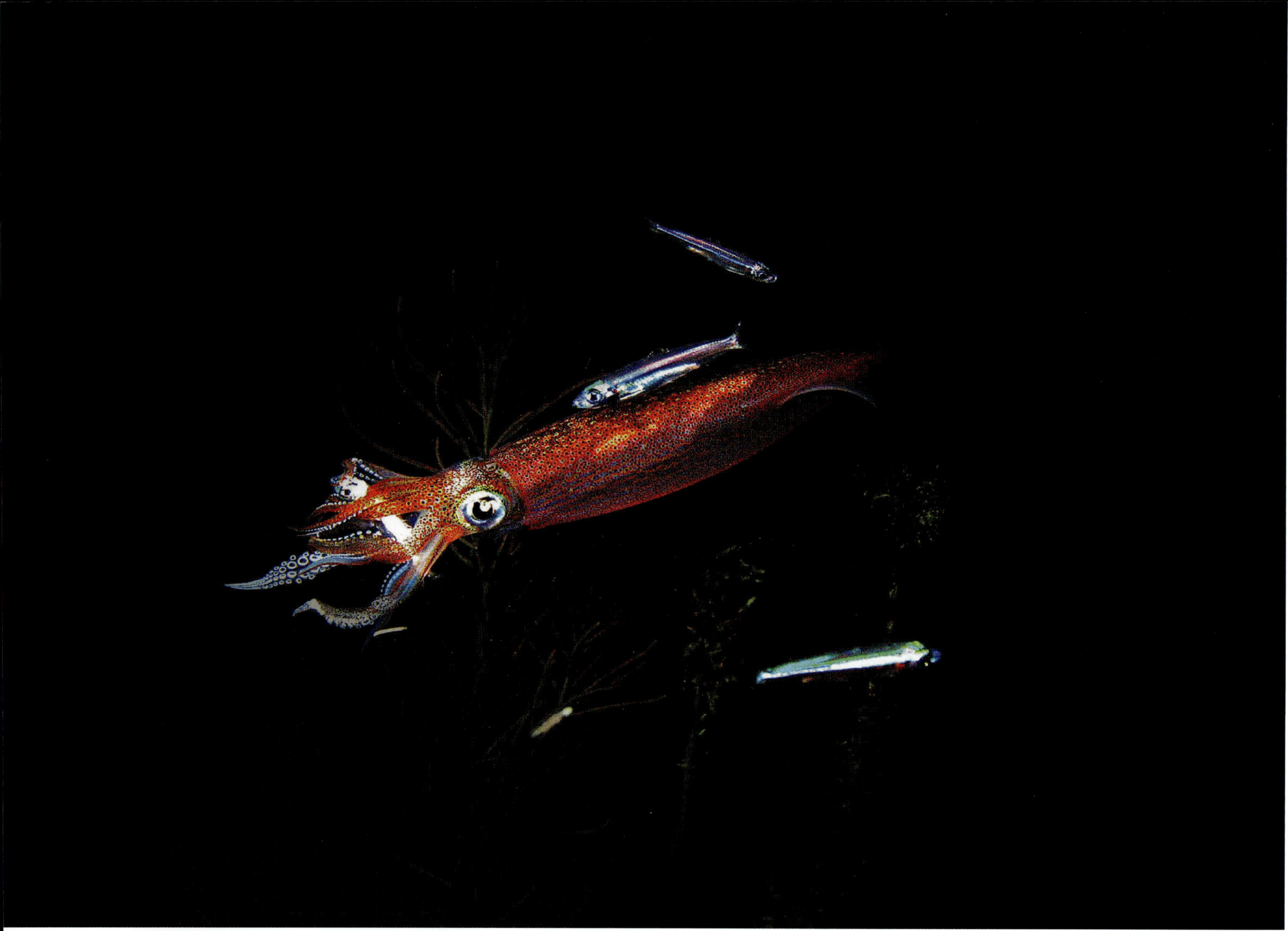

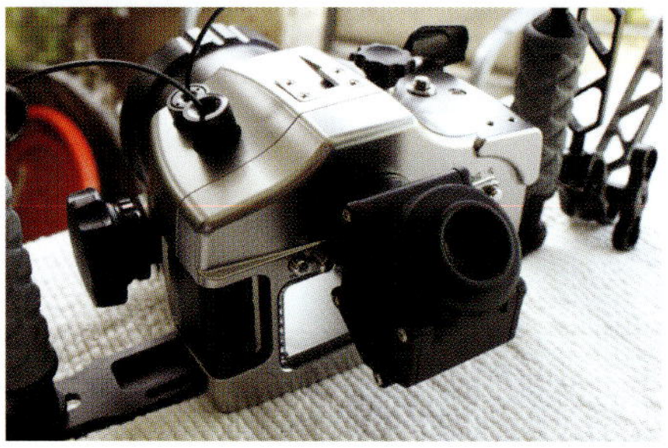

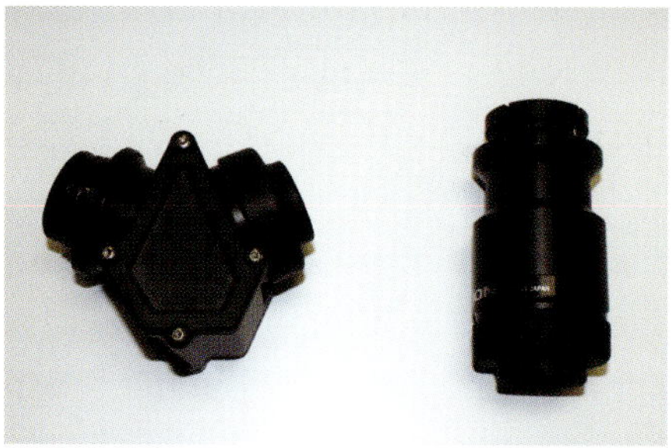

**Top**—This inshore arrow squid, preying, was photographed on a night dive. Exposure: f/4.5, 1/125, and 200 ISO. Focal length 35mm. Photo courtesy of Ryan Marchese. **Bottom left**—A 45 degree add-on viewfinder. Photo courtesy of John Yasaki. **Bottom right**—A straight viewfinder pictured next to a 45 degree viewfinder. Photo courtesy of Steve Philbrook.

There are two drawbacks to its use, though: changing the orientation of the viewfinder to shoot in portrait mode cuts into your reaction time when trying to get a shot, and, as we are used to looking straight into the back of our cameras to view a scene, it can take some time to get used to viewing the scene from an angle.

**Masks.** When you are viewfinding, you will find yet another piece of equipment with a lens. This is the dive mask. Some masks are made with optical-quality glass, which is clearer than the glass used to make our masks. Atomic makes one called Clear-View. Some underwater photographers prefer using a mask with a black skirt. A mask with a black skirt keeps light from coming in from the sides of the mask.

# 3. LIGHTING AND STROBES

When we began in our underwater photography, most of us decided we needed a strobe to restore color or add critical light. We quickly learned that the strobe helped us avoid the backscatter that was caused by our on-camera flash. We also realized that using strobe allowed us to freeze the action in our photographs, which helps us achieve sharpness and focus.

In this chapter, we will take a closer look at the benefits and challenges of working with strobes underwater.

### STROBE SPECIFICATIONS AND FEATURES

Strobe manufacturers provide technical specifications that can help us select and use a strobe to solve a host of problems often encountered underwater (described above). Among these are:

- **The guide number (GN)**—The higher the guide number, the more powerful the strobe is considered to be. (Sometimes a strobe's power is designated in watt-seconds, rather than guide numbers.) We can also use this number to help us establish a correct exposure. (This topic will be addressed in the next section.)
- **Color temperature**—The color temperature of a light source is described in Kelvin (K) units. We know that the color temperature of sunlight (our ambient light source) is around 5500K. When both the artificial light

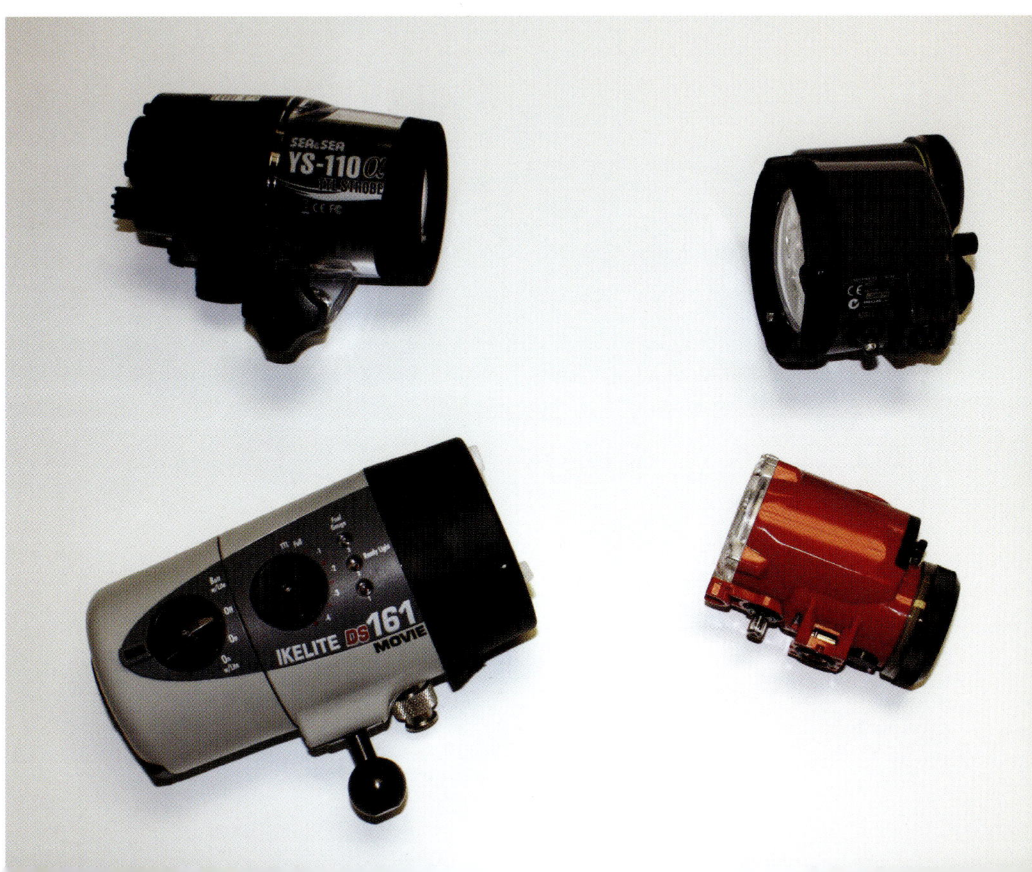


**Right**—Pictured are several strobes from different manufacturers. Photo courtesy of Steve Philbrook and Aquaventure Dive and Photo.

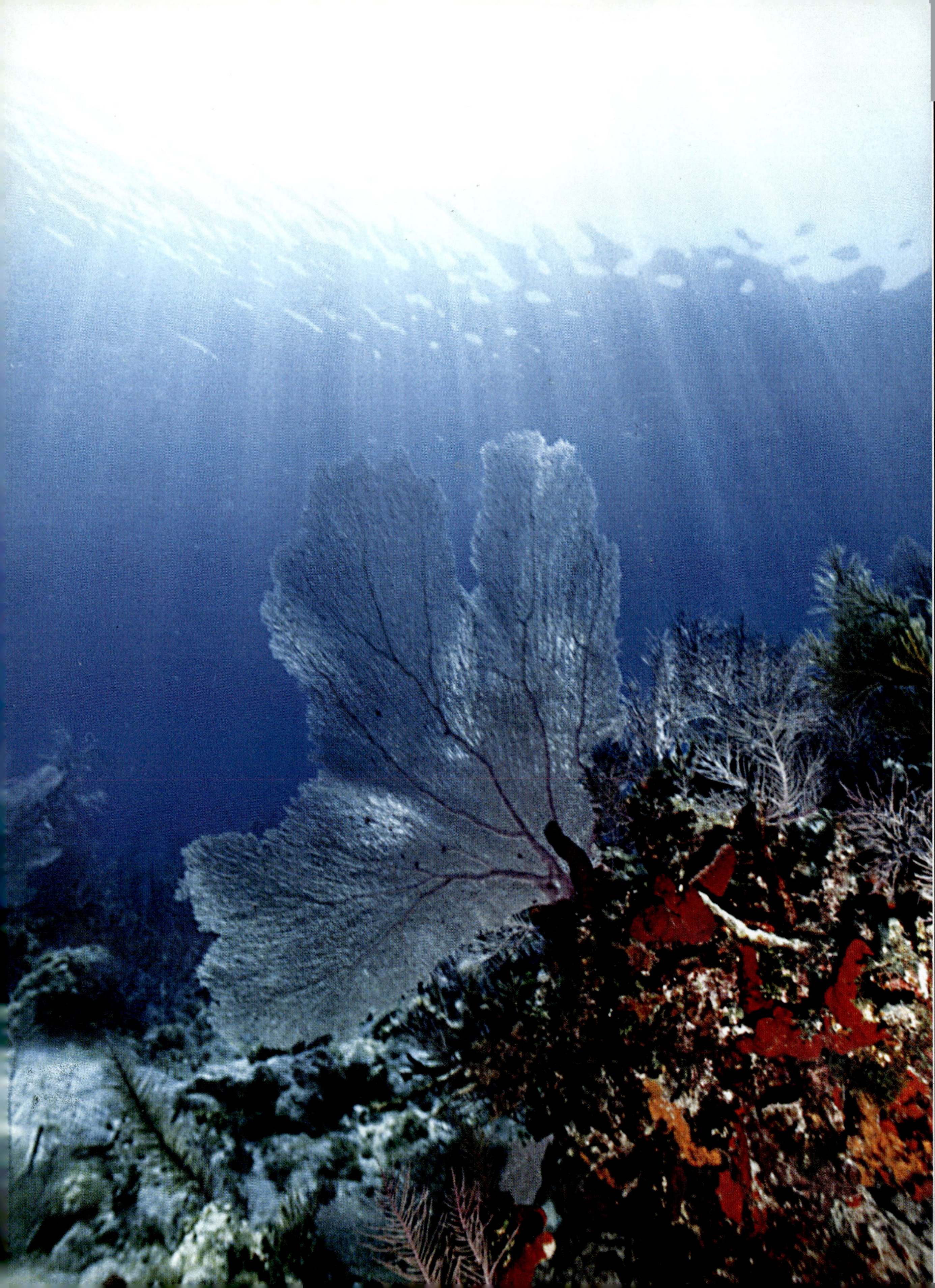

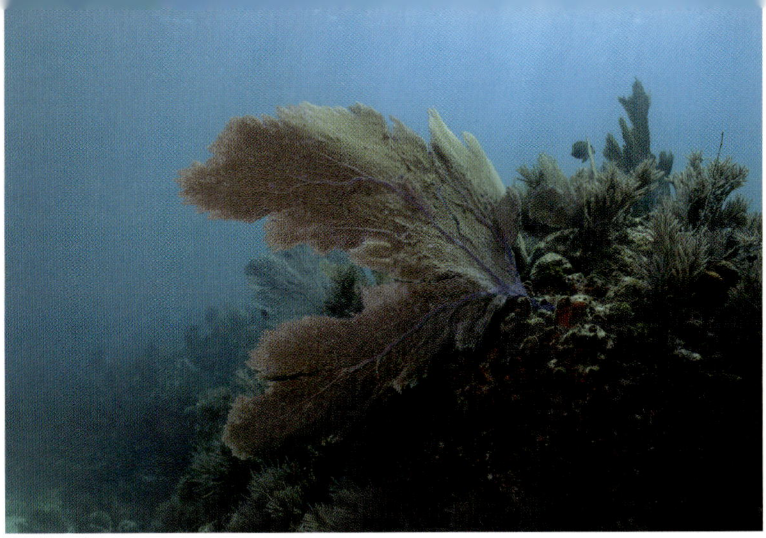

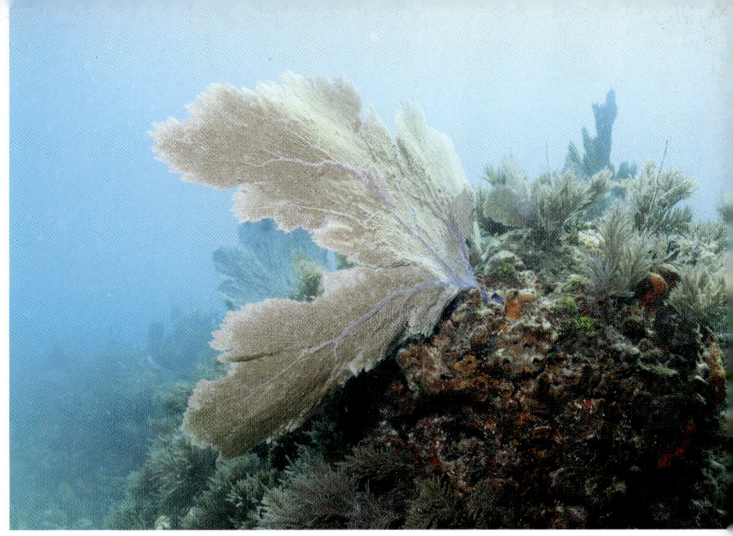

**Facing page**—When ambient light and the strobe's light are balanced, it is difficult to discern whether a strobe was used. Focal length 15mm. **Left**—Not enough strobe was used in this image. **Right**—Too much strobe was used in this image.

source (strobe) and the ambient source (sunlight) have the same color temperature, we can ensure that the colors in scene are recorded as they should appear and that the scene is not impacted by a color cast.

- **TTL flash—**Some strobe units offer through-the-lens (TTL) flash output control. These units are equipped with a light sensor that measures the flash intensity through the lens, then shuts the flash off when a correct exposure is achieved. TTL also stands for "transistor-to-transistor logic."

### BALANCING STROBE AND AMBIENT LIGHT

Ambient light is present in most underwater shooting environments. When we introduce a strobe to enhance the color in our images, freeze subject motion, or avoid backscatter, we have to balance the strobe's output with the ambient light. When this is done successfully, the viewer won't be able to tell a strobe was used in making the photograph. When the lighting is balanced, the photograph will be colorful and natural looking and the image will appear correctly exposed.

If the light we are using is a TTL flash, it will balance the light for us. If not, we'll need to make some calculations that allow us to produce a correct, balanced exposure. There are a few approaches we can take.

**Exposure Values.** Exposure values are a scale of numbers that serve as a shorthand notation of all of the combinations of shutter speed and aperture that will result in the same exposure.

Let's say I am photographing a subject 3 feet away from my camera and strobe. My exposure is f/8 at 1/100 and ISO 100, and my strobe is set at full power. I take the photograph and review it. The image is too bright (overexposed). The settings I used created an exposure, and that exposure has a value. In this example, I am going to give it a value of 0.

Because the first image was overexposed, I will want to reduce the strobe's output, thereby subtracting light from the exposure. One way to do this is to adjust the strobe-to-subject distance. By moving the strobe one foot farther away from the subject, I can reduce the exposure value by one f-stop (conversely, moving the light one foot closer to the subject would increase the

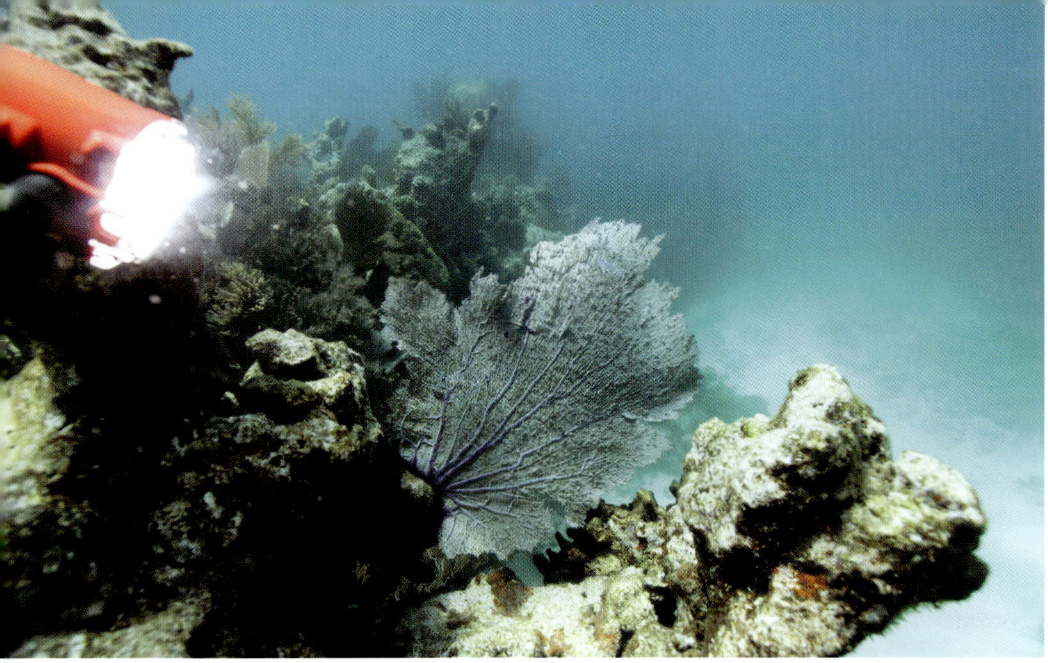

**Left**—When moving the strobe closer to the subject, be sure that it does not end up in the photograph. This mistake is easy to make when using wide angle lenses or handholding the strobe. Photo courtesy of Connie Z Photography, LLC.

exposure value by one stop). This reduced exposure would have an exposure value of −1.

To reduce the strobe's light level and achieve a balanced exposure, I could also decrease the strobe's power via its power setting. Most strobes allow incremental adjustments in f-stops worth of power. In this example, I would adjust the light so that it output one f-stop less power.

There are charts available that list all possible combinations of ISO, shutter speed, and aperture—and their exposure values. You don't need to consult them. The heart of the matter is getting the exposure you are after. The exposure value scale helps you realize how making a change in any one exposure control can increase or decrease the amount of light that will be used to make the exposure. *(Note:* If you want to maintain a consistent exposure value, when you change any one control, you must compensate for the light gained or lost using one or more of the other exposure controls.)

As mentioned earlier, a guide number is used to describe the output power of a strobe. Well, if we want to photograph our subject at a specific aperture and we know what the strobe-to-subject distance is, we can use the guide number to help us make exposure adjustments that allow us to balance the strobe to the ambient light. Let's look at how this works.

Guide numbers are based on an ISO of 100. Let's suppose a strobe has a guide number of 30. My strobe-to-subject distance is 3 feet. To determine the aperture needed to achieve a correct, balanced exposure, I would divide the strobe-to-subject distance into the guide number. In this example, 30/3=10. The correct aperture would be f/10. *(Note:* If you want to use a different ISO, you'll need to compensate for light gained or lost by adjusting the aperture or shutter speed.)

If I had to choose a particular aperture to achieve a specific depth of field, I could use the guide number to determine the strobe-to-subject distance that would result in proper exposure. In keeping with the above example, let's say

I am shooting at ISO 100 and my strobe has a guide number of 30. If I want to shoot at f/16, what should the strobe-to-subject distance be? To obtain this value, I divide the guide number by the aperture—30/16. The strobe should be positioned 1.8 feet from the subject.

A couple caveats need to be mentioned in regard to guide numbers. One is they are given to us by the strobe manufacturer, and the number is sometimes overstated. The second is that guide numbers are based on land or air density, not water, which is 800 times denser. This means that using the formula above is a good start, but our results won't always be right on the mark. Fortunately, we know that a foot of strobe-to-subject distance is equal to approximately one f-stop worth of exposure value. Therefore, no matter how accurate the guide number is, we know that moving the light a foot closer to or farther from the subject will increase or decrease the exposure by one stop. This is a quick way to adjust your exposure without having to change any exposure settings on your camera or lens.

One f-stop worth of ambient light is lost for every 33 feet we descend underwater. So, when I descend 33 feet from whatever depth I am at, I will need to change my aperture, shutter speed, or ISO to compensate for the loss of light.

Earlier, I mentioned that one f-stop worth of ambient light is lost for every 33 feet we descend underwater. So, when I descend 33 feet from whatever depth I am at, I will need to change my aperture, shutter speed, or ISO to compensate for the loss of light.

One last note: shooting in early morning or late afternoon, when the sun is lower in the sky, also results in the loss of an f-stop worth of ambient light. If a correct exposure is achieved with an aperture setting of f/8 when the sun is high in the sky, you will need to open up to f/5.6 to compensate for the loss of ambient light or shoot 1 foot closer to your subjects to ensure a correct exposure.

### COLOR TEMPERATURE AND WHITE BALANCE

Color temperature is used to describe the quality of light a strobe produces. The color temperature of a light source is described in Kelvin (K) units. Sunlight, at midday, for instance, measures between 5000K and 5500K. Our strobes produce light with a color temperature in this range as well. Other light sources have higher or lower color temperatures. Light sources with a lower color temperature produce a "warmer" light. Sources with a higher color temperature have a bluer color cast.

Prior to digital, we bought and shot film that was color balanced for daylight. Some film emulsions, like Velvia, Provia, Sensia and others, grew popular with underwater photographers because they liked how those emulsions rendered the colors in their photographs. Today, we use our camera's white balance settings to control the way that the colors in our scene will appear in the image.

Our cameras offer white balance settings—if we are shooting in ambient light (again, approximately 5500K) and add strobe lighting (again, about 5500K), we can select the daylight, flash, or auto white balance setting on our camera (some cameras allow you to set the balance to 5500K) to ensure that the colors in our image are rendered neutral or, in other words, without a color cast. *(Note:* If you like your color a little warmer or cooler, you can choose a "mismatched" white balance preset. For example, you can select the shade or night white balance preset, even though the ambient/strobe lighting reads like daylight.) You can also manipulate the results in post-production. RAW files can be adjusted with the white balance adjustment tool found in RAW processing/conversion software. JPEGs can be adjusted with the Levels feature of your photo-editing program.

### FIRST-CURTAIN OR SECOND-CURTAIN SYNC?

First-curtain sync is the default setting on most cameras. It is also the default option for most underwater photographers. It certainly is for me. When this setting is used, the flash will discharge immediately when the first curtain is fully open.

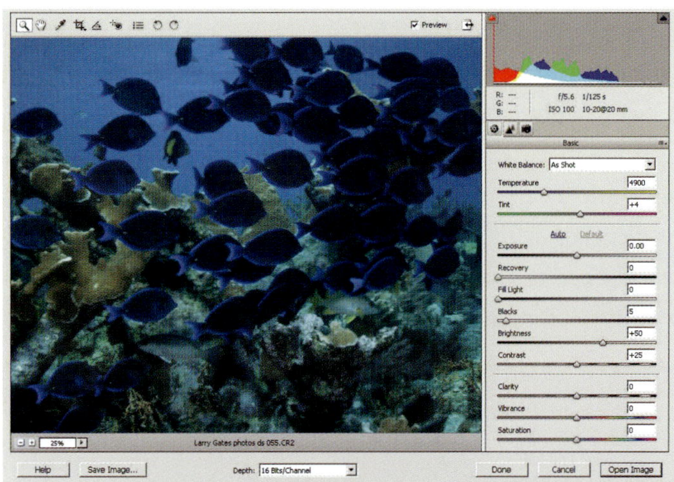


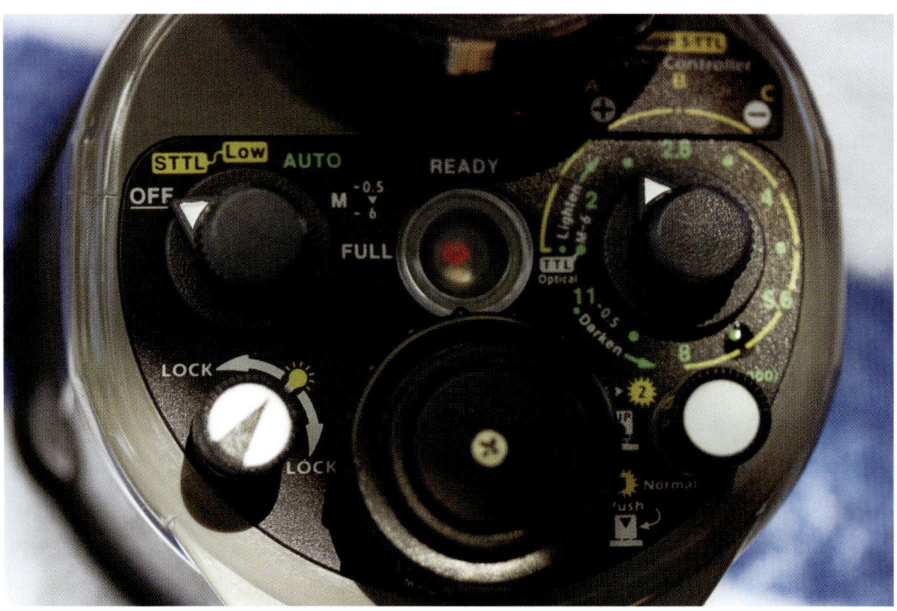


**Top**—RAW image in the RAW reader and its tools for adjusting white balance and color. **Bottom**—Strobe and its power setting controls.

Some cameras allow you to sync with the shutter's second curtain. The flash discharges shortly before the second curtain closes. This setting is rarely used by most underwater photographers. However, you can use it with a slow shutter speed to create an artistic, blurred effect when photographing a moving subject. To gauge the effects, set your camera to the second-curtain sync and photograph a moving subject with a $^1/_{30}$ second shutter speed.

### TTL FLASH CAPABILITY

When used with a compatible camera, a TTL flash system can "read" the scene and fire the flash for the precise duration of time (measured in milliseconds) to ensure a correct exposure. Photographers often refer to "adjusting the power" of the flash. A strobe has only one power, which is described by its guide number and/or in watt-seconds. "Turning up" or "turning down" the flash actually refers to increasing or decreasing the duration of the flash output. The flash can be used at "full power" (e.g., $^1/_{600}$ to $^1/_{25,000}$ second worth of light, depending on the flash unit), or a shorter (decreased) duration.

The strobe's angle of coverage must be equal to or greater than the lens's angle of view so that what the lens "sees" is fully illuminated by the strobe.

Let's move on to some other strobe specifications and learn how these help us work with and govern light—and choose our strobes.

### RECYCLE TIME

Recycle time is the time, measured in seconds, that it takes the strobe's capacitor to recharge and be ready to be fully discharged again. It is measured under the assumption that the strobe was discharged at "full dump" or full power (its longest duration).

The shorter the recycle time, the better. You don't want to risk missing a shot because you were waiting for your strobe to recycle.

You can reduce the strobe's recycle time by using its TTL setting. When the strobe fires at less than full duration, its capacitor does not fully deplete, so the recycle time is shorter. Another way to reduce recycle time is to turn down the output of the strobe when controlling it manually. Of course, when you reduce the power, you will need to make an exposure adjustment to compensate for the lost light.

### ANGLE OF COVERAGE

Angle of coverage is a key consideration in strobe selection. The strobe's angle of coverage must be equal to or greater than the lens's angle of view so that what the lens "sees" is fully illuminated by the strobe. If the angle of coverage is not wide enough, the center of the scene may appear bright and the edges of the scene will appear underexposed.

Today, most strobes provide an angle of coverage that is compatible with the angle of view that macro lenses, standard lenses, and many wide angle lenses allow. Play it safe. Check the strobe manufacturer's specifications for

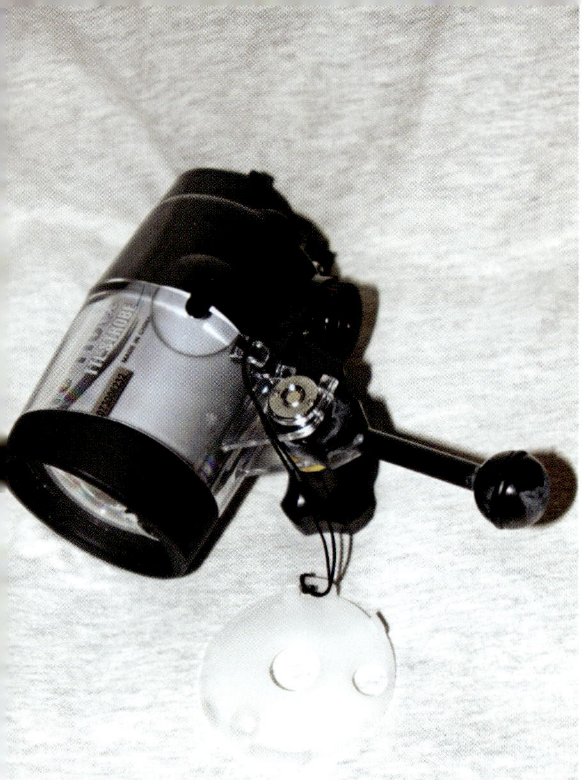

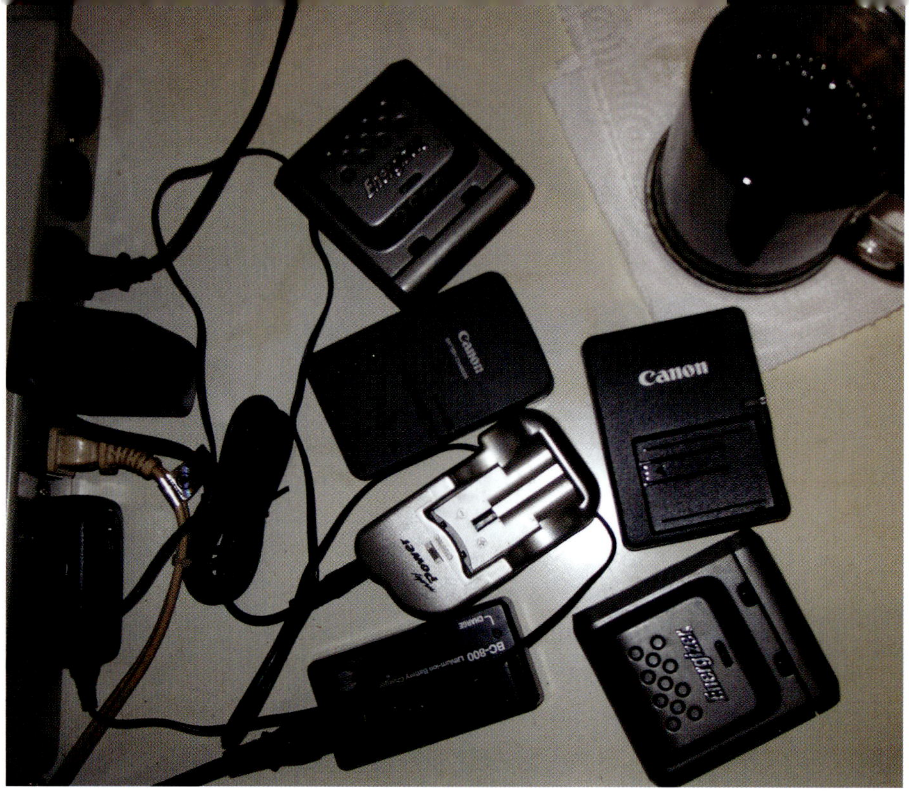


Left—Strobe head with diffuser detached, showing lanyard. **Right**—This photo shows some of the types of chargers we use in our underwater photography.

the angle of view to ensure that it can be used with your lenses before making an investment.

### DIFFUSERS

Most strobes come equipped with a diffuser—a semi-opaque plastic disc that attaches to the strobe's face and spreads out (diffuses) and softens the light, helping to prevent burned-out highlights. The diffuser also increases the strobe's angle of coverage by about 10 percent.

The average diffuser will decrease the strobe's output by roughly one f-stop worth of exposure value.

Diffusers should be attached to the strobe by a lanyard of some sort to prevent their loss. When shooting, if you find that you need to increase the exposure by one f-stop, you can remove the diffuser and let it hang on its lanyard, take the photograph, then replace the diffuser.

### ADVANCES IN STROBE TECHNOLOGY

Strobes were once equipped with just an on/off switch. Many of the strobes on the market today offer incremental power adjustment settings and other interesting features.

There is at least one strobe manufacturer with a strobe that has a control to set the light output in f-stops. The photographer sets the strobe to the same f-stop the camera's lens is set to. (I assume this feature is based on a baseline strobe-to-subject distance, perhaps 3 feet.) I'm also aware of a strobe that allows the photographer to adjust the unit's output incrementally when the strobe is set to TTL. I must admit, the point of that escapes me, because a functioning TTL flash system should preclude the need to do that.

Strobes are now more energy efficient than ever before. By this I do not mean they have become "green." Rather, they can be discharged many more times before the batteries need to be recharged or replaced. For comparison purposes, my very first strobe discharged about 72 times before its recycle time between shots became unbearably long. Most modern strobes will discharge a couple of hundred times or more before the batteries need to be replaced or recharged. This is a good thing because we're not shooting a 36-exposure roll of film anymore. We can shoot hundreds of photos on a dive. The number of flashes per charge is a specification readily available from strobe manufacturers.

Strobes are powered by proprietary rechargeable battery packs or dry cell batteries such as NiMH, which can also be recharged.

Some strobes are equipped with focus lights. These lights, sometimes called modeling lights, can help make focusing easier in lower-light, lower-contrast scenes. Add-on underwater focus lights are also available.

Strobes have improved in many ways. They are more reliable and their specifications are more accurately stated. Ambient light and our shooting conditions, however, have not changed. We still encounter a range of reflectivity among and between the elements in our frame. We're faced with the challenge of exposing a photograph of something extremely shiny and something that is absorbing light like a sponge absorbs water!

In these instances, all you can do is correctly expose your subject and let the rest of the light fall where it may. Check the LCD and histogram, make any necessary adjustments, and get the shot "in the bag." The alternative, of course, is to accept that the light isn't right for making the photograph and move on. Technological advances will never make every opportunity "picture perfect."

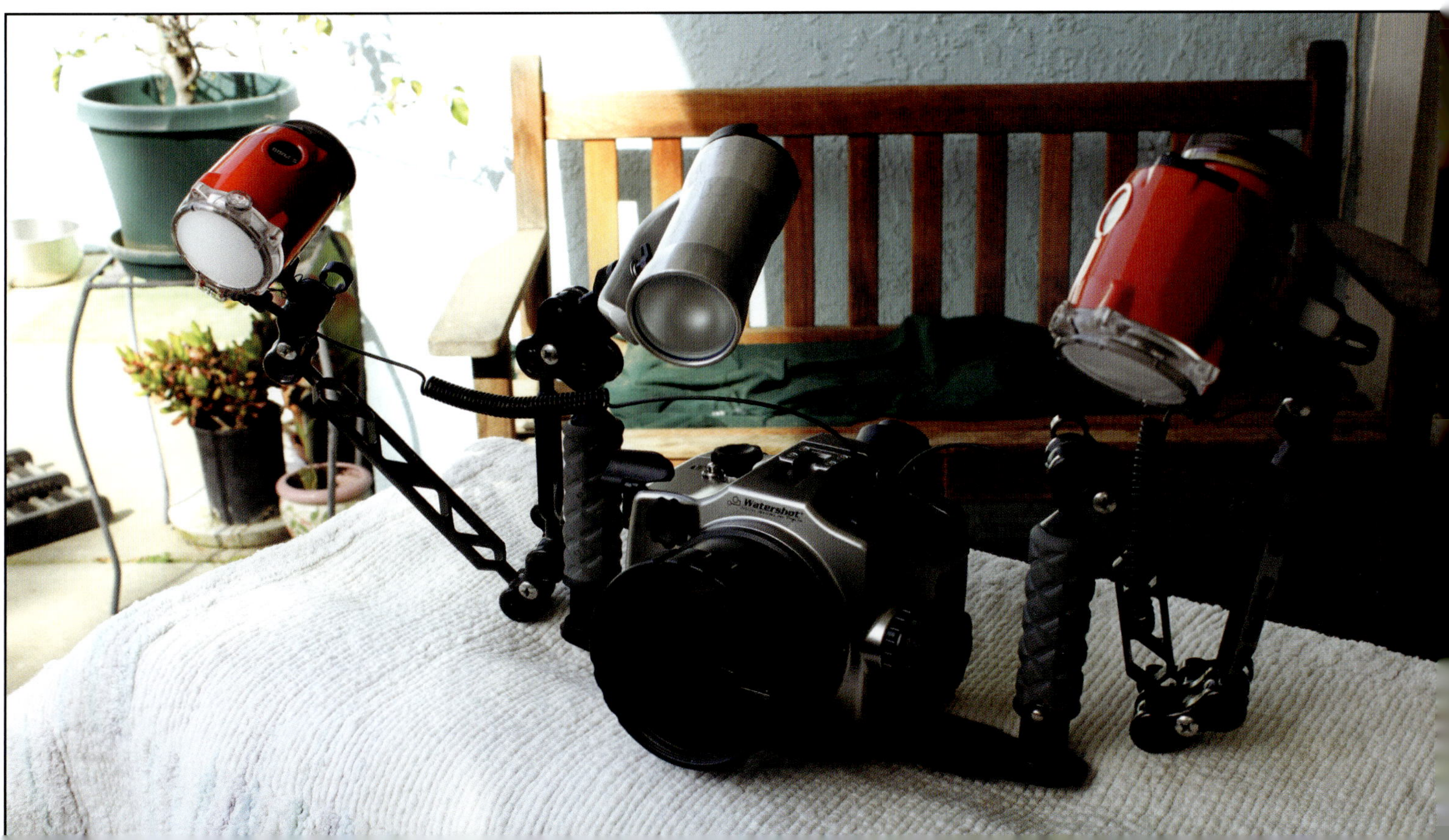

**Right**—Focus light mounted between two strobes. Photo courtesy of John Yasaki.

### TWO STROBES

I once believed that, since there is one sun, one strobe should suffice. I've since learned that there are several good reasons for using two strobes.

Earlier in this chapter, I mentioned that most strobes produce an angle of coverage that is comparable to the angle of view a lens can "see." Well, most strobes have an angle of light in the neighborhood of 100 degrees. Fisheye lenses have an angle of view that approaches 180 degrees. Simple math would indicate it would be difficult to cover a fisheye lens's angle of view with just one strobe.

I love photographing large, colorful reef scenes. When I do, I am usually within 3 feet of the subject and using a lens with at least a 70 degree angle of view. My strobe is off to the left side of my camera on an arm affixed to my camera tray. The strobe has an angle of coverage of at least 90 degrees. If I aim my strobe at what is in front of me, that part of my scene and most of the scene to my left will be well lit. It stands to reason, though, that the scene on

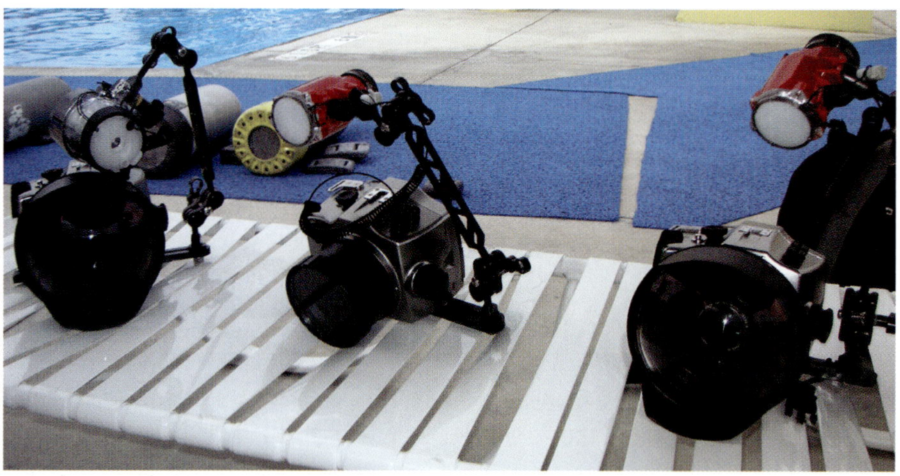

**Top**—Systems with one strobe mounted. **Bottom**—Photographer with camera system outfitted with two strobes.

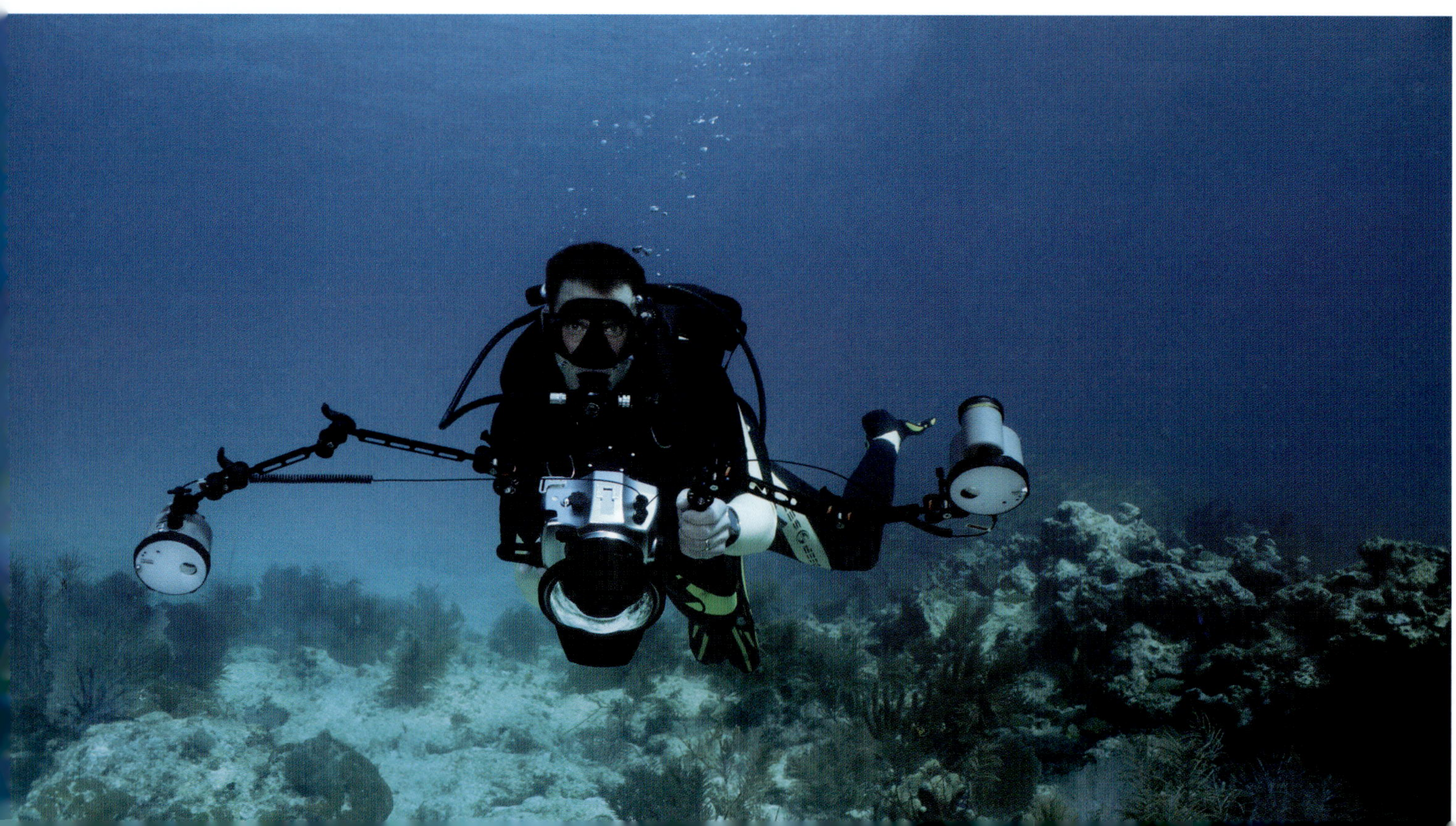

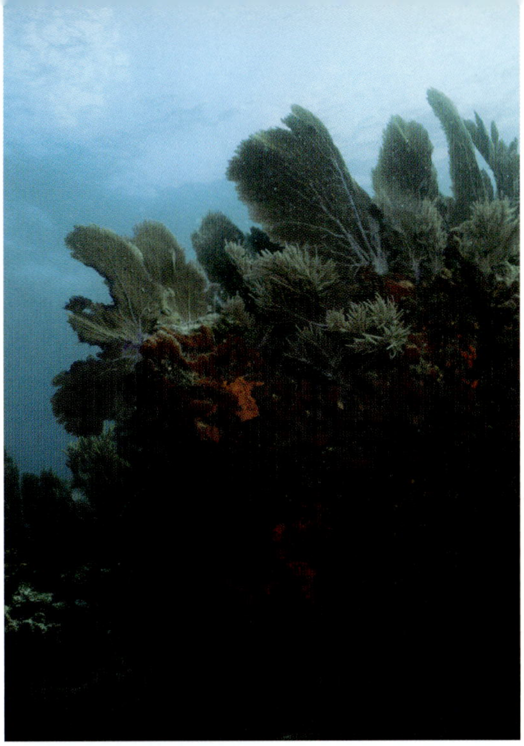
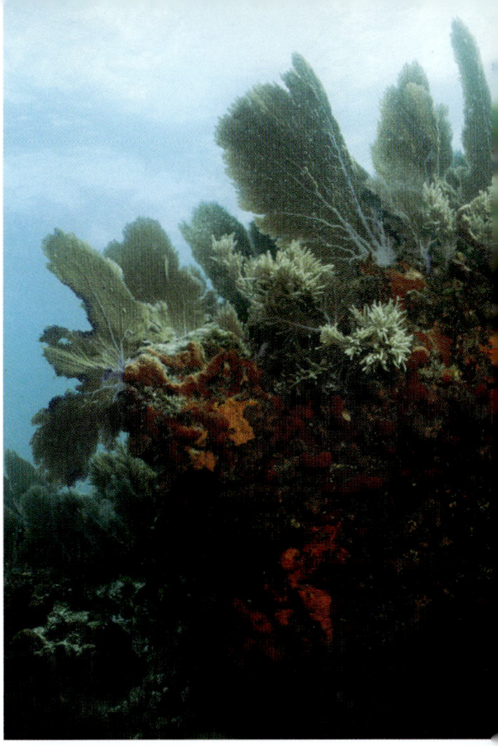
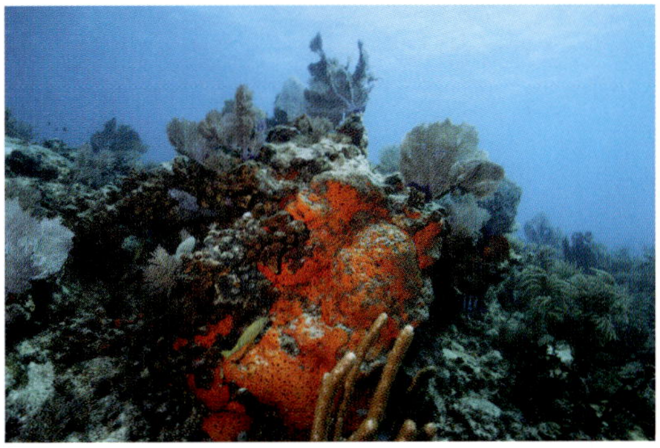
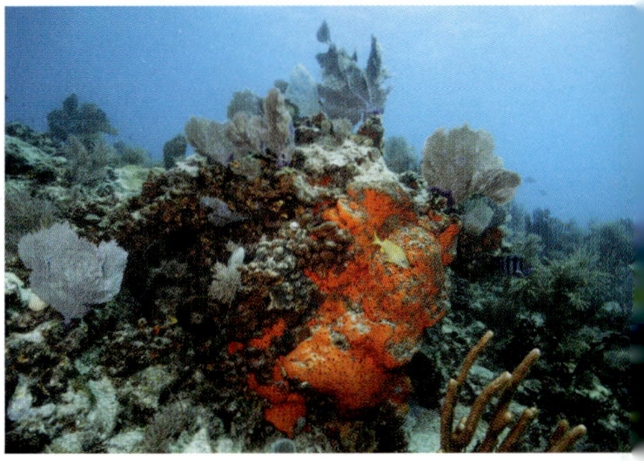

**Top left**—Colors at 3 feet. **Top right**—Colors at 2 feet. **Bottom left**—Reef scene photographed using one strobe. **Bottom right**—The same reef scene photographed using two strobes.

the camera-right side will be underexposed. (The strobe is much farther from this area of the composition and, as mentioned earlier, one f-stop worth of exposure value is lost with every one-foot increase in distance from the light.) Adding a second strobe can create a balanced, properly exposed image.

We know that the closer the subject is to the strobe, the more vibrant its colors will be. For example, a red subject is very richly colored when it is 1 foot from the strobe but appears less colorful at 2 feet. It decreases as we go and, at 5 feet, the subject is almost pale. At a strobe-to-subject distance of 3 feet, my lens covers my reef scene 5 feet out and 5 feet back. The reds on the right side of the scene are not as vibrant as the reds on the left. In other words, I need to put some light on the right side to ensure the color is rendered similarly on both sides of the scene.

There are a couple of other notable benefits to using two strobes: Using two strobes increases the amount of light that's available for the exposure and allows us to use a smaller aperture, increasing our depth of field and image sharpness; with two strobes, you can reduce or eliminate shadows if that is a look you prefer; and having a second strobe means that you have a backup that you can use if something happens to your primary unit.

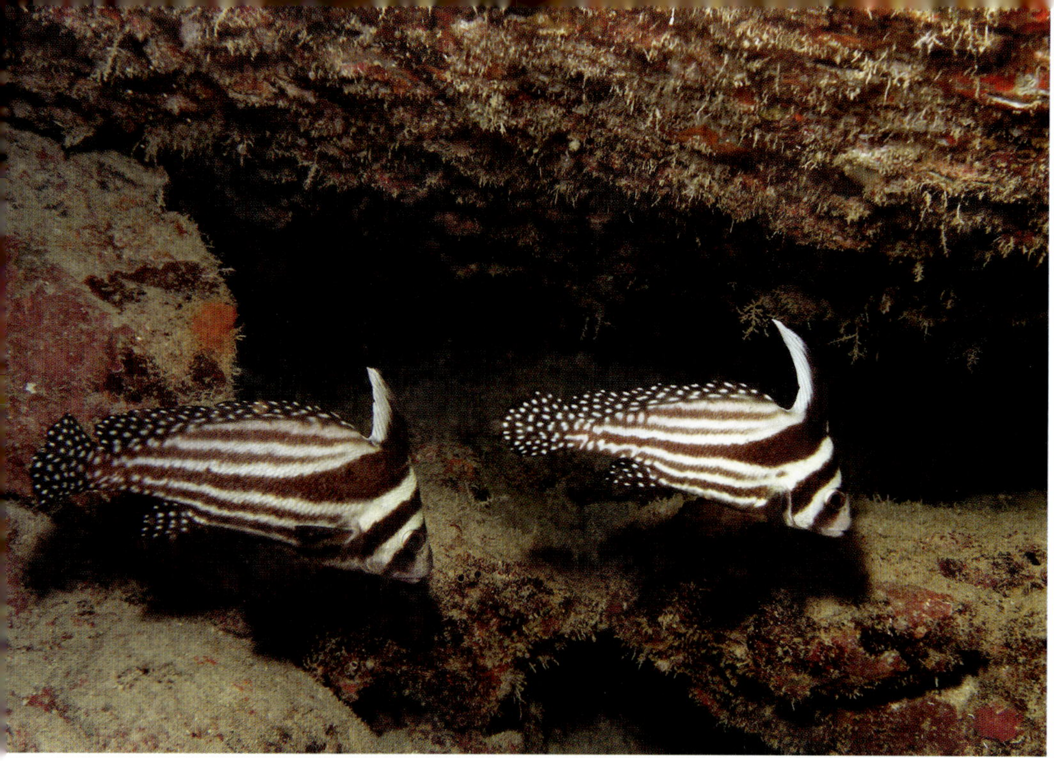

**Left**—As shown here, shadows are not necessarily an unacceptable image attribute.

When two strobes are used, they are mounted on longer strobe arms. This positions the units farther apart, reduces the combined light, and facilitates edge lighting.

Sure, there are benefits to using two strobes. There are also some drawbacks. The use of two strobes will change the camera's buoyancy and therefore *your* buoyancy. Using two strobes will also change the handling characteristics of your camera system. A second strobe and its components will make the system bulkier and create extra drag, which will need to be managed when photographing in currents or surge and in confined areas. Having two strobes adds to the cost of your camera system. Also, adding another strobe means that you have another piece of equipment to care for and travel with. Finally, using a strobe can prevent or reduce backscatter, but using two strobes doubles the odds that backscatter occur.

When using two strobes, it's not critical that they are the same make and model, but there are practical and technical reasons why it is preferable to have two like strobes. From a practicality point of view, you have redundancy and interchangeability. The strobes use the same type of power and sync cords/fiber-optic cables and the same fittings. From a technical viewpoint, using two like strobes means both strobes have the same temperature, power output, angle of coverage, recycle times, and battery life.

Be sure to master one strobe before introducing a second one, as there is a bit of a learning curve involved in adding another light unit.

### A WORD OF CAUTION

When we use two strobes to light a scene, the light may overlap. Where this occurs, more light is added to the exposure. How much? Logic would suggest that it would double. What is your guess? If you guessed about an f-stop worth, you are correct!

How do we compensate for the "extra" strobe output? One way is to reduce the output of the second strobe. (You are really just using it to add light on the right side of the composition.) Another way is to aim both strobes straight ahead or slightly outward (this is called "edge lighting"), rather than in toward the center of the frame. This reduces but does not eliminate the overlap. To make this approach effective, one has to be able to visualize the cones of light the strobes will emit.

## CAMERA AND STROBE: MAKING THE CONNECTION

When adding a strobe to the camera system, we must use a cord or cable to allow communication between the camera and strobe. We must also determine how we will mount and position the strobe to allow for ease in use.

## A SECOND STROBE

Just because we have two strobes mounted and ready to go does not mean that we have to use both units every time we take a photograph. When we do not need that second light, we can turn it off or simply point it over our shoulder and reposition it later.

**Sync Cords or Fiber-Optic Cables?** So, what do we need to acquire and use in order to allow communication between the camera and strobe? Back in the day, if you used a strobe, you used an electrical sync cord. There was no choice; there were no fiber-optic cables.

To use a fiber-optic cable, your camera has to have an on-board flash. To use a sync cord for this link, the strobe used must have a bulkhead that accepts one end of the cord and its fitting, and the housing must have a bulkhead to accept the other end of the sync cord and its fitting. Some strobes come with the ability to use either a fiber-optic cable or a sync cord. If you have a strong preference for one communication link over the other, consider that preference when shopping for a camera. Pro-level dSLRs do not have on-board camera flashes, so we must use an electrical sync cord with a strobe and housing that can accommodate the cord. This means both the strobe and housing need the bulkhead fittings to accommodate the sync cord.

Each option has advantages and disadvantages. Fiber-optic cables are usually less expensive than sync cords. They do not have to be watertight at the strobe end or the housing end. They require the camera to have an on-board flash and are easier to maintain, as there are no O-rings to service. Fiber-optic cables can be finicky, and proper placement of either or both ends must be accomplished or the light will not travel from the camera flash to the strobe sensor.

Sync cords (in my opinion) provide a more solid, robust, and reliable connection between the camera and strobe and are less finicky. They do not require the camera to have an on-board flash, only a hot-shoe mount, so there is never any waiting between shots for the on-board camera flash to recycle. Sync cords can enable the use of the camera's TTL protocol. There are drawbacks, however: sync cords can be damaged by water. Also, either of the two bulkheads needed can leak and cause flooding of either the strobe or the camera housing.

**Attaching the Strobe and Housing Accessories.** There are several components that are used to mate the strobe and the rest of our system. One is a camera tray that mounts to the underside of the housing. Some makers forego trays and opt for handles or fittings that affix to the sides or tops of their

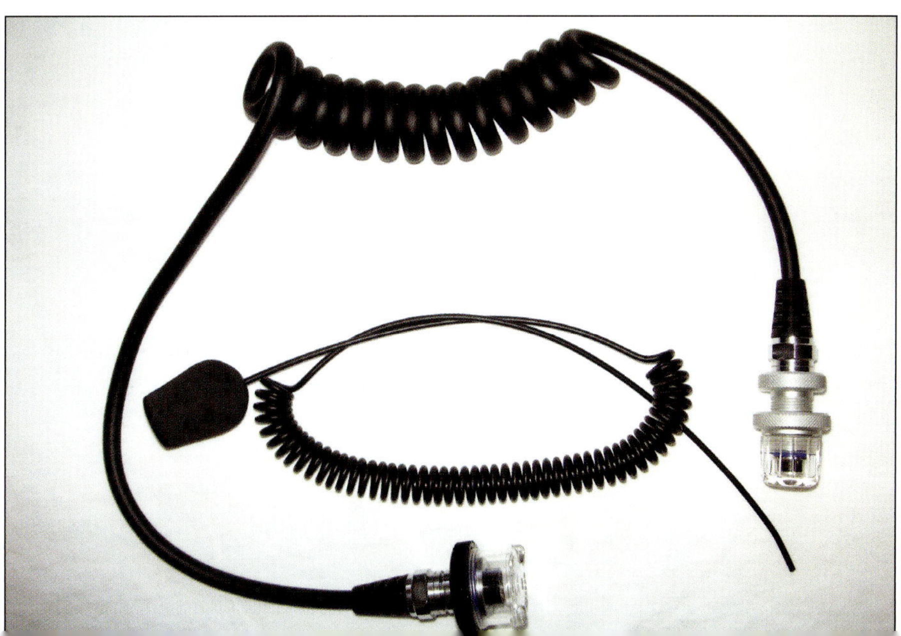

**Right**—Electrical sync cord (top). Fiber-optic cable (bottom).

housings. Trays can also be fitted with handles or an adaptor that attaches to the strobe arm. These options can be configured to suit your personal preference.

At the top of the tray, handle(s), or camera housing, a clamp is added to accept a strobe arm. Strobe arms vary in length. (Additional clamps and arms can be added to suit your preference.) The arm ultimately connects to a strobe head adaptor, which connects to the strobe.

The clamps and arms not only link the strobe to the rest of your system but allow flexibility in placing and aiming the strobes. Once assembled, they articulate much like our shoulders, arms, elbows, wrists, and hands do.

When making baseline equipment choices, I always seem to resort to what worked back in the day. I think this is a logical approach because the equipment used to make images underwater back in the day (about twenty years ago) produced wonderful images. This basic equipment includes a camera (whether amphibious or housed), a tray, a strobe arm, strobe, and electric sync cord. Some shooters, myself included, did without a camera tray and arm assembly and hand-held the strobe. We used our physical body as a substitute to the modern-day articulating arm systems. This worked wonderfully in enabling us to place the light wherever we wanted it, and quickly. The articulating arm systems many photographers use today were designed to mimic the capability of handholding the strobe. They're not required to get a good shot, but you may find that they suit your working habits.

There are several add-ons that can be built into your system. Let's take a look at what is available and the pros/cons associated with their use.

Do you need handles? No. Are they handy? If they have good ergonomics (i.e., they are comfortable to hold and you can reach at least the main controls of the camera housing), yes. I find that I can reach more controls without a handle or handles.

Do you need more than one strobe arm? No. If you have not worked with articulating arms and clamps, you may struggle to get your strobe accurately placed and aimed. Once you have experience using one arm, you should probably add a second one. It will enable you to position the strobe a bit farther to the left or higher above the lens when top lighting is desired. It will also allow you to place the strobe farther to the right side of the lens. A second arm allows you to move the strobe closer to or farther from the subject than does a single arm. I see no need to use more than two arms per strobe.

How long should the strobe arms be? Back in the day, they were not very long. I never measured them, but my best guess is that they ranged in length from 8 to 16 inches. We often use a strobe instead of a flash to help prevent backscatter. To do the job, we need an arm that is long enough to get the strobe away from the camera and off of the lens axis. Generally speaking, the wider the angle of lens used, the longer the strobe arm should be. Most of the one-arm setups I have seen have an 8- or 12-inch arm.

**Top**—Camera tray. **Bottom**—Strobe arm and clamps.

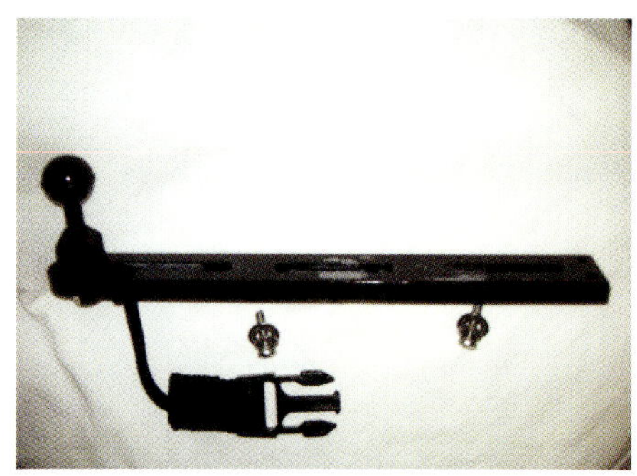

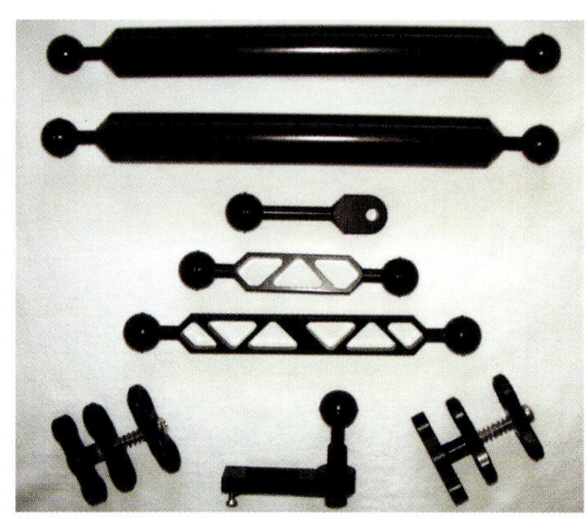

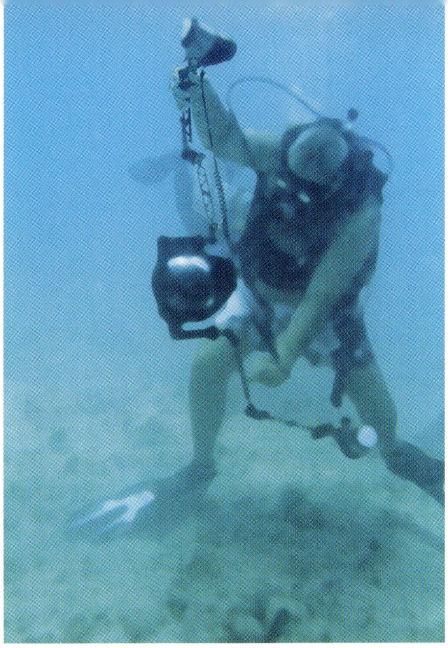

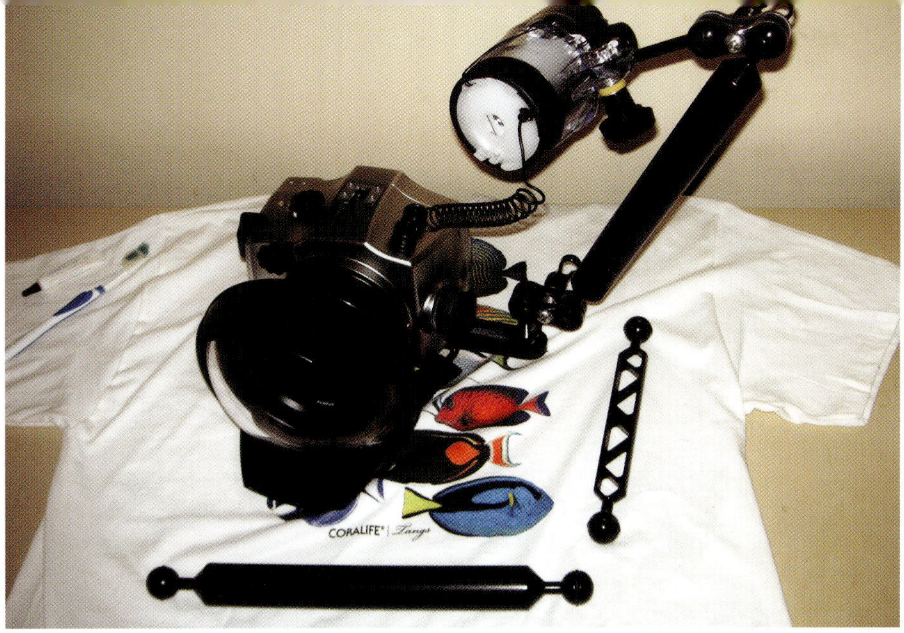


**Left**—At times, it seems we are dealing with Erector Sets in our choice and use of strobe arms. **Right**—System setup with buoyant strobe arm.

When we've mastered the use of one arm, we can adopt a more flexible two-arm system. Though we could use, for example, a 10-inch arm, two 5-inch arms allow you to bring a strobe (or strobes) in closer to the camera. The combination used is somewhat dependent on the angle of view of your lens and how compact you would like your system to be. Some user-friendly combinations are a 5-inch arm and a 3-inch arm, two 5-inch arms, an 8-inch and a 3-inch arm, an 8-inch and a 5-inch arm, and two 8-inch arms.

Another question photographers often ask is, should I buy strobe arms that are positively buoyant or buy floats to make them positively buoyant? The answer depends on how negatively buoyant your camera system is and how comfortable you are with its negative buoyancy. One way to adjust the buoyancy of your camera system is to use buoyant strobe arms or floats for the strobe arms.

My personal preference is for my system to be very slightly negatively buoyant. This is so it will stay put if I need to set it down underwater and will not float up into my face when I clip my camera system to myself.

A downside to having a camera system either negatively or positively buoyant is, it takes more work to handle the camera system. You are either holding it up (if negatively buoyant) or holding it down (if positively buoyant). This can cause arm, wrist, or hand fatigue over the course of multiple days of photo diving.

When we are using two strobes, the conventional wisdom dictates that we should use the same strobe arm configuration on each unit. Perhaps this is due to a desire for symmetry. I choose to arm my second strobe in a way that lets me put its light where I want it.

The components described above are manufactured by strobe and housing manufacturers and third-party manufacturers. Most are standardized and interchangeable. It is better to be safe than sorry, though. Be sure that any items you are considering are compatible with your system before committing to a purchase.

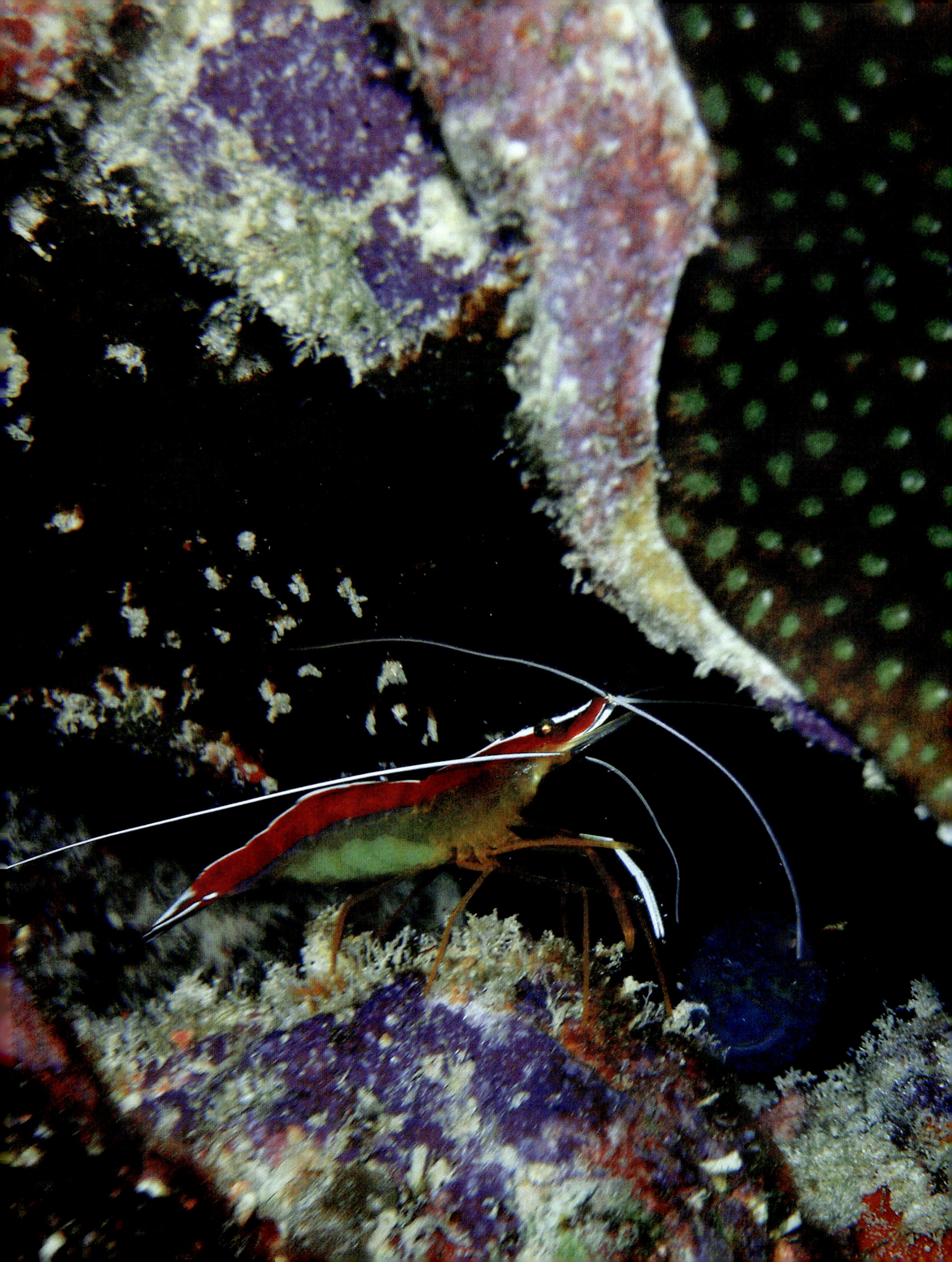

# 4. EQUIPMENT CARE, MAINTENANCE, AND TROUBLESHOOTING

Now that we have all of our advanced underwater photographic equipment in our bags, the next logical concern is, how do we take care of these things? The short answer is, much in the same way that we care for our topside photo gear.

In this chapter, we'll look a little deeper into the topics of equipment care, maintenance, and troubleshooting. This chapter is a critical read, as, even with our use of more advanced equipment, we're likely to run into trouble at some point. Tips for traveling with your gear are included in this chapter as well.

Introducing your camera to temperature extremes can result in condensation forming inside the camera.

*Note:* Though I have taken care to provide good, solid advice for the care and maintenance of your equipment, manufacturers' guidelines should take precedence.

## THE CAMERA, BATTERIES, AND MEMORY CARDS

Keep the following tips in mind to safeguard and baby your camera. Maintenance should then be just a matter of wiping it clean with a soft, clean cloth on occasion.

**Keep It Dry.** Flooding the camera is obviously to be avoided. But smaller amounts of water, like sea spray from the boat, can also negatively impact the camera's functioning.

At day's end, I enjoy a beer with my fellow photographers. While I may bring my camera, I do not set it down on our table. Cameras and (spilled) alcohol don't mix. Have fun, but be careful.

Other liquids, such as cleaning agents and solvents, can cause harm as well. Some liquids, like spray-on sunblock or a mask defogging agent, seem more benign, but I suspect they can cause damage to coatings on lenses or other parts of our equipment.

One unexpected foe is canned air. When air is released from its pressurized container, condensation can result, and you may force water vapor into your camera or lens.

Also, introducing your camera to temperature extremes can result in condensation forming inside the camera.

**Dust and Sand.** In Key Largo, we have coral dust. In other locales, sand or dirt may pose a threat to your equipment. Use common sense and safeguard your camera against these dangers. There are kits and implements available that can be used to clean the sensor and mirrors should the need

**Facing page**—Scarlet Lady Cleaner Shrimp. Photo courtesy of Jeff Boerlacher. Exposure: f/5.6, 1/200, and 100 ISO.

arise. Your best bet, however, may be to consult with a professional camera repair person.

One way to prevent foreign matter from invading your camera body is to ensure that the lens body cap is in place whenever a lens is not mounted.

**Pets.** Keep pets away from your camera and equipment. They shed, lick, sniff, and slobber on things.

**Keep It Clean.** The mirrors in the camera's viewfinder and the camera sensor can be affected by airborne particles when we are changing our lenses. I try to change my lenses in the cleanest, driest possible environment. I also make my changes as quickly as I can. I lay out and organize what I need—new lens, lens caps, etc.—before I begin. This reduces the amount of time the lens elements are exposed to the elements.

**Extreme Heat.** While we may like to work on our tans while on our diving vacations, the camera doesn't need time in the sun. I take care to ensure that my gear is not exposed to heat and sunlight for long periods of time. When my camera system is out in the sun, I'll shade it with a towel. I never leave my camera in the car on a hot, sunny day for extended periods of time.

**Computer Glitches.** Digital cameras are light-sensitive computers, and they suffer from the same glitches that other computers do. In some cases, turning the camera off, waiting a few minutes, then turning it back on will resolve the problem. If this doesn't work, try removing the battery, wait a few minutes or more, reinstall the battery, then turn the camera back on. As a final resort, turn off the camera and remove its battery, memory card, and lens. Wait a few minutes, replace everything, and turn the camera back on. In doing these things, we are, in effect, rebooting the camera.

**Batteries.** When not in use, I periodically recharge my camera battery and spare batteries.

**Memory Cards.** My memory cards are stored in card holders, and I reformat them in the camera, not via the computer.

**Storage.** When not in use, I store my camera equipment in Ziploc bags. I add a silicate packet to each bag and keep them in a cool, dry, dark place. Every few months, I dig the equipment out and fire it up to see that it is still in working order.

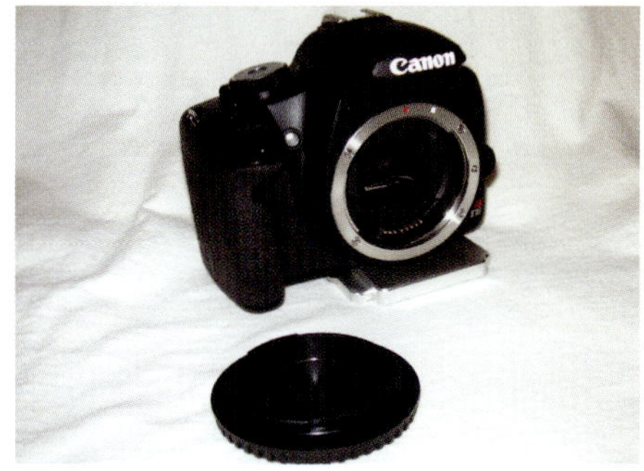


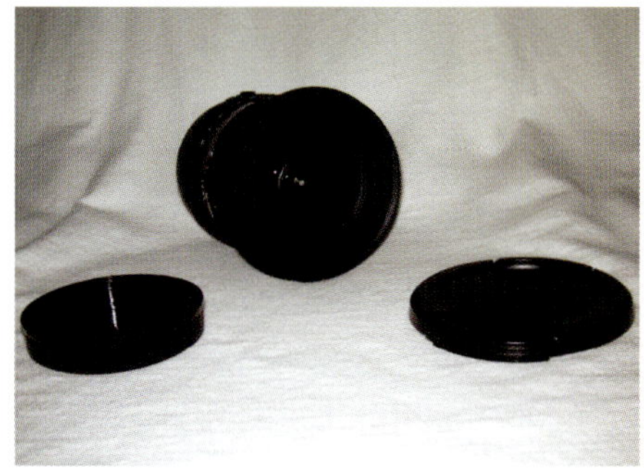

**Top**—The camera body with its body cap. **Bottom**—Lens with its front and rear caps.

## THE LENS

Many of the same commonsense tactics that apply to safeguarding your camera also apply to protecting your lens.

Avoid dropping the lens. Do not set it down where it can fall onto a hard surface.

Keep the lens cap on your lens when not in use and keep foreign matter away from the front and rear of the lens. Avoid getting greasy fingerprints or the lubrication used on O-rings and other seals on the lens, as cleaning them off the lens is a real pain.

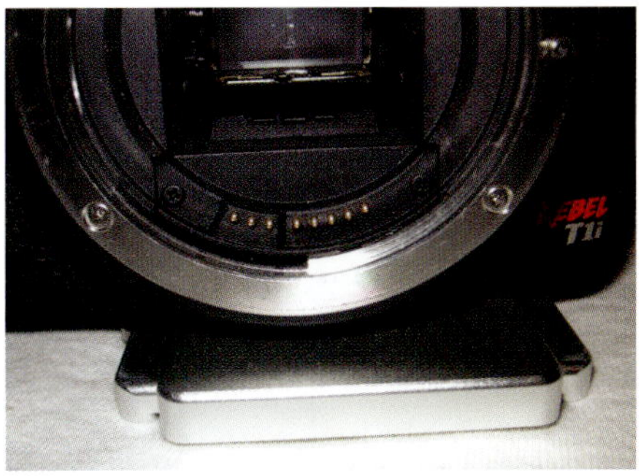

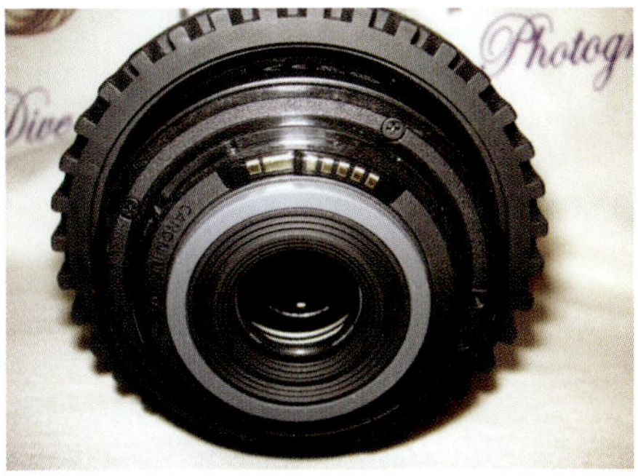

**Top**—Camera's lens contact surfaces. **Bottom**—Lens and its electrical contact surfaces.

Clean your lenses only when they look dirty. Blow lightly on the lens to remove any dust, then wipe it with a microfiber cloth. If the lens has a touch of grease on it, you can apply a liquid lens cleaning agent to a lens tissue and gently scrub, beginning in the center of the lens and working toward its outer edges. Do not allow any of the liquid to run to the edge of the lens where the glass meets the lens body.

Occasionally the lens will fail to communicate with the camera body. This can occur when the lens contact surfaces or the corresponding contact surfaces on the camera body are dirty. Try holding the camera or lens contact-side down and using the eraser end of a pencil to gently rub the contacts clean.

The lens and/or camera body can be damaged during the lens-mounting process. Take your time and be gentle when mounting the lens to the camera body. Be sure to precisely align the components using the index marks as a guide. When turning the lens to lock it into place or remove it, make sure you are turning it the correct direction. Canon's lenses turn clockwise to mount, and Nikon's lenses turn counterclockwise to mount.

When you are doing lens changes, try to think like a surgeon in an operating room. Have your act together and prepare. The longer the process takes, the more risk there is to your system. Don't chat with your dive buddies or have a sandwich during this process.

Unless I absolutely have to change a lens on site, I don't. I use my best guess as to which lens I will need, and I mount it before I am on site.

### THE HOUSING

Aside from camera trays/stays and strobe arms, there is probably not another piece of our underwater camera equipment more durable than our housings, whether made of aluminum or any plastic compounds. While I don't recommend it, dropping one will not automatically ensure damaging it to the point of putting it out of service. I've seen and heard of these housings suffering and surviving terrible abuses and accidents.

This said, care should be taken when handling and using our underwater housings. While the materials they are made of are tough, the controls may not be. A damaged control can put your system out of service and even if it does not, the damage could aid and abet a flood.

**Right**—Aluminum housing.

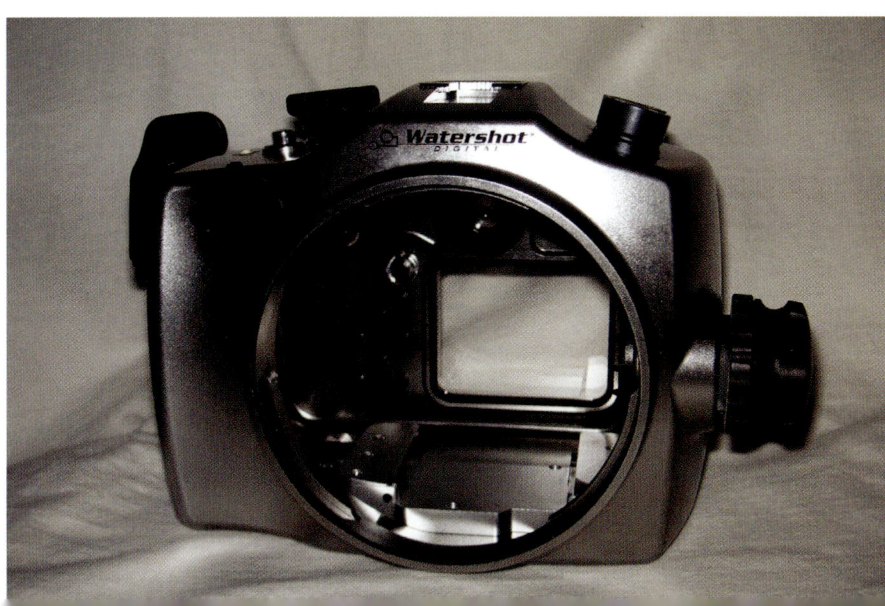

I dive with my housing, as a part of my total underwater camera system, and have it in my hand at all times so that I will be ready should a photographic opportunity present itself. I have a means to secure my camera system to my SCUBA, positioned low so it hangs down and out of the way, should I need the use of two hands.

Pre-dive, I function-check my camera system. Just before entering the water, I dip it in a camera rinse tank (when boat diving) or submerge it briefly (when shore diving) to check for leaks. Leaks are betrayed by a small stream of bubbles emitting from any of the housing's seals or sealing surfaces (the main body seal, the port O-ring, and any controls with shafts that penetrate the housing).

Post-dive, I keep my housing wet until I can give it a long and thorough soak in freshwater. An hour is the minimum soak time, and hours of soak time is better. During the soaking period, I work all the controls several times to try to remove any saltwater (and crystals) from around the control shafts and their O-rings. Once the soak is complete, I let the housing air dry or dry it with a soft towel.

When not in use, I make sure my housing is clean and dry. I remove all of its user-serviceable seals and O-rings and store them in a Ziploc bag labeled with permanent marker. I pack the housing in a plastic bag along with a silicate packet and keep it in a cool, dry, dark place (e.g., on a shelf in my closet).

While most housing makers will recommend servicing any user serviceable O-rings and seals before or after each dive, I generally do a few days' worth of diving before I service mine.

When I want to clean an O-ring or other user-serviceable seal, I run it through my fingers to help remove grit and lubrication, then use a paper towel or a KimWipe. When I want to wash a seal, I use fresh, hot water and take care not to stretch it. Once done, I inspect it to make sure it is clean and has no debris clinging to it. Before I install it, I check for debris again. I look it over once more when I lubricate it. I also check the surfaces that the seal will come in contact with to make sure they are clean and free of debris. I often use a magnifying glass to check the seals and mating surfaces to be doubly sure they are clean.

When I am assembling and readying my system for a dive or caring for any of my photographic equipment, I do so inside a building and under the best lighting I can find. In some cases, this is my resort room's bathroom. I lay everything out before I begin to prevent not installing something I should install. Some advanced underwater photographers rely on a laminated checklist to make sure they do not make a critical error in assembly.

Housing manufacturers offer maintenance recommendations. Annual servicing—which includes the removal and cleaning or replacement of each control and non-user-serviceable seal, plus cleaning the sealing surfaces—is recommended by many.

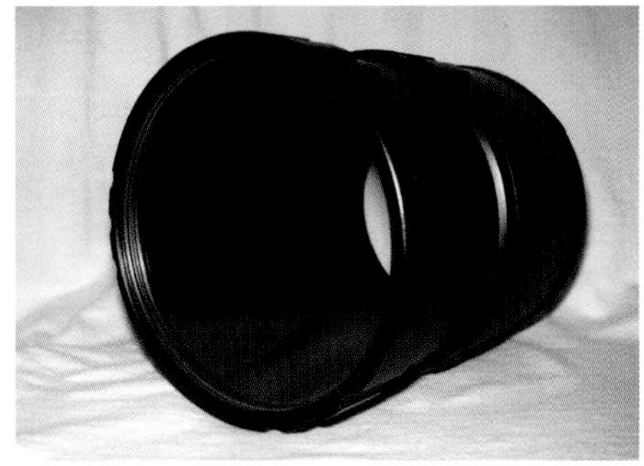

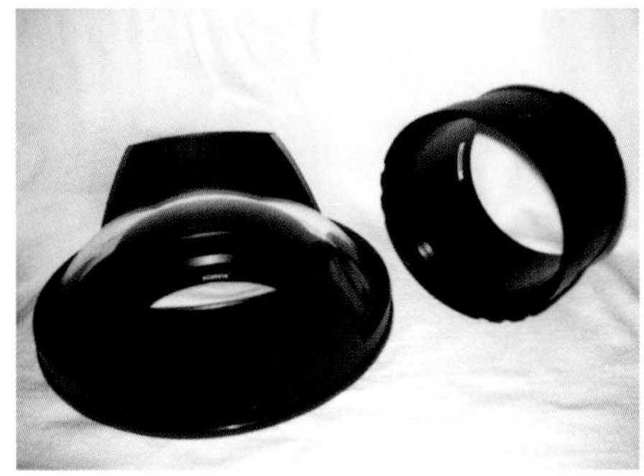

**Top**—A flat port. **Bottom**—A dome port and port extension.

Caring for ports and extensions is straightforward. Clean the inside and outside of ports, whether glass or acrylic, in the same manner in which you protect the lens's front and rear elements.

Protect the port's optics from scratches. Ports can be scratched when you come dangerously close to coral, when you are above water and collide with a solid surface (rigid or foam port covers are available for added protection), or if you do not remove dust or debris from your port prior to cleaning it with a cloth. A minor scratch on the exterior of the port does not result in any loss of image quality, as the water "fills in" tiny scratches.

The housing end of the port should be protected from damage as well. If this is damaged, flooding can result.

I pat my ports dry using a soft, clean cloth. This is because I am never sure what else was in the water and, whatever it is, I don't want it drying and hardening on my lens port's surface.

If you will not be diving for a period of days or longer, remove the port and its O-ring, clean it, and lube it. (I probably lubricate my port O-rings more frequently than I lubricate my main housing seal. This is because doing so makes it easier for me to install and remove the port from the housing.) Dry the components and store them in a labeled Ziploc bag.

### THE STROBE

In my view, strobes are very durable. Yes, they have a face and usually made of glass or acrylic that can be broken, but they are often shielded by a diffuser.

Common sense dictates trying to protect the strobe's face and controls. Take care to avoid dropping the strobe or letting it bang against hard objects.

Follow the strobe manufacturer's recommendations when it comes to maintaining your strobe. The O-ring or seal that makes the battery compartment or battery unit water-tight is typically the only serviceable part.

The strobe should be soaked after use. While the unit is soaking, I work its controls to remove any salt. When the soaking process is complete, I rinse the strobe and let it air dry or dry it with a soft towel.

**Below**—Strobe with its diffuser.

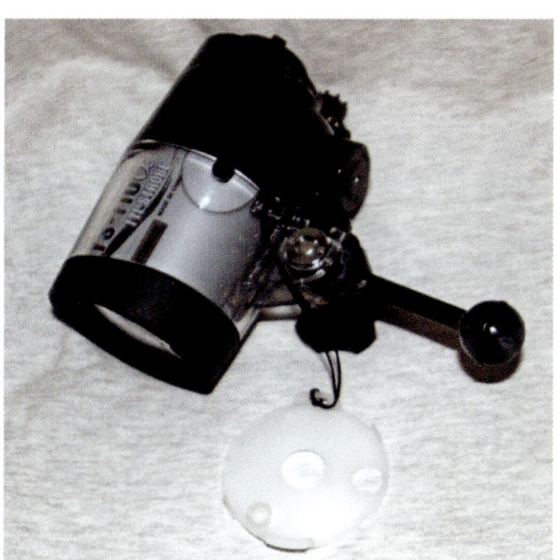

After a day's shooting, remove the batteries from your strobe—even if you think you have sufficient battery power for the next dive. This is because, if the strobe battery compartment incurred a very minor flood, the droplets of water will corrode the battery contacts and wreak havoc. It is best to find out if the strobe endured a minor flood on the day it happened, rather than the next day. Most modern day strobes' battery compartments are sealed from the rest of the strobe. This is a good design because if the compartment floods, a thorough rinsing in freshwater and allowing it to dry may be all that is necessary to make the strobe operational again. *Hint:* If a strobe fires intermittently above or below the water, it may be flooded.

I store my strobes with the O-rings removed and sealed away in a labeled Ziploc bag.

#### FIBER-OPTIC CABLES AND SYNC CORDS

I currently use fiber-optic cables as a means for my strobe to communicate with my camera. These require very little maintenance. I take care to not bend the cables in sharp turns and I try to keep the cable's ends clean and undamaged. I still have a strobe that uses a traditional electrical sync cord, and I treat and care for the cord in the same way, with one additional step: I service the O-rings on each end of the cord.

I've had success in cleaning corrosion from electrical sync cords' metal contact surfaces using Radio Shack's aerosol Precision Electronics Cleaner. It is safe to use around most plastics and leaves no residue.

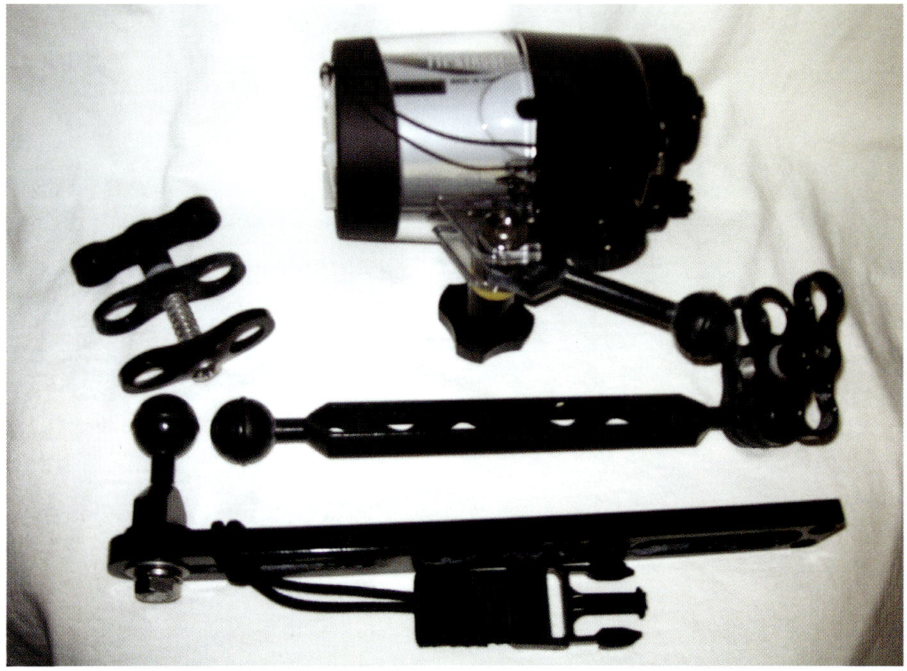

**Above**—Strobe head with gizmos.

#### OTHER CAMERA SYSTEM COMPONENTS

What is left to tend to is the camera tray, strobe arms, their clamps, handles, strobe head adaptors, and various fasteners that hold these together. These components are the easiest to care for and maintain. Rinse them and let them dry.

The strobe arm typically has one or more ball ends that facilitate attaching clamps and allow us to precisely position our strobe or strobes when photographing our subjects. In most cases, there is an O-ring at the ball end's equator. This O-ring should not be lubricated. Its purpose is to provide a soft friction between the ball end and the clamp, and we can adjust that friction by tightening or loosening the clamp. Lubricating the O-ring would prevent the ability to adjust the tension.

When using a housed dSLR camera system and strobe, we end up with a lot of equipment. Some of this stuff just fits together with latches or clamps, and other components are screwed or bolted together. Sometimes a "fixing bolt" is attached to the strobe head to connect a strobe head adaptor. Most times the camera tray is bolted to the housing. In both instances, these bolts are metal. They are often made of a different metal than the strobe head, housing, or other components. Dissimilar metals exposed together to freshwater or saltwater can weld together over time. I learned this lesson the hard way after waiting a year to remove an adaptor from a camera tray. I could not get the job done. My solution was to sacrifice the adaptor, as replacing it was less expensive than replacing the tray. To prevent this, I've learned to periodically (at least once a year) disassemble any components that are fixed together using bolts or screws. Using O-ring lube or lithium grease, I lubricate the threads on these and reassemble them, if I am not storing them.

## TROUBLESHOOTING

Okay gang, we've got all our advanced equipment and we know a bit about how to care for and maintain it. We can apply what we already know about underwater photography using it. So, what can go wrong?

**Floods.** Floods are a major event, and there is no remedy. Some leading causes of floods are incorrect assembly of the housing, port, or strobe; not installing an O-ring; installing an O-ring that is compromised by foreign matter; or damaged/compromised mating surfaces.

Never leave your camera system unattended in a camera rinse container. I've seen camera latches made loose after becoming entangled with sync cords or a part of another camera while being removed from the container. Double check to ensure your housing latches, battery compartment lid, and port are properly locked and in place.

If you are using sync cords, make sure the fittings on each end are completely threaded into the bulkheads of the strobe and housing and fully tightened.

Flooding can also result when an O-ring is improperly seated. To prevent this problem, try this: When pushing and turning one component into another, turn the component that has the O-ring attached backward just a bit before the assembly is complete, then finish the assembly.

**Strobe Issues.** Day in and day out, photographers face problems with their strobes not firing, not syncing with the camera's shutter, or not providing the correct output.

If the strobe is not firing, check to make sure the power switch is in the on position. Some switches can be finicky, and if not turned on to the precise position, the strobe will not fire.

A strobe will fail to fire if there are no batteries installed, they are incorrectly installed, or the batteries are not charged. Always start your diving day with new or freshly charged batteries, and be sure they are correctly installed. Using a mix of different aged and different milli-amp batteries of the same type is not recommended.

Strobes that communicate with the camera via fiber-optic cables are made to work with cameras that pre-flash, as well as those that do not. Ensure your strobe's switch is turned to the position that reflects the camera's capabilities. If either end of a fiber-optic cable is improperly aligned, the flash may also fail to fire. Make sure that the camera end of the cable is clean and it can "see" the output of the camera's flash. Then check to see that the strobe end of the cable is correctly positioned so the strobe's sensor will receive the on-board flash's light as it emits from that end of the fiber-optic cable. Functionality improves when the fiber-optic cable ends are aligned perpendicular to either

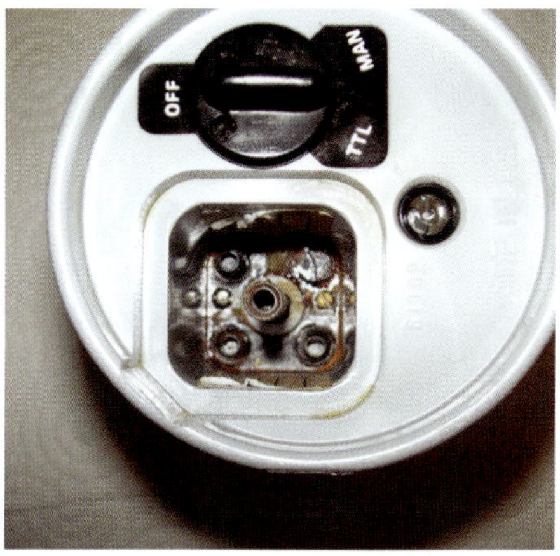


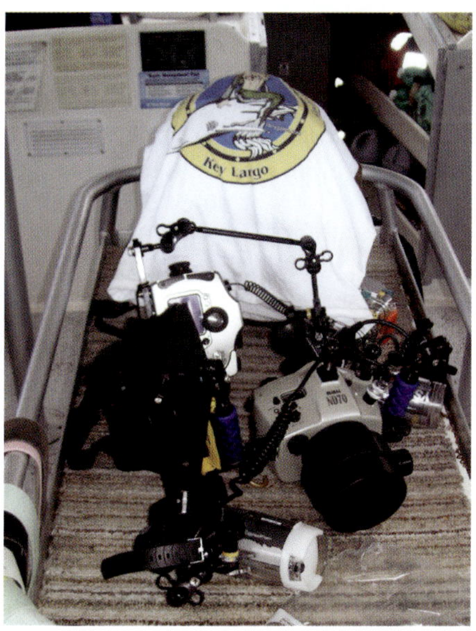


**Top**—Equipment flooding is one seemingly unavoidable aspect of underwater photography. This photo shows the aftermath of a strobe's battery compartment flood. Fortunately, most strobe manufacturers seal the battery compartment off from the unit's electronics. **Bottom**—With only four cameras (systems), what could go wrong?

the camera flash or the strobe sensor. It is also important that each end be clean and not clogged or blocked with or by any foreign matter.

When an electrical sync cord is used, the strobe may not fire if the hot-shoe fitting (which is inside the housing and runs from the bulkhead to the camera's hot shoe) is not firmly or fully in place or has been installed backwards. Also, the strobe may not fire if the sync cord is not correctly threaded into the housing's bulkhead or the strobe's bulkhead. This usually results in damage to the sync cord fittings or the fittings in the housing or strobe bulkheads, so always take care when assembling a system using sync cords. A strobe may not fire if there is internal damage to the sync cord (e.g., a broken wire). This problem is disguised by the insulation surrounding these wires. Substituting a known working cord for the suspect cord will help you determine whether this is the case. Finally, the strobe may not fire or might misfire if a little bit of water got inside either end of the sync cord. Take care to keep these ends dry. If either gets wet, dry it thoroughly. Make sure these ends are dry before assembly, as water in either end can cause a short that can damage the strobe or camera.

You can and should test to see whether your strobe is firing, and in sync with the shutter, by taking a photograph of the strobe. To prevent possible damage to the camera's sensor, photograph only the side of the strobe, rather than pointing the strobe head directly at the lens.

Housed underwater camera systems are an engineering work of art. It is an amazing feat of precision to build a water-tight box that allows us to access all of our camera's controls. When everything is working properly, we can manipulate the controls by rotating, pushing in, or pulling back on a housing control. However, occasionally when we manipulate a housing control, nothing happens. The control shaft may be bent, broken, sticking, or binding, and it may need to be lubricated or cleaned, or the housing may need to be sent in for service or repair (you'll find a list of service and repair centers at the end of this book). In other instances, a simple misalignment between the camera body and the interior of the housing may be to blame. This may be due to the camera not being firmly fixed or affixed securely to its mount within the housing. A misalignment of 1/8-inch is sometimes all it takes to cause a control to not function. In these cases, check to see whether the camera is correctly and securely installed in the housing. If a control binds or otherwise does not work, don't force the issue—just disassemble and inspect.

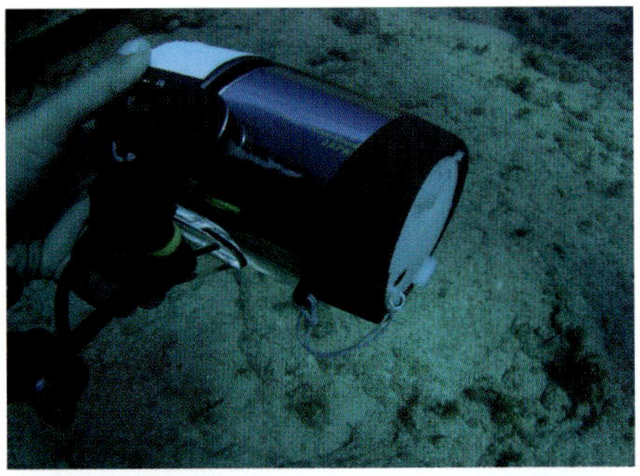

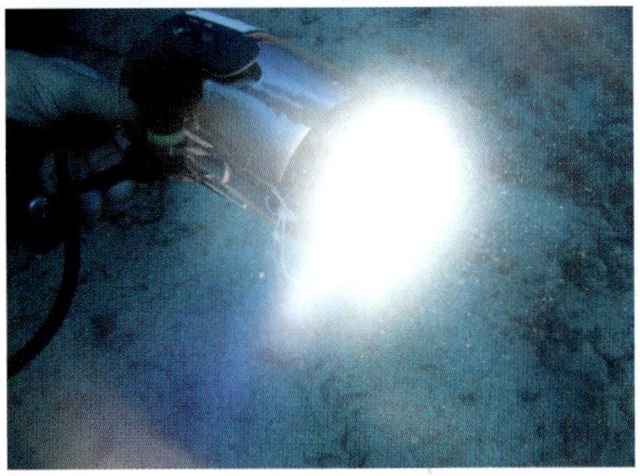

**Top**—The strobe is not firing. **Bottom**—The strobe is firing and in sync with the shutter. **Facing page**—(Top) Outcroppings of coral or a solitary stand of coral are often fish cleaning stations and can make for a good photo opportunity. Just exercise a little patience when you come across one, and see what shows up. Exposure: f/5.6, 1/125, and 100 ISO. Focal length 40mm. (Bottom) Photographing diseased or stressed corals or any aquatic life is a purposeful niche in underwater photography, both for marine study and conservation awareness. Exposure: f/8, 1/125, and 100 ISO. Focal length 18mm.

## PACK YOUR BAGS

We have everything we need and we know how to care for it. We're armed with a few problem-solving tricks that we can rely on if we run into trouble with our equipment's functioning. What do you think? Shall we take all of this on a dive trip? Heck yeah! Let's go diving, and to someplace cool, with clear, warm waters and lots of cool stuff to photograph.

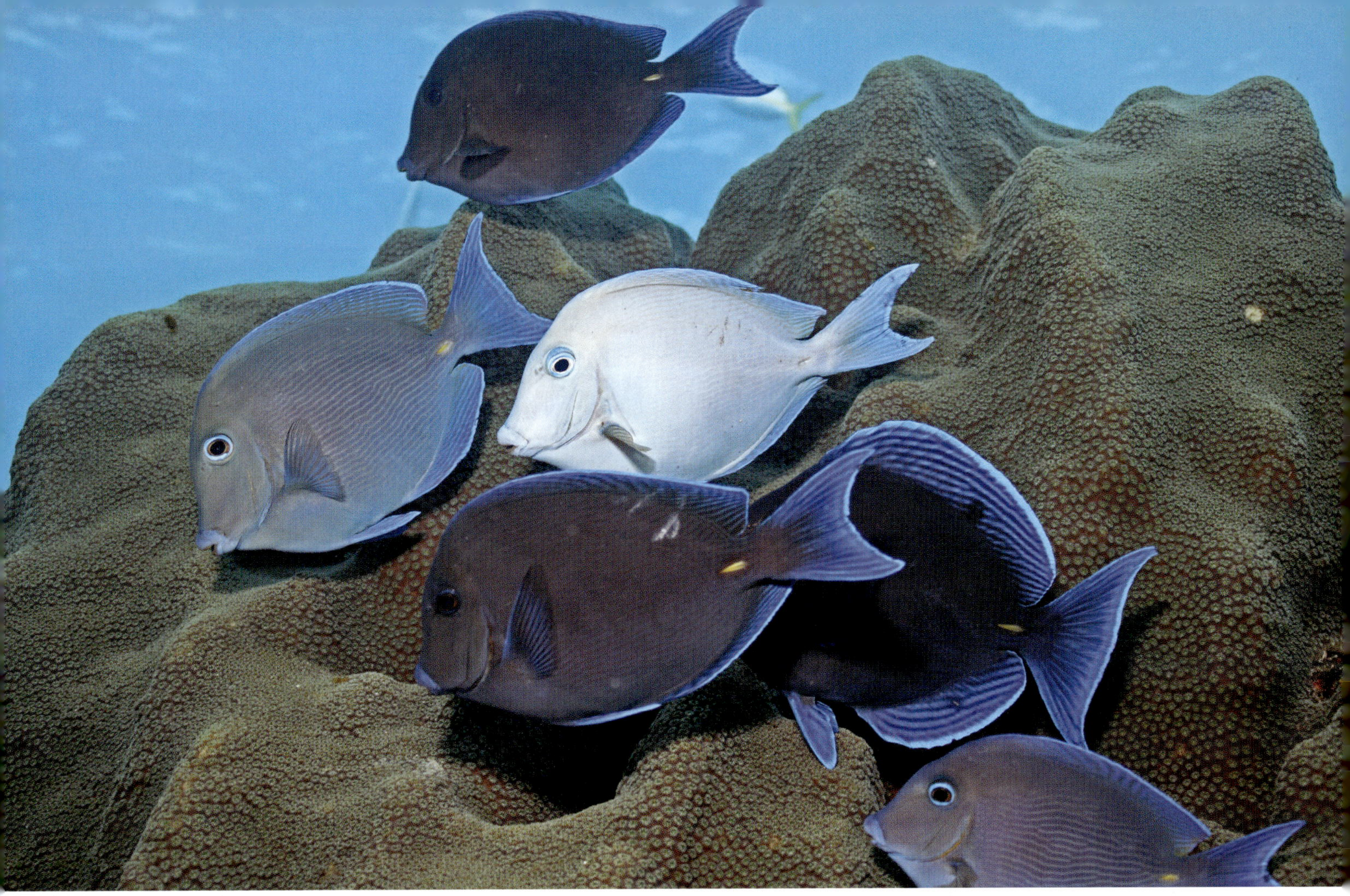

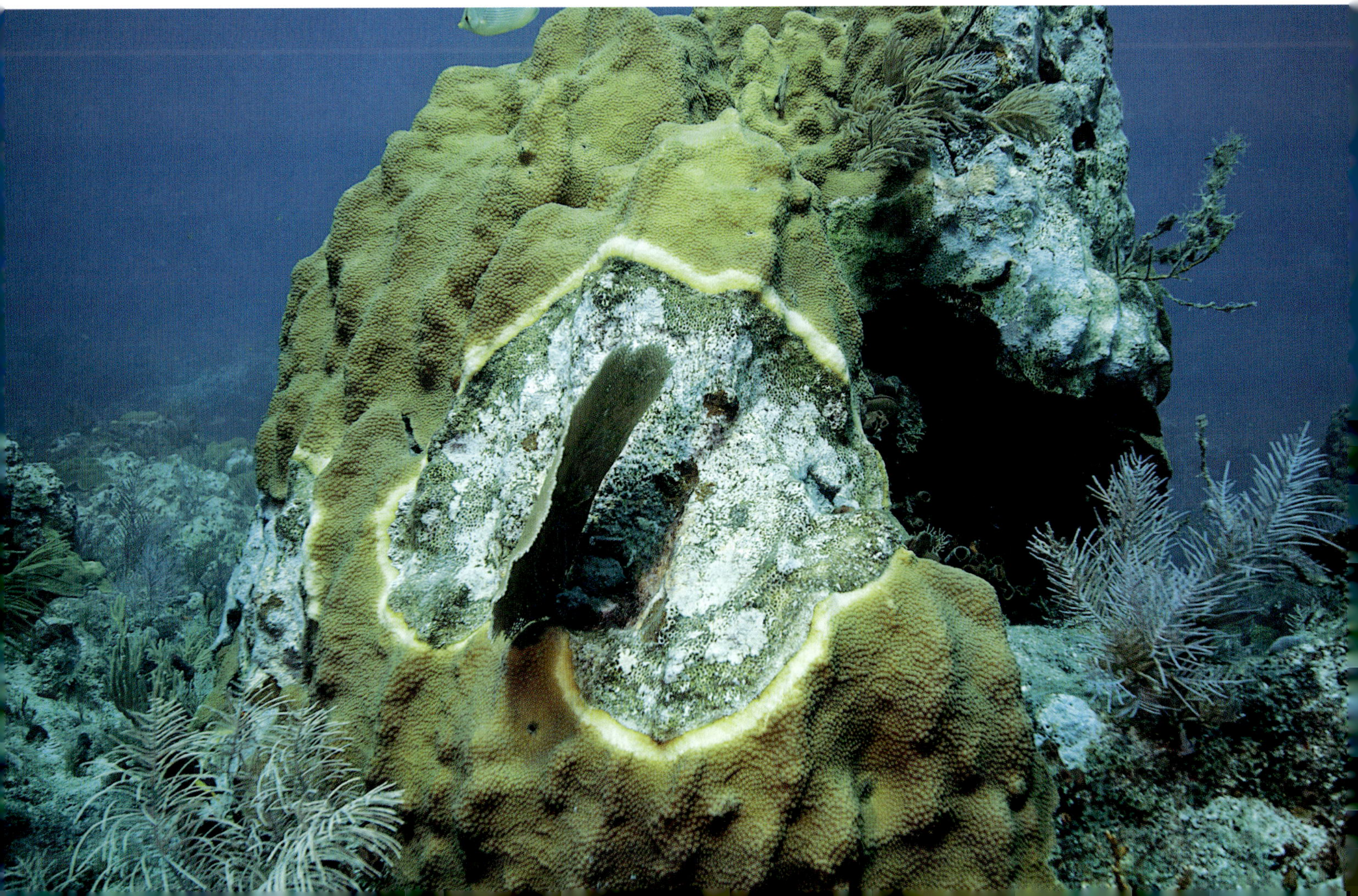

I'm with you, but give me a second to pack my stuff. Here is what I do and why:

My cameras and underwater photographic equipment, along with my scuba gear, are tools that I use to make my living. If I lost them, it would be tough to pay the bills. I often drive to the site of my dive and, when I do, I am in possession of my gear at all times. When I am traveling longer distances, I often fly. I could relinquish control over my things, leaving them in the hands of transportation systems employees, and trust that my gear would meet me, undamaged, at my destination—but I'm not that trusting. So, when I fly, I pack as much of my underwater photographic equipment as I can in a carry-on. My scuba gear and clothing go in my checked luggage. My thinking is that I can rent scuba and buy clothes at my destination if they fail to arrive.

I highly recommend insuring underwater photographic equipment before traveling with it. In fact, it is a good idea to insure your system year around—especially if you're using an expensive housed dSLR system.

I pack my camera with a battery and memory card installed and one lens mounted. These are inside the housing. I keep one port installed on the housing. I remove the O-ring/seal from the housing. This assembly goes in a large plastic bag. I saved the box and shipping materials my housing came in, and I use the Styrofoam it was packaged in to surround my housing/camera/lens/port.

My carry-on bag is not padded. I use clothes for padding and start by layering them on the bottom of the bag. My strobe(s), dome port with extension mounted, lenses, strobe arms, and clamps are wrapped in bubble wrap, which I secure with rubber bands. My battery chargers, spare batteries, O-rings, and other gizmos are packed in labeled Ziploc bags.

Anything that I feel would be of interest to baggage inspectors is packed to allow for easy examination. My electronics are on top and hardware, like arms and such, are packed below. Labeling everything also lets inspectors know what it is they are inspecting.

I always double check the airline's carry-on bag restrictions and make sure my bags do not surpass the size and weight limitations.

Anything that is not critical to my ability to take a photograph (e.g., spare parts and tools) is packed in my checked luggage in labeled Ziploc bags along with my scuba gear, clothing, and other personal items.

There is a wonderful selection and assortment of travel bags available that are wonderfully suited to traveling underwater photographers. Pelican, Storm, and Samsonite make quality hard-side cases and Kata, Lowepro, Canon (and, I suppose, Nikon), and Thinktank offer high-quality soft-sided bags. These are just a starting point. Luggage is probably the last item on your "to buy" list, but it is a necessity.

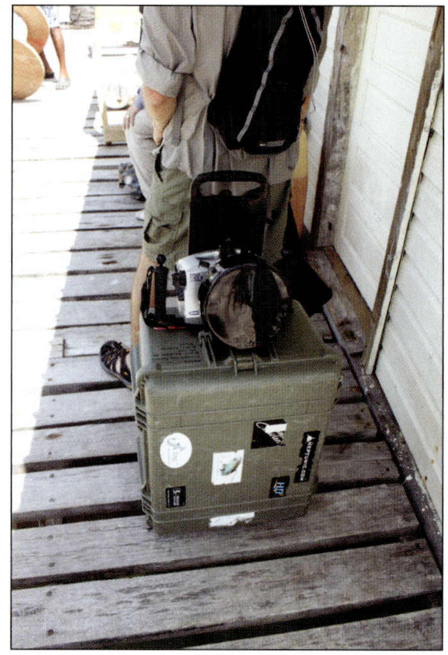

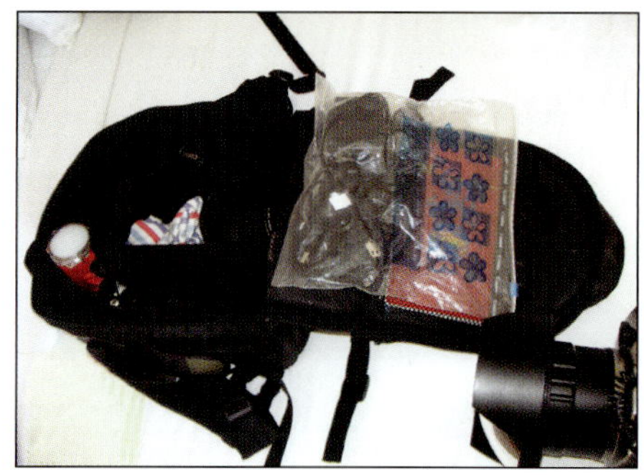

**Top**—A hard-sided case. **Bottom**—A soft-sided case.

# 5. THE SUBJECTS

As we advance in underwater photography, the array of subjects available to us does not change. What changes is the way we photograph these subjects. We acquire more or better equipment that allows us to photograph all of the subjects we encounter, moving beyond shooting just our personal favorites. We also start to explore how specific photographs were taken by other photographers.

In this chapter, we will revisit the subjects we have been photographing all along, but we'll discover some new or different ways of making these photographs. We will investigate some of the artful ways photographs of subjects are taken or made.

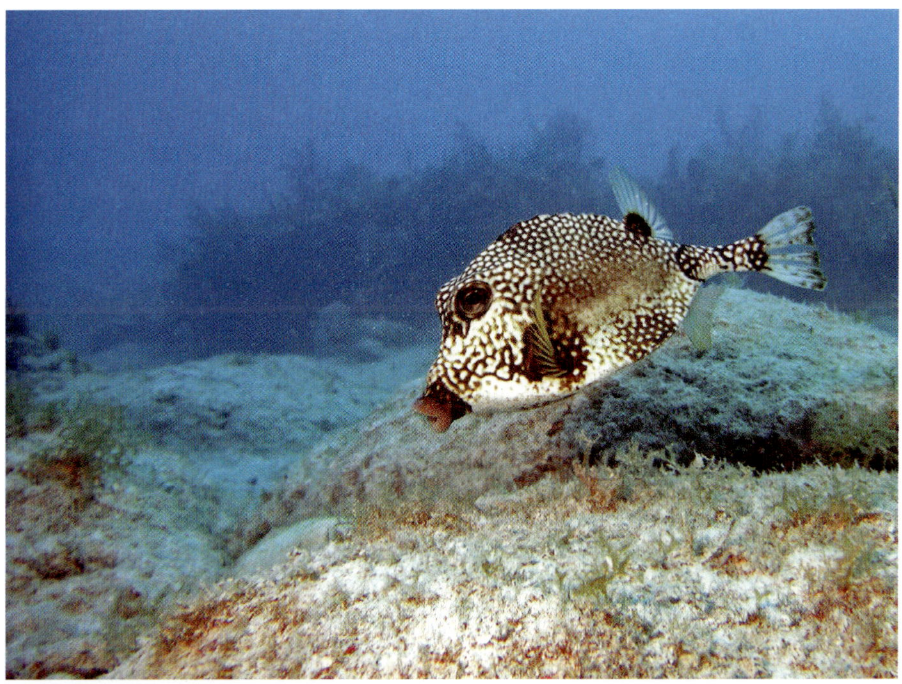

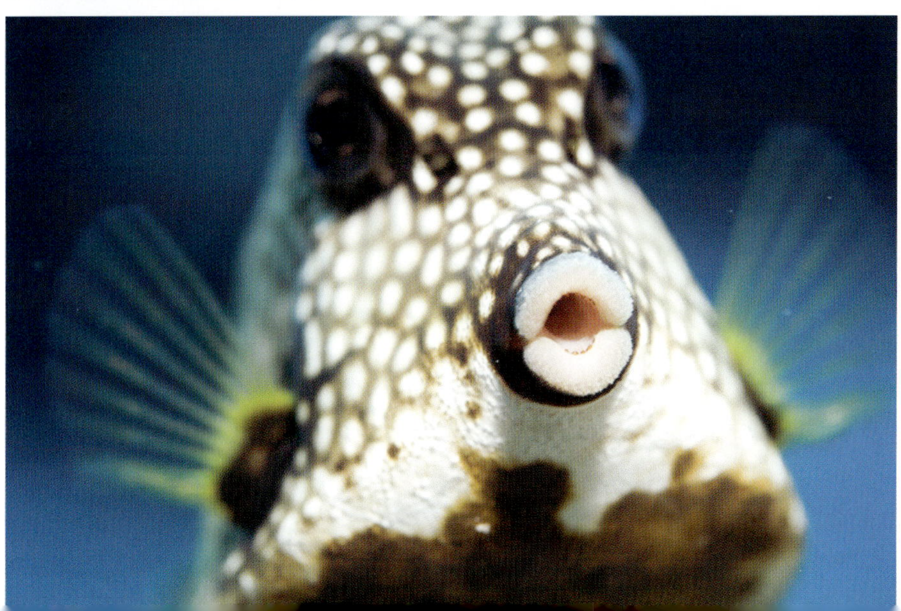

**Top**—A common shot of a Boxfish from my early days in underwater photography. Exposure: f/2.8, $^{1}/_{250}$, and 100 ISO. **Bottom**—This Boxfish photograph evokes more emotion. Exposure: f/6.3, $^{1}/_{125}$, and 100 ISO. Photo courtesy of Mary Moyer.

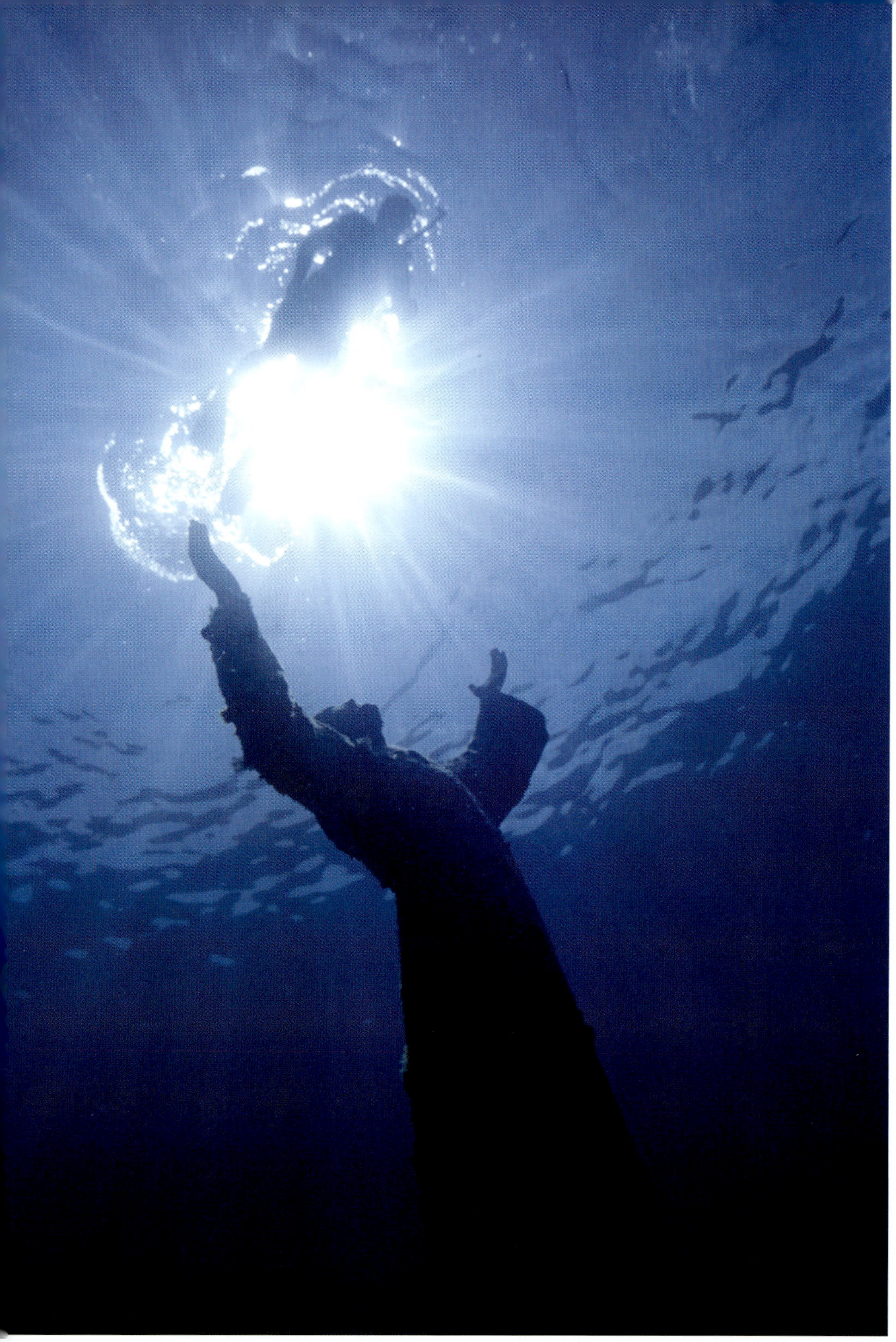

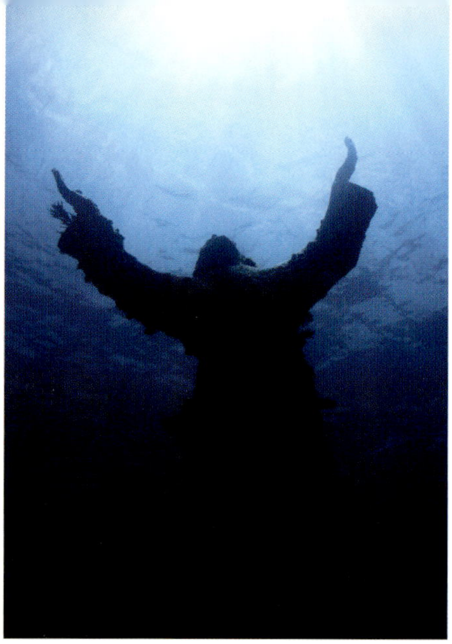

**Left**—Silhouette shot of the famous Christ of the Abyss statue in Key Largo, FL. Exposure: f/22, 1/125, and 100 ISO. No flash. **Right**—A digital-era work-around to shooting silhouettes.

## SILHOUETTES

One option for making a different photo of a common subject is to silhouette the subject. This is what I refer to as a "recipe shot." In other words, you can create the image by following a few simple steps.

Almost anything will make for a good silhouette subject, from a man-made object, to another diver, a turtle, ray, or other fish. One ingredient needed is the sun (preferably high in the sky). Capturing the sun's rays penetrating the water column adds a nice touch. Remember, if you can see the sun's rays, you can capture them.

The trick with the silhouette shot, if there is one, is your position. You want to be able to shoot straight up at—or almost straight up at—your subject. Position yourself so the sun is pretty much behind your subject. That is the hard part—but, at least you are not dependent upon the elements in your composition to become aligned, rather you are aligning yourself with them.

To get the shot, you'll need to use a small aperture. This will cause your subject to appear black or nearly black against the blue water background and sun beyond that. Use a shutter speed of at least $^1/_{90}$ ($^1/_{100}$ or $^1/_{125}$ would be better still). This will help you capture those wonderful sun rays and will help render the water column a richer, deeper blue. Next, set the ISO to 100. Because we do not want any color in our subject, we will not use any strobe lighting for this shot. Finally, all that is left to do is compose the image and take the shot.

The image depicting the statue was taken back in the film era. Shooting into the sun in the digital era poses a problem in that, as of this writing, there are no digital cameras that render those intense highlights produced by the sun very well, if at all. A work-around is to exclude as much of the sun from the composition as possible but still achieve the silhouette.

**Below**—In this photograph, we use parts of the silhouette recipe—a small aperture, fast shutter speed, and ambient light, plus a bit of photo editing, to make an artful capture of an ordinary subject, a Moon Jellyfish.

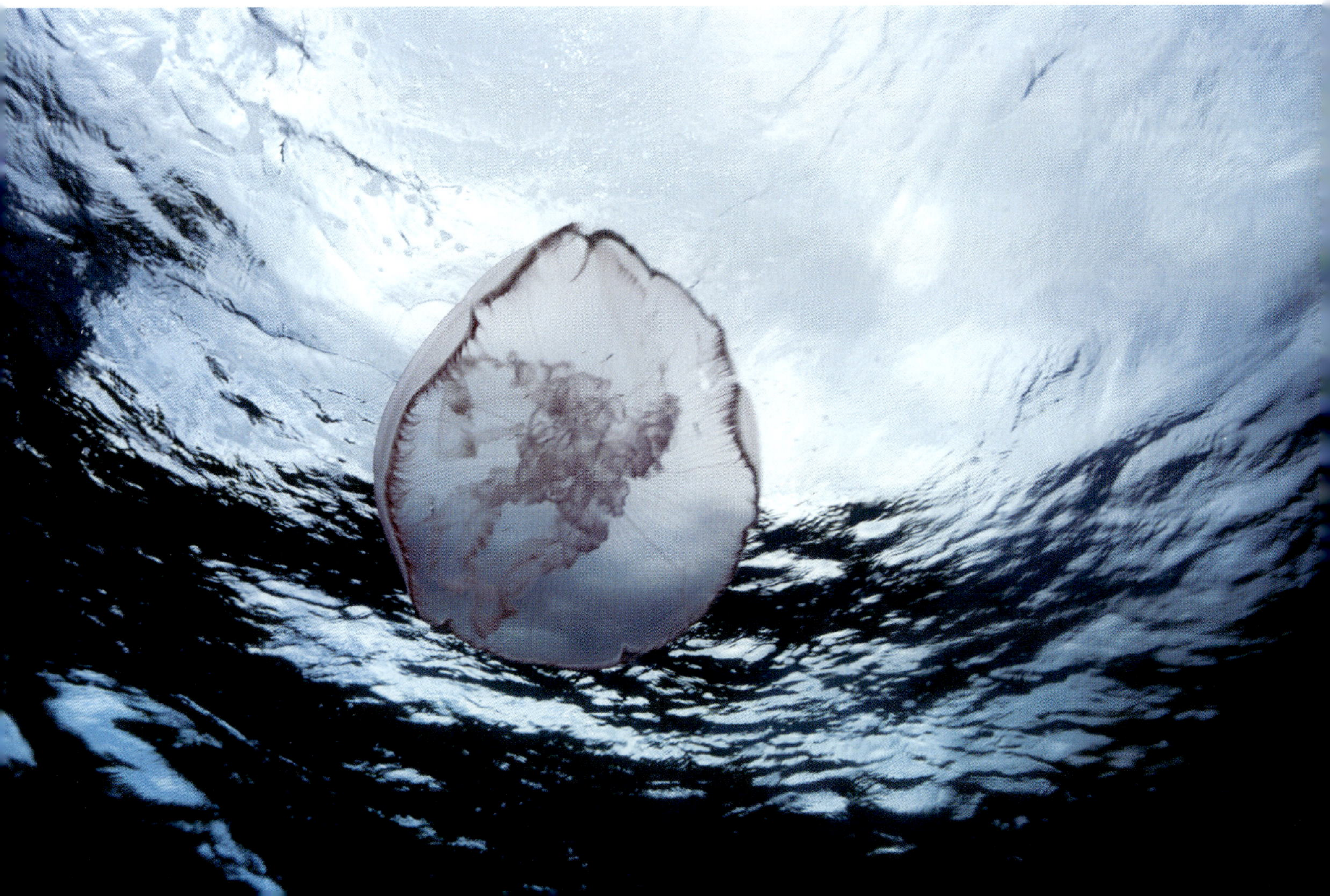

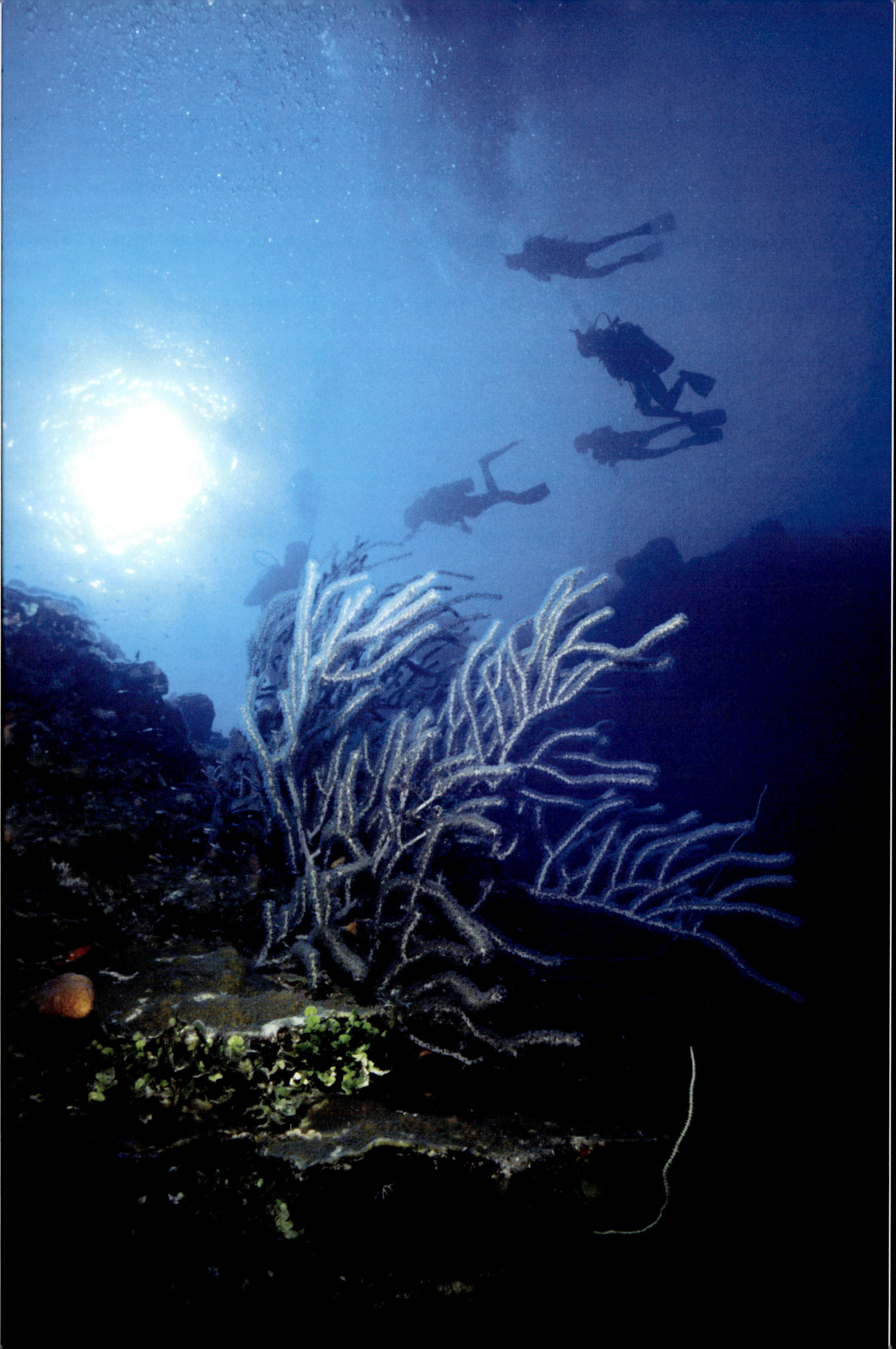

### CLOSE FOCUS/WIDE ANGLE SHOTS

Another favorite technique is one that the late Jim Church coined a close focus/wide angle. (Underwater photographer and film maker Howard Hall calls it a near/far shot.) This type of photograph involves two subjects—a primary subject in the foreground and a secondary subject in the background. The primary subject is in full color and the secondary subject is in silhouette.

The recipe for the shot is similar to the silhouette. There are two differences: First, a strobe is used to bring out the color of the primary subject, while the secondary subject remains in silhouette. Second, these captures are easier to make since a wide angle lens (with its depth of field and angle of view) is used.

To create this type of image, the photographer works very close to the primary subject and strives to expose it correctly and show its color. The photographer uses the sun as a backlight and the distance to the secondary subject to hold the secondary subject in silhouette. In simple terms, he correctly exposes the main subject and lets the rest of the light fall where it may.

As of this writing, there are some photographers experimenting with a new twist on this technique—a macro/close focus image.

### SEPARATION

When we started out in underwater photography, we began to understand the importance of composition. We learned to create images in which the subject stands out from everything else in the frame so it will "pop." To make this happen, we learned to not shoot down at our subject. We sometimes used the water column as negative space to help us achieve separation.

There are other means to achieving separation. One is to allow for a background that is nearly or totally black and void of detail. To do this, we first select the fastest shutter speed that will enable us to sync with the strobe. Next, we get close to the subject so that we can introduce the minimal amount of

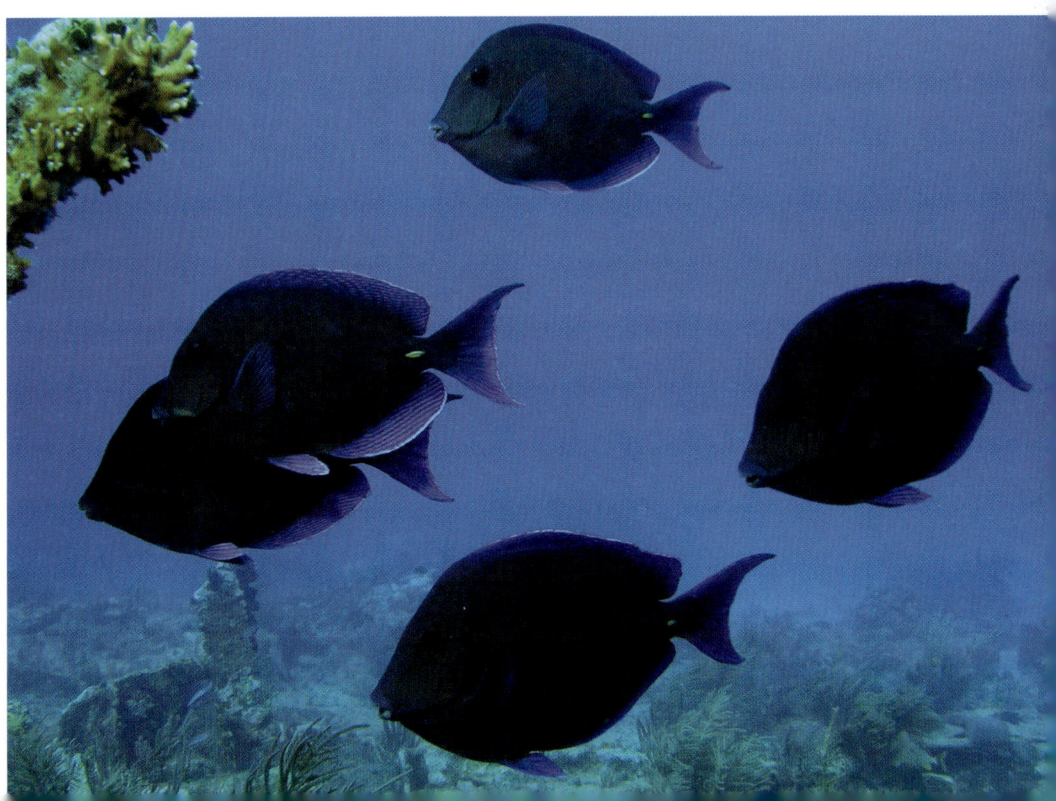

**Facing page**—An example of a close focus/wide angle capture. **Right**—An example of separation. Exposure: f/5.6, $^1/_{125}$, and 100 ISO.

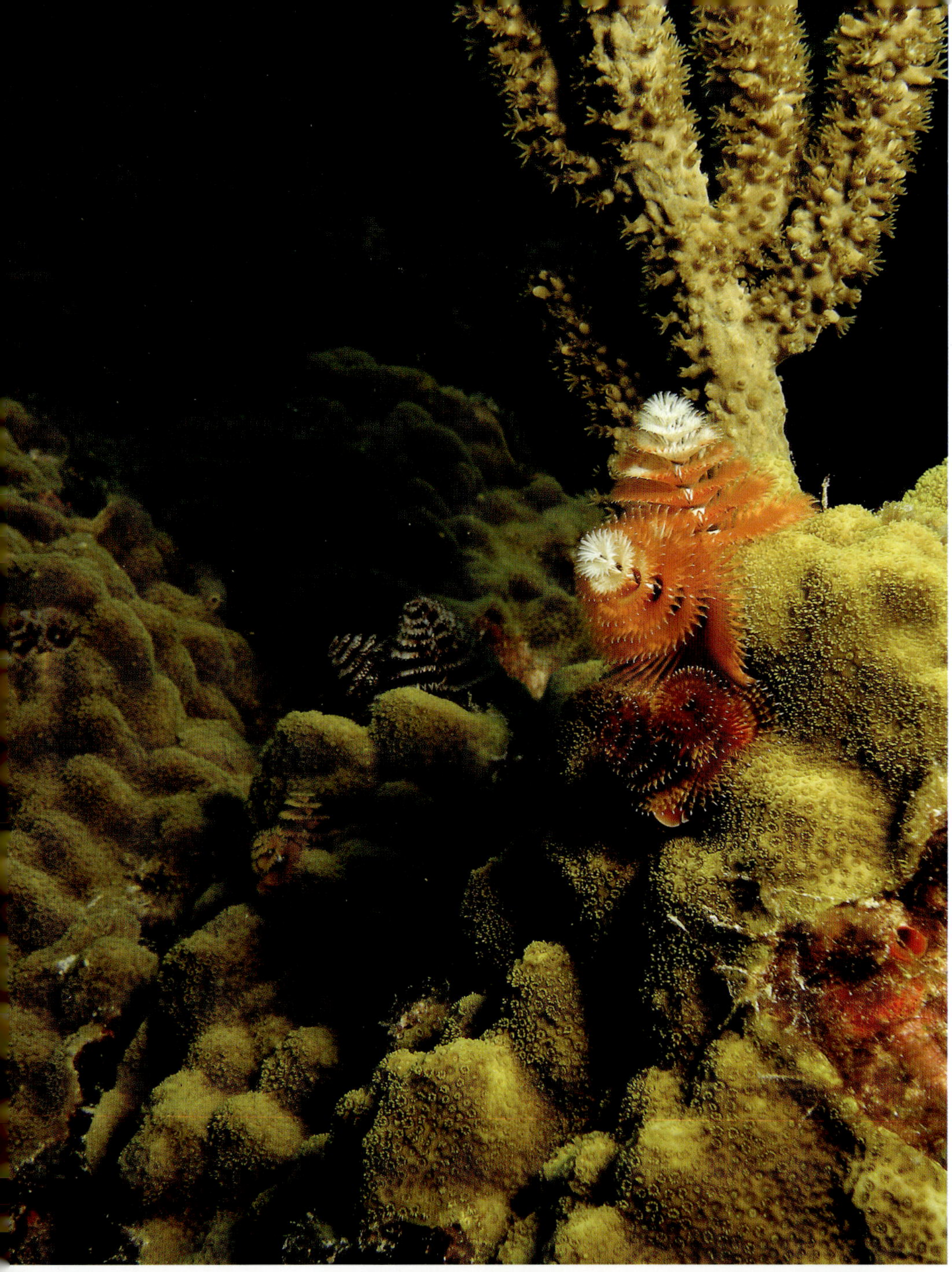

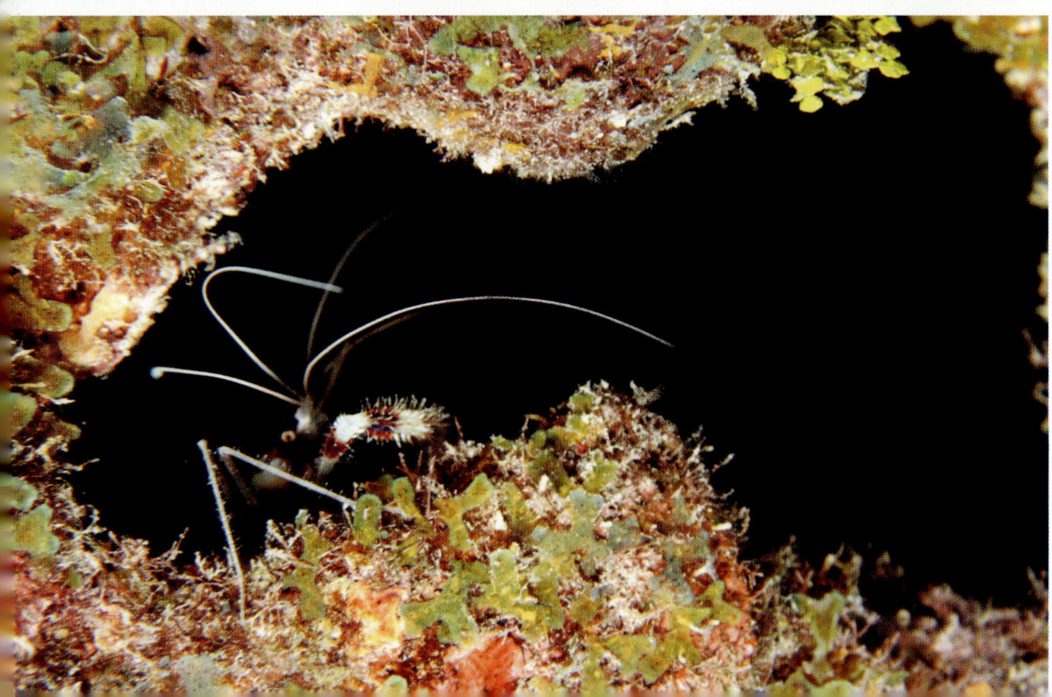

**Top**—A nearly black or pure-black background can help create separation. Exposure: f/8, $^{1}/_{500}$, and ISO 50. **Bottom**—Separation with black in the background. The coral provided a natural frame for the Banded Coral Shrimp. Exposure: f/8, $^{1}/_{125}$, 100 ISO. The photo's dark area was edited for backscatter.

light possible so we are not illuminating what may be in the background. The strobe should be aimed at the primary subject and its output or aperture adjusted for correct exposure.

One of the best ways to achieve a black background is to make sure there is nothing but water behind your subject. This shot is a bit easier to pull off when photographing macro-sized subjects.

Another way to achieve subject separation is to select a large aperture to limit the depth of field.

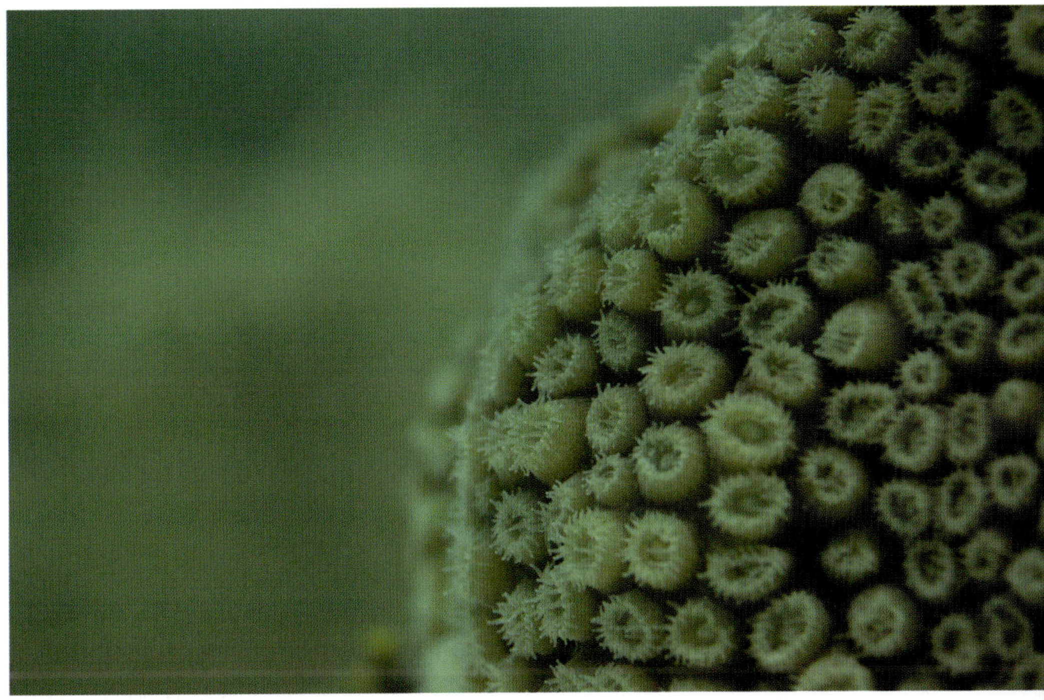

**Top**—An example of using a large aperture to limit depth of field. The extreme blur in the background is referred to as bokeh. Exposure: f/3.5, 1/200, and 200 ISO. **Bottom**—Another example of bokeh. Photo courtesy of Mary Moyer. Exposure: f/8, 1/125, and 100 ISO. Focal length 100mm (the camera had a full-frame sensor).

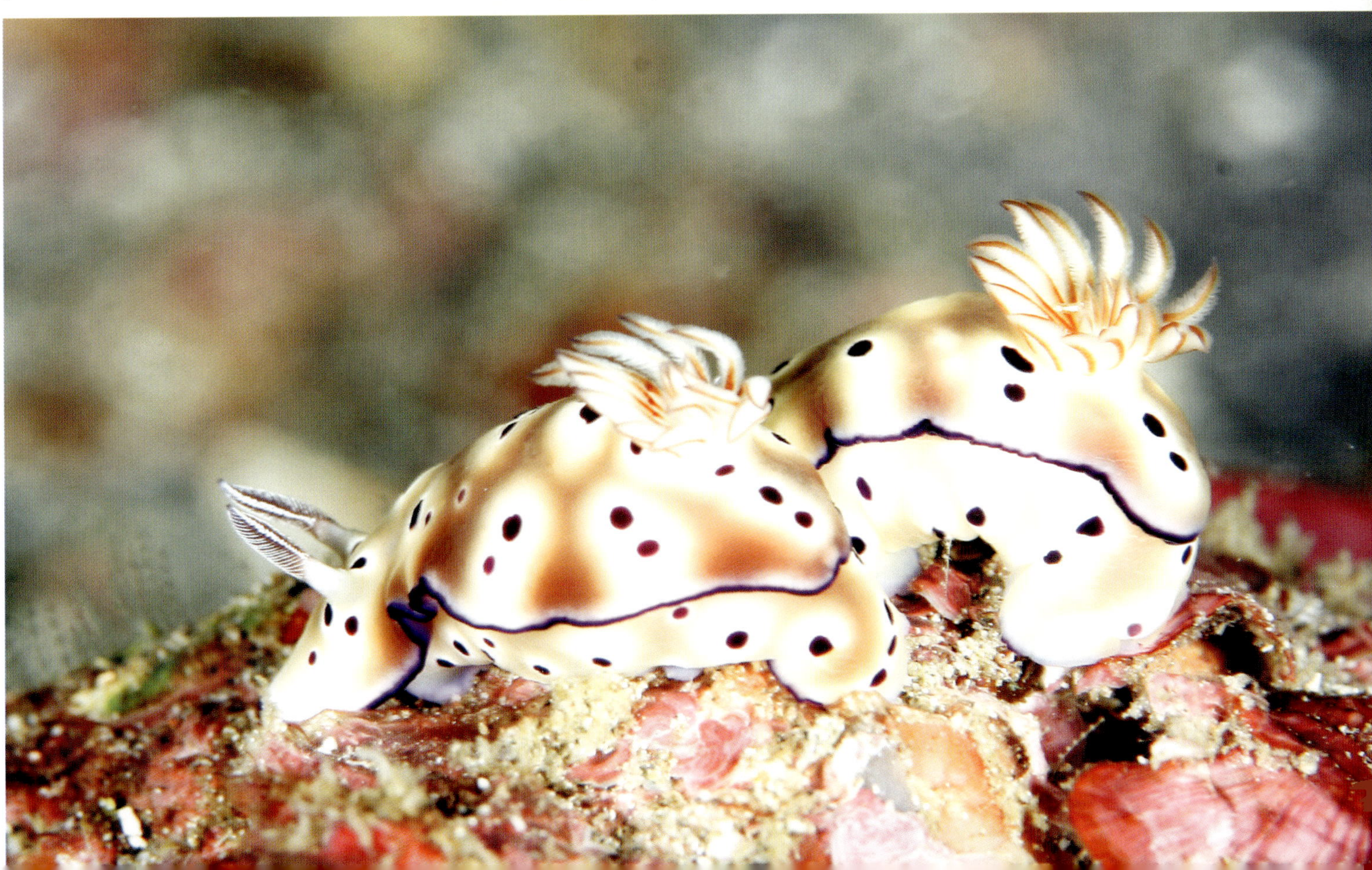

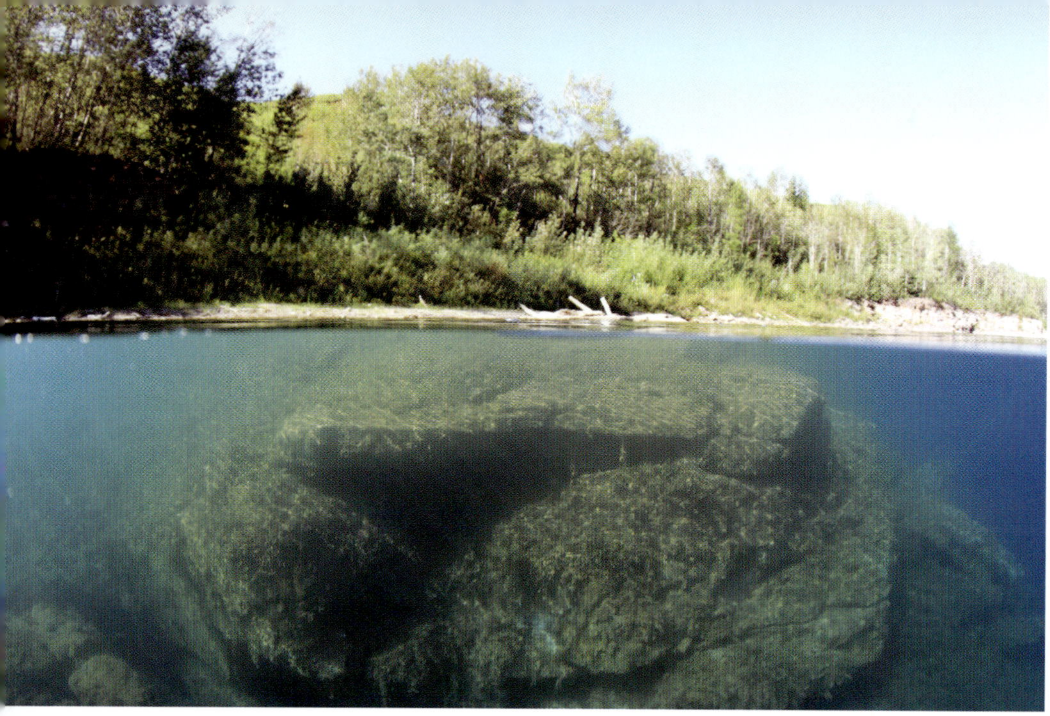

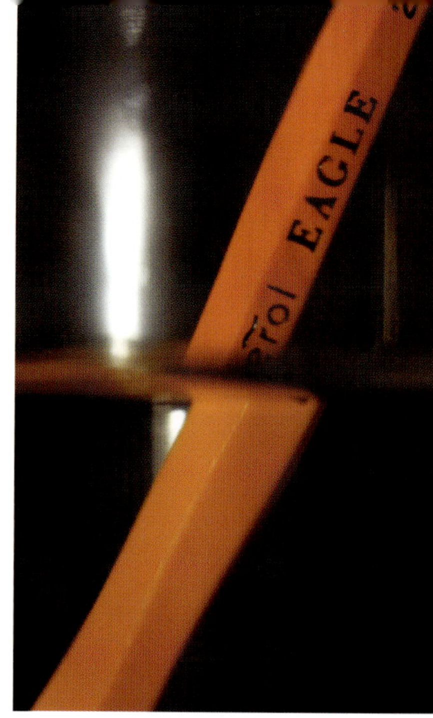


**Left**—An over/under image. Photo courtesy of Steve Philbrook. **Right**—Using a flat port to photograph an over/under photo can result in refraction.

## OVER/UNDER SHOTS

An over/under photograph, sometimes called a "split," can be made with a single subject or a primary and secondary subject. In this type of shot, approximately half of the photograph is above the water and the other half is below the surface.

While an over/under image can be made using a flat port, a dome port is preferred—and the larger the better. There are two reasons for this: using flat ports will cause refraction, and a flat port has a small diameter, making it difficult to hold it halfway underwater. Dome ports do not cause refraction and usually have a larger diameter.

When shooting over/under images where a secondary subject (usually above the water) is in the composition, it is difficult to get that subject in focus. Typically we focus on the underwater subject. The secondary subject can be some distance behind the focus point. Using a small aperture will allow for a greater depth of field, making it easier to render the secondary subject in focus.

This shot is best made with a wide or ultrawide angle lens. These lenses provide an angle of view that will help us frame the subject or subjects. Also, the greater depth of field that lenses that shorter focal lengths lenses allow will help us render the subjects in focus.

To make the image, focus on your primary subject. Because these photos are taken at the surface, we have ample ambient light for exposure. Use strobe, if necessary, to fill in any underwater shadow areas.

Rough surface conditions can make it difficult to hold the port halfway underwater and focus, so it is best to plan to capture these types of shots in calmer, flatter seas. A pool is a great place to practice capturing these images. You're likely to use the pool only on days when there is plenty of ambient light and clear, calm water is a given.

Another difficulty with this type of shot is capturing the decisive moment. Your scene can appear and dissipate rather quickly, so you need to be ready. When a human being is in the photograph, try to preplan their part of the image. In other instances, be on the lookout for the decisive moment and make sure your exposure settings are in the ballpark. Refinements can be made in postproduction.

Be aware that water and its droplets may form on the above-water area of the port. Glass ports shed water more quickly than do acrylic ports when bringing the port up out of the water to make the shot. Sometimes the moisture can be edited out in Photoshop, and other times it can't be and will be the ruin of an otherwise wonderful over/under shot.

This issue was totally frustrating to one of my students, who creates "watershots." Watershots are a unique type of photography. The photogra-

**Top**—An over/under image with a primary and secondary subject. In this instance, the secondary subject is not in focus. Exposure: f/8, 1/125, 100 ISO. 20mm lens and 6-inch dome port. **Bottom**—A swimming pool is a good place to learn the over/under image capture technique. Exposure: f/11, 1/125, and 100 ISO. 18mm lens and 6-inch dome port.

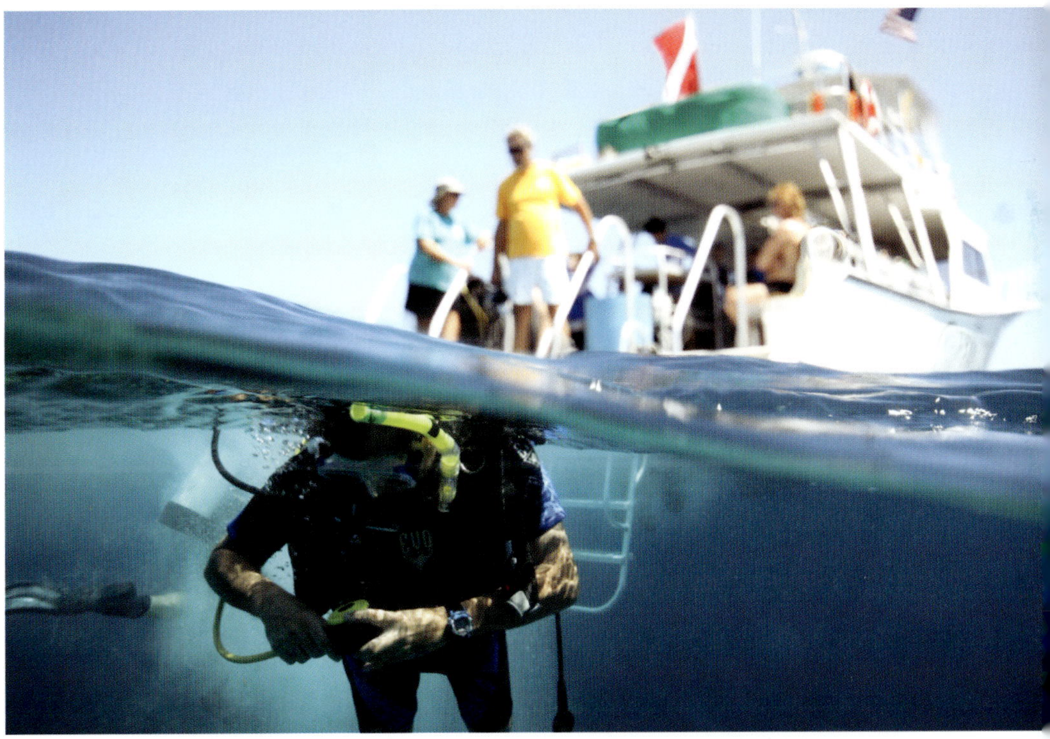

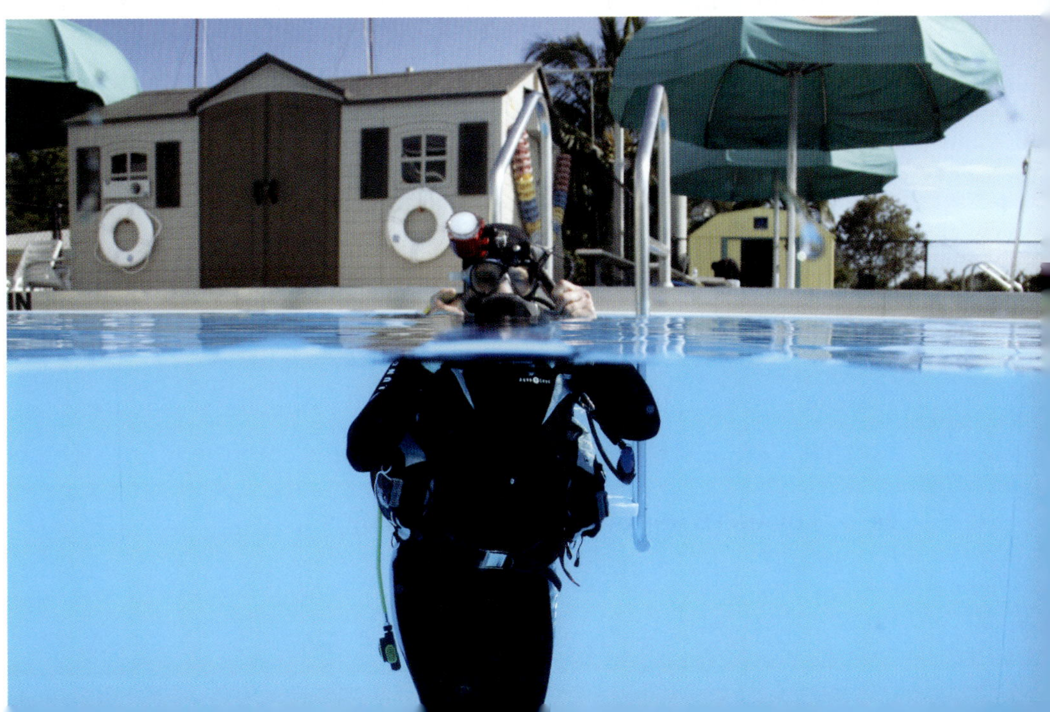

pher is in the water, capturing close-ups of surfers, kite surfers, or wind surfers, for example.

Not being a watershot photographer, yet wanting to be of help, I contacted Steve Ogles, the CEO of Watershot, Inc. His company makes housings for select dSLRs. He also manufactures housings for all kinds of image making equipment, much of it used in the film industry and used under and on the water. He is my age and has been shooting watershots since he was in eleventh grade. If I knew one person who would know how to deal with this problem, it would be Steve.

Steve said, "This is a common problem among surf photographers. Rain-X ain't the answer. Your saliva is the key. So try [the following steps] and see how they work":

1. Make sure there is no oil from fingers on the lens port.
2. Spit on the lens port glass (clean spit, which means you cannot do this after eating).
3. Lick the lens port.
4. Submerge the lens port in the water.
5. Slowly lift it out of the water (there should be a very thin, even sheet of water clinging to the glass).
6. Keep it in the water until ready to shoot.

This process will keep a very thin sheet of water on the lens port while doing over/under shots. Thanks, Steve!

### "REEFLECTIONS"

A "reeflection" (a hybrid of the words "reef" and "reflection") is another fun photograph to make. These are captures of subjects on or near the surface of the water.

Reeflections are easier to make in bright sunlight, with calm water surfaces and a colorful subject. These can also be made using ambient light only. The goal in shooting the reeflection is to achieve a mirrorlike result and/or the mirage of colors and shape of the subject projected on the surface of the water. These types of photographs are challenging to create, but the results can be extraordinary.

Snell's Law is at play in making this type of image, but I will spare you the mathematical explanation. Suffice it to say that, to create the shot, you should be positioned to ensure that the angle between the surface of the water, the subject, and you is no more than 45 degrees.

### ABSTRACT IMAGES

I'm a huge fan of photographing coral, and I typically use a wide angle lens to photograph groups of them as seascapes. However, there are other ways

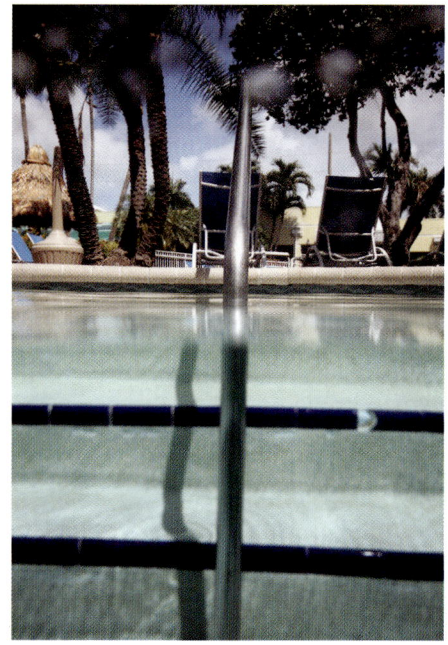

**Above**—As mentioned earlier, a pool is a great place to practice making splits. Pools are also good places for testing combinations of lenses, ports, and extenders. **Facing page**—(Top) Try to create reeflections on days when the waters are clear and calm for the best effects. Exposure: f/8, 1/125, and ISO 100. 10mm focal length. (Bottom) Reeflections are possible at depth when inside caves or caverns with air pockets. In this photograph, the water's surface was found at the entrance to an undersea habitat used for marine research. Exposure: f/4, 1/80, and 100 ISO. 10mm focal length. Strobe lighting.

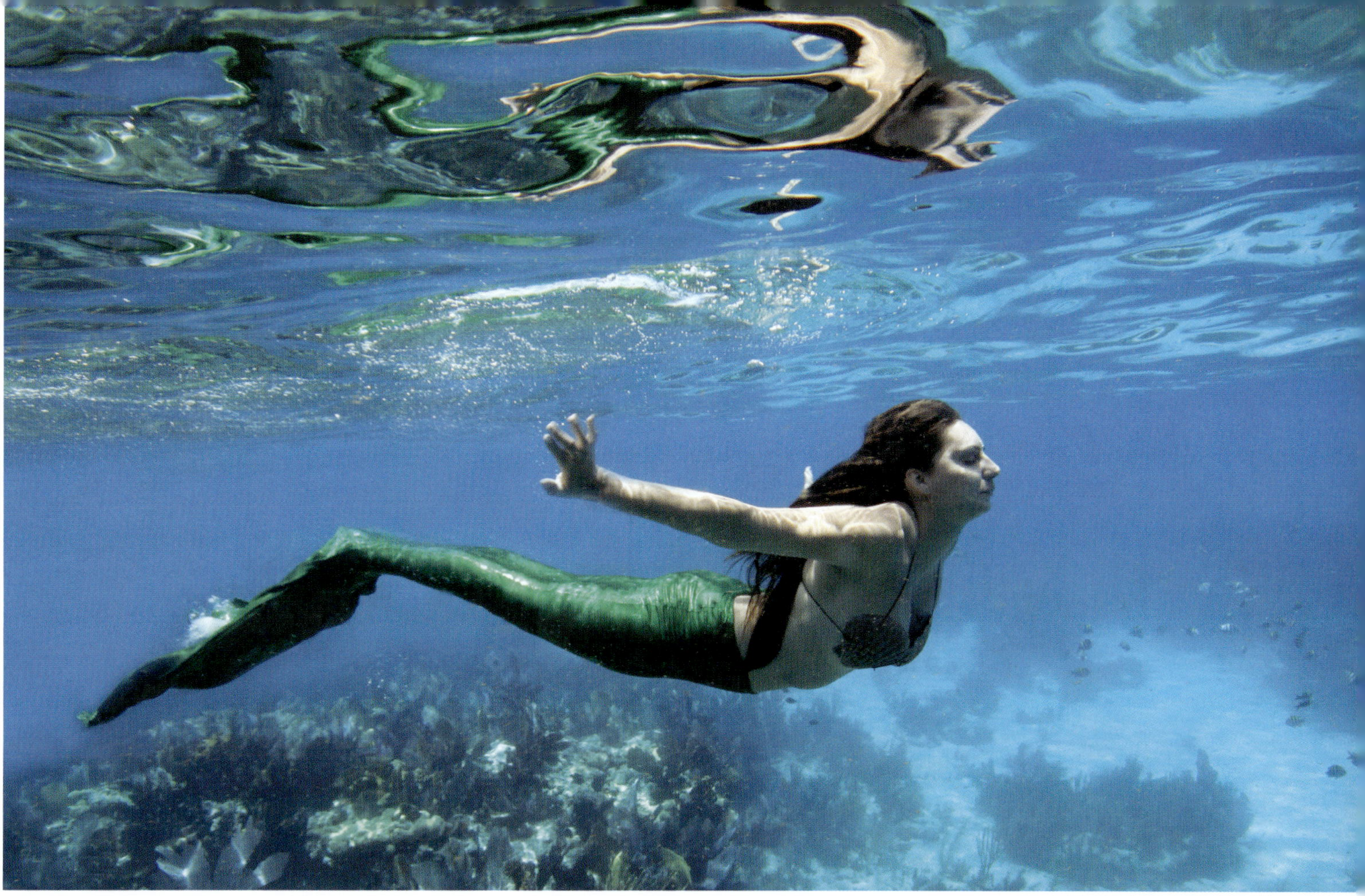

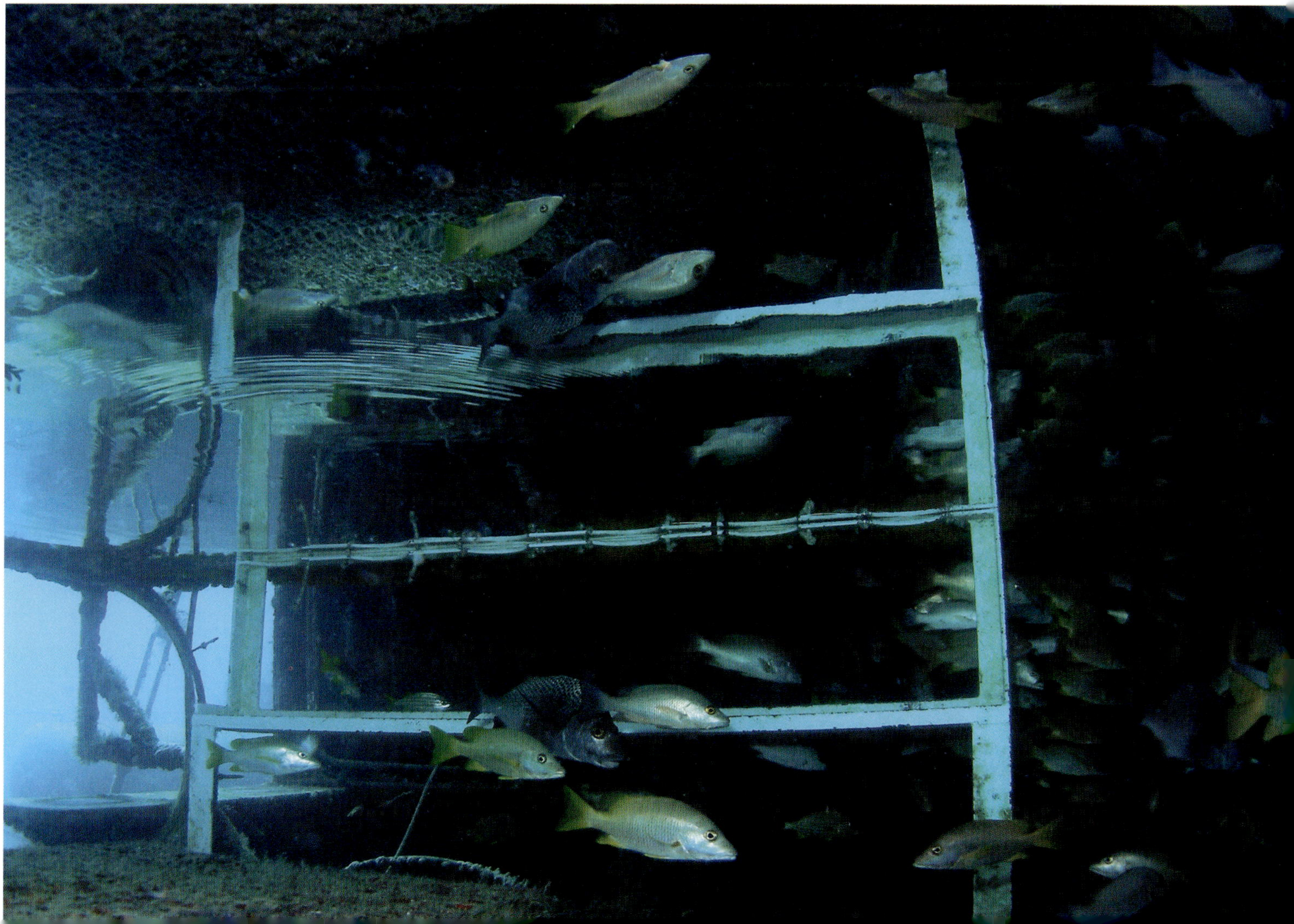

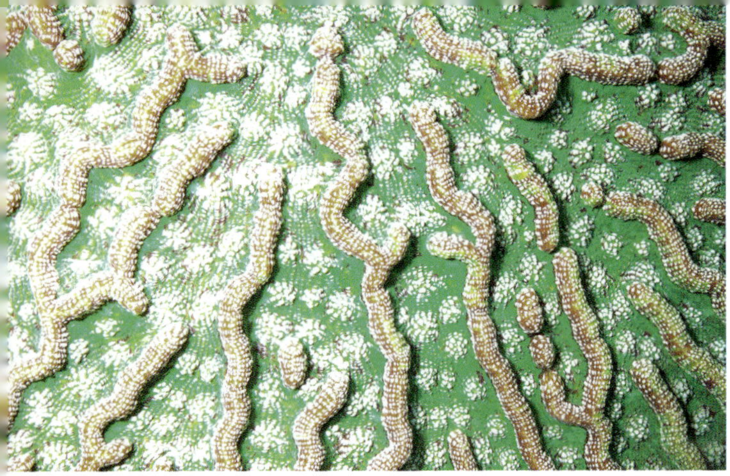

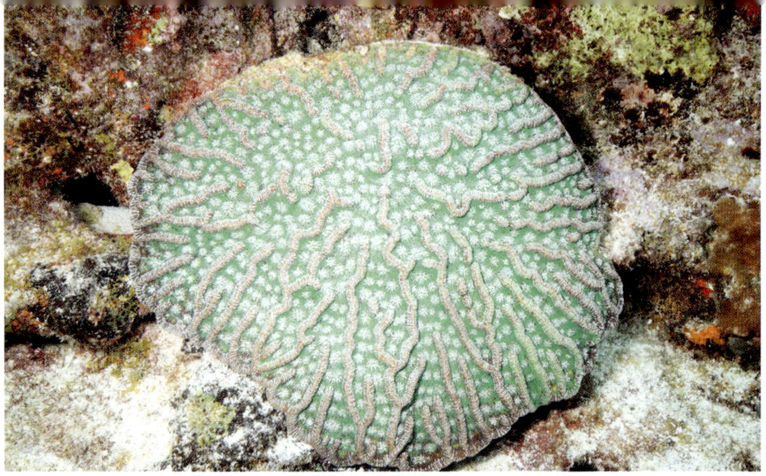

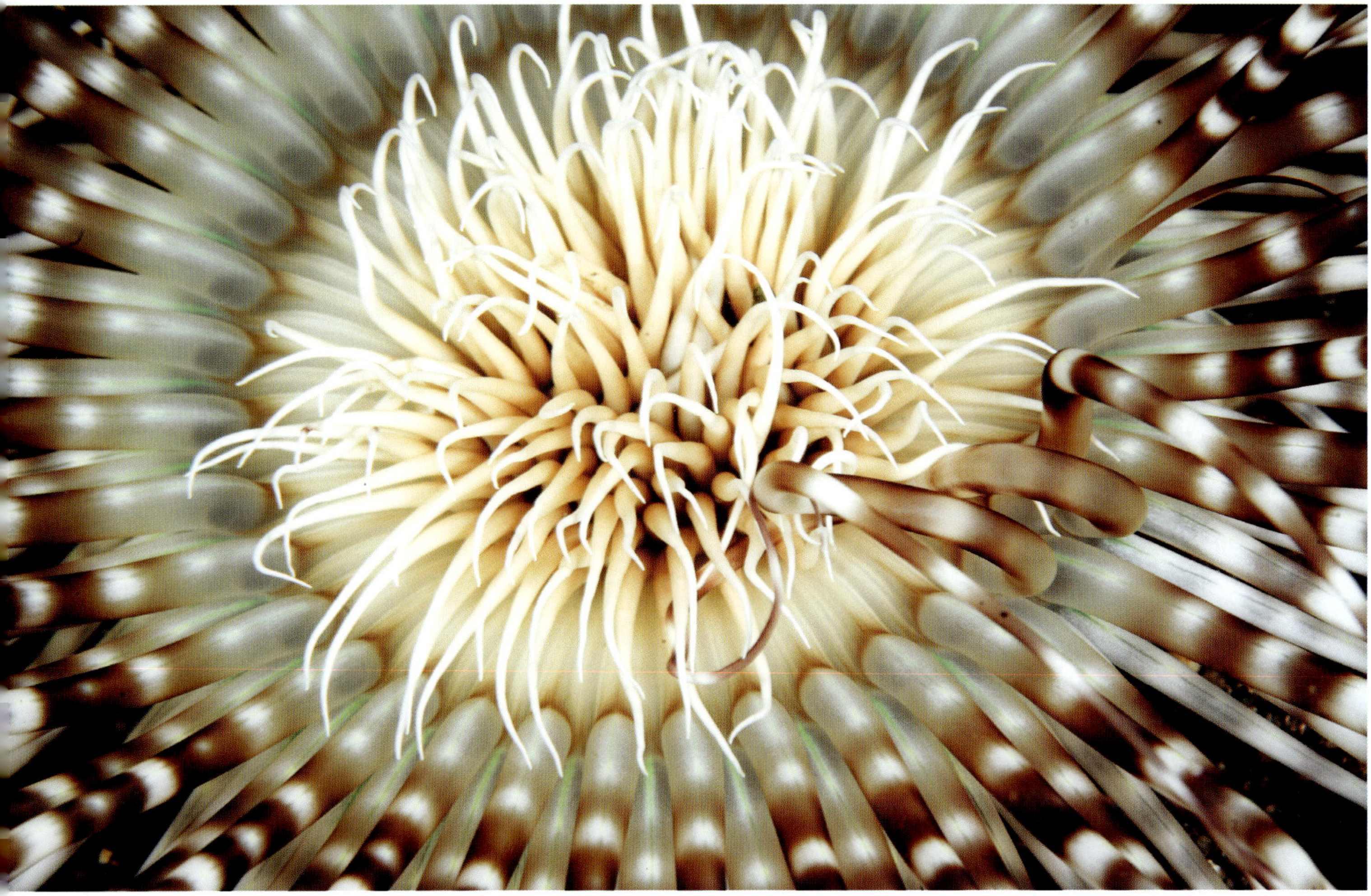

to approach the shot. One is to use a lens with a very narrow angle of view, such as a macro lens, or simply shoot close to the subject and fill the frame to create an abstract image.

Abstracts are not particularly difficult to capture, but they are difficult to see. The photographer has to be moving slowly enough through the water column to recognize the photographic potential in what lies in front of him. These images allow for a great deal of creativity. Experimenting with the strobe's position or lighting the subject differently can result in a more artful abstract.

**Top left**—Abstract. The subject is a Cactus Coral, photographed close. Abstract images typically do not have any negative space in their compositions. Exposure: f/8, 1/125, and 100 ISO. **Top right**—A specimen photograph of a cactus coral. Exposure: f/8, 1/125, and 100 ISO. **Bottom**—Another example of an abstract—the heart of an Anemone. Photo courtesy of Mary Moyer. Exposure: f/14, 1/100, and 100 ISO. 100mm focal length.

### UNUSUAL BEHAVIORS

The more diving and underwater photography we do, the more likely we are to come across or notice unusual marine life behaviors. These behaviors—such as a fish being "cleaned" at the cleaning station, competing with a like species for mating rights, or engaging in predation—make for a great photographic opportunity. We can also make more interesting photographs of fellow divers by capturing their behavior. A closely cropped photograph that includes the eyes of a diver makes for a more interesting photograph than a simple posed shot. These photographs are more compelling than the simple specimen shots we took in our early days. Images like these tell more of a story.

**Top left**—This photo shows a Goliath Grouper being cleaned by a Remora. Exposure: f/4, $^{1}/_{90}$, and 100 ISO. 35mm focal length. **Top right**—The photographer witnessed and captured two Reef Crabs in a dispute over territory. Photo courtesy of Hans DeJager. Exposure: f/5.6, $^{1}/_{125}$, and 100 ISO. Focal length 18mm. **Bottom left**—Here, a Scrawled Filefish preys upon a Moon Jellyfish. Exposure: f/5.6, $^{1}/_{125}$, and 100 ISO. 40mm focal length. **Bottom right**—This photo is of a diver doing something—in this case, the scuba instructor is teaching buddy breathing. Exposure: f/2.8, $^{1}/_{750}$, and 100 ISO. Focal length 28mm. Ambient light.

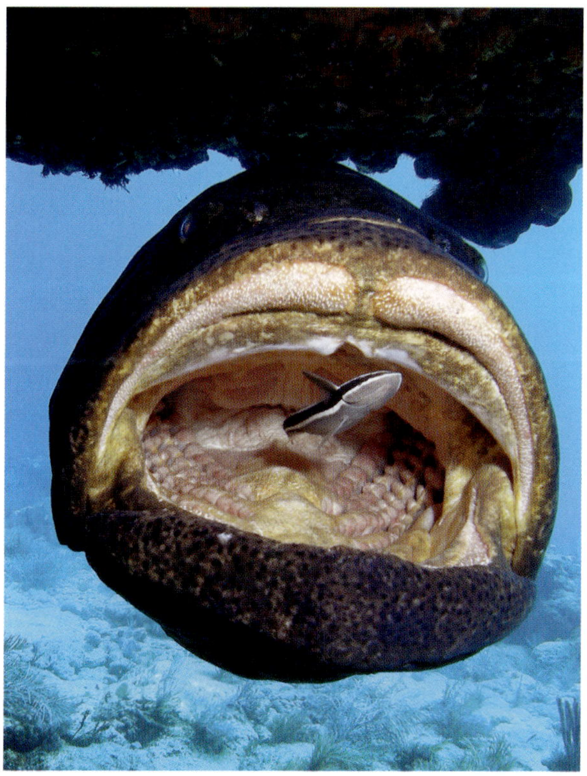

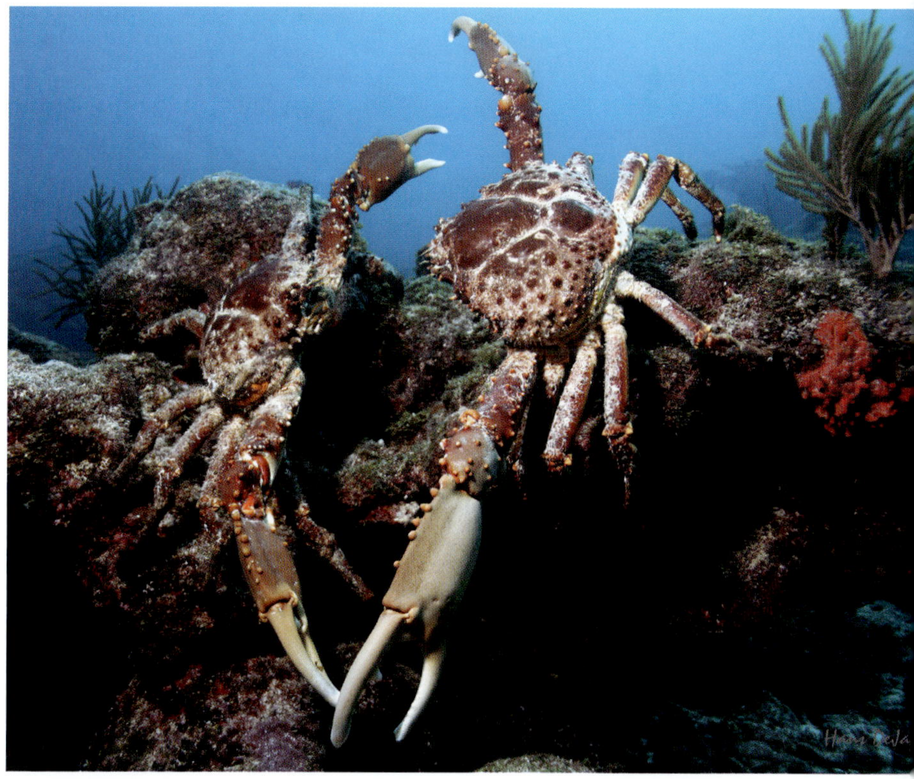

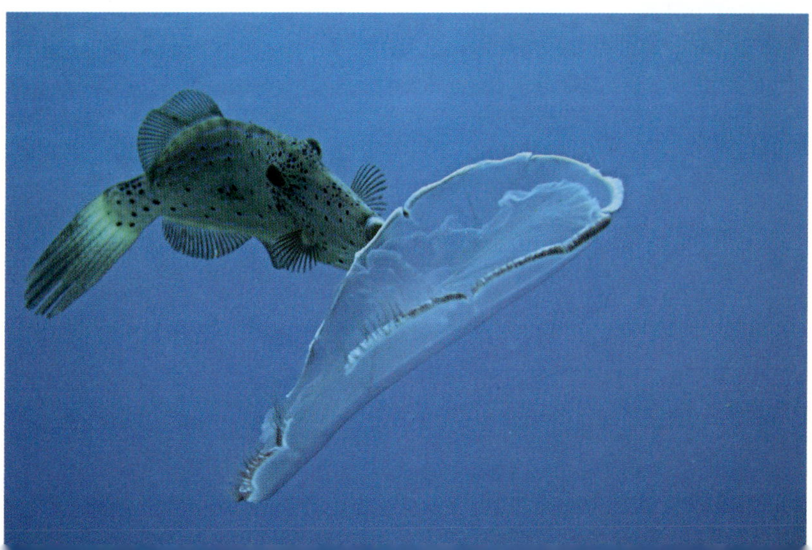

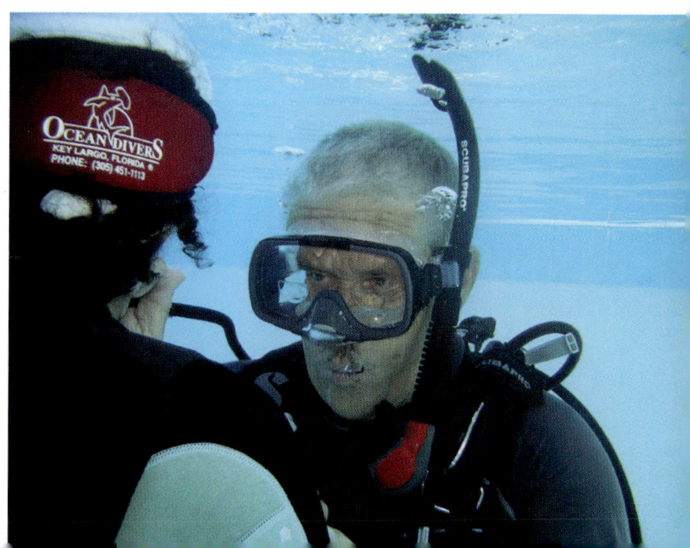

### A DIFFERENT APPROACH

As mentioned early in this chapter, part of our growth as underwater photographers stems from creating images of a wider range of subject matter. The specimens we encounter can be smaller than the size of your pinky fingernail or the size of an aircraft carrier. Photographing them using unique or more specialized approaches—for example, by using a snoot to narrow the angle of light from a strobe to produce a more unique, targeted lighting effect or capturing a scene in black & white rather than in color—can result in images that go far beyond something that simply documents the dive experience.

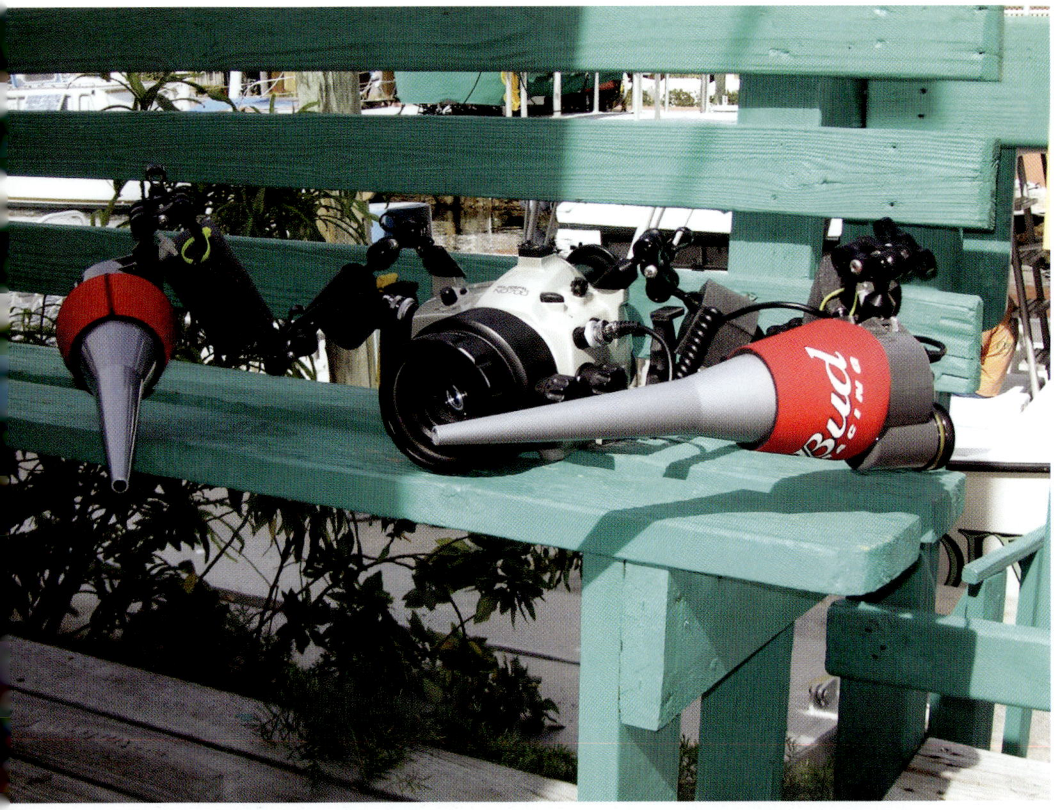


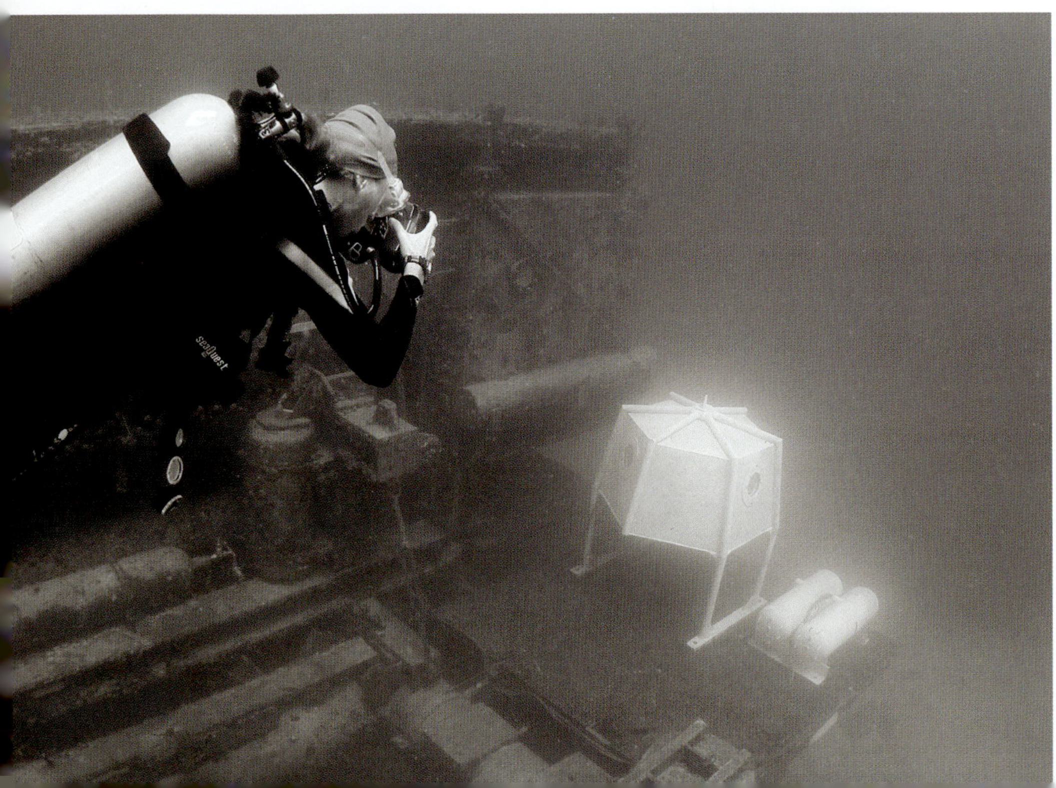

**Top**—Snoots reduce the strobe's angle of light to a very narrow beam that only illuminates the subject. These were made using cozies and plastic oil funnels. **Bottom**—Images can be captured in black & white or converted from color to black & white in postproduction. This image was converted to black & white after the shoot. Exposure: f/4, $^1/_{90}$, and 100 ISO. Focal length 15mm.

# 6. TECHNIQUES FROM ADVANCED UNDERWATER PHOTOGRAPHERS

When my publisher asked me to write a book on advanced underwater photography, the request stopped me in my tracks. The topic is enormous, and I am only one person. Still, I embraced the challenge. I decided to ask other advanced underwater photographers to discuss their work and contribute photographs to build a better, more comprehensive book. (Please understand that, while I consider these folks to be advanced in their underwater photography, they only agree that they are *advancing* and lay no claim to being advanced underwater photographers. I admire their humility and paradoxically, consider that to be a good characteristic of any advancing underwater photographer!) I thank them dearly and have given them credit where their images are used.

This chapter was the most fun for me to write, and I hope you will find reading it equally enjoyable.

### PRACTICE MAKES PERFECT

Before we turn our attention to the advanced techniques photographers are using "in the field," I want to make an important point: As we fin forward in our underwater photography, upgrading and adding new equipment to our camera bags, we find there is little room left in the bag for excuses.

When we get out of practice, we make a beginner's mistakes. The solution is to frequently and regularly engage in underwater photography and keep our skills sharp. Well, if you don't have a coral reef in your backyard and don't live in a place that allows for year-round diving, you can—and should—take advantage of a local diving environment. Many indoor pools can be accessed during the cold winter months. Gaining access to these could be as simple as contacting your local dive store.

With practice, you can improve your technique. When working in a controlled environment like a pool, you can experiment with new things. You can make mistakes and later analyze what went wrong, with minimal expense.

**Left**—Pools can offer a tame, static environment that allows the photographer the time needed to consider where their strobe is aimed. **Right**—A pool also provides a relaxed shooting environment in which we can become familiar with our camera controls and settings.

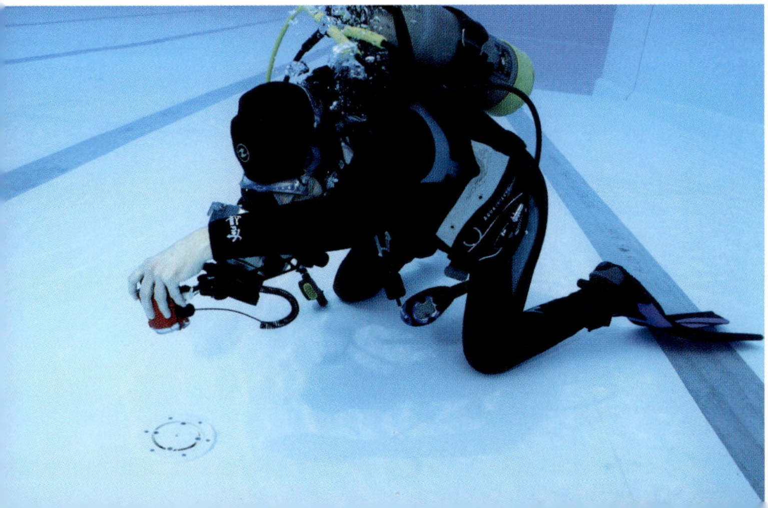

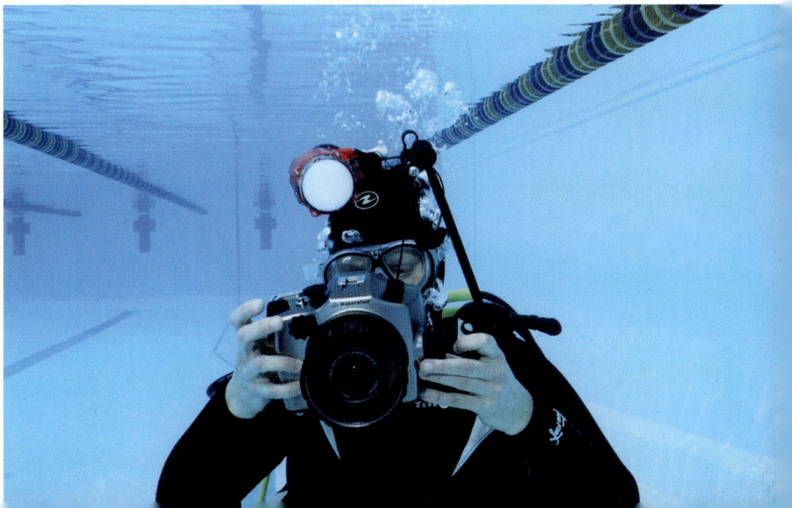

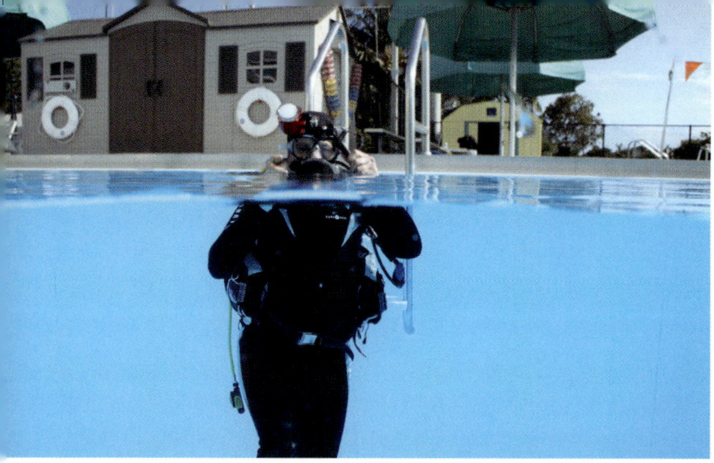

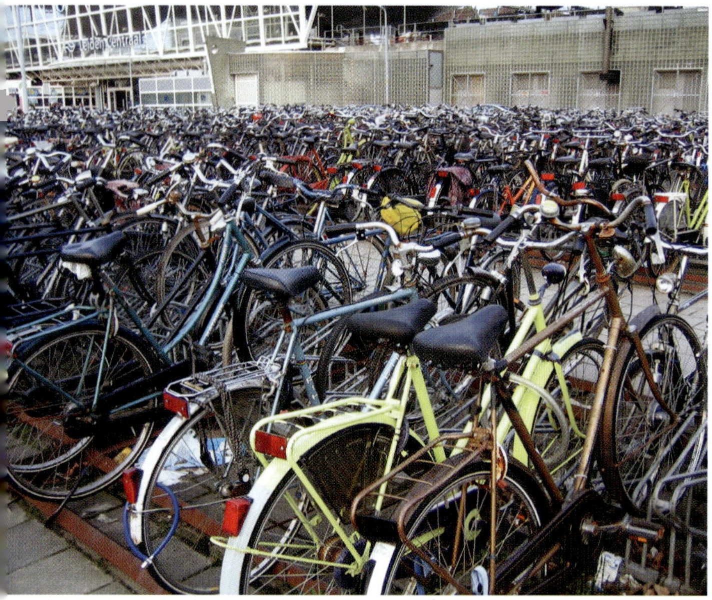

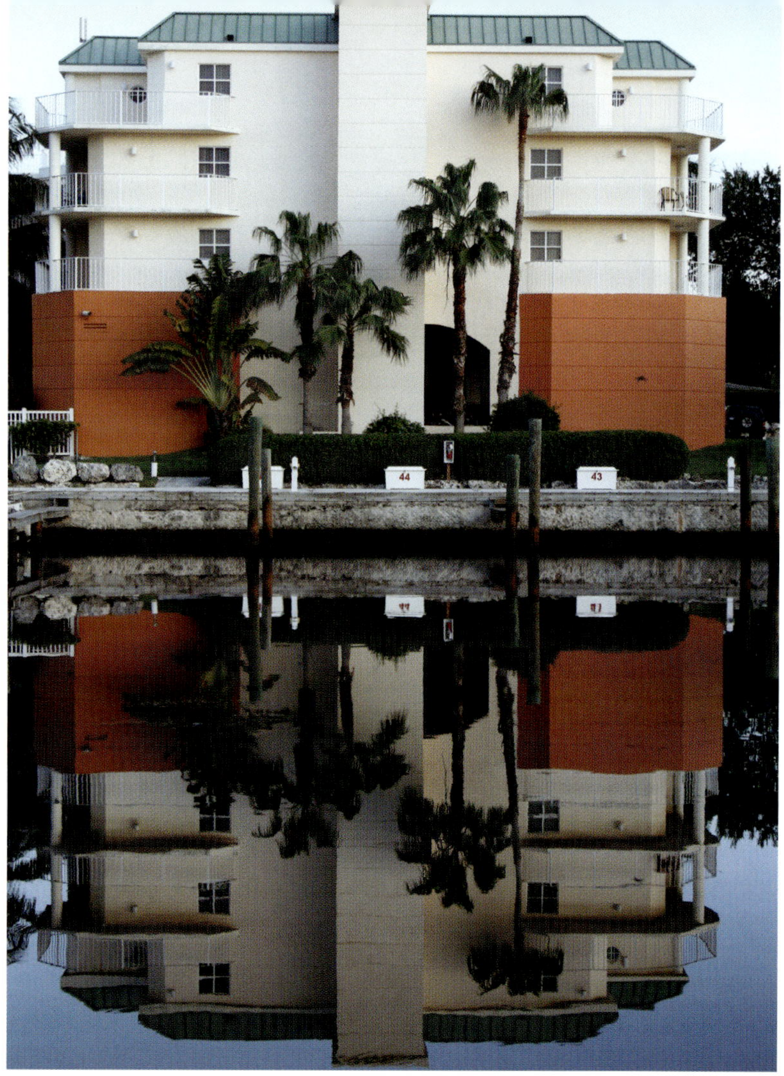

These venues are also closer at hand, more readily accessible, and less costly than photo diving vacations are. They should be employed whenever practical and possible.

When our goal is to improve or advance or keep ourselves in practice, any body of water that we can scuba dive in will more than suffice. The gain in doing these types of photo dives is, you will be ready for the game. That game starts in a body of water that is the end destination of your dive vacation.

Another way to advance in underwater photography is to engage in topside photography. This can involve anything from planning a photo safari somewhere in the world to carrying a camera with you whenever possible. When shooting topside, you maintain your familiarity with your camera and using it. Employ the same carefully made compositional techniques topside that you would use underwater.

Now, let's study some of the techniques used by advanced underwater photographers.

**Top left**—Pools can also be used to experiment in making a different type of photograph, such as an over/under image. **Bottom left**—Even Dutch bikes provide an opportunity to practice your compositional skills. Photo courtesy of Hans DeJager. **Right**—Engaging in above-water photography can help with underwater photography.

# BRIAN BOLTON

Brian shoots his small stuff using a Nikkor 60mm f/2.8 micro lens and his larger subjects using a 10.5mm f/2.8 Nikkor lens. The images that appear here were taken in the Cayman Islands.

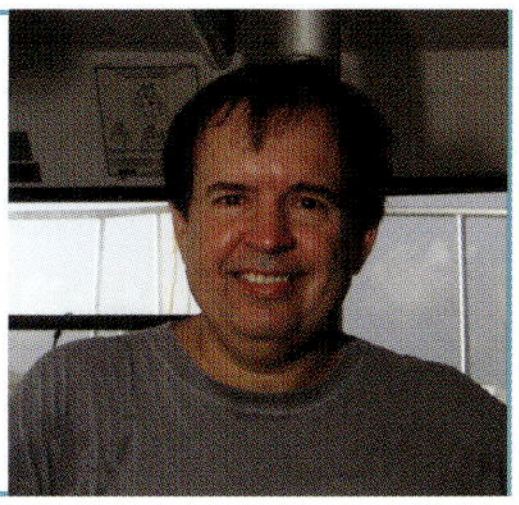

**Photographing the Arrow Crab.** I remember creating the shot very well. It was taken on Bloody Bay Wall in Little Cayman. I was at about 80 feet with my Fuji S2 Pro in an Aquatica housing and one Ikelite Substrobe 100a. I was floating on the wall and needed really good buoyancy control to shoot that. I regulated my buoyancy by breathing.

I began shooting using TTL flash and bracketing perspectives. Next, I set the strobe to manual power and bracketed both exposure and perspectives. One challenge was changing settings while hovering on a wall, dropping down to 2000+ feet, and making ever-so-slight angular shifts from side to side for perspective. I needed to get light onto the Arrow Crab. This was difficult, as it was tucked back into the sponge. I had to stay very calm and relaxed, make small movements, take shallow breaths, and use breathing volume to raise and lower myself in front of the subject. The single most important skill to me is buoyancy control.

**Below**—Arrow Crab in sponge photographed using 60mm Nikkor lens. Exposure: f/27, 1/60, and 100 ISO. Focal length 60mm. Photo courtesy of Brian Bolton.

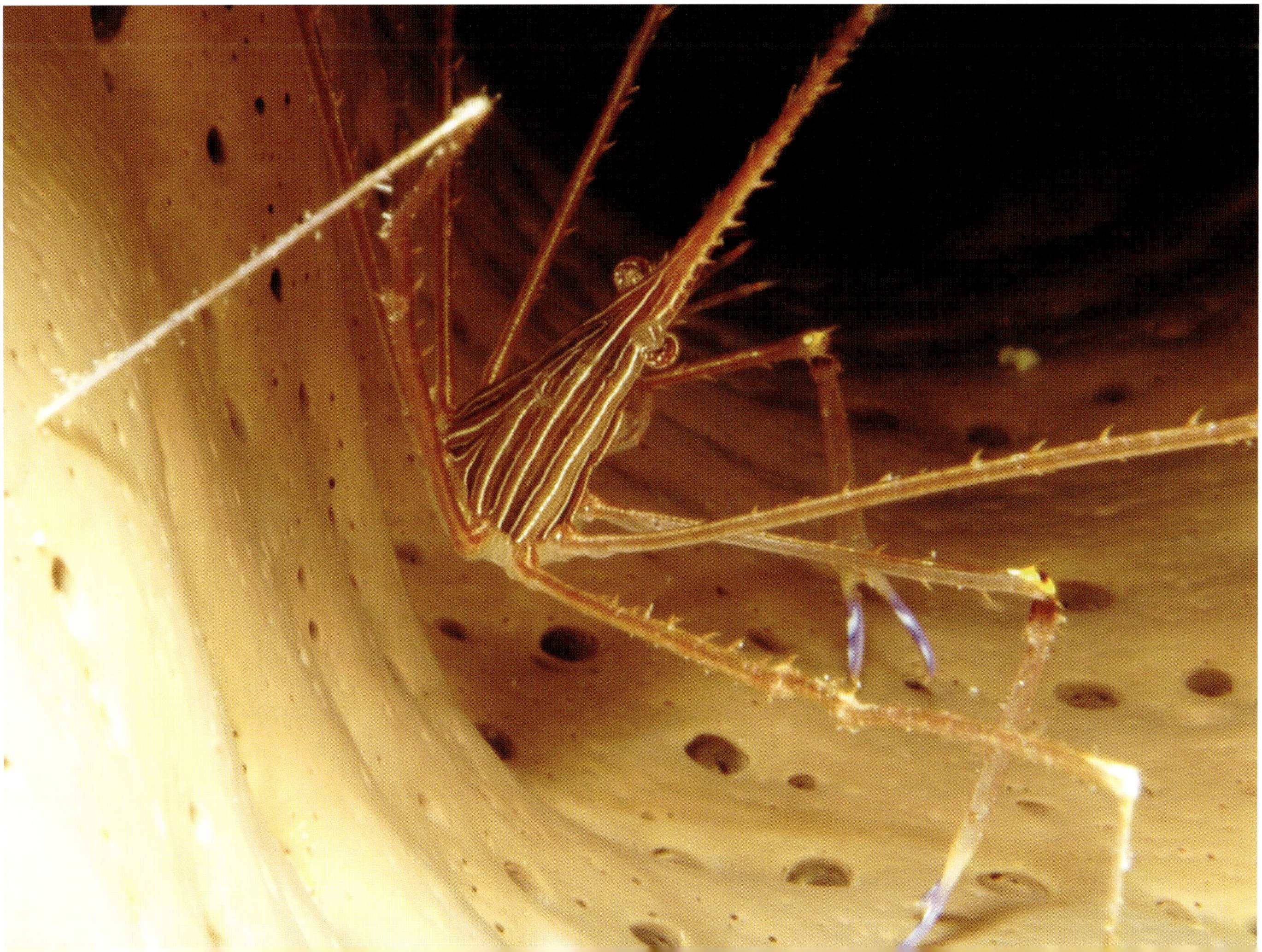

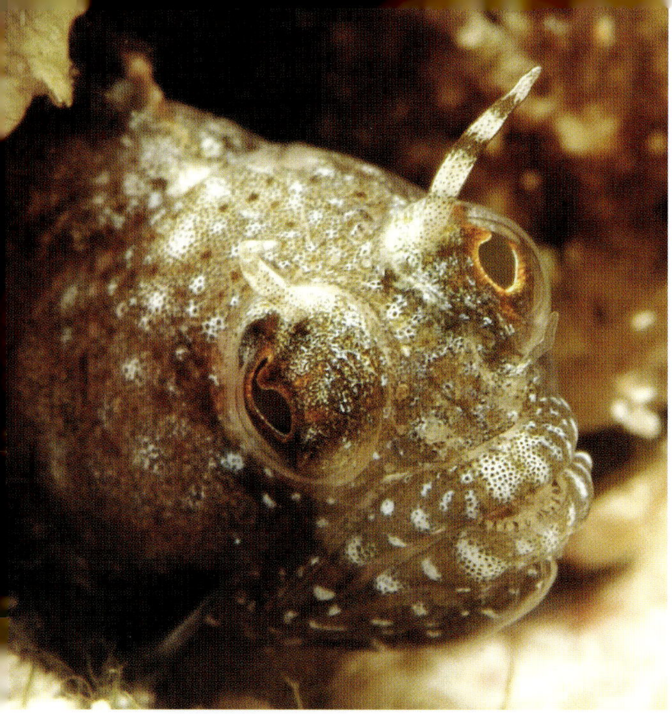
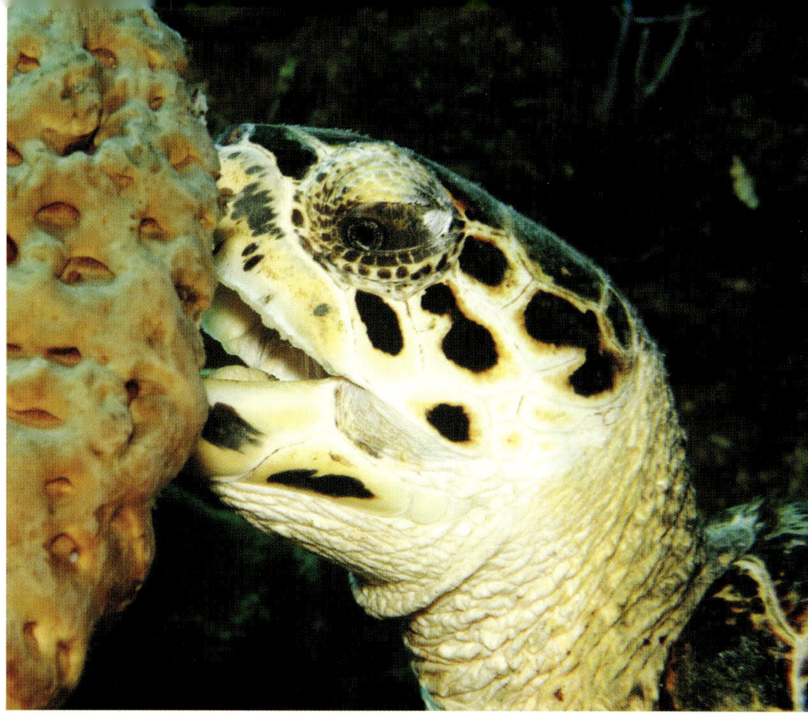
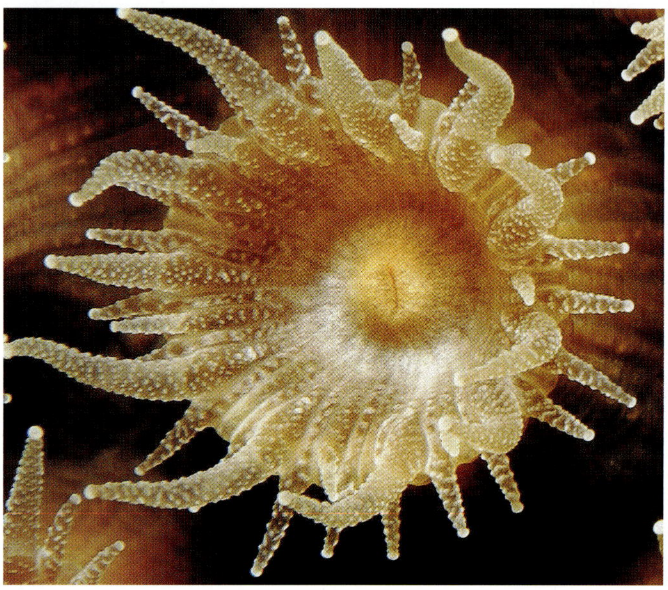
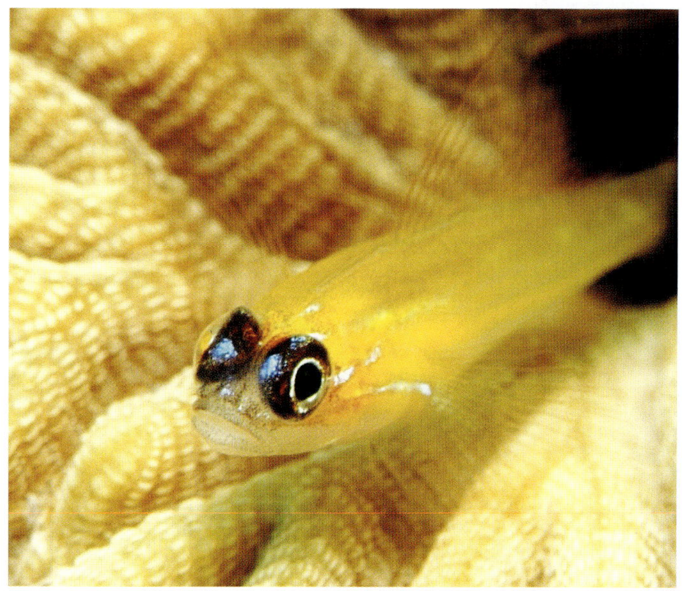

**Top left**—Spiny Sailfin Blenny. Exposure: f/27, 1/60, and 100 ISO. Focal length 60mm. **Top right**—Sea Turtle feeds upon a sponge. Photographed using a Nikkor 60mm lens. Exposure: f/22, 1/60, and 100 ISO. **Bottom left**—Coral polyp photographed during a night dive. Exposure: f/27, 1/60, 100 ISO. Focal length 60mm. **Bottom right**—Peppermint Gobie. Exposure: f/22, 1/60, and 100 ISO. Focal length 60mm. All photos courtesy of Brian Bolton.

I refer to a laminated checklist before every dive to prevent making a mistake such as forgetting to install batteries. The list is small and will fit into the palm of my hand. It is very useful and has saved me money and frustration. Even with it, I have made some bone-headed mistakes, so it is not a substitute for thinking.

# JAN MCGARVA

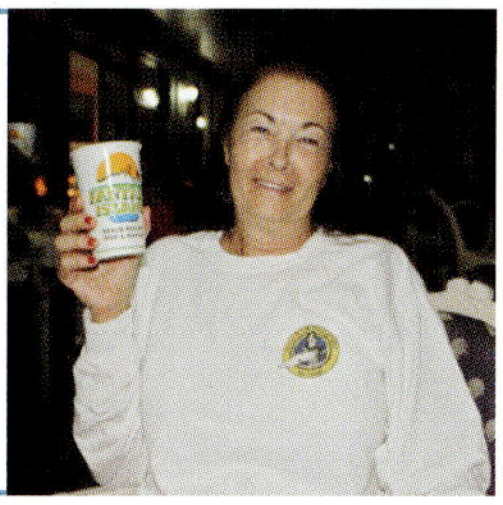

Jan has photo dive experience in the Bahamas, Hawaii, Roatan, and more. She shoots using a Canon T1i in a housing made by Watershot, Inc. She mainly uses an 18–55mm lens with a single strobe.

**The Approach.** I am always looking around for photo opportunities, so most of the time my subject is ahead of me. My first thoughts are to approach slowly, try to contain my excitement, determine the best angle to approach at, and hope that my dive buddy is still with me. At this point, I am also thinking what my favorite photo instructor (Larry Gates) would say to do (like check where your strobe is aimed, shoot from below if you can, check your camera settings, get close, control your buoyancy, etc.). I am also looking at my camera to be sure it is "awake" and that I have selected the settings I want to use for the particular photo.

When I am really excited about a photo op, my first thought is to just get a shot—even if it is not my best. That way, I will have at least captured the moment. On my second and subsequent shots, I try to compose a

**Below**—The Trident is a natural enemy of the Crown of Thorns and is captured here preying on one. Exposure: f/4, $^{1}/_{125}$, and 100 ISO. Focal length 35mm. Photo courtesy of Jan McGarva.

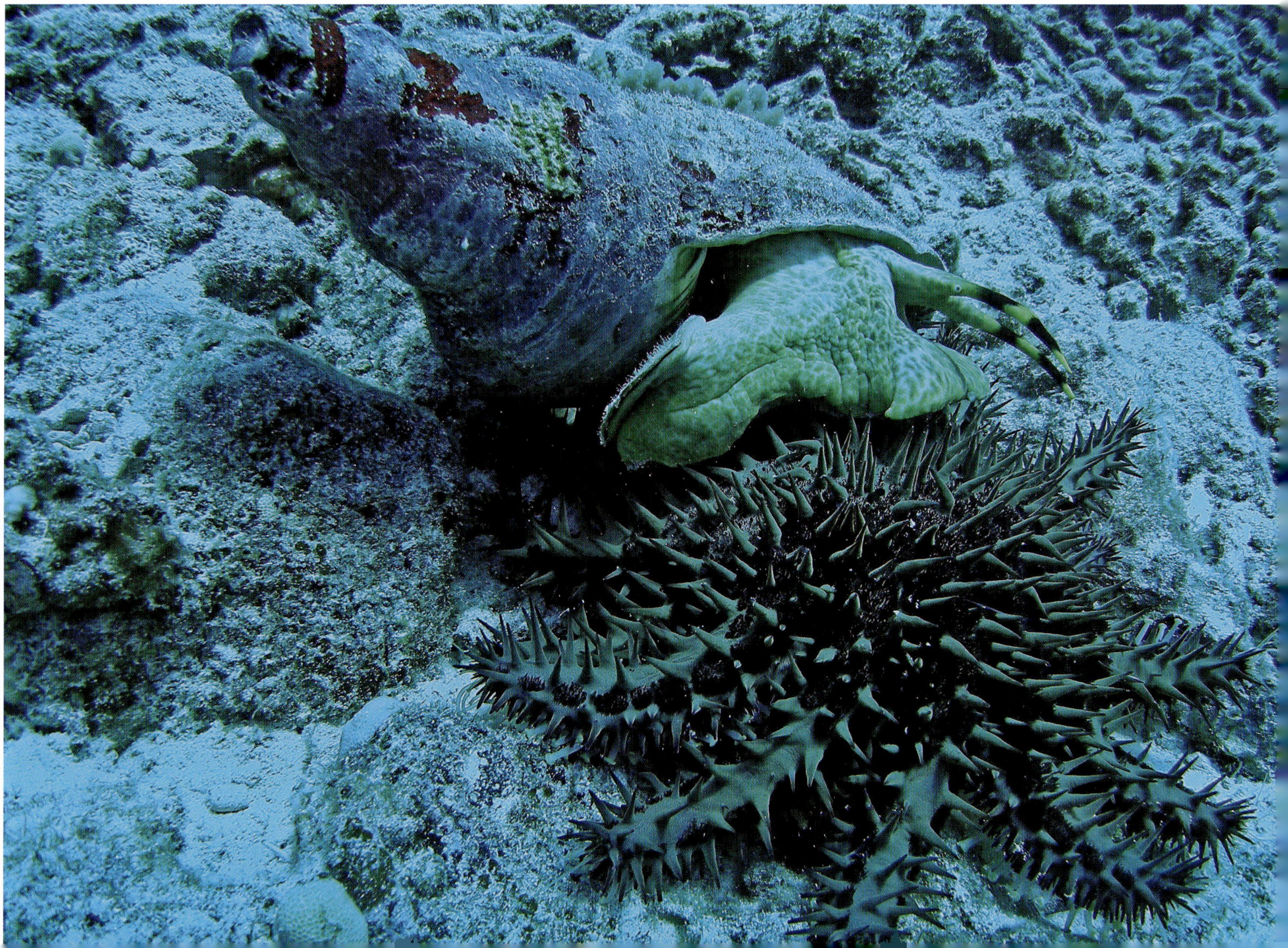

better photo. I also think about where my strobe is while approaching, as I have a bad habit of forgetting to aim my strobe. Other thoughts, like "get close, wait for diver's fins to be out of my frame," etc., also run through my mind. Sometimes I take a photo of a moving subject even if there is a diver's fin, arm, or whatever in the frame. I wouldn't want to miss the photo op because I was waiting for something or someone to get out of my way.

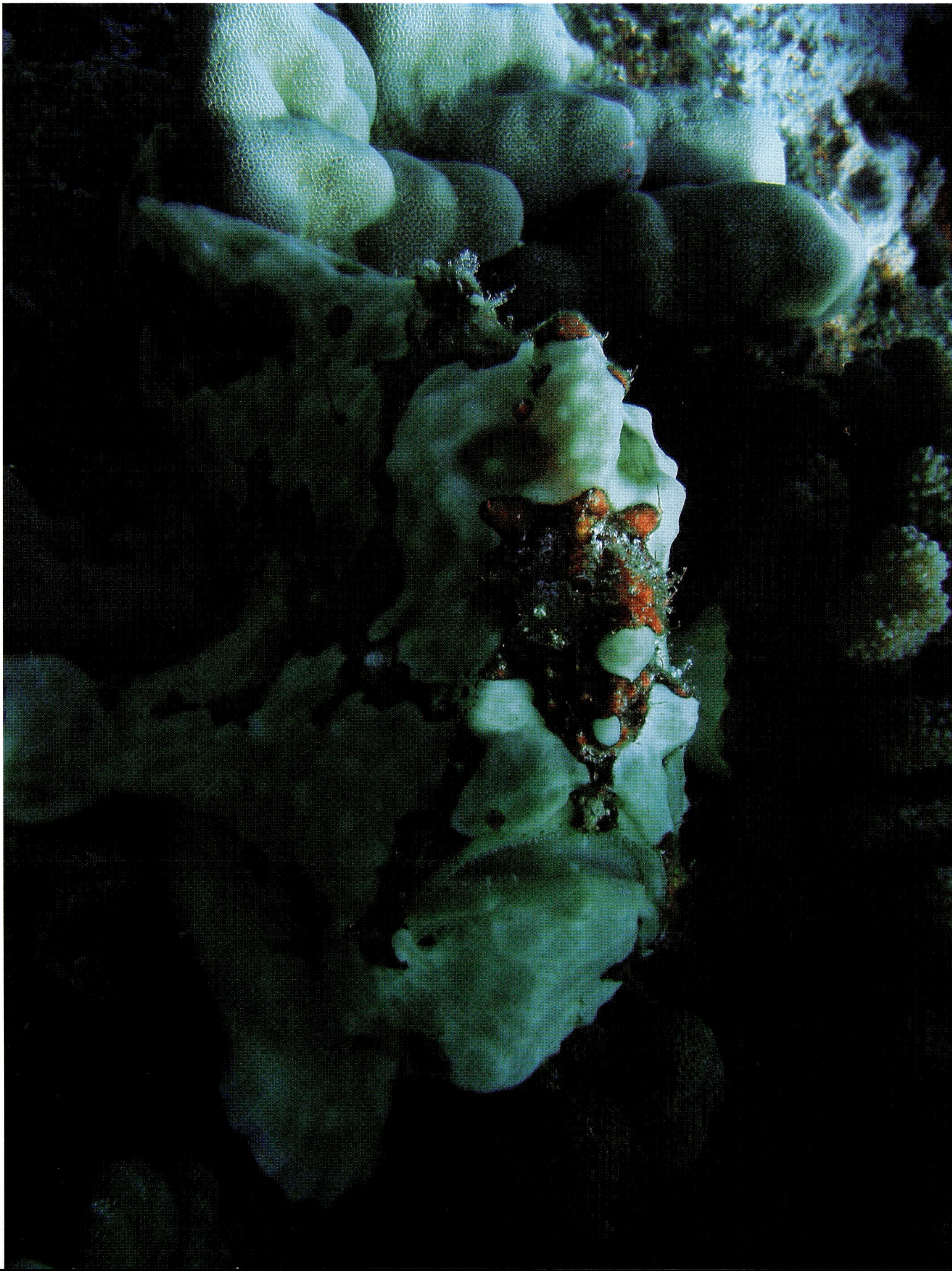

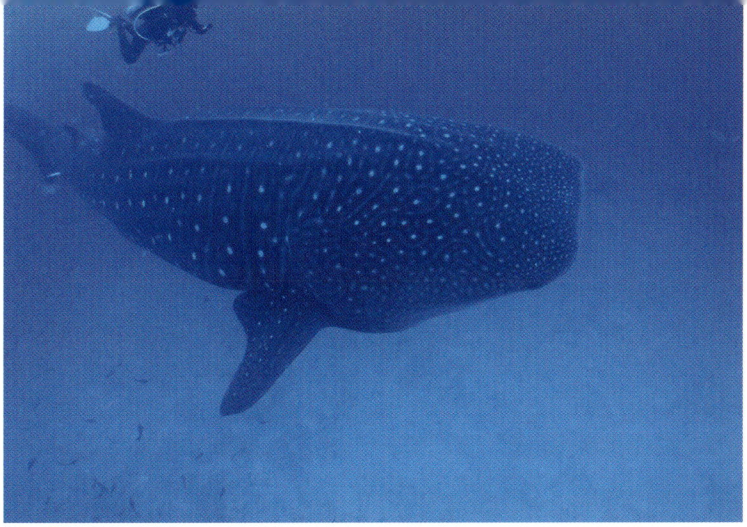

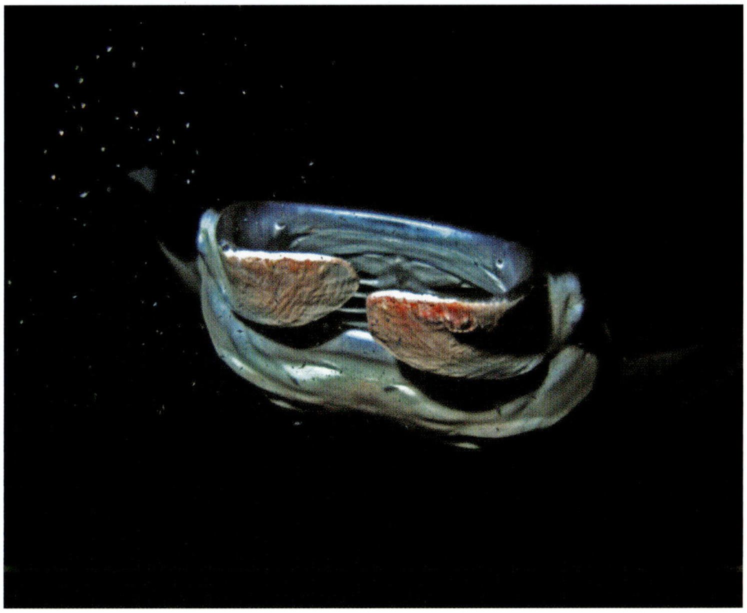

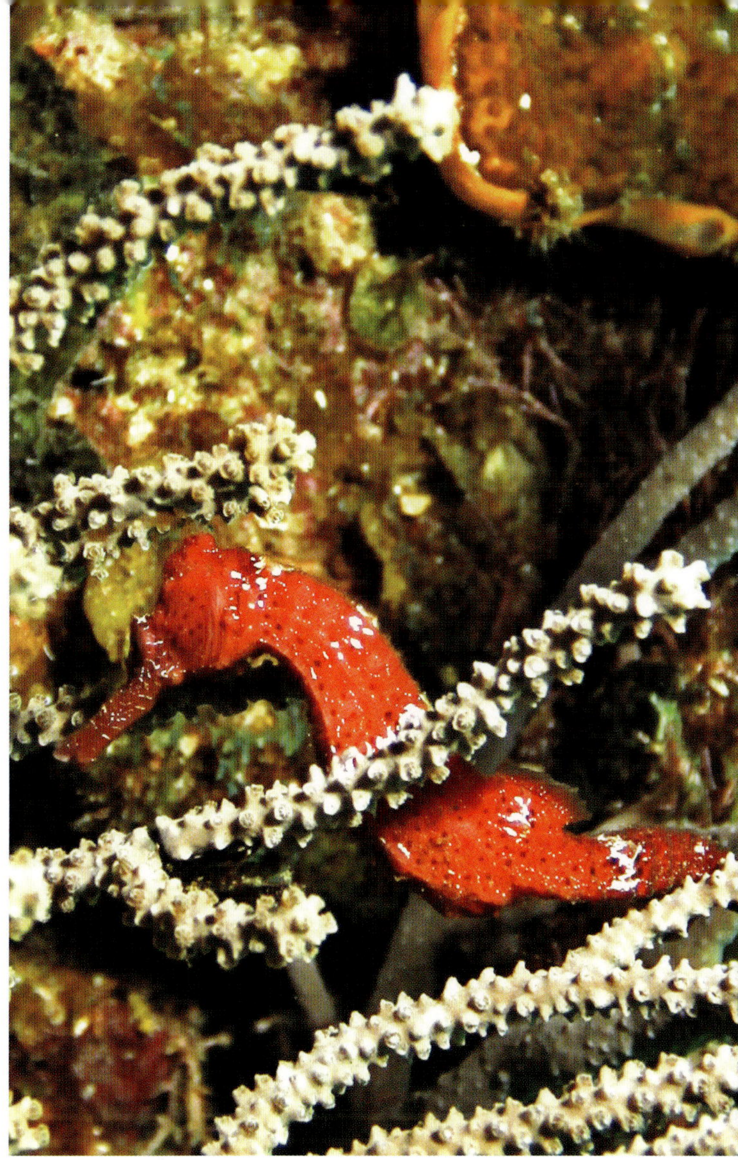

**Facing page**—Frogfish are elusive and blend in very well with the myriad colors and textures of the reef. Exposure: f/4, $^{1}/_{125}$, and 100 ISO. Image captured in Roatan. **Top left**—Traveling to where subjects have a high probability of being seen is important. A trip to the Galapagos Islands resulted in the capture of this Whale Shark. Exposure: f/4, $^{1}/_{60}$, and 100 ISO. Focal length 15mm. **Bottom left**—Manta Ray during night dive in Kona. Exposure: f/2.8, $^{1}/_{60}$, and 100 ISO. **Right**—The Sea Horse is relatively easy to photograph but difficult to find. Exposure: f/3.5, $^{1}/_{125}$, and 100 ISO. Photos courtesy of Jan McGarva.

When photographing pelagic marine life, there is usually deep water and current. My first thoughts with the big stuff are to kick, kick, and kick to get to it, and pace myself so that I can catch up to the big critter for a close-up photo! If you work too hard trying to get to a fast-moving pelagic, you will be too winded to continue and will miss the shot. This is where fitness for diving is important. More than once on the same trip, I was the first one in a group of divers besides the dive master to get to a Whale Shark swimming into the current.

I don't spend a lot of time reviewing my photos in my camera underwater. After I take a photo, I take a quick look at my LCD, check the histogram, and then keep taking more photos. I have seen divers completely miss an Eagle Ray or something swimming overhead because they were busy looking at their LCD screens.

**Night Dives.** I am not fond of doing night dives anymore. Once I have cleaned up and warmed up from my day of diving, I just don't want to get all wet and cold again. However, I *loved* the night dive with the mantas on the Kona Aggressor. I haven't done a night dive since then. Night dives were not allowed in the Galapagos, and I didn't want to get all cold and wet in Roatan after doing three or four dives during the day. Those that went

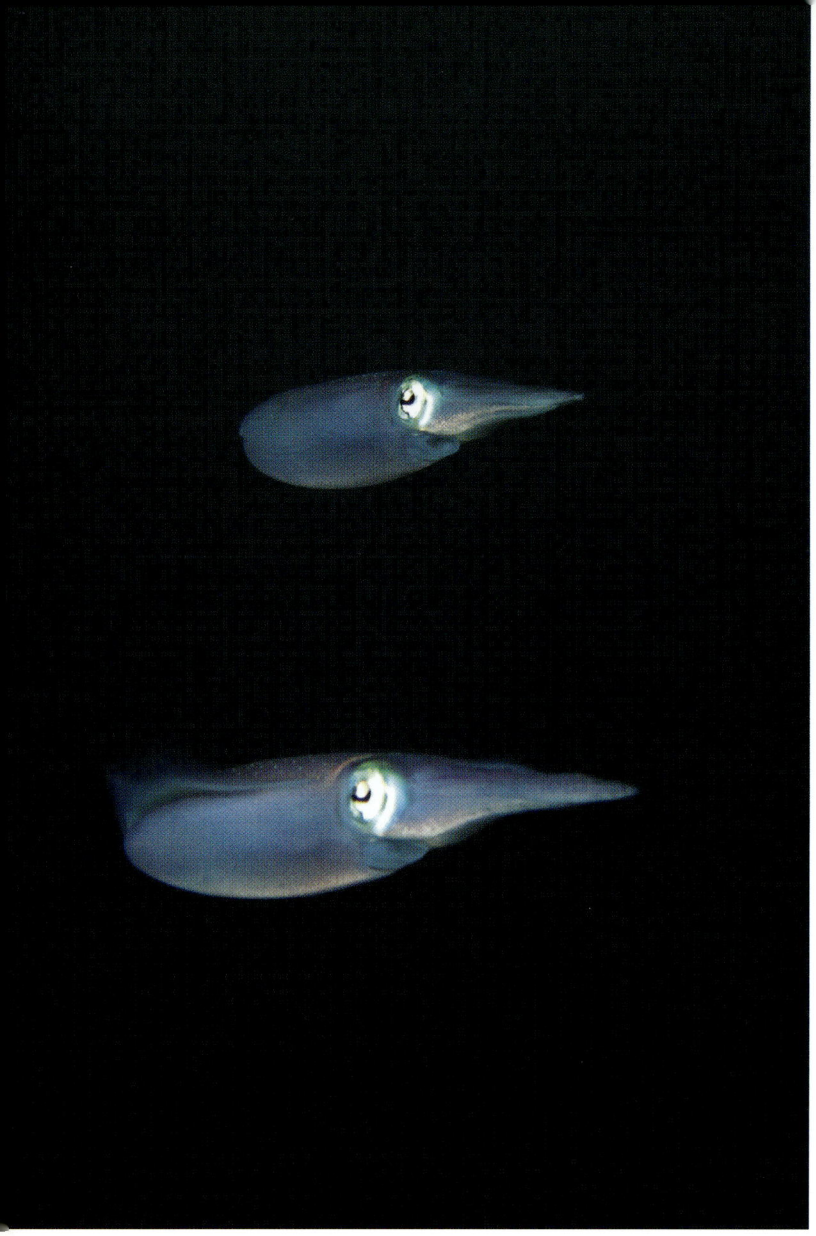

**Left**—Reef Squid photographed at night. Exposure: f/4, 1/100, and 100 ISO. Photo courtesy of Jan McGarva.

on the night dives in Roatan did see some cool stuff, though, and it is probably a worthwhile thing to do at least once.

**Capture Specifications.** I shoot in manual mode. I use ISO 100, a 1/60 shutter speed, and start with f/4 for an aperture. What I did learn from using a point & shoot digital camera at night is that it really helps to have a focus light. I would use that as my primary dive light, as it would be difficult to carry both a dive light and my camera. I use full-powered strobe and, at times, open up the aperture to f/2.8. I still bring along a small dive light as a backup though.

**Etiquette.** One of my biggest peeves is other underwater photographers not using good photo etiquette. There are more and more divers in the water with cameras nowadays, and many don't have a clue. They push their way in for their photos and leave in a cloud of silted, sandy water. They forget that there are others wanting to take a photo too. Once I was the last person in a group to take a photo of a small Splendid Toadfish. Later, when I looked at my photo, my little toadfish was covered in sand from the silted water.

Many divers have cameras. Everyone wants to move in and take a picture of what is being pointed out by a dive master. Many times, after waiting my turn to take a photo, I wouldn't be able to see the subject because divers had silted up the water after they took their photos. Most times I would drop back after everyone left the area for another opportunity to get the photo. Most divers will follow the dive master very closely because they don't want to worry about finding the boat, so it is fairly easy to fall back for a second chance at a shot after the dust has settled.

**Meeting Challenges.** Aiming my strobe properly and having it fire in sync has been one of my biggest issues. The other problem I have is shooting in too-dark areas where the camera has trouble focusing because there isn't enough contrast. I think the solution is to carry a dive light with me to help the camera focus or use the focus light from my strobe. I definitely need to dive with my camera more.

Rob shoots using a Nikon D90 in Ikelite housing. He uses all Nikkor lenses (a 60mm macro, 20mm wide angle, and 17-35mm zoom).

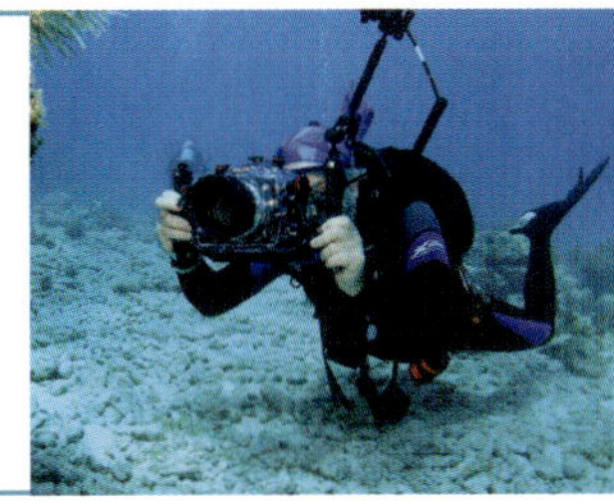

**The Digital Advantage.** I may be the last person Larry knows who made the transition from film to digital photography. That has actually influenced my thought process in the water. I now think about exposure less and think more about composition. With film, it was about a 50-50 between the two; now it's probably more like 80-20 (or higher) in favor of composition. This is for obvious reasons—digital allows for instant feedback, and I can download my pictures and view them on a laptop at night, so by day two or three of the trip, I have a pretty good idea what exposure settings are working well, assuming I'm diving under the same conditions (this was generally the case in Sulawesi, where the images I supplied for this chapter were made). I probably lean a bit more toward underexposing than overexposing. I am comfortable if the images look just a tad underexposed, as that can be easily fixed.

**Conceptualizing the Shot.** When I shoot, I tend to take images that I think my friends will find interesting. For the most part, I am not trying to get a *National Geographic* image—if I get a few pictures that are suitable to blow up and hang on the wall, I'm happy. Taking photos

**Below**—Leaf Scorpion Fish, Sulawesi. Exposure f/11, 1/180, and 200 ISO. Focal length 60mm. Photo courtesy of Rob Stein.

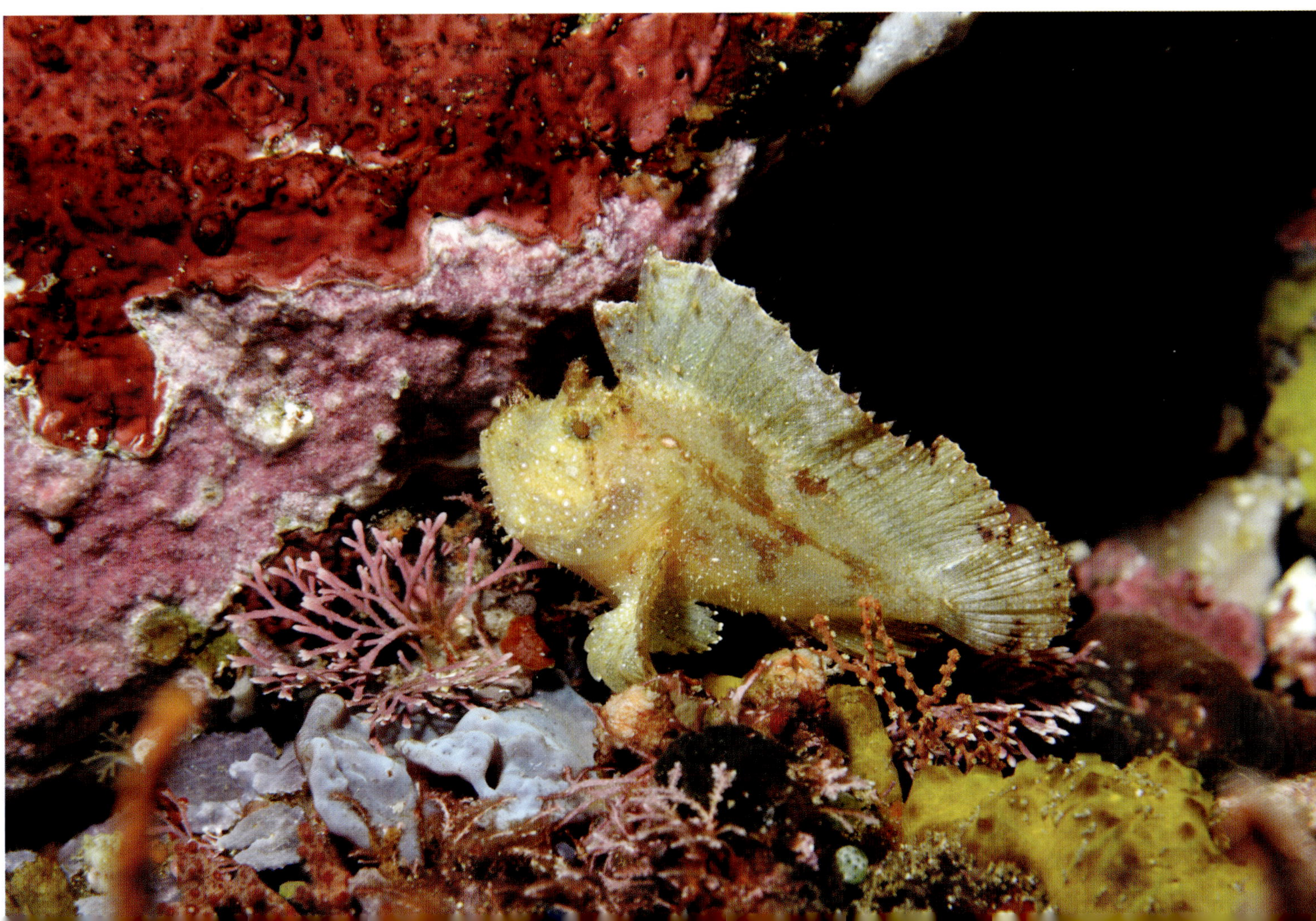

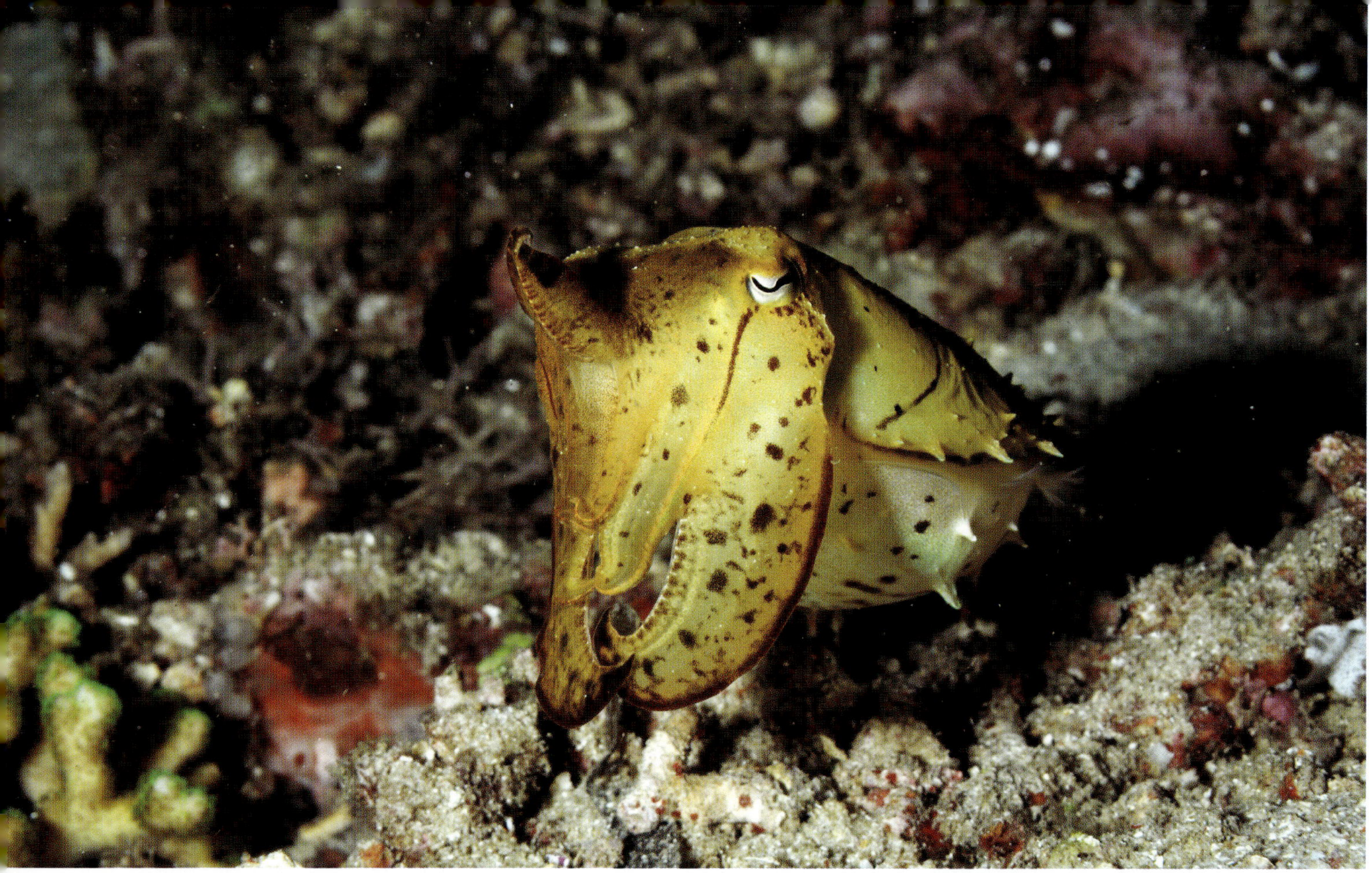

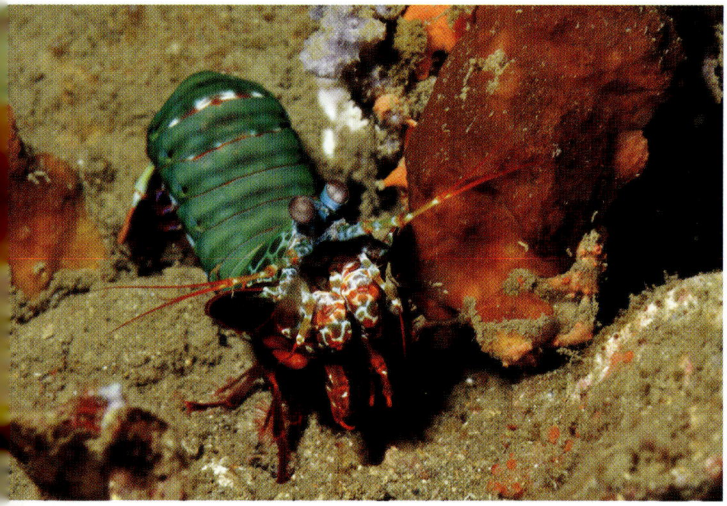

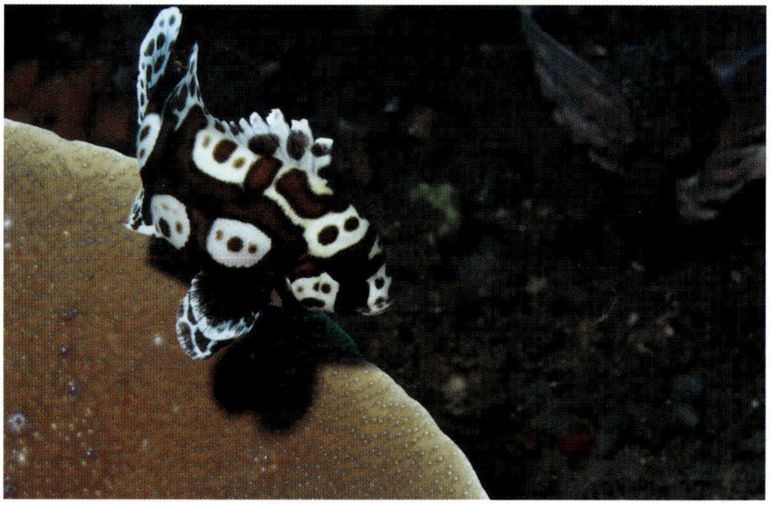

**Top**—Broadclub Cuttlefish, the only large Cuttlefish in the Indo-Pacific, can rapidly and dramatically change color. Exposure: f/16, $^1/_{125}$, and 200 ISO. Focal length 60mm. **Bottom left**—Mantis Shrimp, Sulawesi. Exposure: f/11, $^1/_{125}$, and 200 ISO. Focal length 60mm. **Bottom right**—Juvenile High-Fin Grouper, Sulawesi. Exposure: f/11, $^1/_{125}$, and 200 ISO. Focal length 60mm. Photos courtesy of Rob Stein.

of odd creatures is always great. But one thing I keep in mind is that a lot of the things I see underwater and take for granted are new to my non-diver friends. I also try to remember to take a couple of shots that I can use to "set the scene" if I want to show pictures to friends. More often than not, I don't use these pictures, but it's nice to have them (if nothing else, it triggers my memory about where a group of pictures were taken). So I am not afraid to take a picture of a reef or wreck with a macro lens from a distance—it won't win any awards, but at least I can give people a frame of reference for the macro pictures that follow (e.g., here's the wreck we were diving on).

As for composition, when I am reasonably close to the subject, I will take a picture (it's best to have one in case the subject gets away) and then start moving closer and/or photographing from different angles.

One thing I've found very helpful (and it may be due to the Ikelite housing I use) is the ease of adjusting the strobe's power to bracket the exposure. With the Ikelite strobes set on TTL, there is a control on the back of the housing that can be used to adjust the TTL setting up to +/−2 exposure values. This works great because it's almost a hybrid approach to TTL. If you take a picture at the regular TTL and it looks a bit under- or overexposed, you just turn the knob a bit to add or subtract a fraction of an EV from what the camera thinks is the best exposure. This is especially helpful if you are taking a bunch of pictures in the same lighting conditions. If the lighting changes a bit, that will be compensated for by the TTL, but you still end up with a picture that is exposed as you wanted. The other advantage to this—assuming you are not maxing out the strobe's power—is that if you've found an f-stop and shutter speed that works well for the subjects on that dive, you can keep shooting at those settings with the strobe providing the adjustments for the changes in distance, light, etc. This worked great for the macro subjects in Sulawesi, since all of the pictures were taken within inches to 2 feet of the subject.

**Night Dives.** Night dives are the trickiest for me. Trying to get the camera to focus on a Ghost Pipefish at night (or during the day for that matter) is tough. Using two strobes on night dives is a huge advantage. I take the diffuser off one strobe and manually set the control switch on that strobe to a low setting. I use the strobe as the focus light, and it provides just enough output during the exposure to fill shadows. I leave the diffuser on the primary strobe, keep it angled as I want it for the shot, and set it to TTL (keep in mind, this is all basically for macro work).

**Top left**—The Banggai Cardinalfish, only about 2.5 inches, lives in sheltered areas of coral rubble. This species is one of the most beautiful varieties of Cardinalfish. Exposure f/11, 1/125, and 200 ISO. Focal length 60mm. **Top right**—Clownfish at home within an Anemone. Exposure: f/11, 1/125, and 200 ISO. Focal length 60mm. **Bottom left**—Frogfish. Exposure: f/11, 1/125, and 200 ISO. Focal length 60mm. **Bottom right**—A "Nudie" or Nudibranch or, in scientific terms, *Glossadoris atromarginata.* The black tufts are its lungs (gills), and the things that look like antennae are its "nose" (rhinophores). They are all both male and female, or hermaphroditic, so they don't have to be too picky about sex partners! Exposure: f/13, 1/125, and 200 ISO. Focal length 60mm. Photos courtesy of Rob Stein.

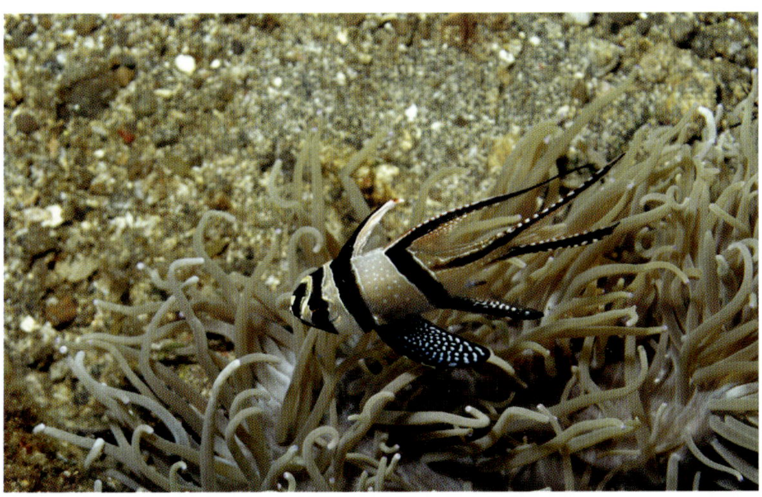

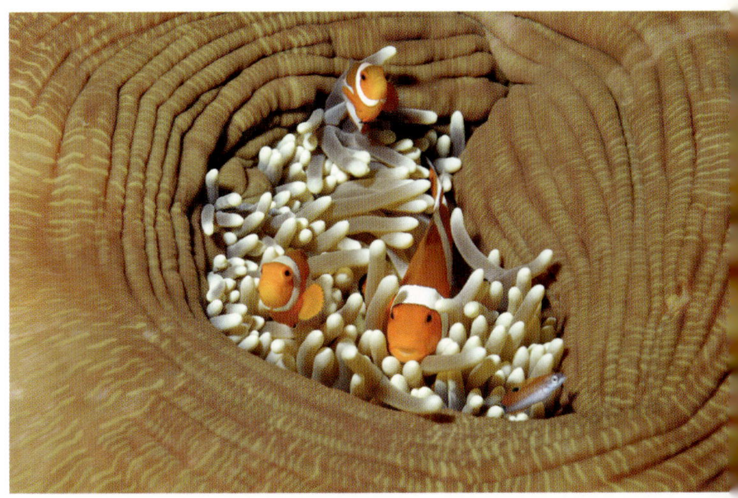

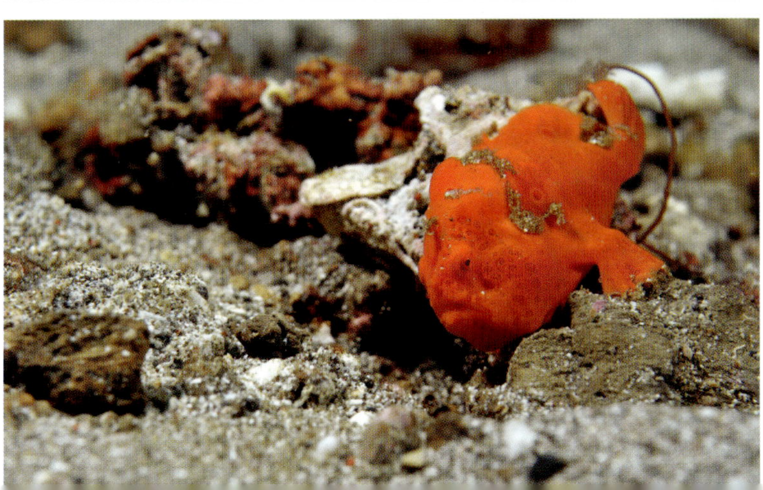

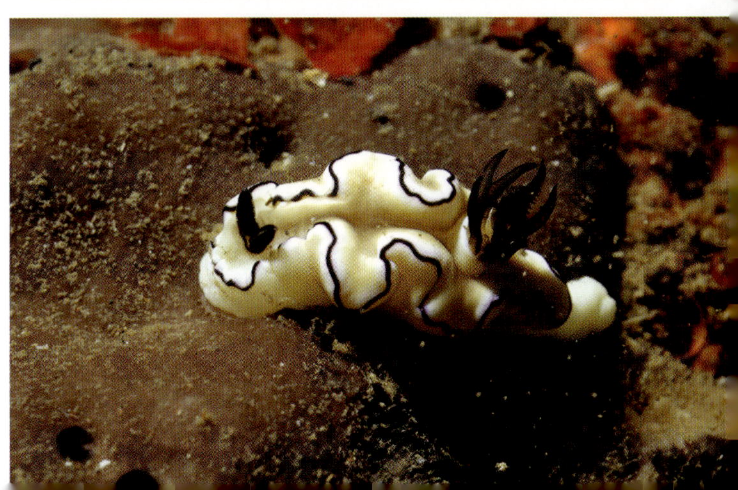

## MARY MOYER

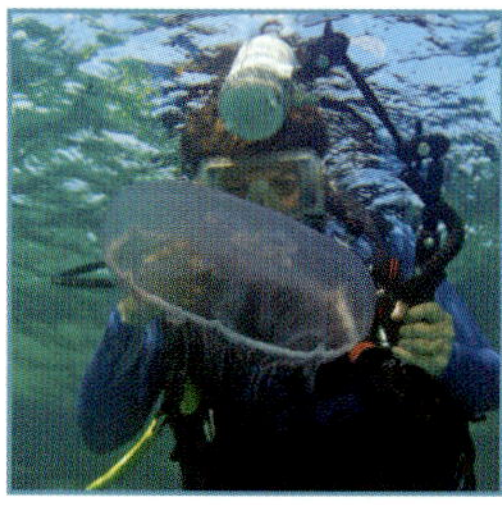

Mary has engaged in underwater photography in places such as the Florida Keys, Alaska, Lembeh, Roatan, Fiji, Bali, Costa Rica, Banda Sea, Monado, and Solomon Islands.

**Lenses.** I am not an expert by any stretch of the imagination, but I have been fortunate to have traveled to dive destinations that offered great opportunities for underwater photography, such as Sulawesi. You definitely want a good macro lens, as all of your muck diving will be macro shots (my personal favorite). I use a Canon EF 100mm. Some of the volcano shots will be wide angle, of course. For those, I use a Canon EF 17–40mm lens. I shoot with a Canon EOS 5D Mk II housed in a Subal housing. I think that if you are fairly new to digital, having a couple of good lenses will keep it simple.

**A Diversity of Subjects.** Sulawesi is one of the premiere destinations for underwater photography. There are a plethora of Nudibranch, Mandarin Fish, Ghost Pipefish, Cuttlefish, Stargazers, Stonefish, Ambon Scorpion Fish, and Mimic Octopus. These subjects are found not on the coral reef but on mucky bottoms, hence the term "muck diving."

When muck diving, it is helpful to have some type of pointer to balance yourself while shooting so you don't have to touch anything and stir up the bottom. We use a large knitting needle. Also because of the remoteness of the destination, some emergency repair items (e.g., a tiny screwdriver, spare O-rings) are essential. I keep dry packs (like the ones placed in pill bottles) in my housing due to the humidity.

**Meeting Challenges.** I recall a particular shot that I was trying to get when we were in the Banda Sea. I had spotted a reddish-brown Leaf Scorpion Fish. Unfortunately, it was surrounded by Stinging Hydroids. No

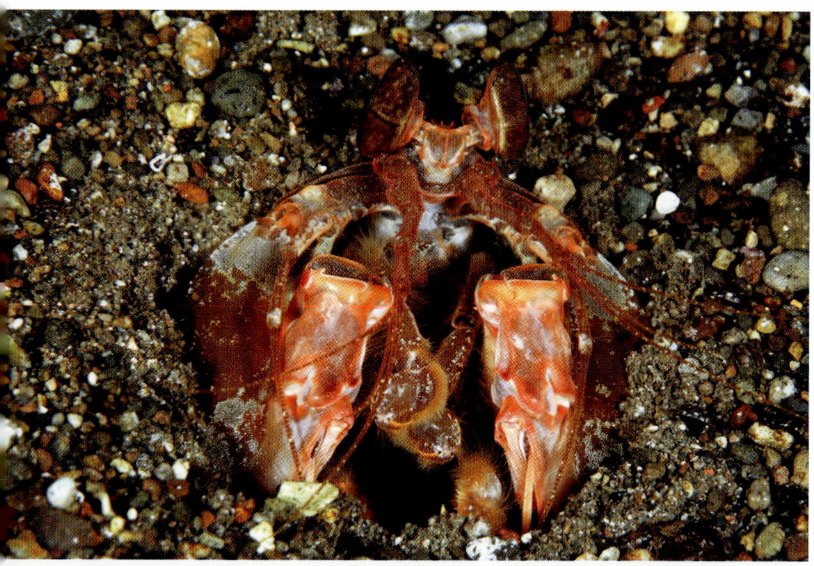

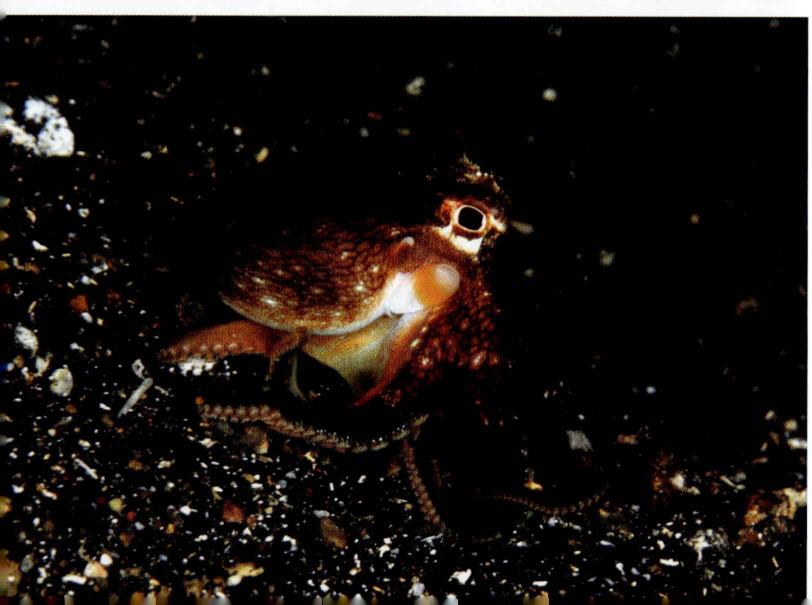

**Top**—Mantis Shrimp. This species is rarely seen out of its burrow in the sand. Its eyesight is extremely acute, and it can even see infrared. Its claws are so fast and strong that it can shatter $^{3}/_{4}$-inch aquarium glass. This also means that it can shatter your dome port or housing, so beware! This was photographed on a dawn dive in Wetong, Indonesia, in the Banda Sea. Exposure: f/14, $^{1}/_{100}$, and 100 ISO. Focal length 100mm. **Bottom**—This is a photograph of a species of octopus simply called sp4. It is found only in Indonesia and lives in coarse, sandy habitats. It was photographed on a night dive off Banda Island in about 20 feet of water. Exposure: f/22, $^{1}/_{125}$, and 100 ISO. Focal length 100mm. Photos courtesy of Mary Moyer.

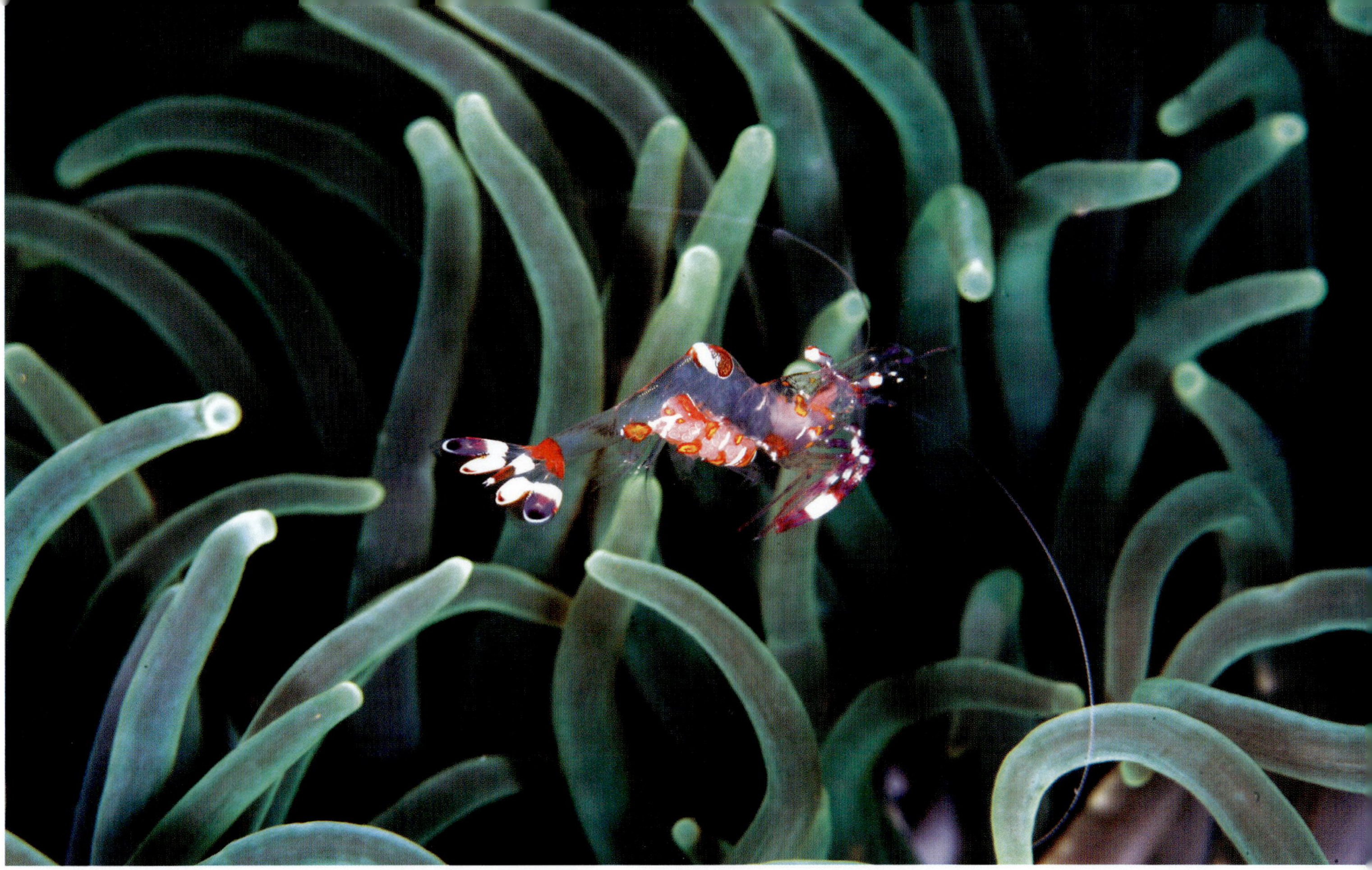

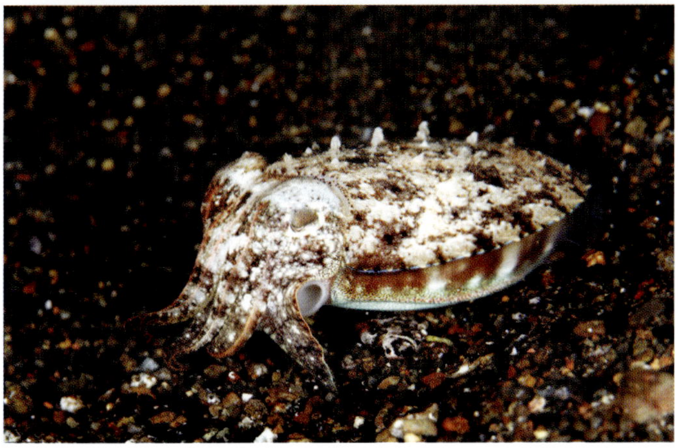

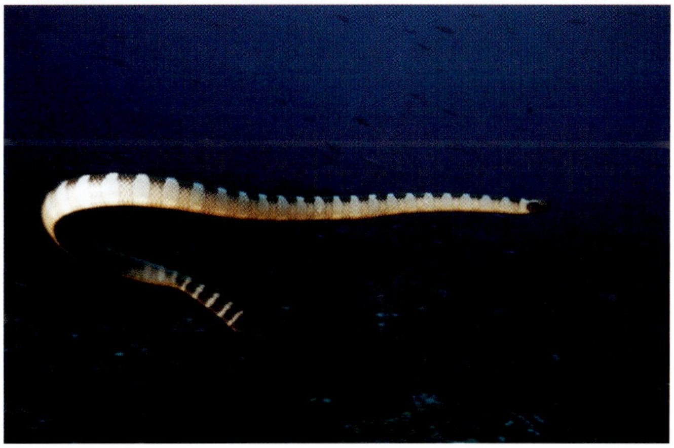

**Top**—Ghost Shrimp. Sometimes you capture things in your frame that are so small that you barely noticed them when you were shooting. Exposure: f/18, $^{1}/_{100}$, and 100 ISO. Focal length 100mm. Photos courtesy of Mary Moyer. **Bottom left**—A photograph of a Papaun Cuttlefish. It is about 10 inches long and was also found on a night dive in Indonesia. One sees many things during night dives that are not normally out during the day. Exposure: f/16, $^{1}/_{60}$, and 100 ISO. Focal length 100mm. **Bottom right**—Sea Snake, Gunnenappe volcano, Banda Sea. Exposure: f/8, $^{1}/_{60}$, and 100 ISO. Focal length 33mm.

matter how I tried, I could not get close enough or get the proper angle to get my shot. This is where having a daring and fearless spouse is advantageous. I showed the fish to my husband and dive buddy, John, and signed to him that there were "stingy things" all around. He took my camera, swam above the scorpion fish, got in a vertical orientation, expelled his air and, while suspended upsidedown, got some awesome shots of our subject! (I treated his minor hydroid stings with hydrocortisone cream.)

When approaching a skittish subject, such as an octopus, I move slowly and begin shooting from farther back

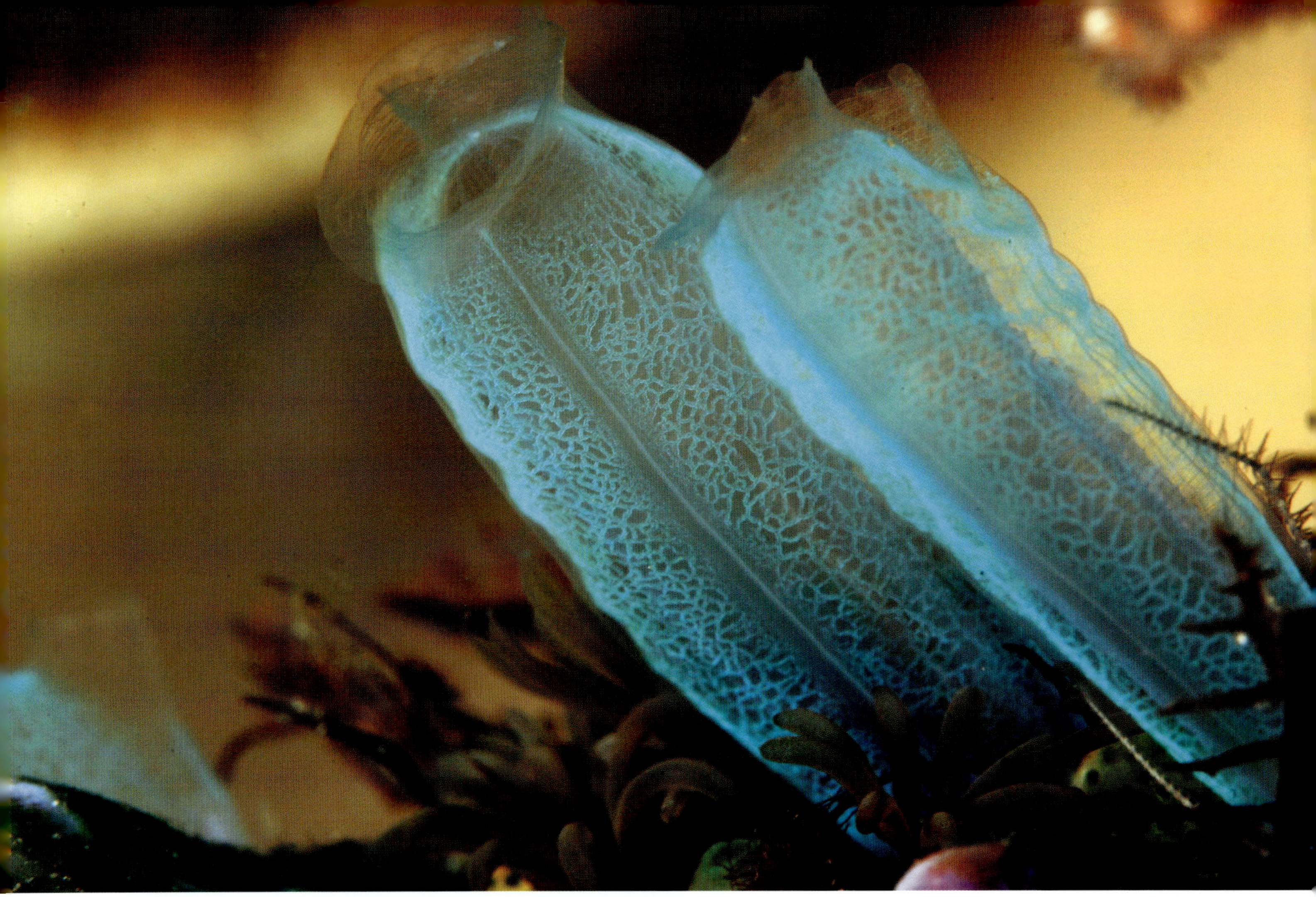

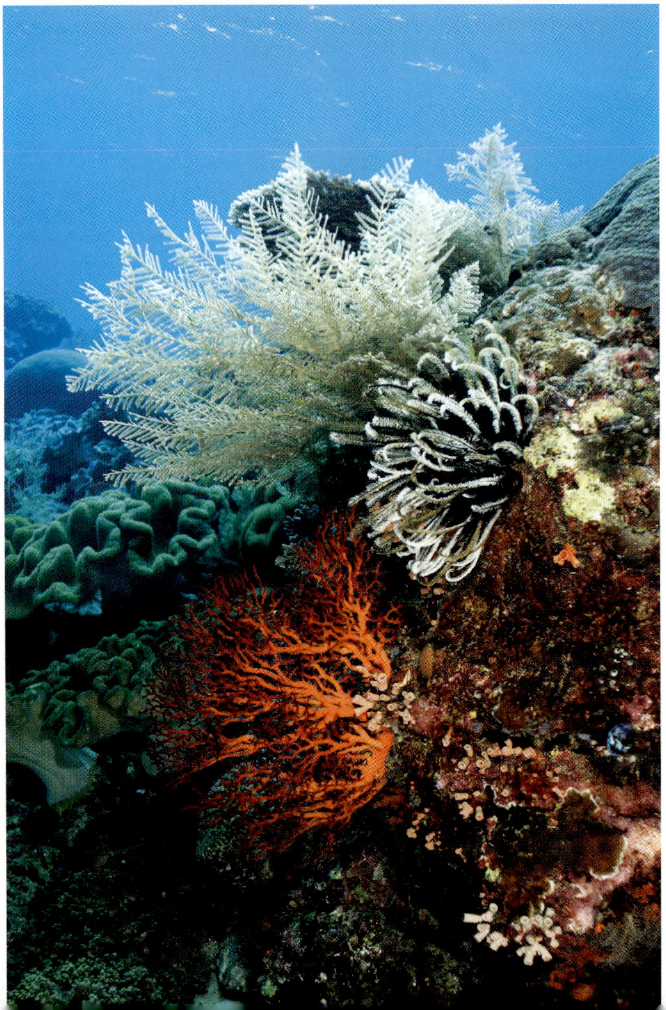

**Top**—Blue Tunicates. Your subject doesn't need to be big, flashy, dangerous, or elusive. Sometimes the most mundane parts of the reef can make awesome photographic opportunities. Exposure: f/14, $^{1}/_{100}$, and 100 ISO. Focal length 100mm. **Bottom**—Coral reef scenic photographed in Fiji. Exposure: f/5.6, $^{1}/_{100}$, and 100 ISO. Focal length 40mm. Photos courtesy of Mary Moyer.

than desired just to make sure that I get a shot. I can always crop later. Then I line up my subject and desired background and shoot a couple of frames. I stop to look at what I have and adjust my aperture as needed. If time and air allow, I will hang out and see if I can catch the subject doing something cool like feeding.

I am kind of a "fish nerd" and I like to find weird critters. That is what keeps my diving and underwater photography fun and exciting. If there were jobs available, I would have become a marine biologist. But for now, it is just a hobby. Being a people doctor pays the bills.

# CONNIE Z PHOTOGRAPHY, LLC

Connie Z shoots with a Canon EOS 500D inside Watershot Inc.'s housing. She uses two strobes when using her ultra-wide 10–22mm lens.

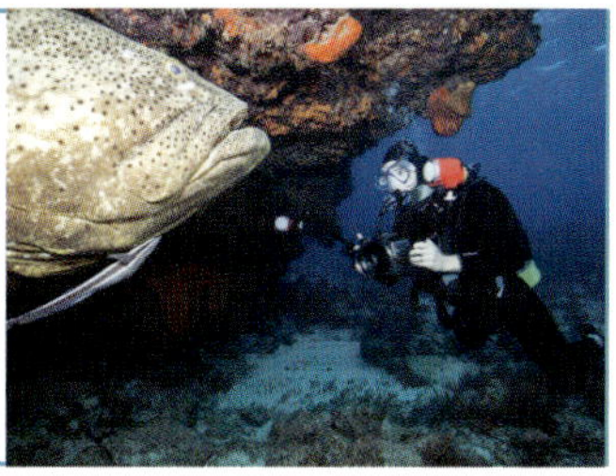

**Pre-Planning.** Before I begin a dive, I think about where I'm going to be and how the predicted conditions (like visibility and surge) might limit or influence what I will shoot. I have three lenses: a 60mm macro, 10–22mm wide angle, and 18–55mm zoom. I plan to commit to either macro images or scenes and choose the lens that will suit the type of images I plan to take. If I plan to capture both image types, I will mount the 18–55mm lens.

**The Dive.** While enjoying the dive, I hunt for something to shoot. I love the hunt-and-discovery aspects and try to remember to look up and around to see what else may be happening in the water column. I've been known to miss cool marine activity, like a spotted Moray Eel that swam past me as I focused on a Scorpion Fish. I don't consider myself very advanced, so I need to pay attention to my position relative to the subject and consider how my strobes will light it. I also check my exposures by looking at the histogram. I shoot different angles from various positions and distances while varying the lighting. Finally, I try to be very careful not to touch

**Below**—Schooling Blue Tang move from coral head to coral head, stopping occasionally to feed. Exposure: f/5.6, 1/125, and 100 ISO. Focal length 35mm. Photo courtesy of Connie Z Photography, LLC.

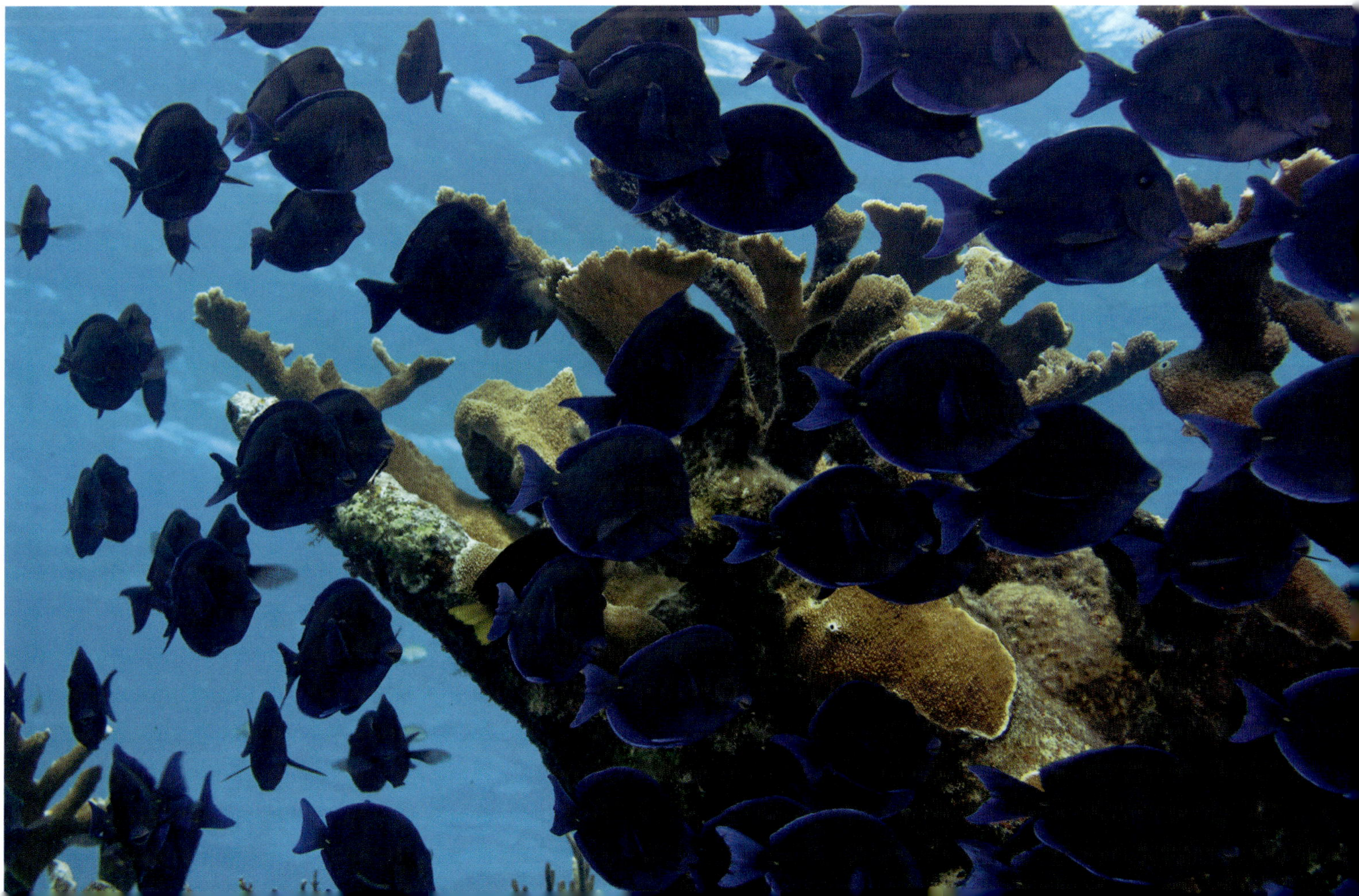

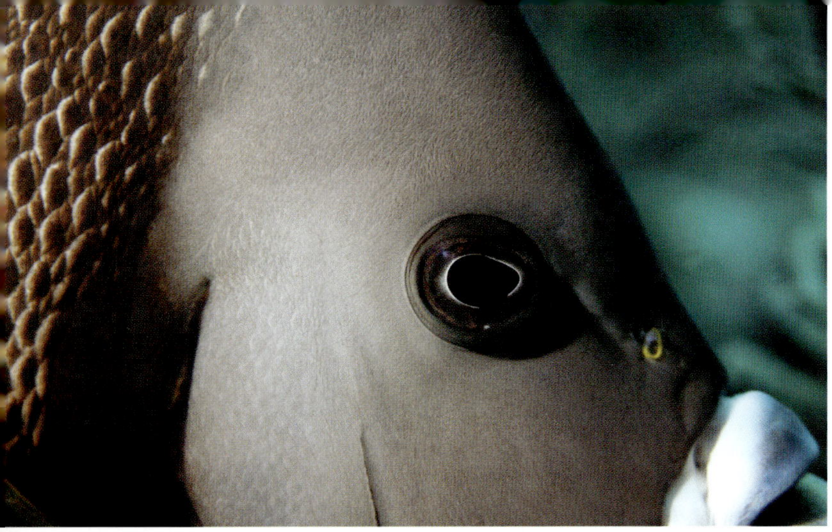

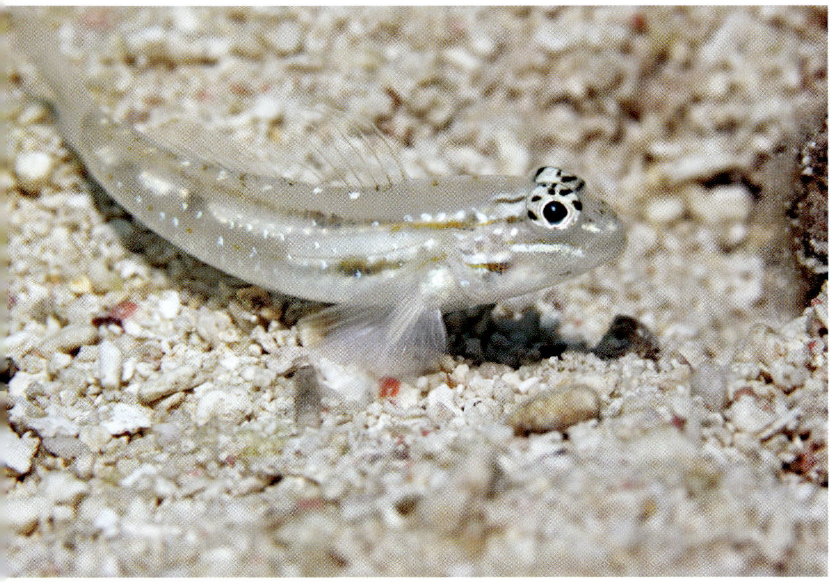

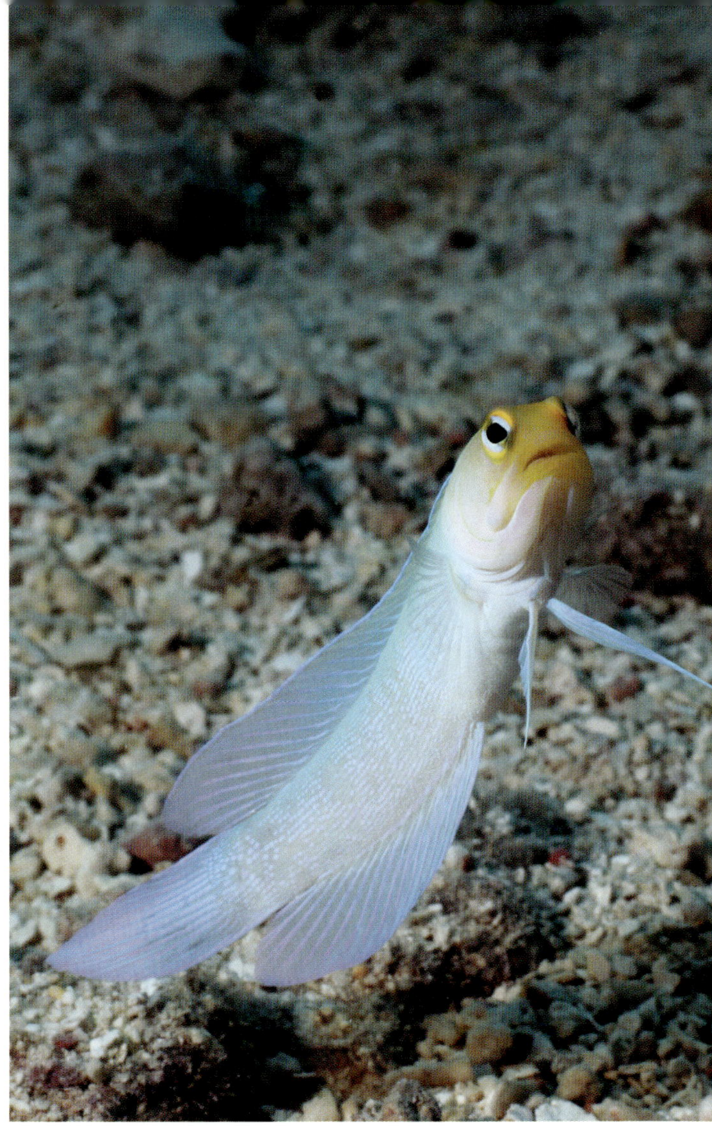

**Top left**—An example of a very tight fish portrait, with the eye of the Grey Angelfish in sharpest focus. Exposure: f/11, 1/125, and 100 ISO. Focal length 60mm. **Bottom left**—Bridled Blenny, approximately 1 inch in length. Exposure: f/6.7, 1/125, and 100 ISO. Focal length 60mm. **Right**—The always-ducking Yellow-Headed Jawfish. Exposure: f/13, 1/125, and 100 ISO. Focal length 60mm. Photos courtesy of Connie Z Photography, LLC.

any of the corals or disturb any of the other wildlife in the area.

Here is the approach I take to get a shot:

1. Find something to shoot.
2. Evaluate how to do it.
3. Start positioning myself by moving closer.
4. Get myself set, either by settling or hovering.
5. Take a shot and check my exposure by looking at the histogram.
6. Adjust and re-shoot.

When photographing a subject, it is important to stick with it and, in the end, if you feel you didn't quite get it, go back and take another quick go at it.

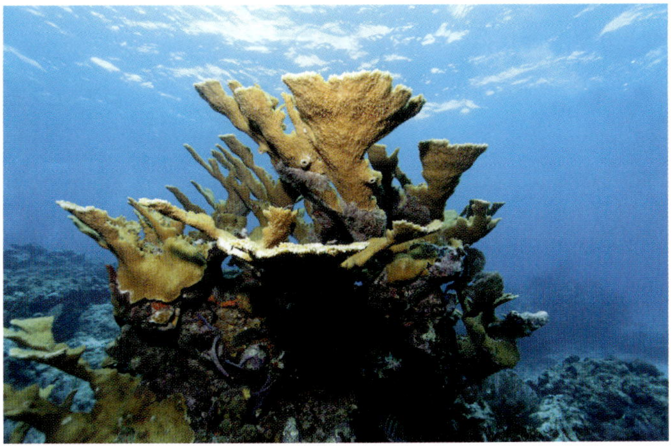

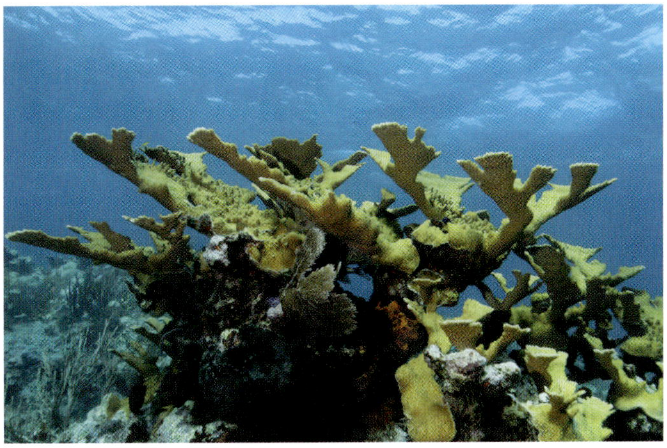

**Left**—Elkhorn coral scenic shot from an upward-facing angle to include Snell's window in the background. Exposure: f/4.5, $^1/_{125}$, and 100 ISO. Focal length 10mm, and inches away from the coral. Connie says, "I prefer to take many shots and take pictures from different levels because I feel the coral color becomes more vibrant at the top. I also need to worry about the nearness of the dome port to the coral. Buoyancy is extremely important, as is the ability to back up a bit if there is current or surge. The scuba handling of myself probably takes more of my concentration than the actual picture taking." **Right**—A different formation of Elkhorn coral, shot straight on from a distance of 1 foot. This perspective gave the water column a totally different look. Also, the light falling on the coral has a different color cast. Exposure: f/8, $^1/_{125}$, and 100 ISO. Focal length 16mm. Photos courtesy of Connie Z Photography, LLC.

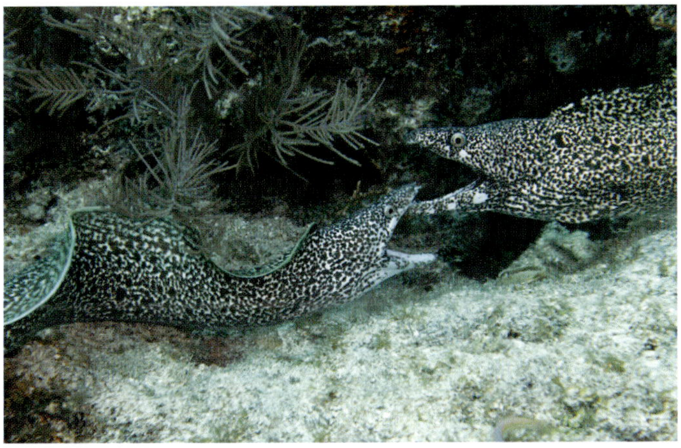

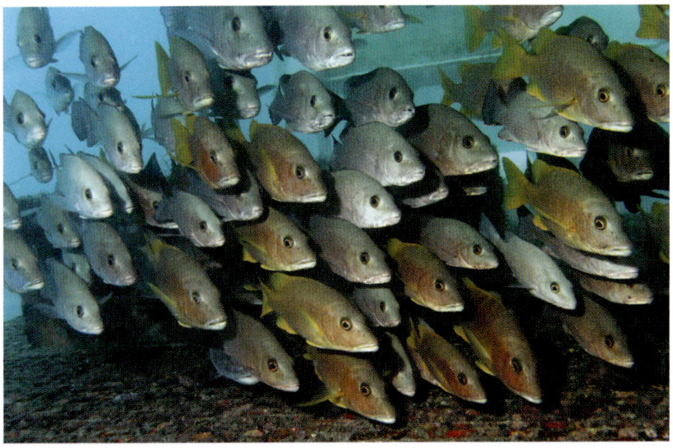

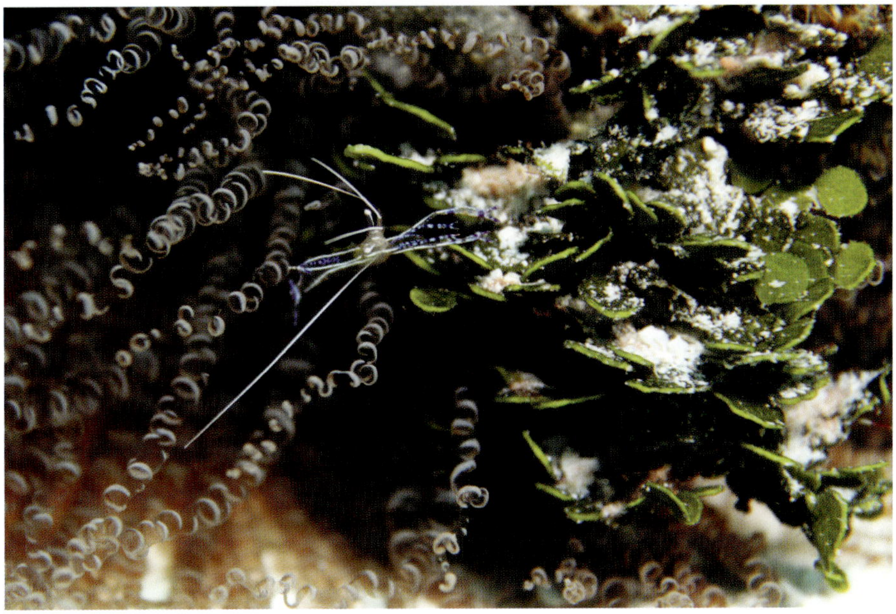

**Above left**—Captured in this photograph is the behavior of two spotted Moray Eels, disputing which has ownership of a dwelling place. Exposure: f/5.6, $^1/_{125}$, and 100 ISO. Focal length 55mm. **Above right**—When taking cover, schooling fish often face the same direction and usually face into any current. Such was the case with this school inhabiting the Aquarius Undersea Habitat near Key Largo, FL. I approach the fish slowly enough so as to not disturb the scene. Exposure: f/5.6, $^1/_{125}$, and 100 ISO. Focal length 25mm. Photo courtesy of Connie Z Photography, LLC. **Right**—Pederson Cleaner Shrimp photographed in Belize. Pederson Shrimp are often found with Corkscrew Anemone. The shrimp antennae provide a leading line to the shrimp in this composition. Connie says, "I try to focus on the eye and have very controlled buoyancy doing so. One small movement, and the shrimp would be out of focus. Aware that these guys won't run away, I know there is plenty of time to carefully settle my position." Exposure: f/4.5, $^1/_{125}$, and 100 ISO. Focal length 60mm. Photos courtesy of Connie Z Photography, LLC.

# JOHN YASAKI

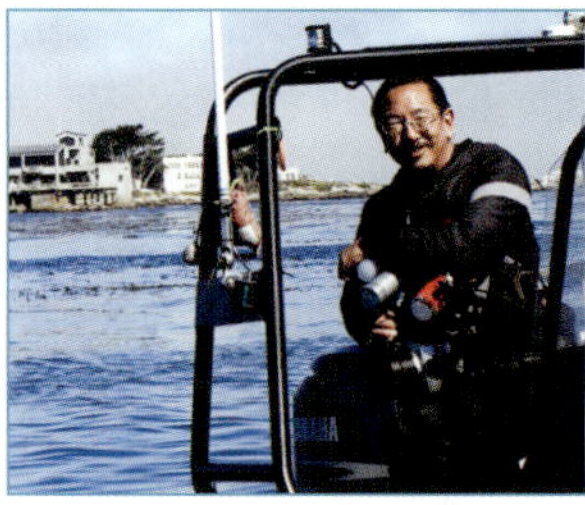

John shoots a Canon dSLR in a Watershot housing and uses twin strobes with a focus light. He primarily engages in macro photography and uses a 60mm macro lens.

*Note:* John is a new friend and fellow diver who is advancing in his underwater photography. I enlisted his help with this book because he dives in an environment that I do not dive in. He lives in California and dives in the colder, darker waters of Monterey. Different diving environments can call for different techniques in underwater photography. He describes his approach below.

**Manual or Auto Focus?** I shoot in a limited visibility, low-light environment. In most cases when I get in the water, everything is moving enough that manual focus would be a liability rather than an asset. I may try it sometime when I find calm water, but I'm satisfied with the auto focus. I might also use manual focus when shooting small gelatinous stuff on the safety stop. Most of those guys don't possess enough inherent contrast for auto focus to lock on.

**Boat or Shore Diving?** I have an 18-foot aluminum-hulled RIB and generally use that for diving. I don't do many beach dives anymore. I'm a bit lazy and don't like carrying all the gear up and down the beach. I will do the occasional beach night dive on the breakwater wall. My

**Below**—A pair of *Heremissenda crassicornis* less than 1 inch in length and on a red-fluted Bryozoa. Exposure: f/16, 1/200, and 400 ISO. Focal length 60mm. Photo courtesy of John Yasaki.

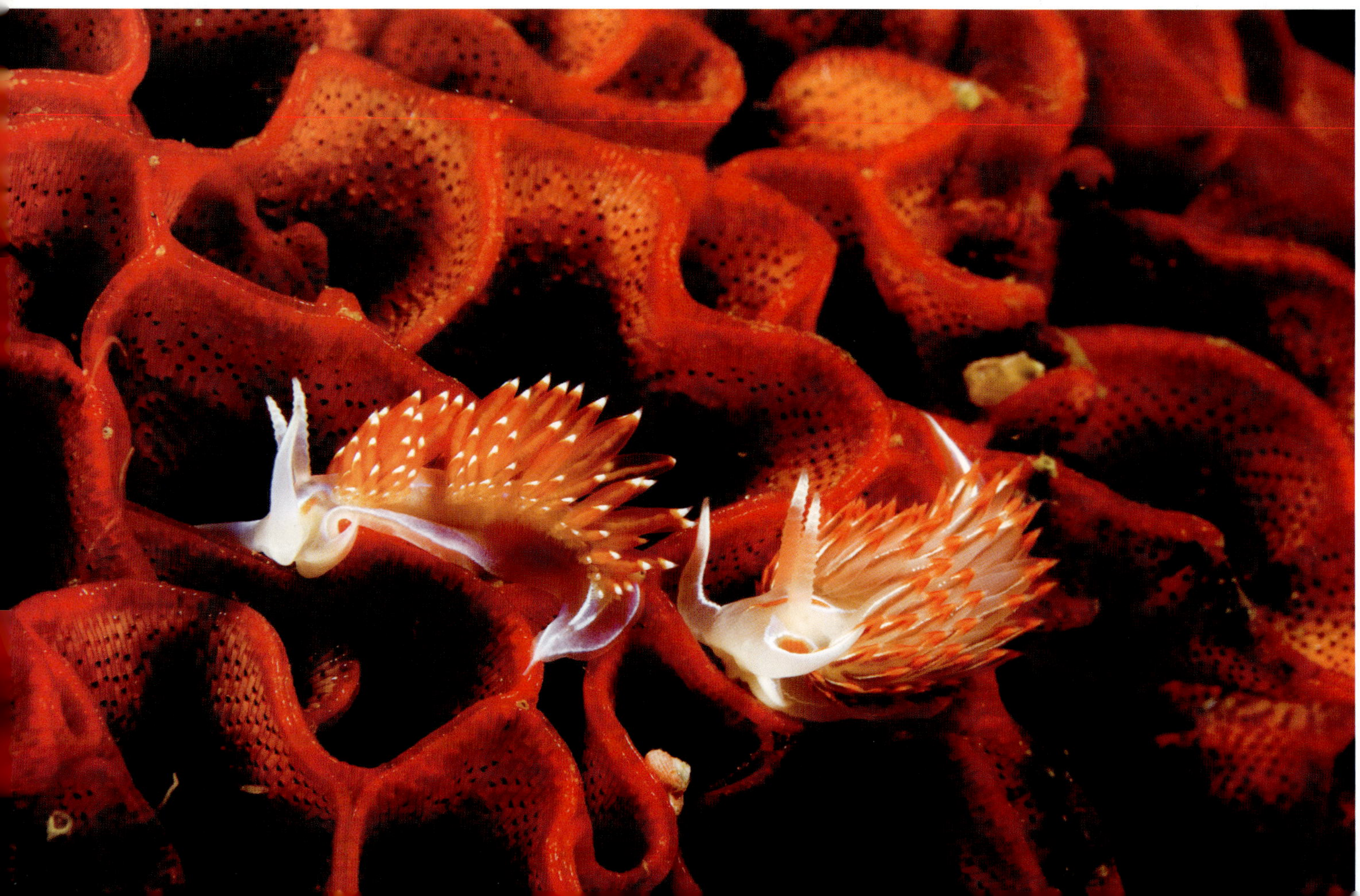

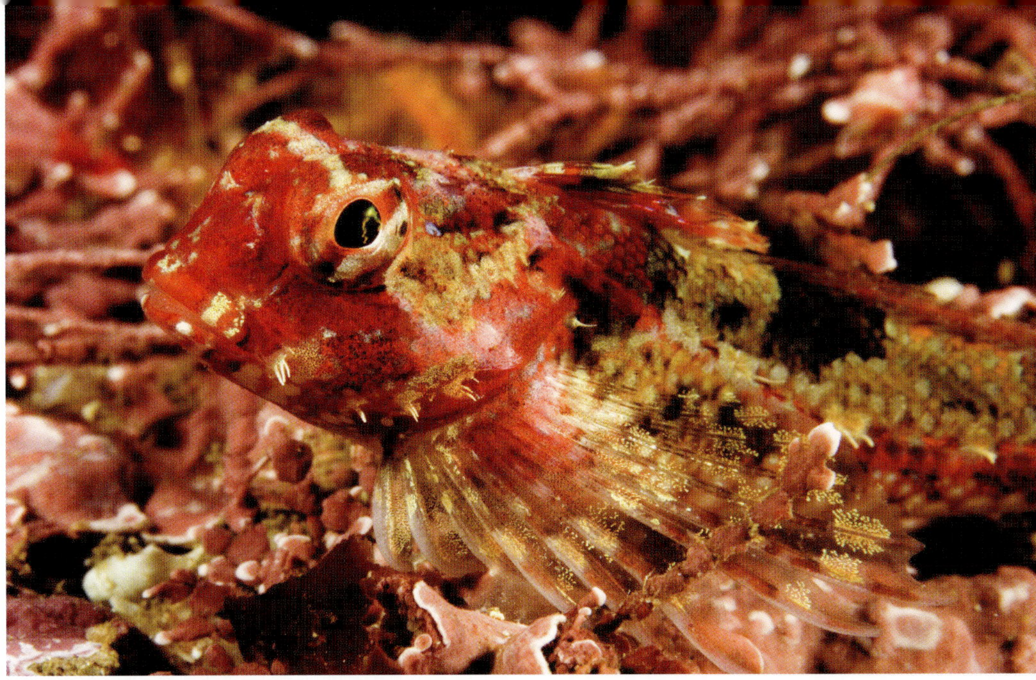

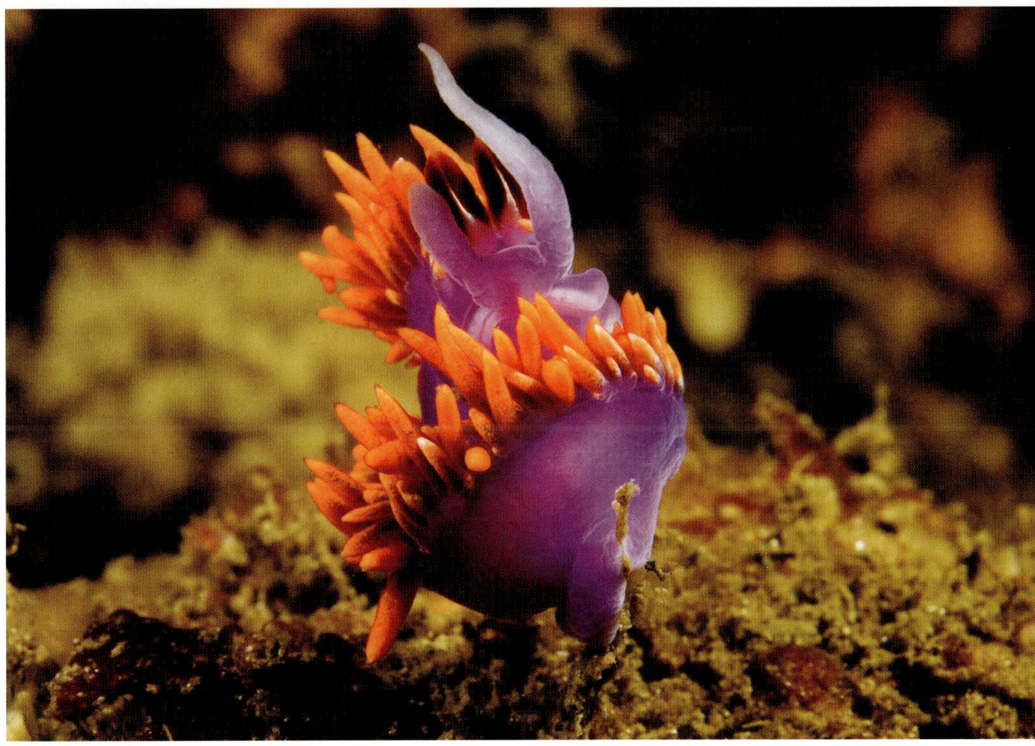

**Top**—Snub-nose Sculpin, *Orthonopias triacis,* a bit over 2 inches in size. Exposure: f/16, 1/200, and 400 ISO. Focal length 60mm. **Bottom**—Spanish Shawl, *Flabellina-iodinea,* measuring a little over 1 inch in length. Exposure: f/14, 1/200, and 400 ISO. Focal length 60mm. Photos courtesy of John Yasaki.

usual technique is to gear up, except for my fins, walk in to chest high, get finned up, and go. Coming out is about the opposite, though I like to be a bit shallower (between waist and chest) to make getting the fins off easier and having enough weight on my feet to walk. My camera pretty much stays in one hand.

I won't go out (beach diving) when the waves are more than shoulder high. Shoulder-high water is usually fairly easy to handle if you use the correct technique, but sometimes you still get hammered.

**Suiting Up.** I wear a dry suit and 3mm wet gloves. I haven't seen a dry glove system I like yet. There is some loss of dexterity with the 3mm gloves, but you get used to it. I've tried 5mm gloves on occasion, but they're just too thick to allow me to work my camera controls.

Our water temps generally range from about 48 to 56, and the average is probably 52. On occasion, the temperature is in the low 60s (El Nino years) or as low as 44. (By the way, 44 degrees is cold even in a dry suit!)

My dive sites tend to be deeper than the ones most people around here dive in. My favorite photo sites on the deep shale are all about 75 to 85 feet. If you throw in some of the other sites I dive often, we're talking about 60 to 110 feet. Occasionally I'll piddle around in shallow waters in the 20 to 40 foot range. There are lots of little critters and encrusting stuff in the shallows—but you won't see them unless conditions are calm.

My dive times are rarely over an hour. Usually it's depth dependent and is in the 40 to 45 minute range.

**Conceptualizing the Shot.** I think about where I need to be to get the right perspective, how skittish the subject will be, what's going to be blocking strobes—stuff like that. If I am photographing a fish, I usually try to get a couple of shots from far away to make sure I at least get an image I can ID from. Then I start working on the artsy shot (or good ID shot).

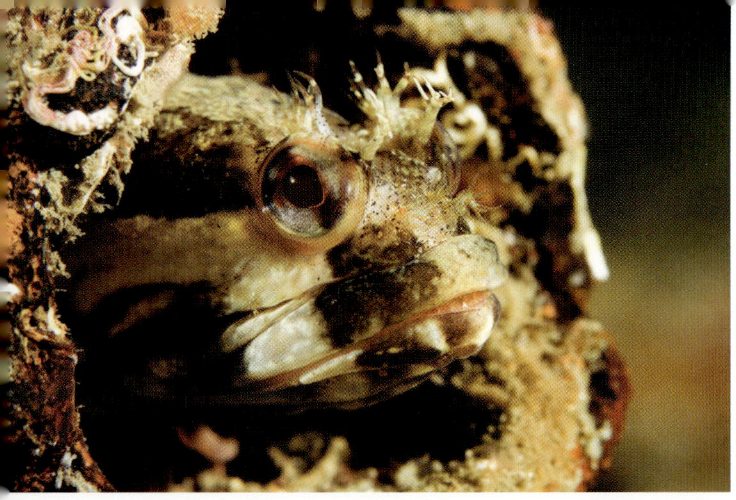
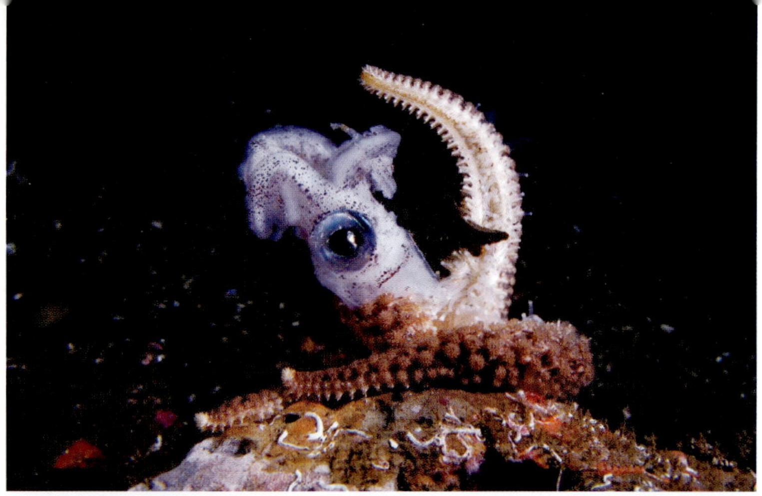
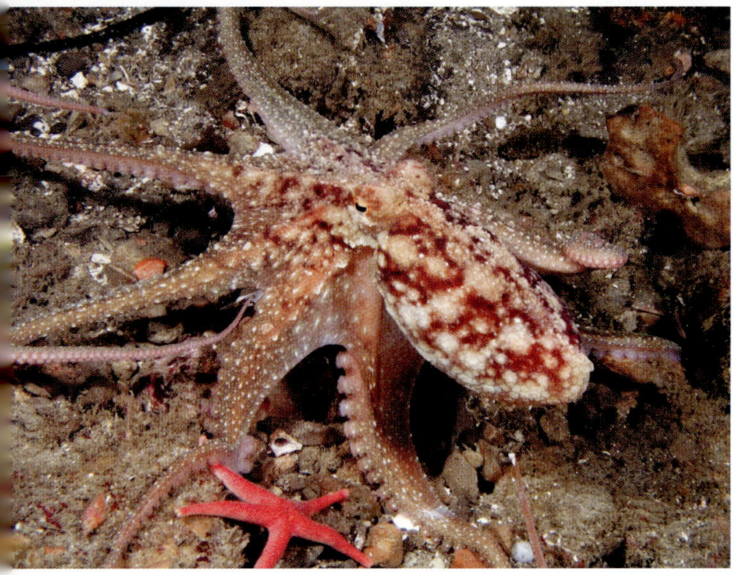
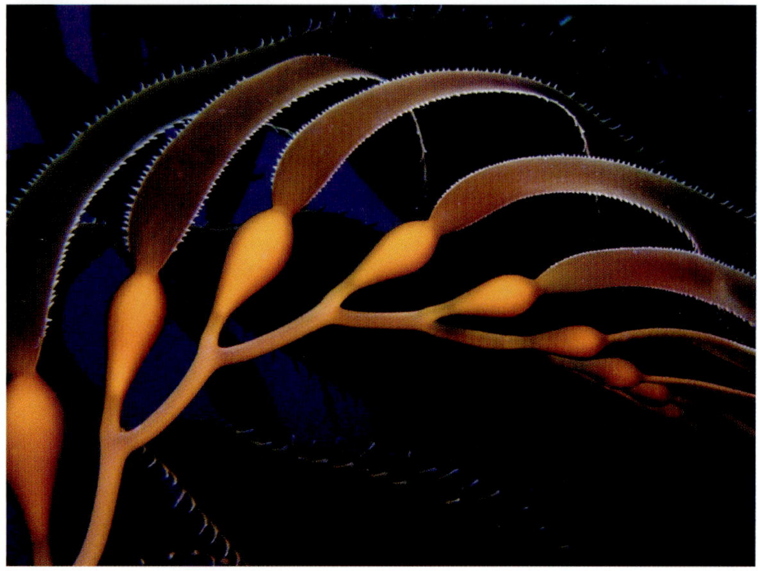

**Top left**—One-Spot Fringehead, *Neoclinus-uniotatus.* Exposure: f/8, $^1/_{200}$, and 400 ISO. Focal length 60mm. **Top right**—Red octopus at 80 feet. Exposure: f/8, $^1/_{125}$, and 64 ISO. Photos courtesy of John Yasaki. **Bottom left**—Sea Star eating a Market Squid. Exposure: f/2.8, $^1/_{125}$, and 64 ISO. **Bottom right**—Giant Kelp, *Macrocystis pyrifera.* Exposure: f/8, $^1/_{125}$, and 100 ISO.

**Challenges.** The limited visibility in the waters I shoot in is due to stuff in the water, and it usually shows up in the images. On a particularly "snotty" day, we may have $^1/_2$-inch chunks of particulate (though they're usually fairly sparse). The limited visibility means that, once you make it to the bottom, there isn't a lot of light on the subject. I *always* have a focus light but only need to use it about a third of the time. It's not that big a deal, but it's something you need to be aware of.

Due to the lack of water clarity, I don't get many opportunities to shoot wide angle images, so that can be a challenge for me.

**Common Mistakes.** I commonly make a number of mistakes: Not working hard enough to get a good perspective, not taking enough shots to make sure I get a decent image, not seeing if something (e.g., algae or critters) is blocking part of the subject, not varying the perspective or lighting or framing when I take multiple shots, not working at backscatter control (Photoshop is our friend!), and probably a bunch of other things.

**Tips.** Get low, get close, and then get even lower and closer. Work hard at lighting the subject with the inner edges of the strobe pools or be prepared for some long Photoshop sessions. Watch the surge so you don't end up crushing your subject.

# ALISON GRACEY

Alison shoots with a Nikon D90 camera with Aquatica housing. She says she loves her camera system to bits, but getting used to it has been challenging.

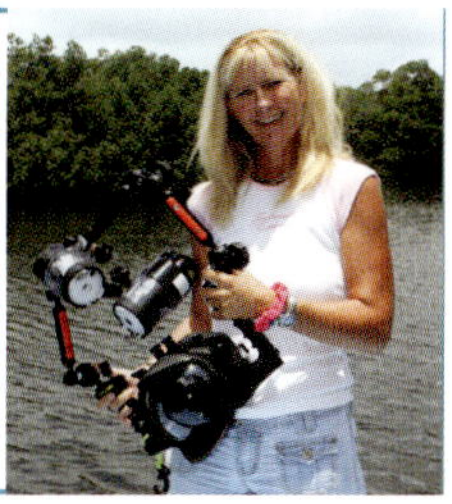

**The Shooting Environment.** In Panama, we don't get the big fish or the crystal-blue water, but there are still a lot of amazing things to photograph. My biggest challenges and wows have been the Sea Horses. I have been shooting them with a 60mm macro lens. Another challenge has been suspension in the water, which can really interfere with macro photography—especially when your lens decides to focus on a suspended particle rather than your subject!

Panama's green water makes lighting a challenge, but I am learning by diving and shooting—and repetition seems to help.

**The Approach.** Once I get over the initial excitement of finding something amazing like a sea horse, I think about my f-stop and where my strobes are pointed. I am always concerned about how long my subject will be in a position where I can shoot it. My first focus has been primarily on macro subjects, but I am gradually broadening my vision and doing a bit more distance work where conditions (visibility) allow—which is not often here in Panama. I frequently dive the same sites. This may sound boring to some, but doing so helps me become familiar with the places where the marine life can be found.

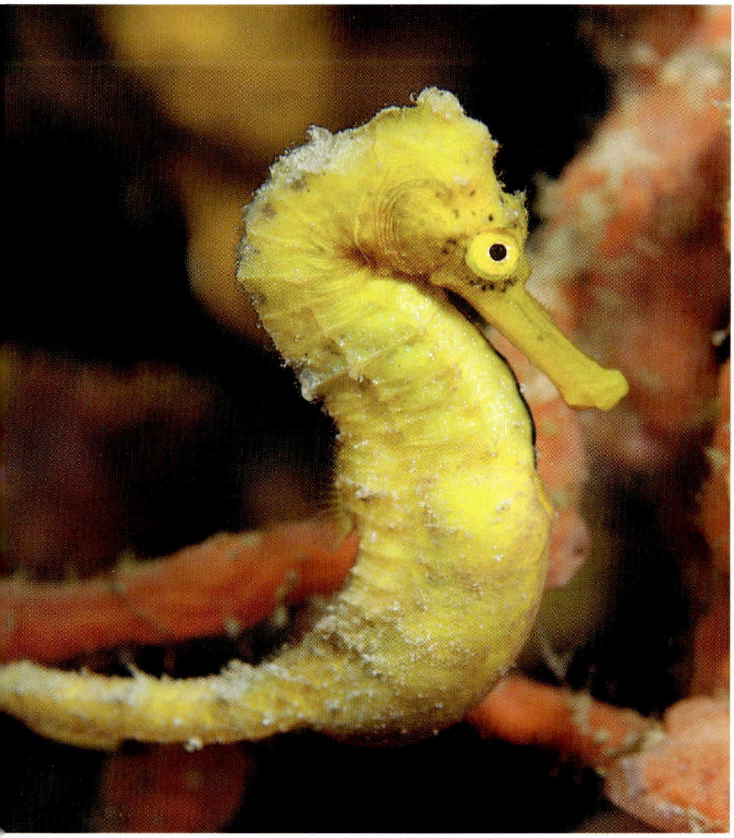

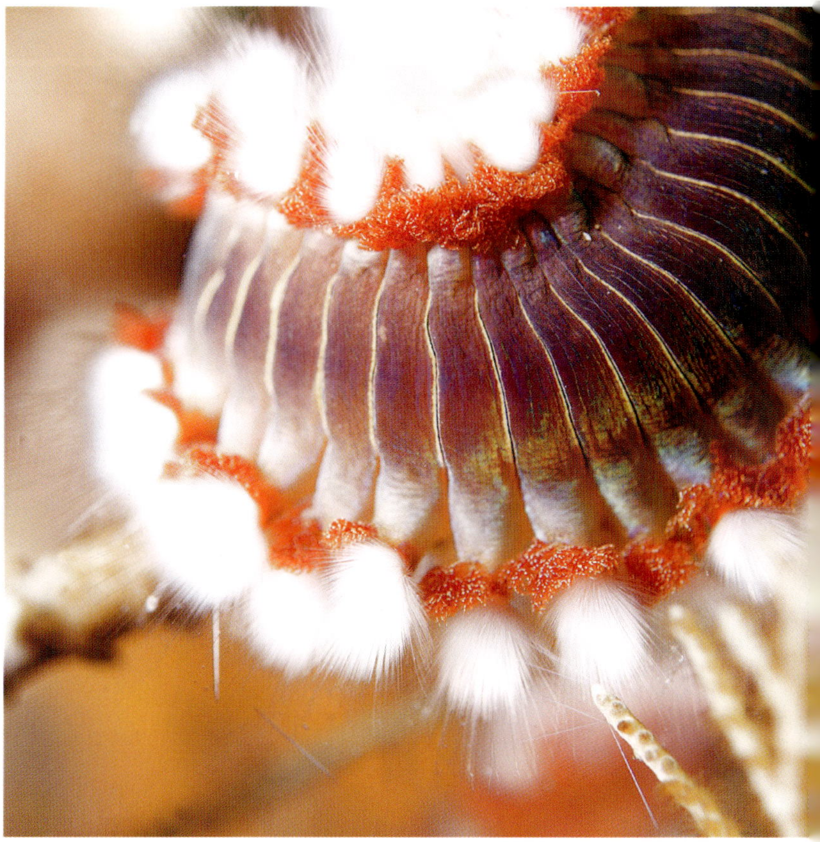

**Left**—Yellow Sea Horse. Exposure: f/5.6, $^1/_{125}$, and 200 ISO. Focal length 60mm. **Right**—The "art" of a Fireworm. Exposure: f/6.3, $^1/_{125}$, and 200 ISO. Focal length 60mm. Photos courtesy of Ali Gracey.

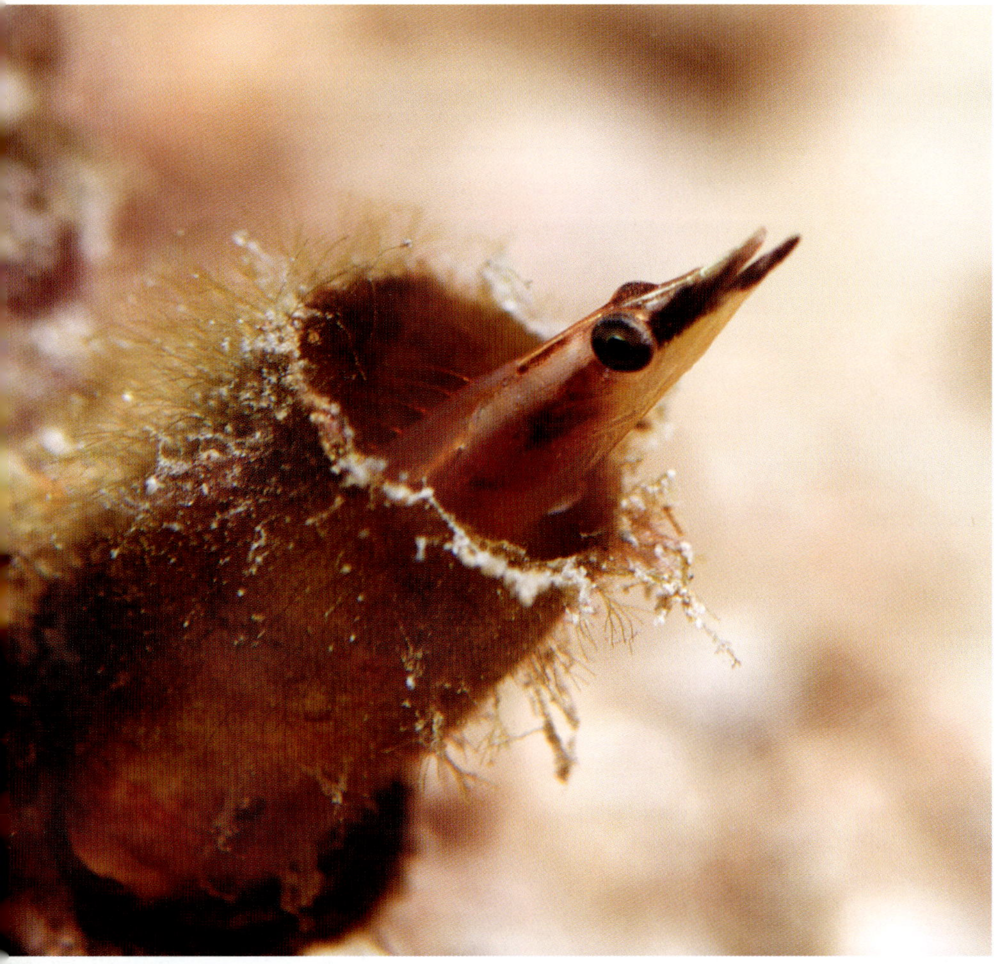

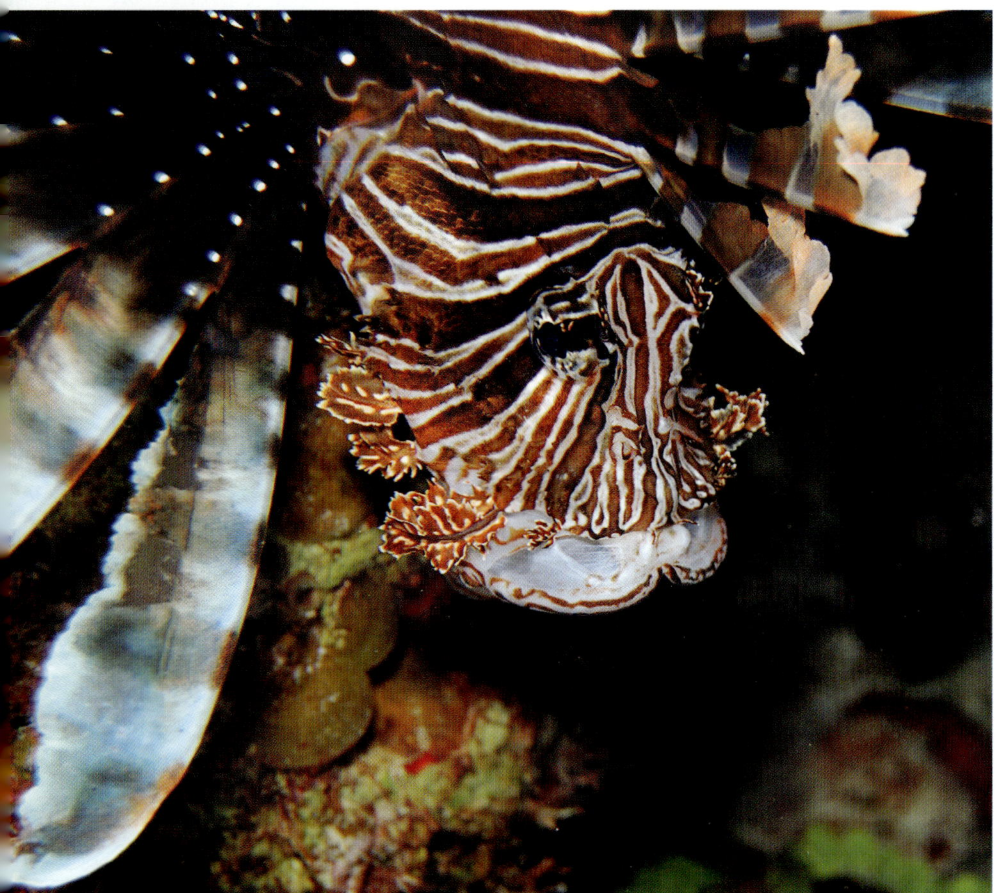

**Left**—(Top) An Arrow Blenny. Exposure: f/5.6, 1/125, and 200 ISO. Focal length 60mm. (Bottom) This portrait of a Lionfish documents their presence in Panamanian waters. Exposure: f/5.6, 1/125, and 100 ISO. Focal length 55mm. Photos courtesy of Ali Gracey.

**Right**—(Top) This Lettuce Slug is as large as they get at around 2 inches. Exposure: f/5.6, 1/125, and 200 ISO. Focal length 60mm. (Center) A sponge provides a home to this thumbnail-sized crab. Exposure: f/6.3, 1/125, and 200 ISO. Focal length 60mm. (Bottom) Like many creatures, this Toadfish blends in very well with its surroundings. In this case, the fish's eye "blew its cover" and caught the eye of the photographer. Exposure: f/5.6, 1/125, and 200 ISO. Focal length 60mm. Photos courtesy of Ali Gracey.

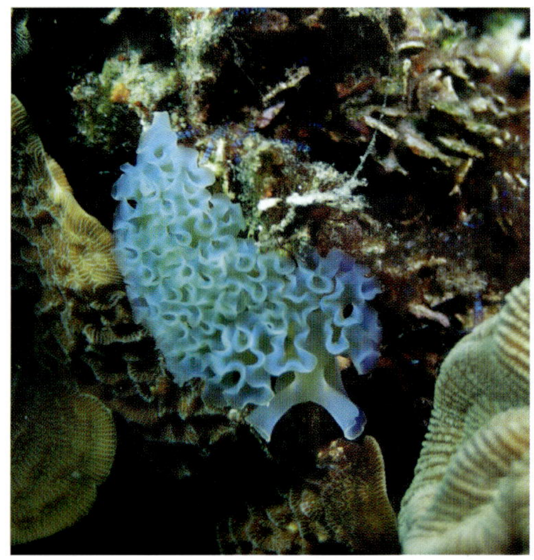

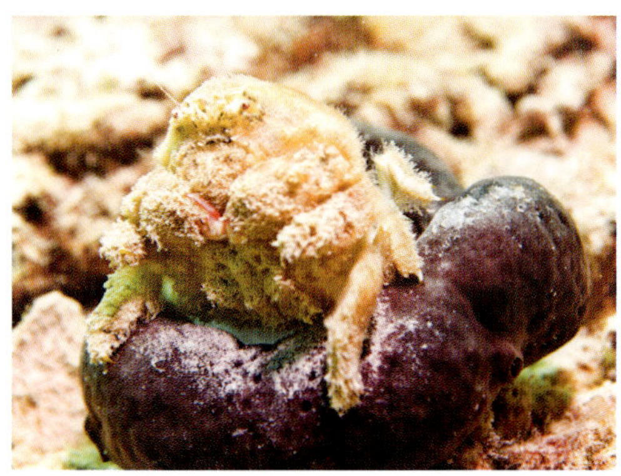

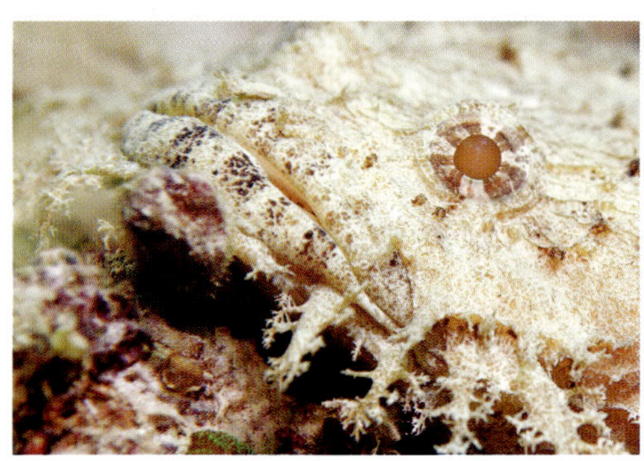

## STEVE MINOR

Steve Minor uses a Canon SLR in a housing made by Seatool. He favors his 18–55mm zoom lens. When not shooting stills, he uses his Sony HDR-SR12E video camera in an Ikelite housing.

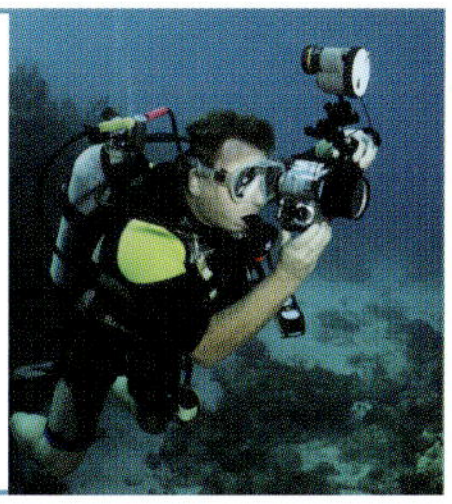

**Pre-Planning.** I cannot be sure what my subject will be when I take that leap into the water. All I know is that I will be presented with a variety of subjects at different depths, in different lighting conditions, and that each will require a different reaction time.

For me, the subject opportunities fall into three groups. I approach all of them with my equipment adjusted to my standard settings.

The first group are those subjects that allow me to compose shots from different angles and different settings. I enjoy this group because I can get instant feedback and adjust the strobe position and/or camera settings. When photographing this group, I will almost certainly get a "keeper" image.

The second group of subjects are those that are fast-moving or easily spooked. These require a great deal of stalking. In this scenario, my abilities as a scuba diver are tested as much as my ability to take a great shot. As my buoyancy control has improved, I've been able to capture some of my favorite images. Again, if I have time, I will experiment with the settings.

When working with these subjects, my knowledge of my equipment is put to the test, as the quick reaction time that is required does not allow me the luxury of thinking about and looking for the correct button to press. I enjoy the challenge of photographing subjects in this group. Getting a "keeper" is extremely satisfying because of all of the work involved in getting it.

The third group are those subjects that appear out of nowhere and only allow me a shot or two before they disappear. Here, reaction time is crucial. My aperture and shutter speed settings are the farthest things from

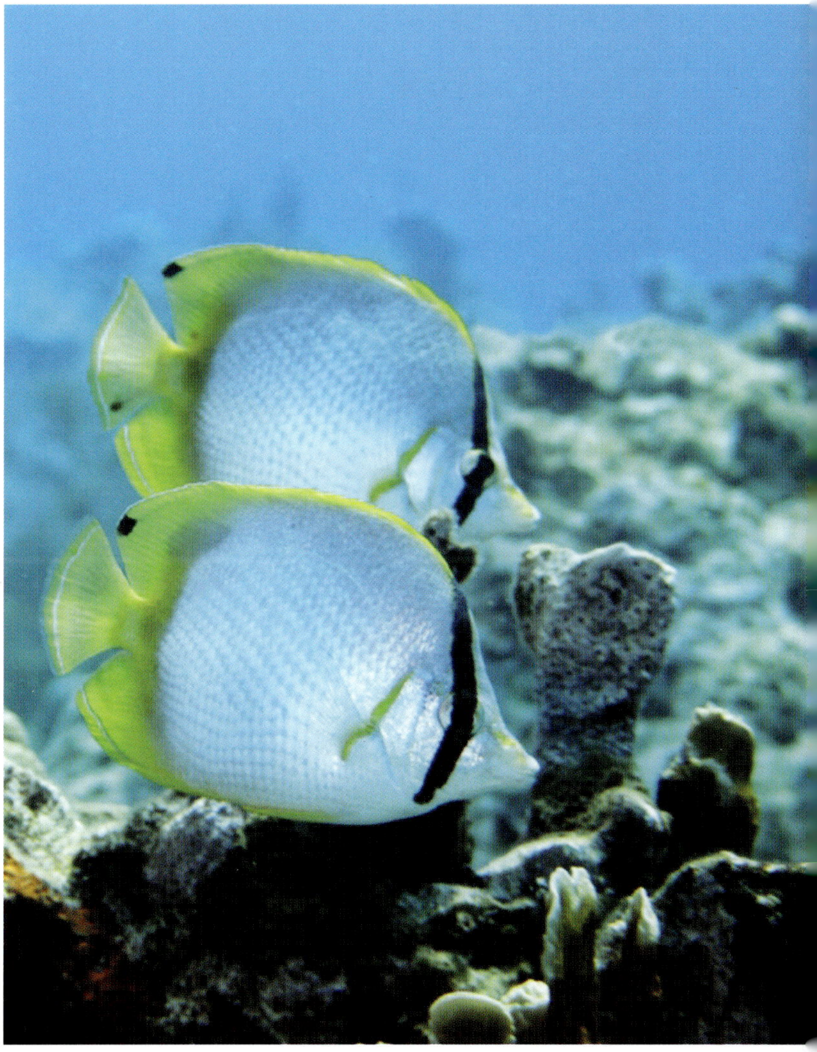

**Above**—Mates for life. Exposure: f/3.5, $^{1}/_{125}$, and 100 ISO. Focal length 55mm. Photo courtesy of Steve Minor.

my mind. I just hope that my standard settings will do the job. It is a challenge for me to manage my excitement and think about getting the best composition—especially when the subject is not one I come across on most dives. Some of my "keeper" images of subjects in this group have come down to luck. In other words, I was in the right place at the right time and my standard settings worked in the given conditions.

There are times when you come across magnificent subjects but, for whatever reason, the conditions just don't favor attempting a shot. When this happens, I look away from the viewfinder and just watch in fascination. Somehow I can still remember these moments without a picture to keep.

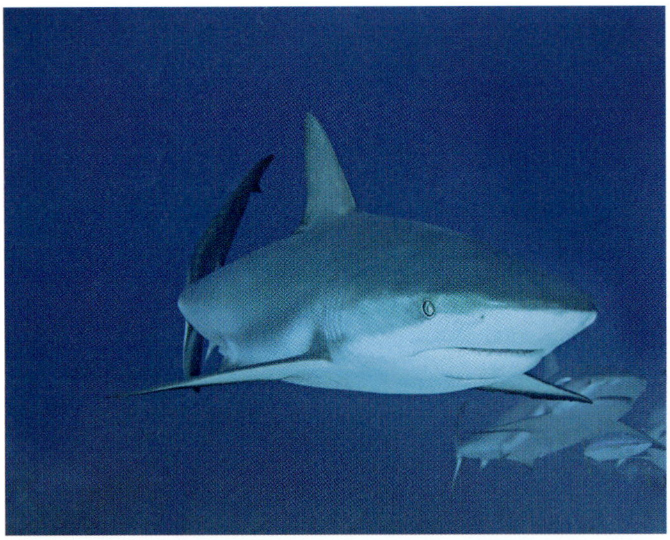

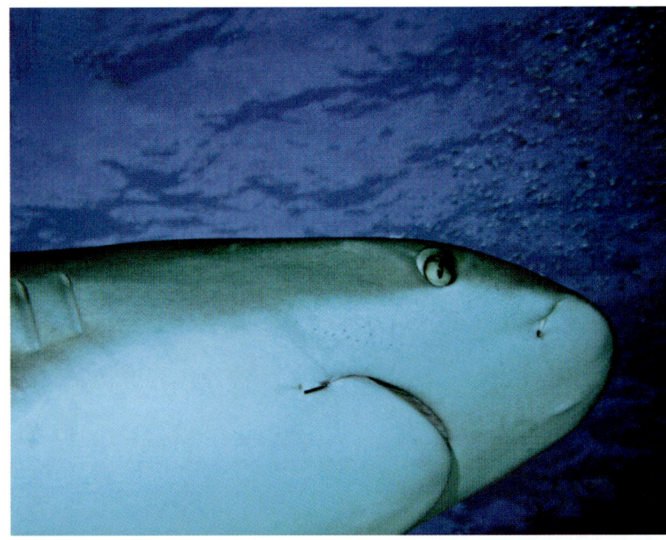

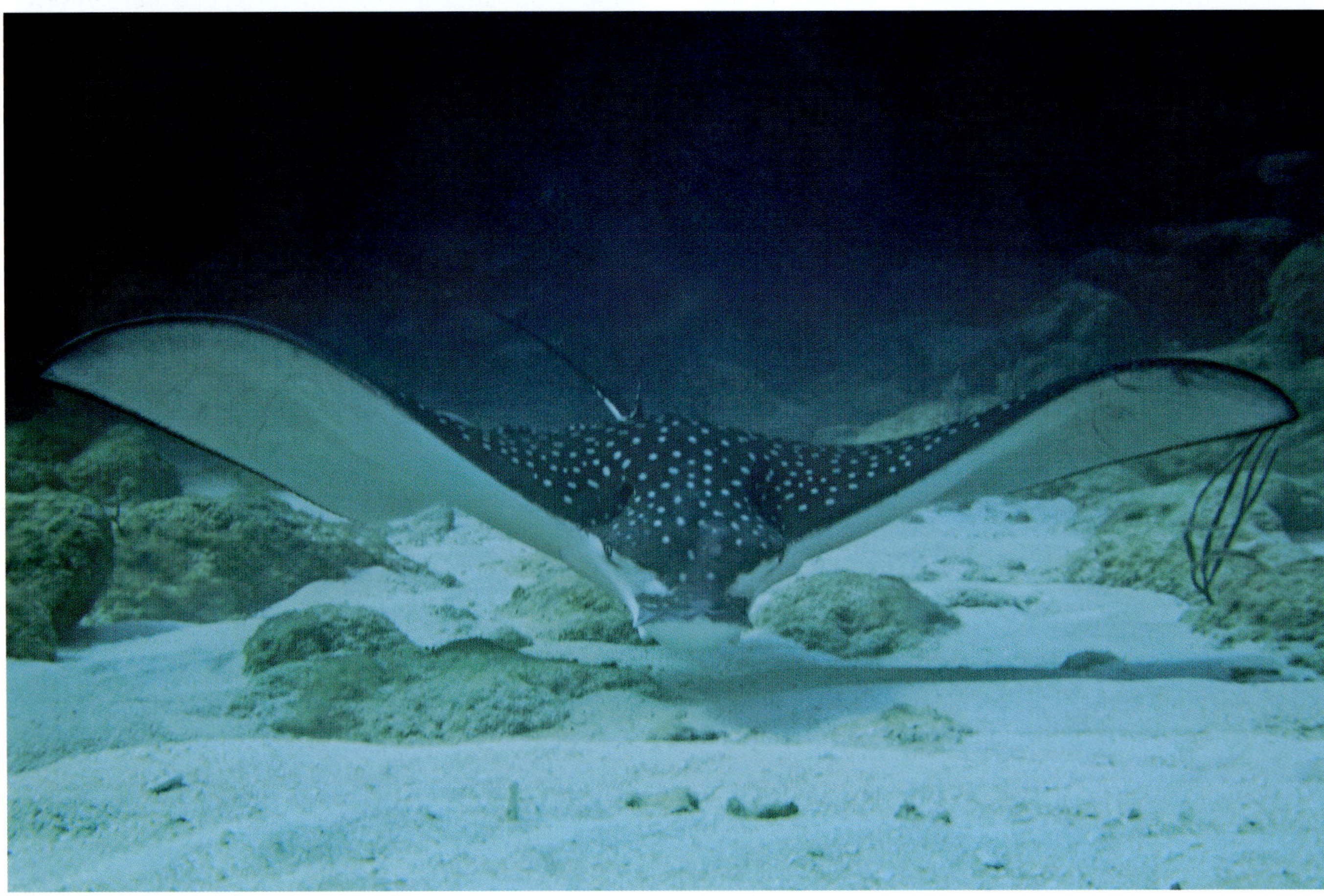

**Top left**—Close encounter. Exposure: f/6.7, 1/125, and 100 ISO. **Top right**—Closer encounter. Exposure: f/8, 1/125, and 100 ISO. Focal length 55mm. **Bottom**—Eagle Ray coming through! Exposure: f/5.6, 1/125, and 100 ISO. Focal length 55mm. Photos courtesy of Steve Minor.

# 7. AFTER THE DIVE

Not all of us live near the coral reef or other inland dive sites. Most of us are unable to do underwater photography frequently and on a moment's notice, much less year round. Most of us can dive just a few times a year. So, what do we do when we're unable to dive and take pictures? We work with them in photo-editing and organizing programs and share them, of course! That's what underwater photographers do.

## WORKFLOW

The means we use to organize, edit, and publish/share/distribute/sell and retrieve our photographs is called the workflow.

There are a few tools we need in order to conduct and manage the workflow. We need a computer, a means to download our photos onto it, and a software program or application to help us organize, edit, and output our photographs.

*Note:* The sample workflow that follows was designed for use with a Canon camera, Windows platform, and programs primarily from Adobe. However, it can be adapted for use with other cameras, platforms, and software. This workflow speaks to working with RAW files as well as the more commonly used JPEG files.

**Download.** The first step in the process is to download the image files on the camera's memory card to a newly created folder onto the computer's hard drive. Create a descriptive label for the folder. It can be named by date, location, subject, etc. I name my folders with "who and when" or "where

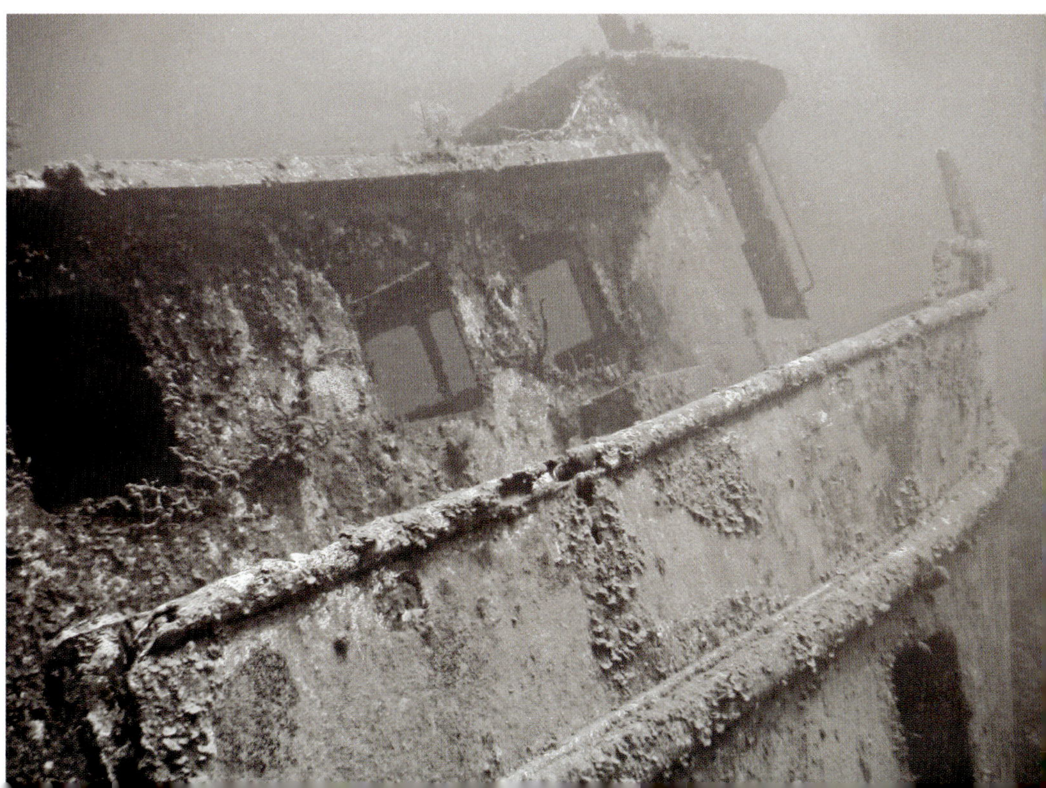

**Right**—Shipwrecks make good subjects for black & white photography. To get a substantial amount of the ship in the frame, the photographer must often shoot from too far away to capture color—so why not just make the capture in greyscale? Exposure: f/3.5, 1/125, and 100 ISO. Focal length 20mm. Photo courtesy of Mary Moyer.

and when" descriptors. *(Note:* I choose not to organize my images via imaging software because not all programs play nice with each other and some will cause you to wrestle with them when it comes time to access the files.)

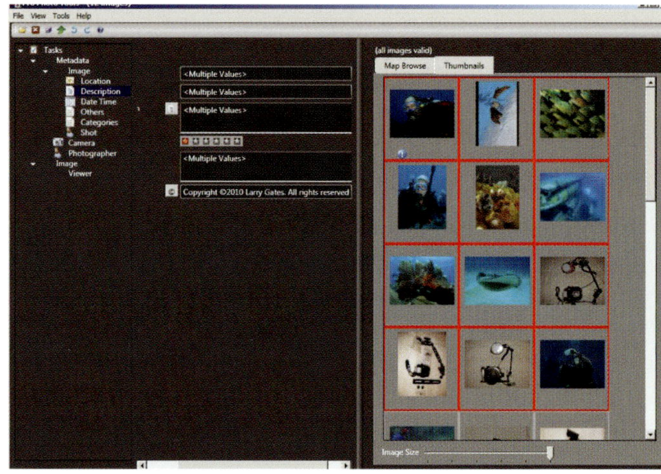


Leave the data on the memory card for now.

If your camera did not embed your copyright info into the files' metadata, then embed this info using a photo-editing program. Microsoft's Pro Photo Tools is one, Irfanview is another, and both are free.

Back up the folder to another storage device or copy it to a CD or DVD. I use an external hard drive. Once this is done, it is safe to delete the files from the memory card. I do so by inserting the memory card in the camera and formatting the card.

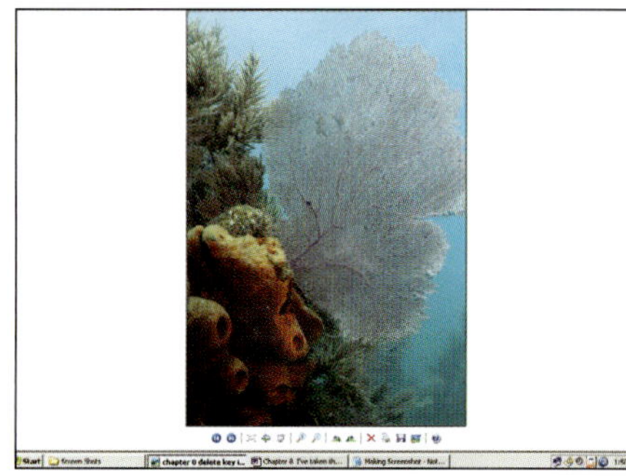

Top—Embed copyright information in the image metadata. **Bottom**—This photo is a candidate for deletion. I got an incomplete image of the otherwise acceptable scene of a Purple Seafan complemented by the sponge color.

**Review the Images.** Working from the newly created folder on the computer, perform a three-pass review of the images. During the first pass, look to see what you've got in the can. During the second pass, make sure the image is in focus, correctly exposed, nicely composed, and of an interesting subject. If it isn't, send it to the trash bin. When you are trying to decide whether to keep or delete an image, ask yourself if you got what you wanted in the image and what you are going to do with the picture.

Being a harsh critic will result in keeping far fewer photographs, but the keepers will be easier to manage and will make a much richer portfolio.

During the third pass-through, we are still looking to delete images. If we did our job during the shoot, we should be looking at several versions of the same subject or scene. Our job at this point is to pick the best one. Ask yourself if there is more than one reason why you should keep a photo (or multiple photos) of a subject. If there isn't, delete it.

**Image Editing and Retouching.** Now that we've scaled our image inventory back to only the best shots, it is time to finesse them a bit to make them look their best. If your photo was captured in RAW, then your first edits will be completed in the RAW file area of the editor or in a RAW file converter/reader. If the capture was made in JPEG, then you will open the file using your photo editing software.

I capture using either JPEG or RAW + JPEG. When I've captured both, I begin the editing process with the RAW version, as edits to the RAW file are nondestructive. When finished, I open the edited RAW in a photo-editing program. When this is done, the photograph and edits made in RAW are applied and the file is converted to another file format, such as PSD. The RAW file itself remains in its original unaltered/unedited state.

When working with a JPEG file, my first step is to duplicate the image. Once this is done, I close the original image, send it back to its folder, and save the duplicate in the TIFF format. *(Note:* When RAW files are opened in an Adobe program, they open as PSD files.)

At this stage, I must decide whether or not to crop the image. I still believe it is best to crop with my fins and compose in-camera. However, today's dSLRs create large file sizes that allow us to crop to improve the composition and still have enough image data to make a substantial sized print. In the vast majority of instances, I maintain the aspect ratio of the camera sensor when cropping for composition.

I do not want to fill my hard drives with files cropped for every conceivable print size. So, in instances when the print size I want has a different aspect ratio than my camera's sensor, I leave the cropping to the person who makes the print. I can collaborate with my printer if there is a decision to make as to what ends up being cropped out in order to make the print of a given size work.

My next step is to touch up my photograph, if necessary, and remove distracting particulate matter. Most photo-editing programs have a clone tool or healing brush, and either can be used to make this edit.

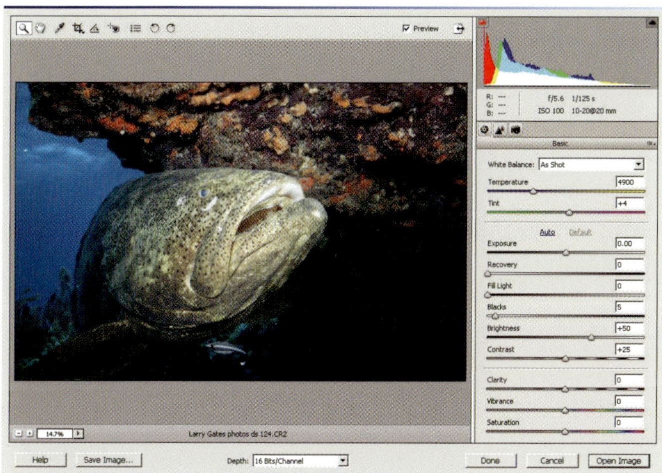


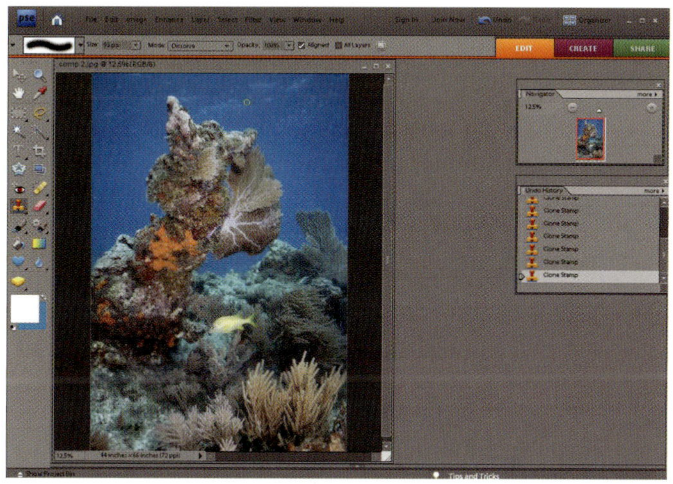


**Left**—RAW file opened in a RAW file reader/editor. **Right**—JPEG file opened in a photo-editing program.

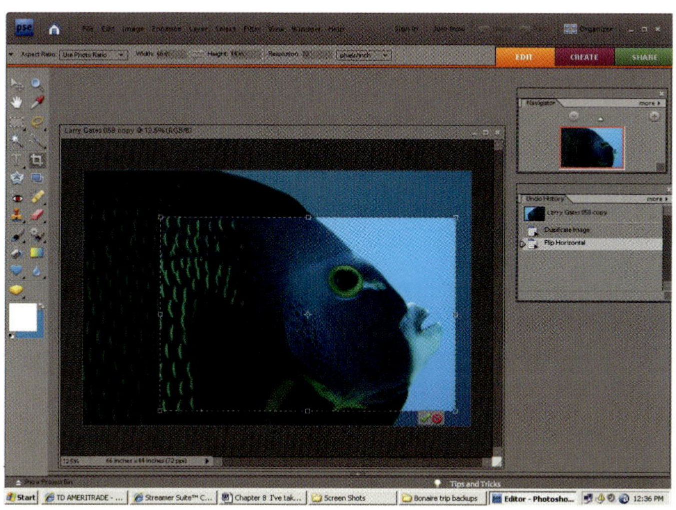


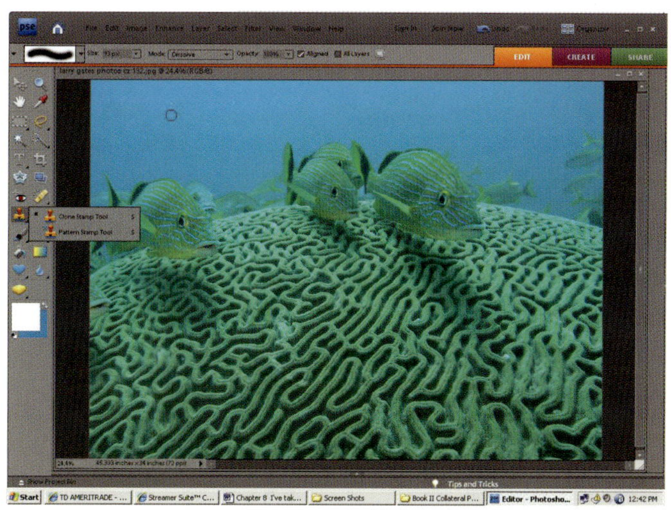


**Left**—Cropping the photograph. Every photo-editing program I'm familiar with has a crop tool. **Right**—Editing out backscatter with the Clone tool.

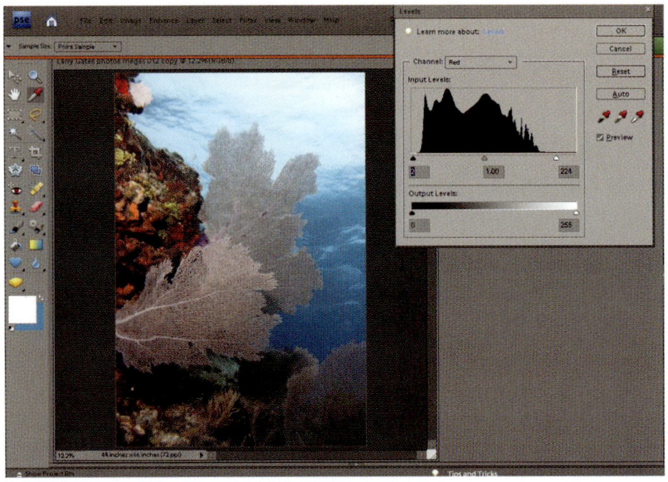

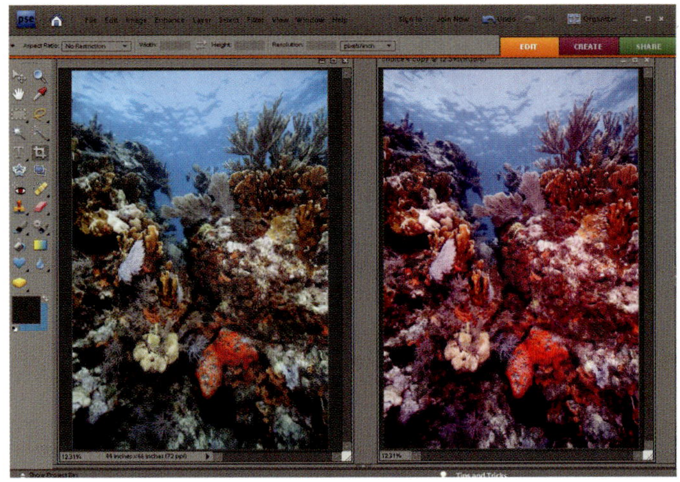

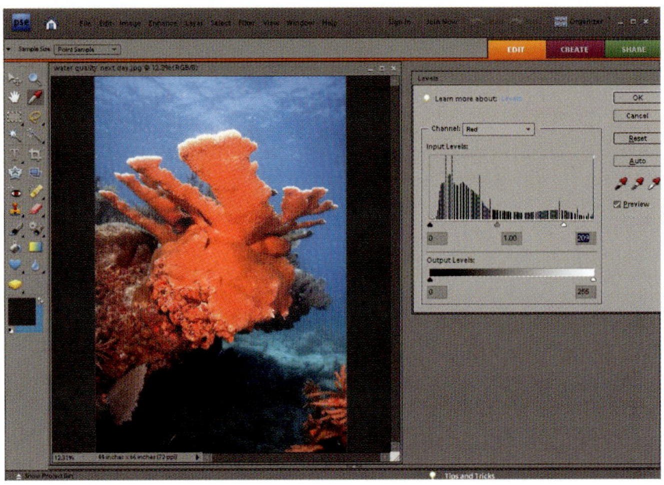

**Top left**—Using the Levels feature in the editing stage to adjust for exposure and color balance. **Top right**—The photograph on the left is edited in an acceptable manner. The photograph on the right is over-edited. **Bottom**—In this photo, the red channel was over-edited. There are reds in the lower-right corner of the photo, where there were none. Also, overworking the red channel can wash out highlight areas in the photo, such as the leading edge of the Elkhorn coral. Finally, Elkhorn coral is not really that color.

I do this edit now because if the photograph cannot be successfully touched up, it is not likely worth doing further edits to it.

*Adjusting Exposure and Color Balance.* My next step is to investigate whether the photograph can be improved by a tweak of the photo's exposure and color balance. My favorite tool for this is Levels (in Adobe products). Another tool sometimes employed is Curves (also Adobe). RAW files should be judged in the RAW reader, and enhancements should be made using its tools. Lightroom (v. 3) offers effective tools for adjusting the white balance, exposure, or color balance of JPEG or RAW files.

Adobe's Shadows and Highlights and Brightness and Contrast adjustments are weaker tools, as they do not allow for fine adjustments. However, they can still be useful in some situations.

When adjusting for color (white balance in this context), I work with individual color channels—the red channel, green channel, and blue channel—rather than the composite RGB channel.

Avoid over-adjusting any of the color channels. To gauge the effectiveness of the adjustment, look at the edited image. Does it look right? Next, look at the histogram to make sure that the data looks good (more on this below).

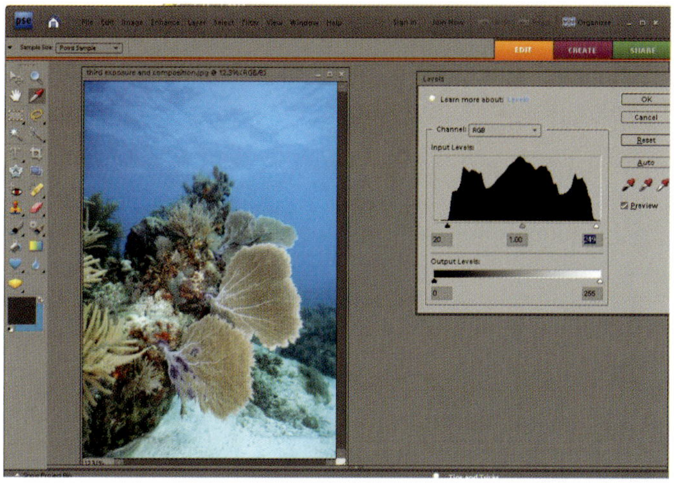

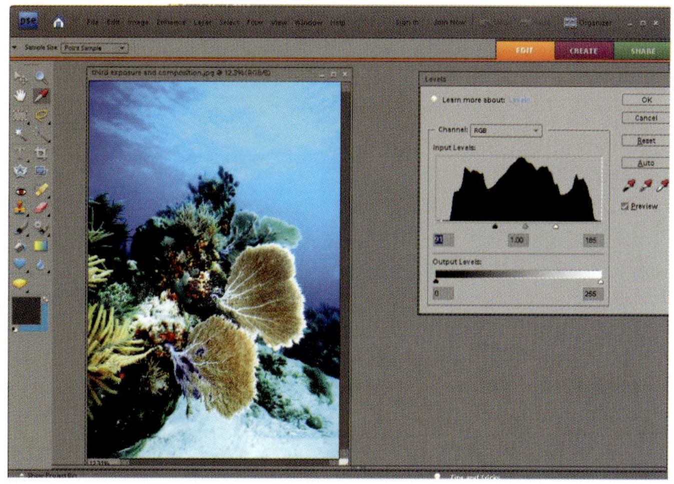

**Left**—The histogram shows the data is not extending from 0 to 255. In these instances, we can move the sliders inward so that they meet up with the start and end points of the data. **Right**—In some cases, moving the sliders under the data can result in an over-edited photograph.

## A CALIBRATED MONITOR

When working with our images, a calibrated monitor is essential. Monitors come calibrated for use in an office environment (e.g., to view documents, not photographs), so we will need to make some adjustments to ensure our monitors accurately display our image colors as they were captured. There are various monitor-calibration utilities on the market (a simple Google search will yield many options), and some monitors come with their own calibration utilities.

Keep in mind that the color your monitor displays may change as it ages. This means that you should periodically re-calibrate your monitor to ensure that what you see is what you get.

Red is the first color we lose in underwater photography and try to restore in postproduction. We are usually good to go with blue and green. In postproduction, we sometimes are tempted to conjure up the reds we've lost. Unfortunately, overworking the red color channel can have some undesirable—if not horrific—results.

A histogram is a graphical representation of all of the tones in an image. In a histogram, 0 is equivalent to black and 255 represents white. In photographs where there is little or no detail in the shadow areas (underexposure), the data will run off the left side of the scale. In images where there is no detail in the highlights (overexposure), the data will run off the right side of the graph.

Ideally, all of the data in the histogram will begin and end at the 0 and 255 points. Where it is stacked up along the scale is less critical. Data may be stacked on the left side of the histogram if there were many darker areas within the photograph.

We can adjust the sliders under the histogram to affect the exposure. For example, if the data does not reach the 0 end of the scale, we can move the slider at that end of the scale toward the right until it is positioned under the data's starting point. It is not mandatory that the sliders be adjusted to this position. Sometimes we can produce the look we are after by moving the slider a little closer to the start/end of the data.

*Sharpening.* The next step is to sharpen the image. The amount of sharpening required for an image depends on its intended use. One sharpens to one degree for print purposes and to another degree for online publication. Because of this, you may want to leave the images in this folder unsharpened until you know how they will be used.

I very rarely sharpen my photographs because I do not see well enough to gauge the results of my editing (unless I grossly oversharpen). I don't want my sharpening talents (or lack thereof) to interfere with the talents of my printer, who may decide to sharpen the photograph before making a print.

The Unsharp Mask filter shows a preview window and three sliders—Amount, Radius, and Threshold.

My friend, professional photographer Theresa Stack, recommends using the two-two-two method when preparing for Web distribution: 200% for Amount, .2 for Radius, and 2 for Threshold.

One printer told me that when sharpening, he will begin by using settings of 100% for Amount, .2 to .5 for Radius, and 2 to 5 for Threshold and adjust from there, if needed. Do not to oversharpen, as doing so will result in noise.

Finally, sharpening is not a cure for focusing errors.

*Key-Wording.* The final step in this part of the workflow is to keyword the photo. Key-wording can be done on an individual photo; if you are key-wording a group of similar photos (e.g., corals, or fish, or divers), you can use the batch process feature to make the task quicker and easier. If not done

## COLOR CALIBRATION AND COLOR SPACES

Unfortunately, there is more to achieving accurate color rendition in your images than simply calibrating your monitor. To produce an image with colors that do our subject and scene justice, we must make sure all of the devices we use in our workflow are operating in the same color space.

Our eyes can perceive a wide gamut of colors, tones, shades, highlights, and shadows. Unfortunately, the devices we use to capture, edit, and output our photographs are more limited.

Digital cameras are light-sensitive computers that record color in binary code (0s and 1s). Any of the devices in our workflow that render color use a color space—a system that maps out these 0s and 1s to try to reproduce, as accurately as possible, the colors we saw and recorded with our cameras. A variety of color spaces exist, and each has a unique gamut of color. To ensure the image color is rendered properly in the output stage, we must ensure that all of the devices used in our workflow use the same color space.

So, what color space do we choose? The color space with the widest gamut is generally the best bet, provided all of the devices in our workflow are capable of handling the gamut of the selected color space. Note that color spaces with a very wide gamut, such as ProPhoto, can cause problems. Because the monitor may be able to show more colors and tones than can be printed with ink on paper, color shifts may result. Color shifts can also occur if one converts from one profile to another, as the conversion simply uses the nearest match within the new gamut.

Most devices handle the sRGB and Adobe RBG color spaces. The sRGB color space works very well for outputting to a computer monitor and for displaying images on the Internet. Adobe RGB has a wider gamut. So long as the printer supports the color space, it can be a good choice for images that will be printed.

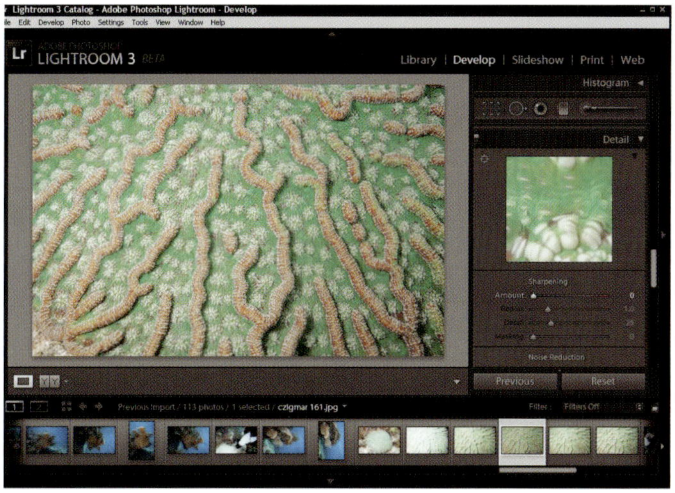


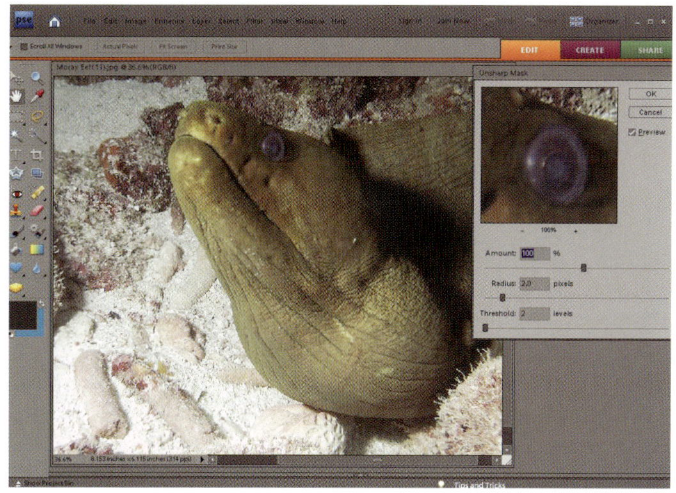

**Left**—Sharpening tool and its adjustments. **Right**—Sharpening using the Unsharp Mask (USM).

previously, copyright information can be added to the photograph's metadata at this stage as well.

In another person's workflow, key-wording may be done much earlier. I am only interested in key-wording keepers, so I key-word later in my workflow.

*Saving the Edited File.* Once done, the edited file is saved to the folder that contains the original photograph. The shoot folder will contain the original image (RAW, JPEG, or both) and the edited version, saved in the PSD or TIFF format.

When I am going to use a photograph, I duplicate the TIFF or PSD file and convert it to JPEG. If the image will be used on the Web, I downsize the file, add my watermark, and save the image. I create a folder to house the edited JPEG image(s) for the specific use (Web, print, stock images, book projects, etc.).

*Programs and Applications.* A myriad of photo-editing and organizing programs/applications exist that help us in our workflow. There are many that can handle much of the process and many that tackle one step or aspect best. While most work quite well for processing individual files and most can do some batch processing, others offer more types of batch processing.

What follows is a short list of some of these programs and applications, along with a brief description of their forte.

The mother of all photo-editing and organizing programs is Adobe's Creative Suite (CS). This suite, which includes a powerful image-editing program—Photoshop, can help us with our workflow from start to finish. CS is a comparatively expensive package, and some of its programs are not necessarily needed in our workflow.

Adobe also offers Photoshop Elements, a lighter-weight, less expensive version of Photoshop. In my opinion, the program offers all of the image-editing tools we need in our workflow (plus some we don't, like special effects filters). It can also be used to help us organize our images.

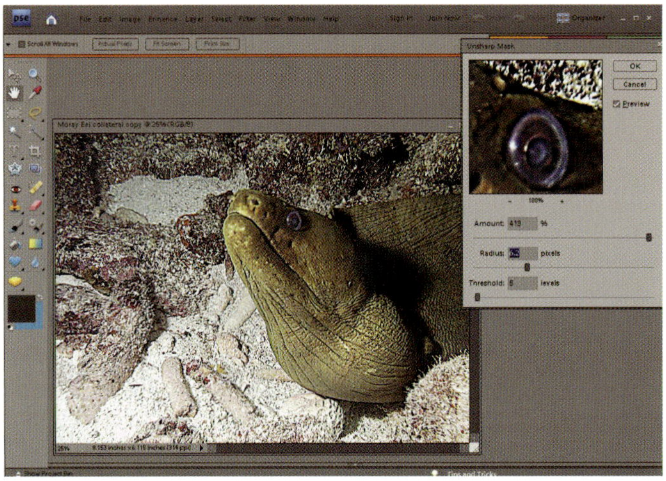

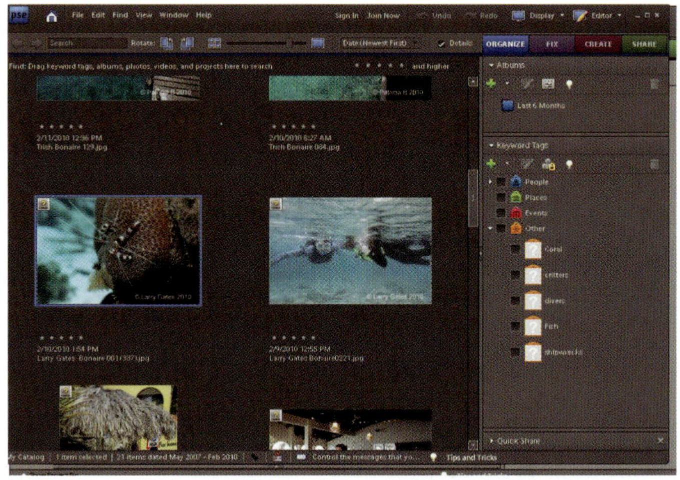

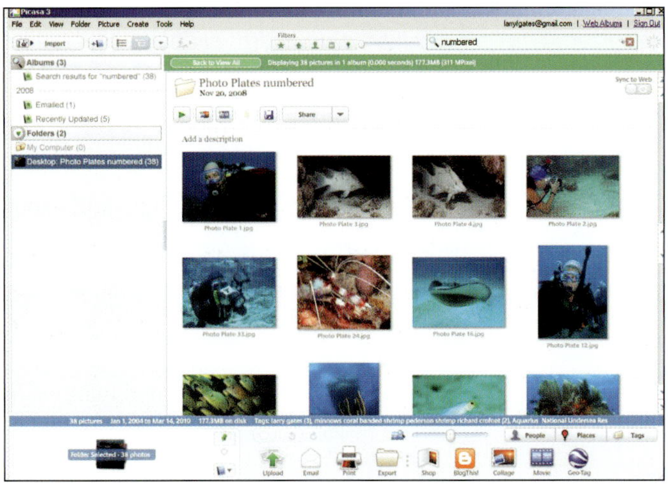


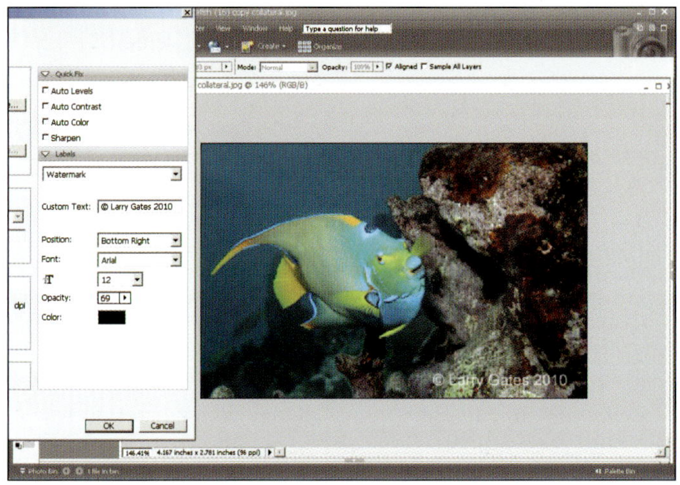


**Top left**—A photograph that suffered the effects of over-editing. In this case, it was the Unsharp Mask that created noise. **Top right**—Photo being key-worded. **Bottom left**—Picasa is a photo organizer/retriever program. **Bottom right**—A watermark can be added to the photo in the image-editing process. This watermarked image shows copyright protection and ownership.

Adobe Lightroom is a photo-organizing program with an ever-increasing number of photo-editing features built into each version. This program is capable of meeting most if not all of our workflow needs. It offers an elegant batch processing feature.

I use Lightroom for the bulk of my editing, Elements for the rest, and Picasa for "photo finding."

These Adobe software products are available for both Windows and Mac platforms.

GIMP (GNU Image Manipulation Program) is the open-source community's version of Photoshop. It is a general-purpose image editor that will function on Windows and Mac platforms as well as Linux distributions.

Mac/Apple's entrée into the photo-editing and organizing arena is Aperture. The program also contains a browser. It falls somewhere between Adobe's Photoshop and Lightroom in terms of features and function and provides all of the tools required to handle your workflow.

Mac's iPhoto allows you to browse, organize, edit, and share your images. It is similar to Windows' Photo and Fax viewer.

The above-mentioned programs or applications can meet or surpass our basic workflow needs. The following is a short list of programs or applications that are more specialized in handling particular aspects of our workflow:

Photo Mechanic, by Camera Bits, is a program that is designed for working with groups of photos. It is used to sort, tag (with copyright info and key wording, IPTC data, and fields), and make comparisons between photos. It also offers the ability to batch process. It is not a photo-editing program.

Irfanview is a photo viewer that also offers photo-editing tools and allows for batch processing and editing IPTC and other metadata.

Picasa, a free download from Google, is primarily a photo-retrieval program. It has editing features, but other programs and their editing tools are more robust. In my view, Picasa's long suit in this card game is helping to find a photo.

Once Picasa is installed, and from then on each time it is opened, it scans the computer's drives and locates all image files and folders. It builds a database of where the images are located on the computer. Its internal search engine will find a photo based on keywords or folder names. Alternatively, you can scroll through the folders of thumbnails to find the desired image.

Once opened, it displays two windows: The left window is a view of folders containing photos. The window on the right displays thumbnails of photos beginning with the last folder viewed using Picasa.

**Editing or Manipulating?** As we advance our skills in using photo-editing programs, we have a choice to make. Do we want a reputation for being a good shooter or a good photo editor? We can have both, as long as we stop short of manipulation. If you become known as one who manipulates photographs, your viewers

## METADATA

Metadata provides information about our image files. It can tell us who created the file, when it was created, the size of the photo in megabytes, the dimension of the image in pixels, and more. The means to viewing this information will depend on the program or application used. Consult the program's Help files to determine where and how to access the data.

EXIF (Exchangeable Image File Format) data, a subset of metadata, is embedded in a photograph at the time of capture. It allows us to see the exposure settings used when the photograph was taken. We no longer need to remember to record our exposure settings.

We can add information to the metadata by opening a file and going to File>File Info in Photoshop. There we will find various tabs that allow us to describe the photograph and name the person or group that has proprietary rights to it, assign a copyright status, add a key word to help us organize and retrieve our files, and more.

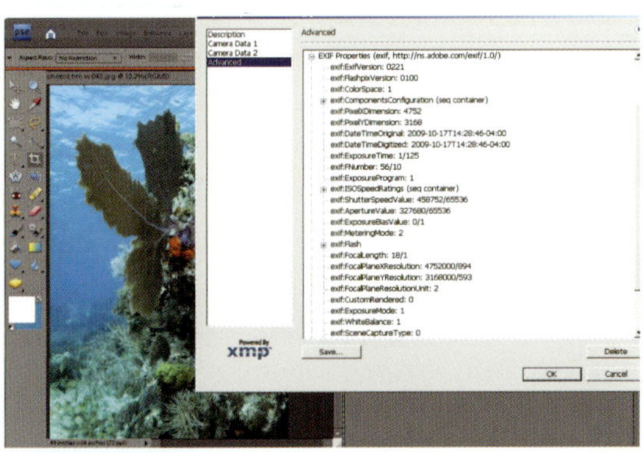

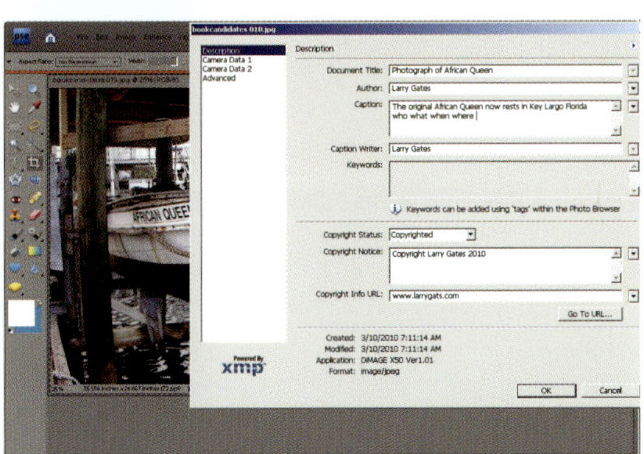

**Top**—Exploring metadata and, in this case, the image file's EXIF data. **Bottom**—IPTC Photo metadata is comprised of text fields describing the photograph and who has proprietary rights to it.

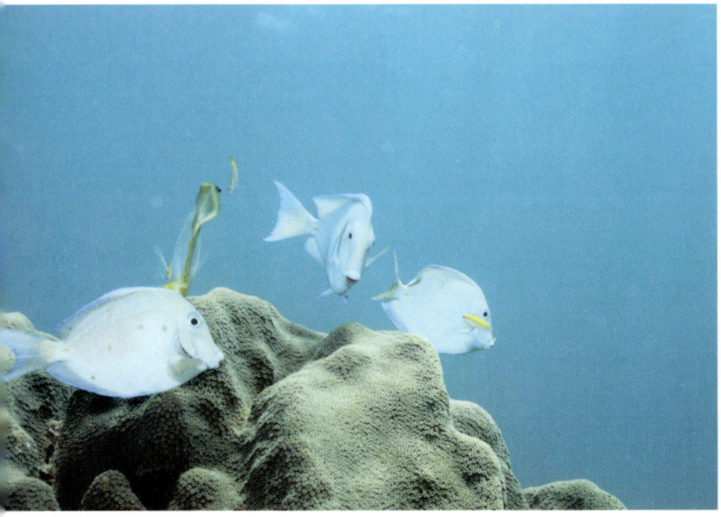

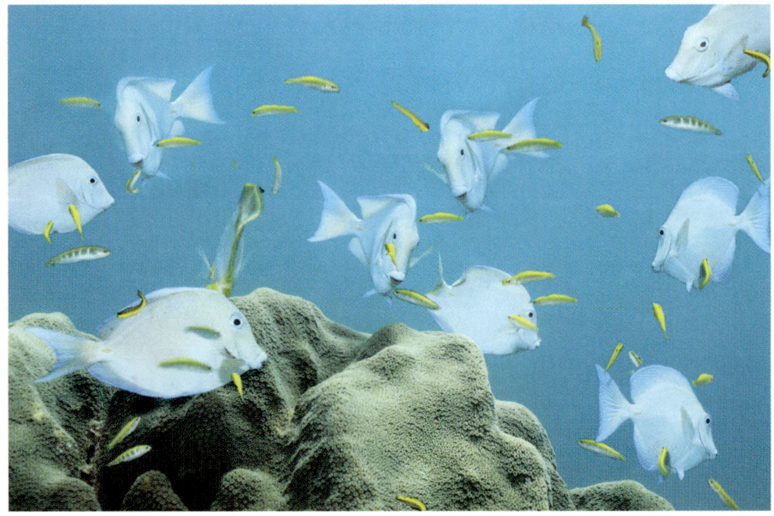

may wonder whether they are looking at something that really happened at that time and place or something you created on your computer.

Always be up front with your viewers. When you have retouched an image to bring out its best qualities, make this known. When an image is manipulated (like in the example above), share this fact with the viewers. (Most of the photographs in this book have been edited. With the exception of one photograph identified in this chapter, none have been manipulated.)

**Left**—What really happened at the given time and place. **Right**—Manipulation of what really happened at the time and place.

### PRICING YOUR IMAGES

Pricing is difficult for many photographers, as the "right price" for an image is somewhat dependent on the buyer or audience. For example, you may elect to charge a charitable organization less for an image they plan to use for a campaign than you would a corporate client who wants to spice up their magazine ad.

No matter what, do not give your work away—literally or figuratively. Asking too little for your work devalues it and cheapens the perceived value of underwater photography as a whole.

There are free online resources that may help you develop a pricing strategy for your images. Another helpful resource is Cradoc fotoSoftware's fotoQuote Pro.

If these options fail you, ask a professional photographer for guidance on what your photographs are worth. It may be embarrassing to ask for help, but keep in mind that the photographer has a vested interest in offering you guidance. Helping you develop an appropriate pricing system will help keep the market strong.

### KEEP IT ON THE LEVEL

Marketing photography services or photographs is a business. Should you decide to market your photography, be sure to establish a bona fide business—one that meets legal requirements.

# CONCLUSION

## MOVING FORWARD

No matter where we are in our pursuit of becoming advanced—or *more* advanced—underwater photographers, we can more easily reach our goals if we have patience. Great shots do not come easy. Yes, once in a while we get lucky and are in the right place at the right time. More often though, a great image is the result of using the right equipment, ensuring that it functions as it should, and making sure that we practice and keep our skills sharp. Shooting consistently well has much to do with shooting regularly. I live in Key Largo, the diving capital of the world, but when I am unable to shoot for whatever reason, it seems as if I am starting all over again when I enter the underwater realm.

As we evolve in our underwater photography, we take fewer yet better images. We learn to know whether or not capturing a good photograph is possible when we first encounter the scene and subject.

Once back in the water, I need to try to settle down and slow down. I want to focus on the task at hand—to take more than ordinary, run-of-the-mill photographs, and have fun while doing so. If I can do this, I will create at least one image that is a keeper—every time. As we evolve in our underwater photography, we take fewer yet better images. We learn to know whether or not capturing a good photograph is possible when we first encounter the scene and subject.

I find I take some of my nicest photos by starting out my dive, just enjoying the fact that I am diving and in a very wonderful place. As I descend into the depths, I find myself in a Zen-like frame of mind. I begin to look around, almost casually, for subjects. Even if I don't immediately see prospective subjects, I try to enjoy the moment. It is cool to scuba dive with my camera. If something appears, hopefully I will have the right equipment and technique to make the photograph. I know I am armed with the right attitude.

There are times when I am on a mission to photograph a specific subject. I may need an example to show my students later. During these times, I am applying my equipment and technique in tried-and-true ways to capture the photograph. I am not advancing. My growth as an artist comes when I am free to take chances, try new things, and fail—then simply try to improve.

I do not consider myself to be very creative. But when I am just diving with my camera with no particular mission or subject in mind, I often witness something ordinary and try to create something special from it. Sometimes I experiment with the lighting, expose for an artistic effect, or try a more artful composition. The things that come to mind sometimes yield great results.

There are also more formal ways to gain ground in your underwater photography. You can take a course in underwater photography, participate in an

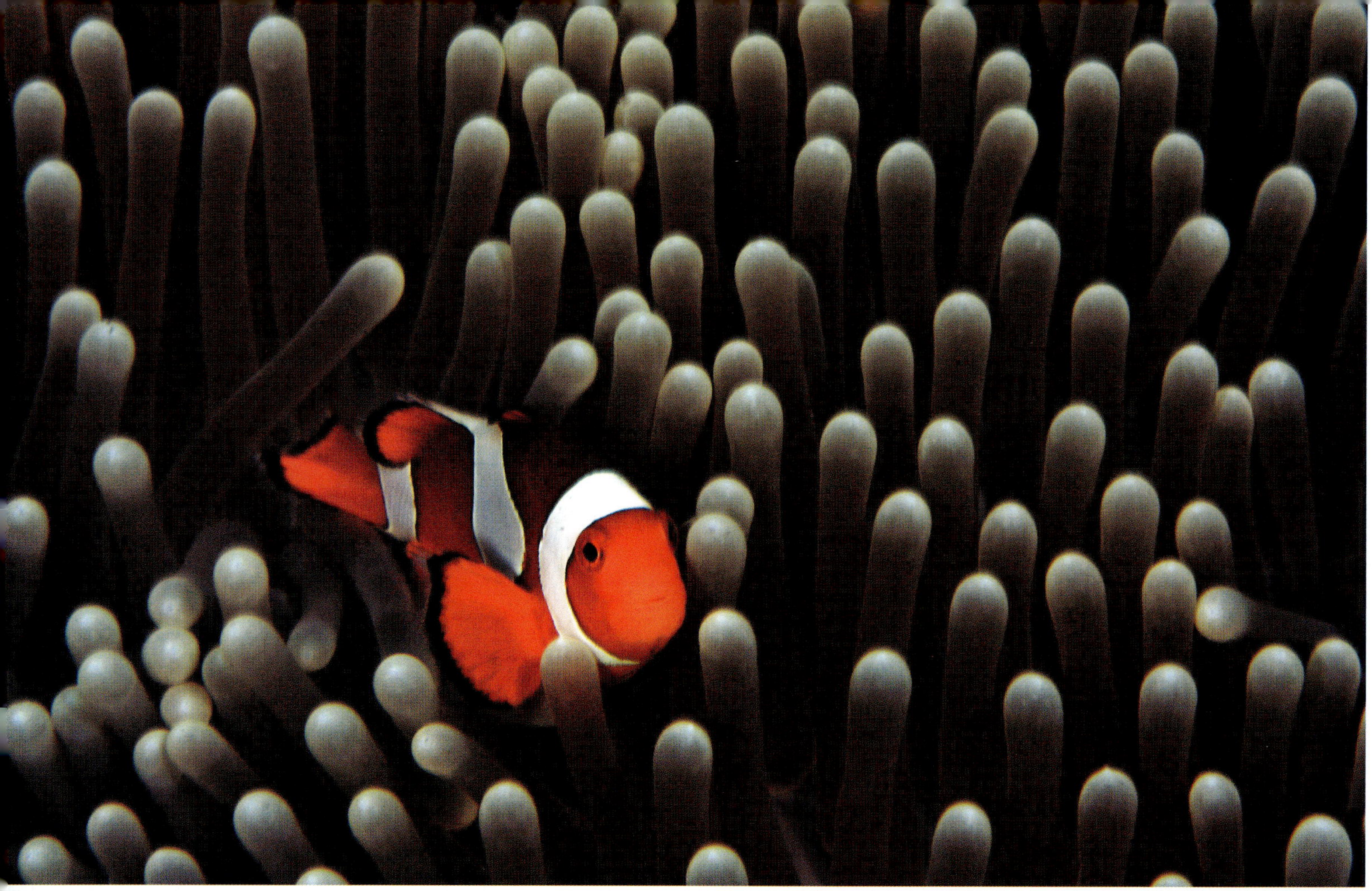

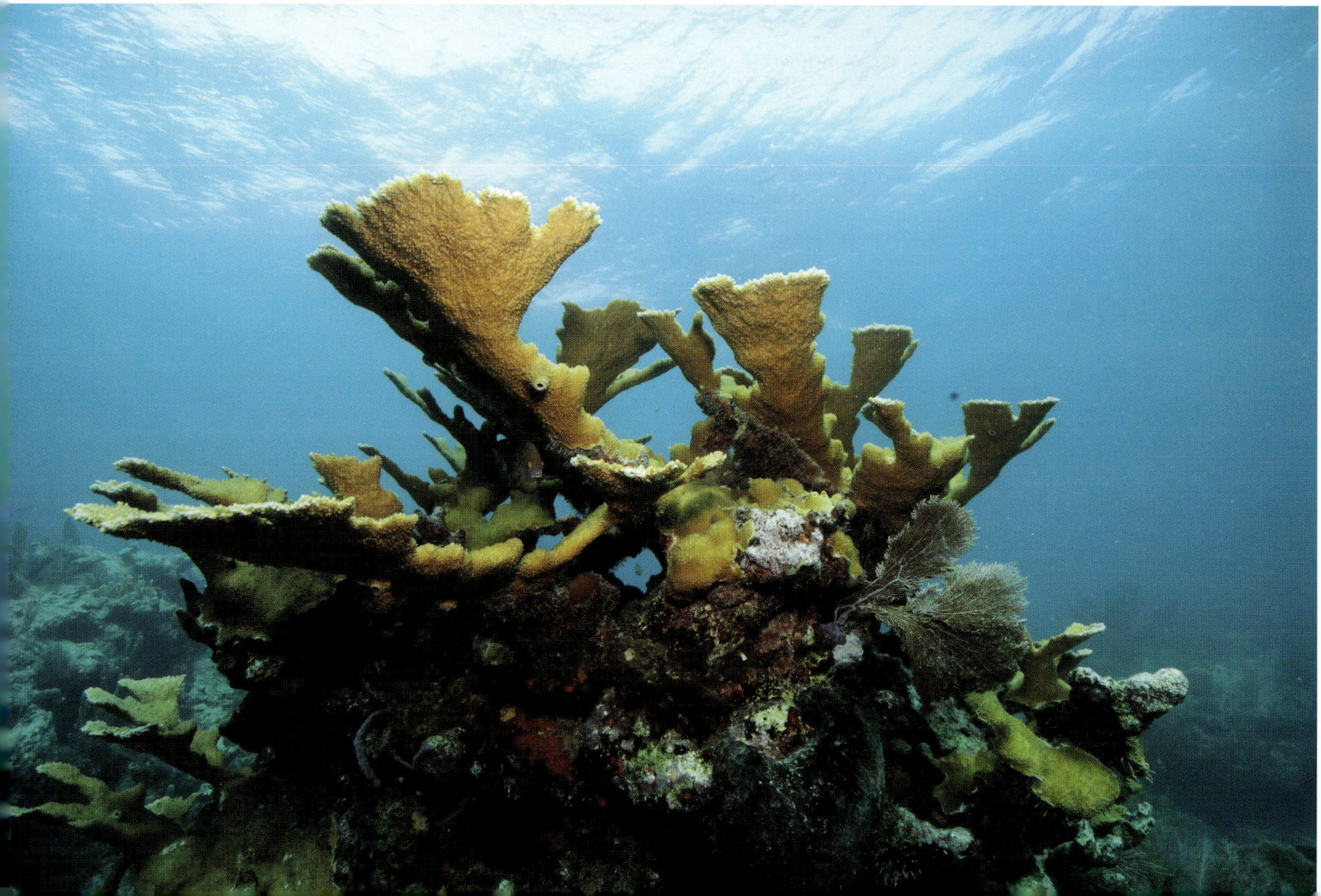

underwater photography workshop or seminar, and engage a professional to help you with your underwater photography in general, or a specific aspect of it.

Travel will take you to subject-rich environments that offer plenty of opportunities to improve your underwater photography. If you travel to a place that is popular with other underwater photographers, you can also learn by sharing your experiences.

### LOOKING BACK

Most of the photographs featured in this book were taken using a housed dSLR camera system. Some were taken using a full-featured digital point & shoot camera system, a few were taken with a simple point & shoot digital camera, and fewer still were taken with a 35mm amphibious film camera. None were taken with a top-of-the-line, professional-level camera. None of

**Facing page**—(Top) "Nemo" and friends, captured in the Banda Sea. Exposure: Exposure: f/22, 1/100, and 100 ISO. Focal length 100mm. Photo courtesy of Mary Moyer. (Bottom) Elkhorn Coral is a fast-growing species, but stands of it are rare and, consequently, it is a worthy subject. **Top**—Goliath Groupers, a protected species, can grow to be huge in size and weight. Capturing smaller subjects in the frame can help you illustrate the Goliath Grouper's size. Exposure: f/5.6, 1/125, and 100 ISO. **Bottom**—Different dive locations offer different photographic opportunities. This photograph of a Sea Horse was taken in Roatan. Photo courtesy of Jan McGarva. Exposure: f/4.5, 1/200, and 200 ISO. Focal length 100mm.

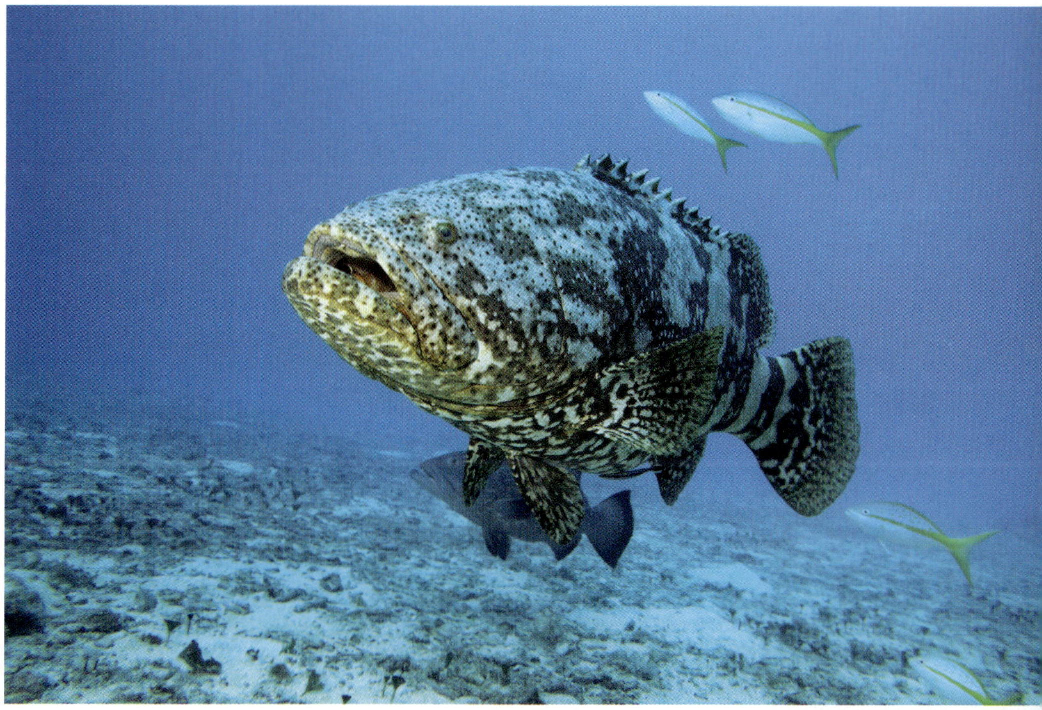

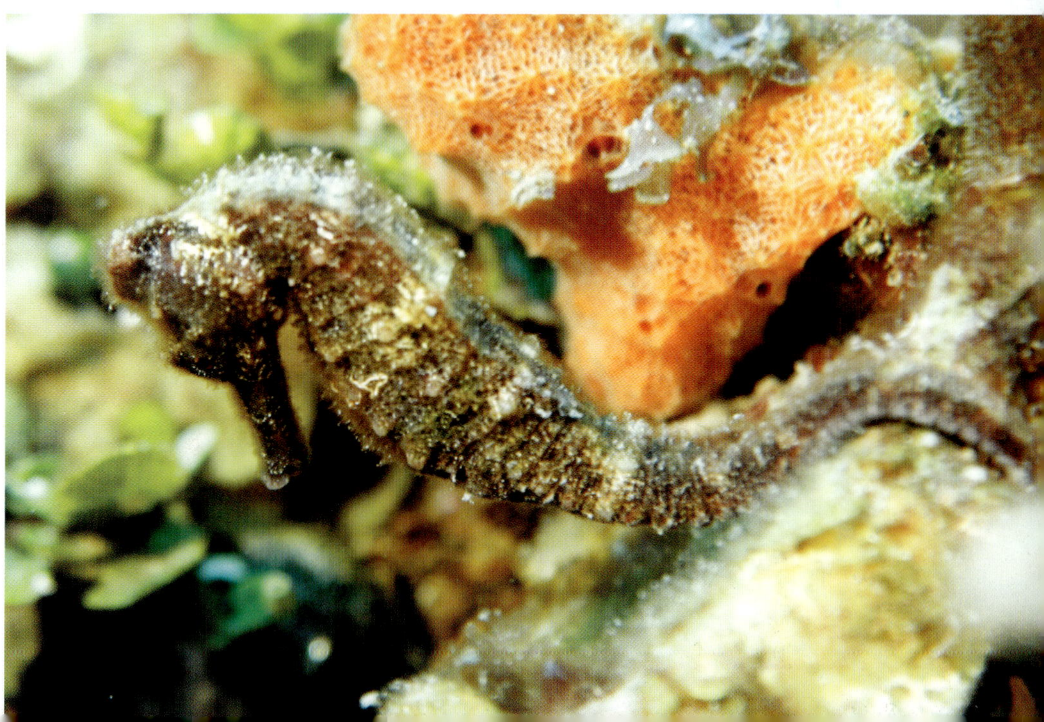

the images in this book were made with the most expensive housings, ports, and strobes. Some of the images in this book were made with a pro-quality lens, but most were not. This proves you don't need state-of-the-art equipment to produce great images.

The photographs of large subjects were taken using lenses with focal lengths of 20mm or shorter. Medium-sized subjects were photographed using lenses with focal lengths between 20mm and 60mm. Small subjects were photographed using lenses with a focal length of 50mm to 105mm. The images of colorful subjects were shot from within 5 feet of the subject.

**Top left**—The Spanish Shawl is one of the most colorful of the sea slugs. Focal length 60mm. Exposure: f/16, 1/200, and 400 ISO. Photo courtesy of John Yasaki. **Top right**—Midnight Octopus. Exposure: f/3.5, 1/160, and 100 ISO. Focal length 28mm. **Bottom**—This small Pufferfish is a candidate for a macro lens, which allows for close focusing and lets you get close so the small subject fills a good proportion of the frame. Exposure: f/8, 1/125, and 200 ISO.

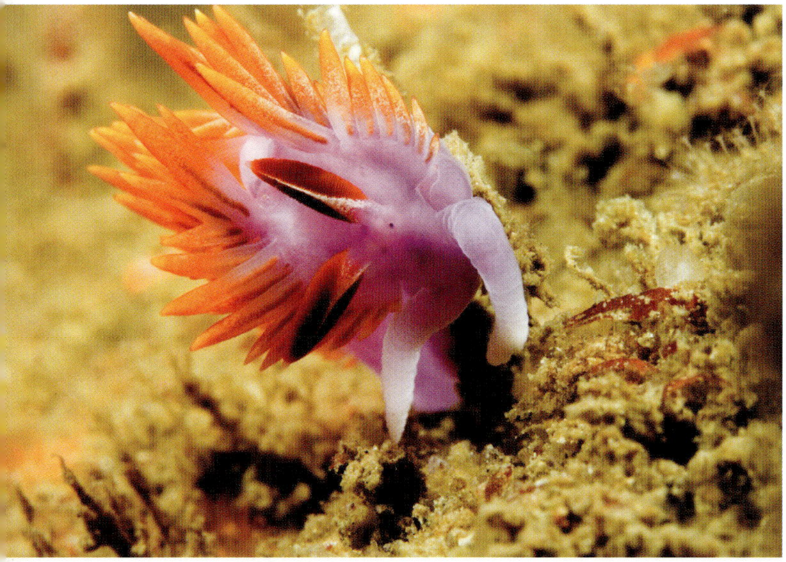

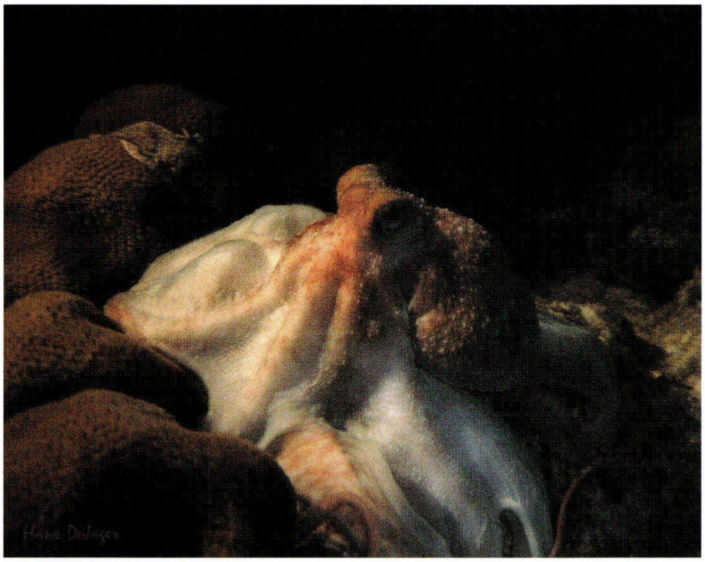

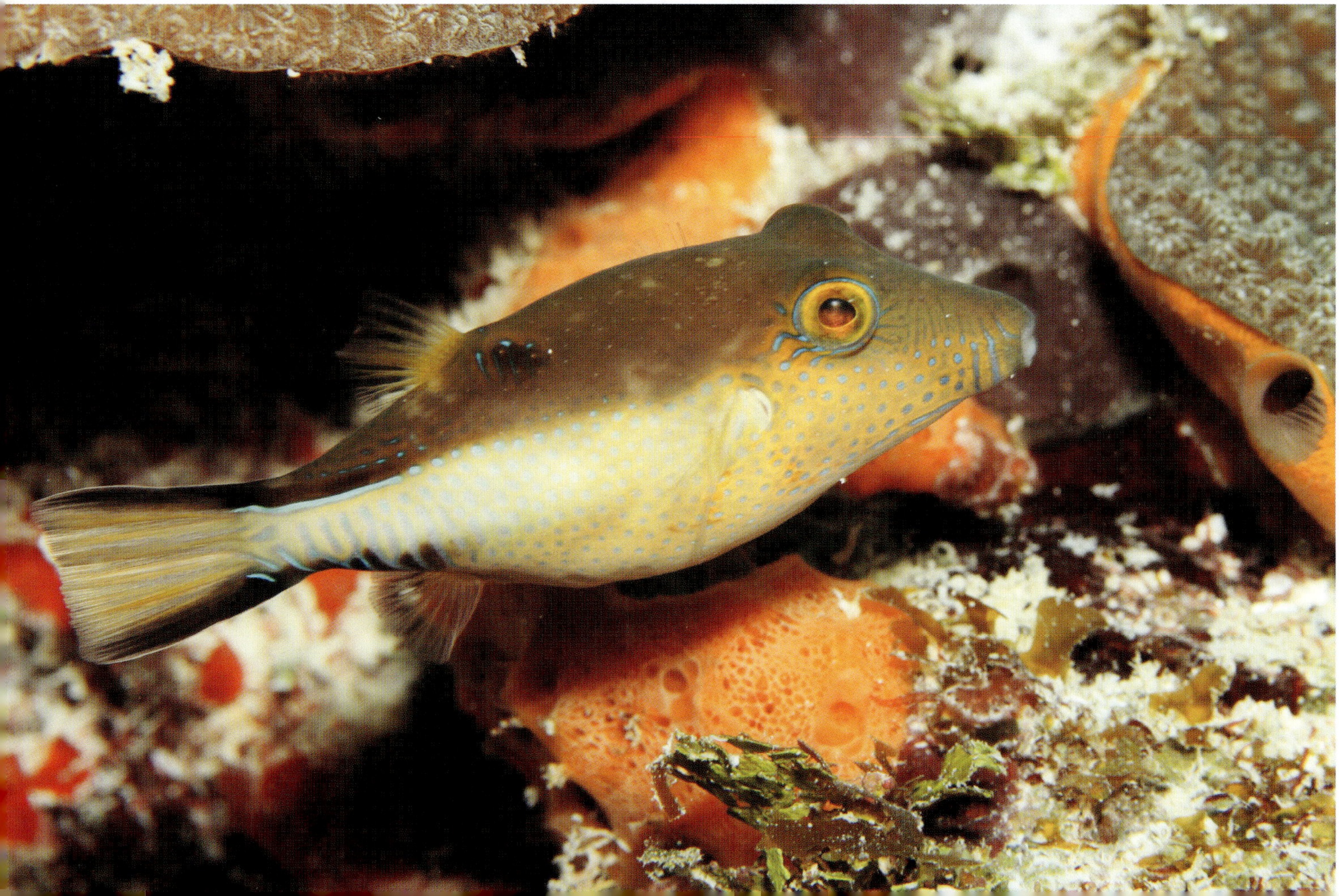

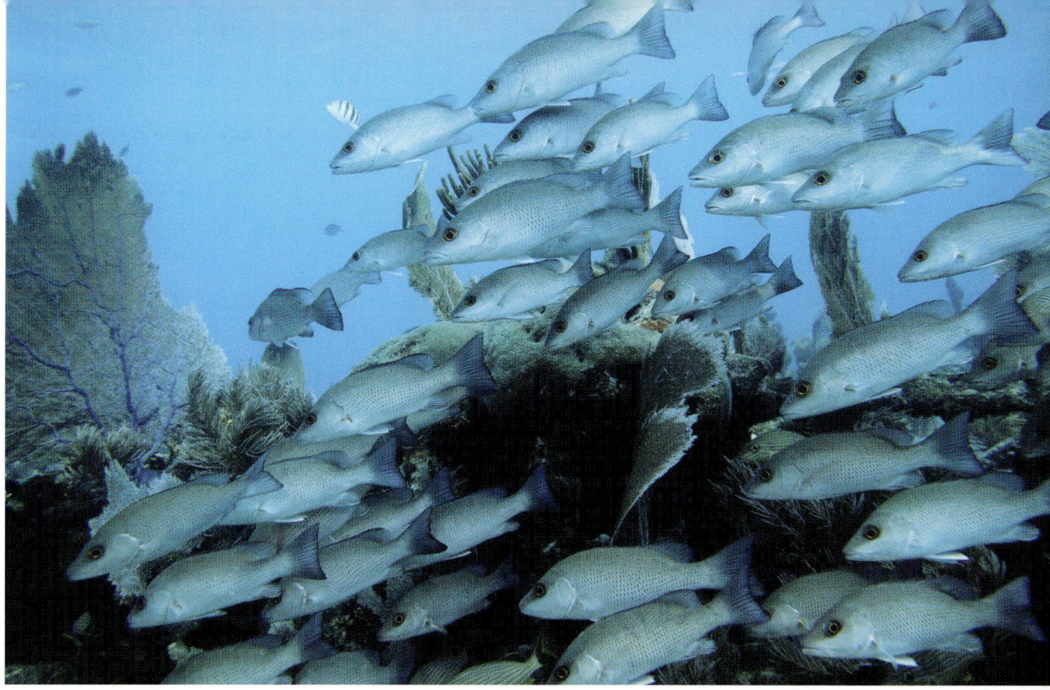

**Top**—One compositional theme is to capture a photograph of a school of fish, all facing the same direction and tightly grouped. Exposure: f/4.5, 1/125, and 100 ISO. **Bottom**—Being an advanced underwater photographer requires patience. This Porcupine Fish had been swimming all over the wreck, then it finally approached the patient photographer. Exposure: f/8, 1/125, and 100 ISO. Focal length 28mm.

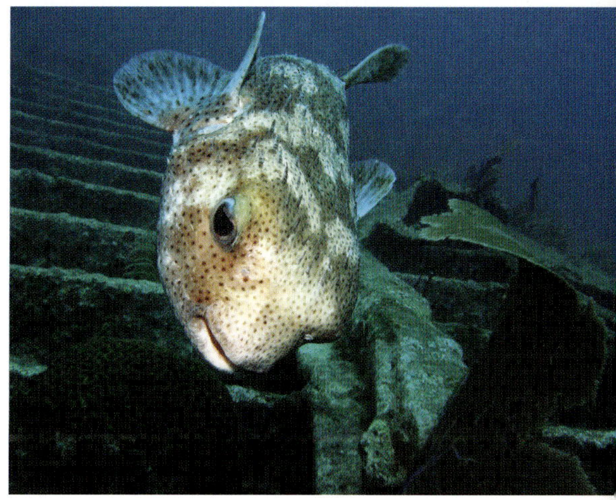

Many of the photographs are displayed with their respective exposure data—the f/stop, shutter speed, and ISO. In some cases, the dive location is noted as well.

With these specifications in mind, take another look through the images. When you review the photographs, ask yourself which lens was likely used, or what lens would be best to use, to make that photograph. Look for technical flaws in the images—such as washed-out highlights—and ask yourself how you might have avoided them.

Determine what vantage point you would choose and how you would get into position to get the shot. Where could you find such subjects? How could you get the photograph?

Think about what equipment you would need and what you would have to do to make that photograph yourself. Determine what vantage point you would choose and how you would get into position to get the shot. Where could you find such subjects? How could you get the photograph, or perhaps a better one, or one just as nice but composed a bit differently?

By now, you should be able to answer most, if not all, of these questions. Picture yourself as the underwater photographic version of a loaded weapon. All you need to do is point yourself at your subject, hit the target, and get the shot. You can be that person. You only need to have the right tools. You have the proper and necessary diving skills. You have the knowledge of the techniques. Now you need to be on location.

Be patient with yourself. Good shooting to you!

# APPENDIX: CAMERA SERVICE AND REPAIR

### AQUATICA

**Backscatter**
225 Cannery Row
Monterey, CA 93940
831.645.1082
Fax: 831.375.1526
sales@backscatter.com
www.backscatter.com

**Pacific Housing Repair**
820 Park Row #600
Salinas, CA 93901
831.751.3885
pacifichsg@redshift.com
www.pacifichousingrepair.com

**Underwater Camera Repair**
21912 SW 95 Place
Cutler Bay, FL 33190
305.234.0903
Fax: 305.234.0907
mikem@underwatercamerarepair.com
www.nikonosrepair.com

### CANON

**Canon U.S.A., Inc.**
800.652.2666

### IKELITE

**Ikelite Underwater Systems**
Attn: Repair Department
50 W 33rd St.
Indianapolis, IN 46208
317.923.4523

### INON

**Reef Photo & Video**
3320 NE 32nd St.
Ft. Lauderdale, FL 33308
954.537.0644
www.reefphoto.com

### NAUTICAM

**Reef Photo & Video**
3320 NE 32nd St.
Ft. Lauderdale, FL 33308
954.537.0644
www.reefphoto.com

### NIKON

**Nikon, Inc.**
800.645.6678
8:00AM–2:00AM ET, seven days a week

*East of the Mississippi River:*
*Nikon Inc. Photo & Digital Svc.*
*Nikon Inc. Factory Service*
*1300 Walt Whitman Rd.*
*Melville, NY 11747*

*West of the Mississippi River:*
*Nikon Inc. Photo & Digital Svc.*
*Nikon Inc. Factory Service*
*841 Apollo St., Suite 100*
*El Segundo, CA 90245-4721*

### NIKONOS

**Underwater Camera Repair**
21912 SW 95 Place
Cutler Bay, FL 33190
305.234.0903
Fax: 305.234.0907
www.nikonosrepair.com

### OLYMPUS

**Olympus**
800.622.6372
Fax: 631.881.6580

*East Coast*
*Olympus Imaging America Inc.*
*Attn: Product Repair*
*400 Rabro Dr.*
*Hauppauge, NY 11788-4258*

*West Coast*
*Olympus Imaging America Inc.*
*Attn: Product Repair*
*10805 Holder St., Suite 170*
*Cypress, CA 90630-5145*

### SEA&SEA

**Sea&Sea**
2380 Mira Mar Ave.
Long Beach, CA 90815
877.973.2732
service@seaandsea.com

### SEACAM

**Underwater Camera Repair**
21912 SW 95 Place
Cutler Bay, FL 33190
305.234.0903
Fax: 305.234.0907
mikem@underwatercamerarepair.com
www.nikonosrepair.com

### SEATOOL

**Reef Photo & Video**
3320 NE 32nd St.
Ft. Lauderdale, FL 33308
954.537.0644
www.reefphoto.com

### SIGMA

**Sigma Corporation of America**
Attn: Service Department
15 Fleetwood Ct.
Ronkonkoma, NY 11779
800.896.6858, 9:00–5:00 ET,
Monday through Friday
Fax: 631.585.1895
info@sigmaphoto.com

### SUBAL

**Backscatter**
225 Cannery Row
Monterey, CA 93940
831.645.1082
Fax: 831.375.1526
sales@backscatter.com
www.backscatter.com

**Pacific Housing Repair**
820 Park Row #600
Salinas, CA 93901
831.751.3885
pacifichsg@redshift.com
www.pacifichousingrepair.com

**Reef Photo & Video**
3320 NE 32nd St.
Ft. Lauderdale, FL 33308
954.537.0644
www.reefphoto.com

**Underwater Camera Repair**
21912 SW 95 Place
Cutler Bay, FL 33190
305.234.0903
Fax: 305.234.0907
mikem@underwatercamerarepair.com
www.nikonosrepair.com

### WATERSHOT

**Watershot, Inc.**
828 H Ave.
Coronado, CA 92118-2522
619-437-1489
619-437-8107
tim@watershot.com
786.547.3049

# INDEX

OTHER BOOKS FROM

# Amherst Media®

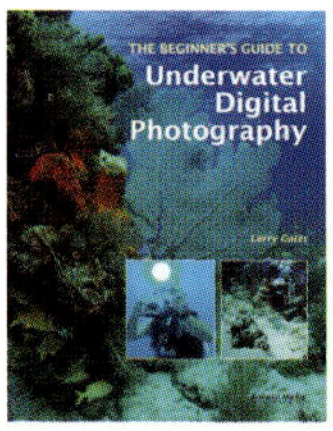


THE BEGINNER'S GUIDE TO

## Underwater Digital Photography

*Larry Gates*

Written for the "regular guy" photographer, this book shows you how to make smart technical and creative decisions. *$34.95 list, 8.5x11, 128p, 160 color images, index, order no. 1911.*

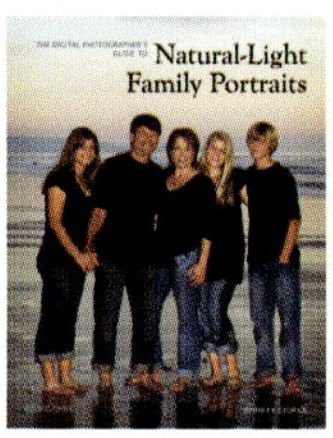


THE DIGITAL PHOTOGRAPHER'S GUIDE TO

## Natural-Light Family Portraits

*Jennifer George*

Learn how using natural light and fun, meaningful locations can help you create cherished portraits and bigger sales. *$34.95 list, 8.5x11, 128p, 180 color images, index, order no. 1937.*

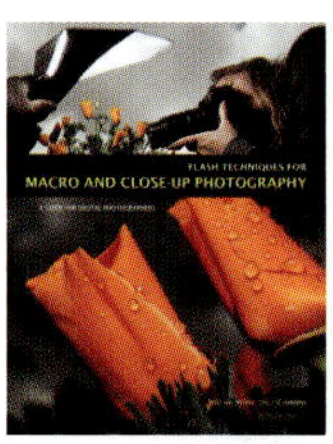

## Flash Techniques for Macro and Close-up Photography

*Rod and Robin Deutschmann*

Master the technical skill-set you need to create beautifully lit images that transcend our daily vision of the world. *$34.95 list, 8.5x11, 128p, 300 color images, index, order no. 1938.*

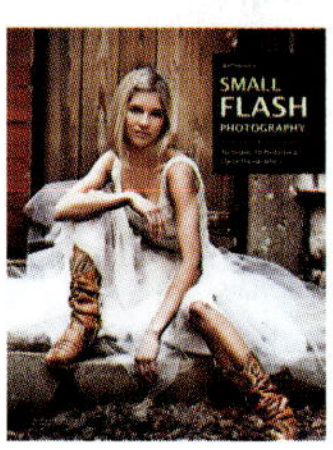


BILL HURTER'S

## Small Flash Photography

From selecting gear, to placing the small flash units, to ensuring proper flash settings and communication, this book shows you how to take advantage of this new approach to lighting. *$34.95 list, 8.5x11, 128p, 180 color photos and diagrams, index, order no. 1936.*

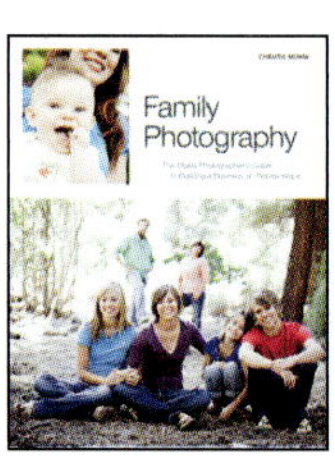


## Family Photography

THE DIGITAL PHOTOGRAPHER'S GUIDE TO BUILDING A BUSINESS ON RELATIONSHIPS

*Christie Mumm*

Build client relationships that allow you to capture clients' life-cycle milestones, from births, to high-school pictures, to weddings. *$34.95 list, 8.5x11, 128p, 220 color images, index, order no. 1941.*

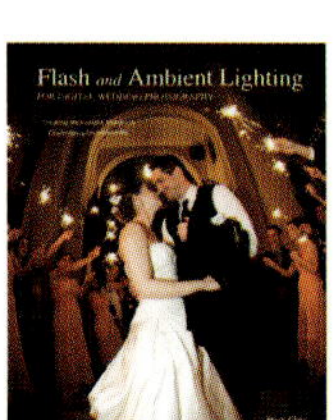


## Flash and Ambient Lighting for Digital Wedding Photography

*Mark Chen*

Meet every lighting challenge with these tips for shooting with flash, ambient light, or flash and ambient light together. *$34.95 list, 8.5x11, 128p, 200 color photos and diagrams, index, order no. 1942.*

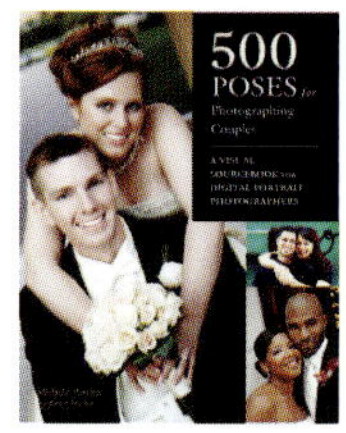


## 500 Poses for Photographing Couples

*Michelle Perkins*

Overcome the challenges of posing couples with this visual sourcebook, showcasing an array of head-and-shoulders, three-quarter, full-length, and seated and standing poses. *$34.95 list, 8.5x11, 128p, 500 color images, order no. 1943.*

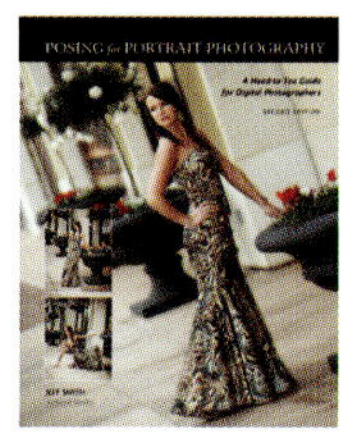

## Posing for Portrait Photography

A HEAD-TO-TOE GUIDE FOR DIGITAL PHOTOGRAPHERS, 2ND ED.

*Jeff Smith*

This book will show you how to correct the most common figure problems, design poses that look natural, and craft images clients are sure to love *$34.95 list, 8.5x11, 128p, 200 color images, index, order no. 1944.*

## MORE PHOTO BOOKS ARE AVAILABLE


Amherst Media®
PO BOX 586
BUFFALO, NY 14226 USA


Individuals: If possible, purchase books from an Amherst Media retailer. Contact us for the dealer nearest you, or visit our web site and use our dealer locater. To order direct, visit our web site, or send a check/money order with a note listing the books you want and your shipping address. All major credit cards are also accepted. For domestic and international shipping rates, please visit our web site or contact us at the numbers listed below. New York state residents add 8.75% sales tax.

*Dealers, distributors & colleges:* Write, call, or fax to place orders. For price information, contact Amherst Media or an Amherst Media sales representative. Net 30 days.


(800) 622-3278 or (716) 874-4450
Fax: (716) 874-4508


*All prices, publication dates, and specifications are subject to change without notice. Prices are in U.S. dollars. Payment in U.S. funds only.*

WWW.AMHERSTMEDIA.COM

FOR A COMPLETE CATALOG OF BOOKS AND ADDITIONAL INFORMATION